To Jacqui
Live for Now
the Moment
much Love
Garri

SURVIVING

7/7 London Bombings & Beyond

MY AUTOBIOGRAPHY

Garri Holness
With June-Elleni Laine

www.spiritlevelpublishing.com

ISBN 978-0-9934774-0-9

Cover Design and Typeset by Lucianne Soley
www.luciannesoley.co.uk

First paperback edition printed 2015 in the United Kingdom
by **Spirit Level Publishing**

Spirit Level is a symbol of levelness and stability. Spirit Level Publishing intends to provide a level platform for spiritually conscious, practical books and publications that offer insights and motivational ideas to a general readership. Although every precaution has been taken in the preparation of this book, the publisher and authors assume no responsibility for errors or omissions. Neither is any liability assumed for damages resulting from the use of this information contained herein.

Spirit Level Publishing is an imprint of
Dark Horse Publications Ltd , Greater London UK

For the Goddess that was Vera Holness

MY ROCK

MY MOTIVATION

MY INSPIRATION

MY MOTHER

“

TO LIVE
WILL BE AN
AWFULLY BIG
ADVENTURE.

”

PETER PAN

The Boy Who Lived in Two Worlds

by J.M. Barrie

PREFACE

When a person experiences a shock or adversity such as a near-death experience, loss of a limb, disfigurement, death of a loved one, excommunication, redundancy, savage Media attack, or a paranormal experience, it can change their lives completely and be the catalyst that starts them on a spiritual quest. However, it's very few men who could face all of these things together, triggered by a deliberate act of terrorism and manage not only to survive, but also to re-emerge with a positive mental attitude. You are warmly invited to read about such a man.

This man is Garri Holness, and his remarkable autobiography makes for a compelling read. It presents an explicit, heart-rending, edgy filmic-style narrative of his life that takes the reader on a roller coaster ride of raw emotions.

Within its pages we find a shy, creative, funny, caring and considerate man, who shows extreme care and loving support for his Mother. We catch glimpses of his childhood in Brixton in the eighties and his struggle to break free from the stigma of a youth custody sentence. We are shown how he finds his salvation in music and how his dogged determination brings him back from the brink of death and devastation, to a place of healing and compassion.

Today he bravely chooses positive thinking despite adversity, to rise above the savage press articles he still faces on the Internet. His aim is to help uplift and inspire others who find themselves in a dark place, but can't find the motivation to break free. *Surviving 7/7 The London Bombings & Beyond* can make you laugh as well as cry, and you may even appreciate the 'lickle' Jamaican Patois included, with a glossary in the back to keep you in the know!

*Please note that although the people in this book are all real, some of their names have been changed to respect their privacy.

6th July 2005 11:00am
Advertising Agency Holborn London

The tension builds and you can almost hear a pin drop as most of my colleagues huddle around the TV holding their breath.

"The games of the 30th Olympiad in 2012 are awarded to the City of London!" Cheers explode as they announce London's bid for The 2012 Olympic Games is successful! The excitement builds and the buzz is contagious. Whatever work was being done in my department grinds to a halt as everyone joins in the jubilation.

The mood is electric and I can't help smiling as a couple of the guys come over and offer me a high five. A woman shrieks excitedly, "I can't believe it, I live in East London I'm definitely gonna go, I hope I can get tickets!" A guy replies, "Don't worry love, you're not alone they must know locals will want tickets, do you think they will ballot them?"

"I dunno, but I'm gonna try my best to get some." Her face is hopeful.

One of the young interns leaps over his seat and starts waving his arms in the air to get attention. "I'm going to be an Olympian watch this." he encourages the others to join him as he creates his own Olympic event, 'The Backward Chairs Race' They take turns to roll each other along as fast as they can on their office chairs shrieking and laughing as he acts out manic air brushing, as if to remove anything standing in the way of the chairs that would potentially slow them down.

My deadline is too tight to join in, as I have to reconcile my work by the end of the day, so I laugh with them, but when I notice it's getting a bit out of control, I offer words of caution. "Slow down guys, one of you could get hurt." They ignore me and carry on regardless, getting more and more animated.

Billy comes over to my desk and stands watching the ever-growing commotion, smiling and shaking his head. He looks at me still busy trying to finish my work and frowns slightly, "Garri, what's up? Aren't you pleased about The Games?"

I smile looking up from my computer screen, "Yeah, yeah of course I am Bill, but I've got work to do, unlike some other people!" I laugh, but then look at him more seriously, "I do have some concerns about security though."

"Why do you say that Garri? Don't put a downer on it."

"No, no I'm not putting a downer on it Mate, I'm just saying, I feel the volume of tourists that will come here will be easy pickings. I've seen it before at big events like Carnival when people fall prey to pick pockets and such like, so security has to be on point. That's all I'm saying."

He looks at me thoughtfully. "Hmmm, yeah I see what you mean, I didn't think of that. It's a good opportunity to regenerate East London though, isn't it?"

"Yeah man, fantastic opportunity, I can't wait." I smile, Billy's phone rings so he rushes back to his desk and I'm left to carry on putting the time-sheet data in SAP.

The Manager's voice shouting from the corridor distracts me.

"Come on you lot, move along back to work." His voice is light hearted and only half serious, so I reply joining in the fun.

"Yeah but they've only got seven years to perfect their new Olympic event!" They laugh all the more, and the high level of excitement subdues only slightly as everyone tries to calm down. Knowing them, a long liquid lunch is on the cards.

The Games coming to London, makes me wish I'd been able to pursue my interest in Athletics, I was pretty good at track and field events when I was at school. Maybe I could have been an Olympian! That would have been exciting and I know Mum would have been proud.

After I get back from my lunchtime workout at the Gym, the afternoon passes quickly and after double-checking the SAP codes and W.B.S numbers I'm finished for the day and ready to leave. I join the Commuter Rat-Race at around 5:15pm, as everyone rushes to get home.

I feel upbeat about the Games as I head off to see Mum at the Nursing Home as usual. She loves to watch the Jamaican Athletics team compete. If she's not asleep when I get there, I'll tell her the news and I'm sure she'll be pleased.

Mum's been confined to a Nursing Home for the last three years trying to recover from a severe stoke, which sadly has left her paralysed down the left side. Then after a second stroke on the right side, she continues to suffer with epileptic fits. I see her almost every evening after work as well as at weekends to do what I can to support her recovery, often combing out her hair and washing her face. Sometimes I can tell it's such a relief when I moisten her dry lips with a damp flannel, it must be frustrating not being able to eat or drink anything. I remember the time when I dabbed her mouth with Jerk Chicken and her whole face lit up as she licked her lips.

As I arrive at Russell Square Station there's already a queue to get in. The lifts are very slow, so I charge down the spiral stairs two or three at a time, down and down until finally I'm at the bottom and manage to catch the next train by the skin of my teeth. The black rubber seal on each side of the closing doors catches my arm on the way through and leaves a mark.

As I get to King's Cross they've changed the platform at the last minute, so I hurry up the stairs as fast as I can, over the bridge and down the other side. Determined to catch my train, I make a final leap down the last four steps, but unfortunately a guy is coming the other way and we collide! He falls back heavily onto the floor and I nearly end up on top of him.

"Sorry Mate! You okay?" I regain my balance and offer him my hand to help him up. He looks pissed off but unhurt.

"Yeah it's alright, I'm okay, but you need to slow down mate!"

"Are you sure you're okay? I'm so sorry!" I smile, but he keeps a straight face, raises his hand palm open to end the conversation and rushes off. I'm late now, but as luck would have it my train is delayed so I jump on board.

6th July 2005 18:30
Knollys Road Nursing Home Norwood

When I arrive there's no one at reception, so I sign in anyway and go straight up. Climbing the few flights of stairs to Mum's room, it's easy to remember the strong, powerful, feisty woman that she was for so many years, and I feel sad that Mum has to go through this now. I look in from the doorway hoping for one of the 'Golden Moments' when she shows glimpses of who she used to be. But as I walk into her room, her eyes are closed and she looks so, so, peaceful, I don't want to disturb her. I put my gym bag down near the door and quietly walk over to her bed.

"I'm not troubling you today Mummy Holness," I whisper as I move a wispy curl of hair away from her brow and kiss her forehead. "See you tomorrow Me Big Darlin'." I feel torn. I don't want to leave her, yet I don't want to wake her either, so I stand at the doorway, unwilling to leave, just staring at her. The clock ticks quietly on the wall, the sound of her breathing peacefully, the peg feed that's inserted into Mum's stomach makes an electronic sound as it switches on to administer the required dose of liquid food; I take it all in silently.

I hate leaving Mum, I remember when she nearly fell off her bed just as I was arriving one evening. When she saw me at the door, her eyes lit up then she called out *Garri!* Until that point she hadn't said anything since her stroke in May 2002. As I ran over to help her, it was fantastic to hear her voice after so long, but a terrible shock that she nearly fell. It still plays on my mind, so much so, that it's a wrench to leave her every time since then. Let me stay positive though, I'll see her tomorrow and spend more time with her then, she might be awake as well.

7th July 2005 06:30am
Croydon Home

I wake up just before the alarm and stretch out my body still feeling the affects of the gym as well as running down all those the steps at Russell Square yesterday. I remember the guy I knocked over at King's Cross and cringe, poor guy! After breakfast I sort out what to wear and decide on blue, yeah it's a blue day and my blue trainers with the divided big toe section are my current favourites. Quick shower, shave and sort out my hair, after checking myself in the mirror I'm good to go.

7th July 2005 07:30 am
East Croydon Railway Station

I arrive in plenty of time for my morning commute up to work and contemplate the day ahead while waiting for my train, I wonder what today will bring. Oh yeah! I'm taking Jane to the gym, what workout shall I do with her? The platform fills up around me with more and more half-asleep commuters, some holding polystyrene cups awkwardly out in front, as they totter along with phones stuck to their ears, trying hard not to spill their coffee.

It's a warm day and I wish I'd remembered to bring a bottle of water with me; it gets hot on the Tube. When the train pulls in, I hurry to get on-board, find a seat and place my gym bag on the floor at my feet. Sitting back, I rest my eyes thinking about the lovely Halle who I met recently on this very train. Unfortunately, I won't see her today as she's gone on holiday. Anyway, I feel lucky to get a seat this morning as I plan my day in the office and look forward to seeing Mum after work. I may even pop in to see my mate Carlton and get involved in some music later.

7th July 2005 08:37am
London King's Cross Railway Station

It's a lovely sunny morning and everyone seems pleased about the Olympics, which creates a buzz in London. The thought of walking to work crosses my mind, but I decide against it. Instead, I hurry through the manic crowds towards the Underground to catch a tube to Russell Square.

7th July 2005 08:45am
London King's Cross Underground Station

Crushed in a sea of bodies that is the rush hour on the London Underground, I can't even get near to the first Piccadilly Line train that rolls in. As the second train approaches, also tightly packed, I head for a gap towards the front of the train, but as I'm about to board a blonde woman pushes in and squeezes on the train in front of me. I tap her lightly on the shoulder,

"Have a nice day love." She glances back and does a double take as if to say something, but the train closes it's doors and rolls away into the tunnel with her still peering strangely through the window at me.

I'm one of the first to get on the next train. Tall enough to look over most people's heads, I watch as commuters file in hurriedly through the open doors as if there's not a second to loose. Hairs bristle on the back of my neck as I get the sense of being stared at. I look round quickly trying to see who it is, as the train fills up around me.

A man's voice shouting from the crowded platform distracts me. "Excuse me, can some of you move along please?"

"Where d'you want us to go mate, on the roof?" I reply without missing a beat. There's a ripple of chuckles, followed by a final surge before the doors close as the last few desperate passengers push to get on regardless. Shoved back and forth I put my bag on the floor between my legs, so I can grab the yellow upright handrail and stand more firmly. As the train finally closes its doors and jerks into action, arms push in around me trying to grab the handrail too.

It's extremely hot and airless in this carriage, and I smell an unpleasant mixture of stale breath, coffee, tobacco and body odour veiled with the scent of perfume. Tightly packed together like sardines in a can, at least

I only have one stop to go to work. A bead of sweat trickles down my brow towards my eye, I quickly wipe it away muttering under my breath. "Chaa man! I shudda walked!"

As we roll away from the station the familiar droning hum of the train gaining momentum builds up, as we enter the mouth of the tunnel. I quickly scan the Newspaper Headlines of passengers seated along the row next to me. London is buzzing with news about the Olympic Games. I feel the pressure on my ears as the train starts to picks up speed, when *'BOOM!'* A sudden explosion and intense *flash* of light bursts through the carriage, and forces me headfirst into the handrail as we grind to a halt.

Darkness claims the carriage and an eerie silence looms. Still holding on tight, I look around desperately trying to catch a glimpse of something, anything, in the pitch-black. A feeling of dread grips me as I realise something serious just happened; I see nothing, I hear nothing.

My eyes close as a miraculous sense of calm suddenly surrounds me. My inner voice takes over, *'I've gotta stay focused, I've gotta stay focused, I've gotta stay calm.'* And I know my life depends on that.

7th July 2005 09:05am
London King's Cross Underground Station

When I open my eyes I'm on the floor. Black smoke laced with the sickly stench of melted plastic and burnt hair assaults my senses. The dense fumes hang around me in the darkness stinging my eyes and inside my nose. The unbearable heat is suffocating and as I struggle to breathe there's an unpleasant taste in the air. Overhead, exposed wires spark erratically sending out flashes of light that cut through the dark smog. A sense of claustrophobia wells up in my psyche as the carcass of the train seems to squeeze in around me like a make shift coffin.

Overcome by fumes I cough to clear my throat causing a powdery residue to shower down from my hair over my face and into my eyes. "What the hell's that?" Blinking frantically I quickly try to wipe it off, but the more I disturb it, the more it rains down on me. My attention shifts towards the flashes of light overhead that momentarily illuminate the destruction, I catch glimpses of uprooted and mangled seats amongst uncoupled light fittings that hang down clinging onto bare wires, and then I'm plunged back into the depths of darkness again. The tell tale signs of a serious incident are apparent, but I can't work out what the hell happened or where the other passengers are; I feel uneasy and disturbingly alone.

Suddenly a distraught scream breaks the deathly silence. "I've lost my legs!" My body jumps in shock. "I've lost my legs!" She shrieks again. Instantly there's a weird sense of relief that I'm no longer alone, until the terrible realisation of what she actually says hits me. There's a call to action deep in the pit of my stomach, I know in this moment I have to get up and help her.

Before attempting to stand I scan my legs, trying desperately to see as the random flashes of light reveal that my trousers are torn and there's a gaping void where my left shin should be. 'What the fuck's happened?' When I grab my bare foot I don't even notice my trainers are gone, but I know something's very wrong as my leg folds up towards me at an impossible angle. 'Shit!' I frantically scratch at my heel… There's a vague sensation, somehow comforting yet making no logical sense. I'm confused; nothing makes sense as I expand my awareness outwards again. Strange muted sounds and vibrations stream in steadily and the more aware I become, the more unbelievable the scene that emerges around me appears to be. What happened? I can't work it out.

Then I remember the woman who screamed. Even though I know I can't walk, I have to do something, so I shout back to her. "Don't worry love, you're not alone, I've lost part of my leg too, but keep calm we're going to get out. They must know we're down here!" No reply, nothing but cruel silence followed by an immediate sense of loss.

The urgent need to connect with somebody fuels me, but it's too dark to see much. Then I remember my phone; fumbling into what's left of my trouser pocket I find it. Although the screen's shattered, it shines a constant dim light that I can use to guide my search for others and maybe a place to sit and wait for help. As I drag my body along the floor my hands become wet and sticky, I assume from coffee spilled when the train stopped, but then I feel something I can't understand. The dim light reveals a dismembered arm covered in blood and I freeze.

The horrifying realisation hits me that I've been dragging myself through my fellow passenger's mutilated limbs, torn flesh and blood. It's a struggle to believe what's in front of me now as I register a pile of dismembered bodies and the smell of death. Distressed and nauseated I quickly pull the neck of my t-shirt up and over my nose to mask my face. As I continue along on autopilot trying to switch off to the terrible truth, I instinctively move more carefully and respectfully through the bodies and debris around me. Every so often I'm compelled to stop and engage with fellow passengers, duty-bound to realign limbs that poke out at awkward angles, whilst offering words of support to anyone who may still be alive.

Looking back along the carriage reveals little, there's only a diffused glow from emergency lighting coming in from the tunnel. Any level surface is covered with what looks like tiny lights twinkling eerily through the smoke and gloom. On closer inspection I realise it's shattered glass from the windows reflecting the intermittent light that flashes overhead, causing it to sparkle like diamonds nestling in small clusters.

I try to take in a long, deep breath but the heat, humidity and fumes make it difficult to breathe at all. I'm forced to take short shallow breaths, which heighten my distress. Then, in sheer desperation, I have to say something positive, whether anyone can hear me or not, I don't care I have to speak up.

"Keep calm, they must know we're down here, so just keep calm everyone."

"Yeah, that's right we should all keep calm, are you alright over there?" Instantly elevated by the unexpected reply, I find a new sense of hope that others may be alive too. "Yeah, I'm okay thanks, just uncomfortable." Sounds of muffled movement are followed by an outline coming towards me through the darkness. "Hello, my name's Alison." I reach out my hand towards her as she approaches, "Hi Alison, I'm Garri, good to meet you." We shake hands; strangers brought together in a bond of mutual survival.

"Right Garri, if you're okay let me go check if anyone else needs my help and I'll come back to you in a minute." Alison walks away into the darkness, and in this moment I'm so thankful that at least *she* can walk.

Trying to haul my battered body towards an undamaged seat I realise my foot is attached to my leg by nothing more than threads of skin, so I have to carry it carefully if I have any chance of saving it. Feeling weaker and weaker as I go on, I don't know how much longer I can hold out and for the first time, the ultimate question arises, 'Am I gonna die here?'

20th November 1985 11:30am
London The Old Bailey Courthouse

Shock sets in and I feel sick to my stomach as I try to grasp what happened. After nine months in custody awaiting trial including my eighteenth birthday last month, I'm now in the bowels of the Old Bailey, where they used to hang prisoners. The merciless energy is intimidating as I'm escorted along a dark tunnel-like corridor to see my Mum in the visitor's room. I get an odd sense of relief from banging my shoulder against the wall, again and again as we go along, perhaps trying to wake up from this unbelievable nightmare. How could I get seven years for something I didn't do? I'll still be locked up for my nineteenth birthday, my twentieth, and twenty-first! How am I gonna cope? Seven Years!

Another detainee is being led along the corridor towards us, he's older than me, maybe about thirty, but he appears calm and aloof. As we get closer I sense he's tough, a proper villain. The long scar on his face hardens his appearance; his whole demeanour suggests that prison is not new to him.

"He just got fourteen." His warden whispers to mine as they pass yet the man remains nonchalant. This is my first glimpse of life on the inside and it troubles me. As we approach the visitor's room, the timely sight of Mum through the window brings instant relief.

7th July 2005 09:25am
London King's Cross Underground Station

As I open my eyes I see Alison coming back towards me, she's like a beacon of hope in the darkness. "Okay Paul how you doing?"

"Paul? My name's not Paul, it's Garri."

"Oh yes sorry Garri."

"I'm not so good Alison, I feel faint." I get the sense Alison ties something around my damaged leg. "Okay lets see if we can find somewhere to sit you up off the floor." Alison being with me feels supportive as we move slowly through the devastation in our search for an upright seat away from the worst of the debris.

At last we find a section of undamaged seats. With my back up against the base I raise my arms placing my palms carefully onto the seat above and somehow manage to hoist myself up using all my strength. Once on the edge I shuffle back to get comfortable, placing what's left of my left leg over the armrest, in an attempt to support it and help stop the bleeding.

As I try to rest back, I remember Mum's ring on a chain around my neck, my stomach turns over as I quickly feel for it. Found it! I try to wipe it clean with my T-shirt but I'm covered in a film of dirt. With it nestled safely in the palm of my hand, thoughts of Mum rush in.

I have to stay alive to look after Mummy; she needs me! What if being with her at the nursing home last night is the last time I'll ever see her? I could die right here underground. A mother's worst nightmare must be losing a child. No! I can't let that happen. I won't let it happen! The voice in my head gets stronger and motivates me. *'You will get out of here Garri! I know you will!'* The voice may be strong but my body feels weaker and weaker.

April 2002 Early Morning
St. Thomas Hospital A&E

Rushing to get to the hospital because Mum's had a stroke. I'm upset, panicking, trying to get there quickly because my phone was on silent when my brothers were calling me. Finally inside A&E, I catch sight of Mum unconscious on a stretcher next to a nurse and my brothers trying to fill in a form. I rush over; they aren't sure how to answer some of the questions, so I offer help straight away because I know Mums details; I do her paperwork.

Once the form is complete, I sense Hector is annoyed with me. It must have been frustrating trying to get hold of me with no reply. I feel bad, like I've let Mum down after everything she's done for me. She's been with me every step of the way and I wasn't there for her when she needed me. A tear wells up and escapes down my cheek, but I quickly catch it and wipe it away; I'm here now and I'll do all I can to help her.

7th July 2005 09:40am
London King's Cross Underground Station

Alison jolts me back to my senses and I realise I desperately need her help to stay alive. "I know I've lost my leg, but listen, if I close my eyes I need you to slap me, I can't die here. I mean it Alison please slap my face, I've got to stay awake, okay?"

"Okay Garri don't worry, I will if that's what you need."

"Thanks." I struggle to keep my eyes open for a while, but it's not easy.

September 1993 Evening
Brixton Town Hall

I'm MC-ing with my crew Total Eclipse, at a social event. The music sounds wicked booming out of the new speaker boxes we made and I'm well pleased. We take turns being on the mic keeping the crowd entertained, dancing and having a few drinks. A girl comes in upset and tells us our friend Eric is having a heated argument with some boys outside, so we all rush out to help him. I feel the alcohol pumping quickly through my veins, and things get a bit woozy as I run as fast as I can to find Eric. I don't see one of the troublemakers with his leg outstretched until I fall over him, as if in slow motion, my head hits the floor and bounces several times before I black out.

7th July 2005 09:55am
London King's Cross Underground Station

Slap! "Garri, wake up!"

"What? Oh yeah... thanks Alison."

Awake again, I sit quietly staring into the devastated train, as my eyes grow more accustomed to the darkness, I see something move at the far end of the carriage. A dark silhouette starts coming forwards out of nowhere. It leaps along frantically from seat to seat and as it gets closer I can make out the shape of a man who seems completely out of control and certainly on a collision course with us if he keeps coming. I have to do something! "Slow down! What the fuck are you doing? Slow down! You're gonna hurt somebody!" Oblivious to my enraged yelling, the man continues towards us even faster. I put my energy into one last desperate yell attempting to stop him, "I SAID SLOW DOWN MAN!" but he keeps coming closer and closer until at the last second, he just manages an emergency stop nearly falling on top of me. Getting ready to make more noise, I shine the light from my phone towards him and he freezes just like a rabbit caught in headlights, wide-eyed and looking very shocked to see us. I sense confusion and desperation; it resonates deep inside me. I can't see his features clearly but get an impression he's in his late twenties or early thirties, hidden beneath a mass of dark curly hair, and a moustache; his trance like stare unnerves me. Who is this man? Where has he come from? And, why is he running through the train wreck like a wild man?

Alison calmly stands up and somehow manages to guide him slowly around my leg beckoning him to the floor. Without a word he quickly rushes away in the direction of the tunnel, and disappears into the darkness. Alison and

I exchange a confused frown, but we don't find anything to say about him.

After this ordeal I really need to lie down and look for something I can rest my head on; there's a bag on the opposite seats but I can't reach it. "Alison could you get that bag for me please, I want to rest my head on it?"

"Don't worry about the bag Garri, here just rest your head on my lap if you like." She's so sweet, a real Angel but as I lay down, I realise I'm on her bare legs and sense we both feel awkward. Too embarrassed to relax, I decide it may be better to go back down on the floor and rest my head on the seat. Once I sit up Alison goes to check on other passengers seated further along the carriage.

I'm growing more and more fidgety, but daren't lay down as I'm convinced that if I fall asleep I'll be left here to die. I put my hand down to the floor feeling for a space to get down, but I'm sickened to feel a fusion of body parts in amongst the debris. I try to continue my search further along, but it feels like the floor all around me is covered. I decide it's better to stay on the seat so I slowly shuffle back to the end seat where I can rest back sitting up. Finally I reach the end seat and place what remains of my left leg under the armrest. It feels good to sit upright and brings a slight relief. Battling to keep my eyes open, I fear I'm losing the will to go on, but then Alison comes back just in time. I call out to her with a sense of desperation.

"Alison, Alison, I'm drifting!"

"Garri... Garri!" *Slap!* Alison brings me back to my senses again.

This time I'm determined I'm going to survive, so instead of fearing the worst, I try to visualise rescue. I close my eyes and imagine that they're taking me out of here. It calms me for quite a while, until the discomfort in my body overwhelms me again and I'm compelled to move. I find myself back on the floor regardless of what I may be sitting on. With every passing minute, the carriage feels smaller and smaller, as if it crushes in around me, imprisoning me, making me feel powerless and out of control. That old feeling of isolation, despair, and restriction takes me back to a place I know only too well.

20th November 1985
Prison Van Leaving The Old Bailey Courthouse

Imprisoned in a 'sweat-box' struggling to peer out through a small, reinforced window, I catch glimpses of my family going crazy in the street outside trying to get to me. As the van moves away they run after me, but I lose sight of them, consumed by the crowd. The van stops abruptly at a red light so they chase after it again; I catch another glimpse as they frantically bang on the side. I try to wave from the window, only to feel the handcuffs bite in. I make a fist and grab my injured wrist trying to ease the pain.

7th July 2005 10:10am
London King's Cross Underground Station

With my hand closed tightly around my phone I open my eyes feeling relieved the light is still working. Although it's dim, it's the only constant source of light I have and it's comforting; something I can control. Aware that I'm drifting in and out of consciousness, I can't tell the difference between the real and the imaginary. A light shines in the distance, but then its gone. Is it real? Could it be rescue or maybe I'm dead and it's an Angel coming for me, who knows? There it is again; it's small and bright but it's too far away to be sure.

April 1989 09:00am
Aylesbury Youth Custody Centre

Unexpectedly the door opens and my Prison Officer appears with his usual air of authority; yet today he must be in a good mood because he grins as he comes in. "Come with me." He escorts me out of my cell and I can't help but feel anxious as he leads me down the corridor. Is it my family? Is it a solicitor visit, am I being moved again? I'm very uneasy not knowing what's happening, but this is how things are in here and I have to grin and bear it.

7th July 2005 10:15am
London King's Cross Underground Station

Straining to look along the carriage, I'm pretty sure I can see a light moving from one side to the other, then another light and another. I call out towards the lights. "What's happening?" No answer, but now my attention is solely focused on the lights as I decide it has to be rescue and a sense of relief begins to ease my anxiety. My body starts relaxing, but I realise that although they may be coming, they're moving painfully slowly. I mutter under my breath in sheer frustration. "Aw come on man, why is it taking so long?" Feeling restless and irritated not knowing what's happening, I just want to get out now. I know I can't last much longer.

April 1989 09:30am
Aylesbury Youth Custody Probationers Office

"Take a seat Garri," the Probation Officer requests with a twinkle in her eye. I smile back and sit down feeling calmer.

"Do you know why you're here?"

"Nope."

"Well I'll tell you, it's good news. Your parole's been granted!"

"Really? That is good news. At long last!" I feel elated inside, but in the circumstances I must stay calm. Although I thought it could be parole, I dared not get my hopes up too high. I'll save my celebration for when I actually walk out of here.

"Would you like to use the phone to call your mother?"

I call, "Hello Mum, it's me…"

7th July 2005 10:25am
London King's Cross Underground Station

"What's happening? Why is it taking them so long?" I mumble again under my breath, but this time to my surprise I hear a voice inside my head loud and clear. *'They're coming! Remember the woman who lost her legs? She needs help and there are others as well that need help, just stay calm, they'll get to you soon enough.'*

It helps to know what's going on, although I don't know or care where that information came from, or how real it is. It's probably only my imagination, but let me save the little strength I have left. No point wasting it getting upset, there's nothing more to do other than rest back and try to stay calm.

"Are you okay?" Someone leans down over me with a torch.

"Yeah, yeah I'm okay." A knee jerk reaction to say I'm still alive, not a true account of how I am, so my rescuer keeps walking past me looking for others; I can't find the strength to say anything else. It's disheartening, like I've been waiting in a long queue and get to the door only to find the queue goes on further inside. I try to comfort myself, they know I'm alive it won't be long now.

17th May 1989 06:30am
Aylesbury Youth Custody Centre

The sound of keys rattling wakes me and I hear the clunk of solid metal locks being undone one after the other. Every morning it's the same old story, but today it's different, today I'm excited. I'm about to leave this chapter of my life and I can't wait to get out. I see freedom just up ahead; there's a light at the end of the tunnel and it feels good. I get ready to say goodbye to the Man dem and the 'lock down' of youth custody! I couldn't be more cheerful as I dutifully empty my slop bucket for the very last time. After strip washing thoroughly in my cell to remove all traces of this place, I eat breakfast leisurely knowing I can afford to relax and take it easy; porridge toast and tea has a new sweetness to it this morning!

7th July 2005 10:35am
London King's Cross Underground Station

Regaining my senses I can feel people around me. "Can you walk?" a distant voice shouts.

"Yes I can walk." Alison replies; she's still here beside me. What an Angel!

"Come on then let's get you out."

"I'm not leaving Garri alone, I'm staying with him."

I must be the last one left in here alive.

"Don't worry, he's *Priority One*, and he'll be right behind you." I sense someone approach and suddenly feel the sensation of a needle being embedded in my left arm. Some kind of sheet is pushed underneath me and they lift me up. My wait to leave this hellhole is over and my eyes close, finally the last one out but safe now; finally I can let go!

17th May 1989 10:00am
Aylesbury Youth Custody Centre

Having collected my stuff, and all dressed up in my new clothes Mum brought in, I'm feeling good. The Prison Officer leads me to the front gate and opens it. I can see life on the outside!

"Okay Garri, take care, but next time you come, bring a friend!"

"I ain't coming back." I shout with confidence.

"Yeah, they all say that!" He laughs. Although I can't get out quick enough, when I look back at the large heavy metal gate closing firmly behind me, I suddenly feel unsure. I wonder how I'm going to fit back into my community with a conviction hanging over me.

7th July 2005 11:05am
The Royal Free Hospital A&E

The boundaries of dreaming and reality are blurred. With sirens still blaring I'm dispatched from the Ambulance and wheeled through double doors that reflect the flashing blue emergency lights. Inside the Hospital several doctors and nurses rush towards me from the haze. I can't hear much of what's being said but I'm focused on my leg. "Can you save my leg?" I don't hear anything so I ask again louder, "Can you save it?"

"We don't know yet, if we can we will, but if we try to save your leg, your life may be in danger."

"Argh no!" I feel numb, but I know it's a sacrifice I must make, I have to survive.

"We'll do the best we can, okay?" They sound sincere.

"Okay, okay I get it, if you gotta take my foot you gotta take it, as long as you save me." Now I know I'm in God's hands!

Spring 1974
Stockwell Park Estate Burrow House Brixton

Dad, filled with bravado, challenges us to a race! My brothers and I laugh him off. Him with the metal implant in his leg, thinking he can run faster than us! He even offers to give us a head start, which makes us laugh even more! But it seems he's serious, so we agree and get ready for the race with Dad at the back giving us the promised head start. He counts us in.

"Unno Ready, Steady, Go!" I start running as fast as I can and within seconds Dad passes me with ease and then in turn passes both my brothers aged eleven and thirteen to win the race just as he said he could. "Unno kyaan run, unno ah pickney and me a big man!" It's with great pride, I realise Dad is still strong, and in that moment he's an inspiration to me. Even though Dad has a metal plate in his leg, he can still run fast!

11th July 2005
The Royal Free Hospital A&E

Squinting through blurry eyes, two shadows float up on either side of me, they pass from one side to the other and then I clearly hear Mums' voice.

"Garri wake up! Garri get up! Garri!"

No longer underground, but in a white room that I don't recognise, I wonder if I'm dead. As I become aware of my body, the first thing I feel is something attached to my neck. A dressing as large as my hand covers it and as I explore further I find an array of other dressings. As I look down I can't even see my left leg, there's a box shape over it covered by white sheet.

Distant sounds of movement and muffled voices give me the idea that I'm in hospital. There's a stack of medical equipment flashing, bleeping and carrying on, then I realise it's all attached to me! Touching my head causes a 'déjà vu' moment, as black soot falls down from my hair just as it did underground, and as I try to brush it away, I'm aware of someone sitting beside my bed. It's Fitzroy my cousin, who gets to his feet straight away and looks at me. His lips are moving but no sound is coming out, he looks so worried.

"Fitzroy, you alright man? I can't hear you?"

"Me! I'm alright, but how are you Man?" His voice sounds muffled even though it looks like he's shouting; maybe it's a dream?

Suddenly there are people everywhere, swarming in like bees around a honey pot, I feel overwhelmed as I try to take in what's happening. An escalating sense of distress wells up as I start to realise it's not a dream and it must be serious. Then I see the familiar face of my oldest brother Hector, he brings me a welcome sense of security as he leans over and touches my arm smiling. His calm energy comforts me as he speaks. "How you feeling Bruv?"

"Bwoy, I'm alright you know, guess I'm lucky to be here?"

"Yeah man and you'll be okay, just stay calm."

I breathe slowly as I focus on his words; I so needed to hear that.

"What happened Bruv?"

"Garri Mate, Suicide Bombers." Hector shakes his head sadly without taking his eyes off me.

"What?" I pause, it's hard to grasp what he says, but it sinks in slowly. I can hardly focus enough to say anything else. I guess I must be drugged up to the eyeballs as well.

I look around slowly taking in the sea of faces all looking at me, each one with lips moving, but the volume must be turned down, God knows what they're saying. I smile as the familiar faces of family and several work colleagues come into focus along with a few of the Man dem from the Endz. It's surprising to see them collide together as never before in a melting pot of flavours, cultures, colours and creeds. Then amidst them all, I notice a clean-cut white man in a dark suit who I don't recognise. As he approaches, I do recognise the warrant card that he quickly flashes under my nose.

Anxiety makes knots in the pit of my stomach and as he talks, I only catch a small sections of what he says as I focus hard on his mouth. "Is there anything you need to tell me Garri?" I feel defensive, as my negative experiences of the Police kicks in. I blurt out a salad of disjointed words that I just can't control. "Yes I should tell you something… yes, I mean no … it's not even, but yes I think I must… to tell you." I try to whisper discretely about the thing that's always at the back of my mind. "I've got a conviction."

He smiles awkwardly and puts his hand to cover his mouth so only I can see as he whispers back. "How long ago was that Garri?" He seems different I feel his empathy.

"About twenty, yeah around that, twenty years ago."

"Ah, nothing to worry about now mate, if anyone gives you problems about it, give me a shout, I'll deal with it. Now then, can you talk about what happened, do you remember anything suspicious before the Bombing?"

"What?" I can't hear him or take in anything else he says, but I feel much better now he knows about my conviction. He backs off disappearing behind my visitors.

I feel a strong need to reassure everyone, including myself, that I'm okay, they must have gathered here wondering if I'm gonna die or something. As they come closer I try to say something but it's not easy to speak. I recognise a security guard from work, who sits down beside me but it seems like he's talking nonsense at a hundred miles an hour. I can't understand a word he says. I wonder if there's something wrong with him. As I look around it dawns on me that there's something wrong with me, I can't hear much. I ask for a pen and paper so I can communicate explaining that I can't hear. Before he moves away I write, *'He talk too much and too quick.'* And he holds it up laughing for the others to see. Someone shouts, "Well he ain't lost his sense of humour has he?" and it feels good to get a laugh!

Next Tina* from work approaches, "Bloody Hell Garri, it's been really strange seeing you lying here without a smile on your face for five days. I don't think I've ever seen you without a smile before."

"What? Five days?" Her words sink in and shake me up! The true severity of my situation strikes home with a massive thud!

Overwhelmed, exhausted and in need of comfort, I turn my thoughts inwards towards Mum and close my eyes.

12th July 2005 08.00am
The Royal Free Hospital A&E

I wake up realising I'm in hospital and remember being woken up in the night by a drunken party going on outside, which I'm pretty sure wasn't a dream. I catch sight of a nurse coming up the ward. "Morning Nurse, can you help me please?"

"Morning Garri, what can I do for you my lovely?"

"What was all that noise outside my window last night?"

"What noise?"

"Rattling and clanking bottles, people laughing, singing and carrying on? Sounded like a drunken party."

"*Tut*, no party out there," she laughs, "no one can get into the Hospital grounds at night dear, maybe you heard the refuse shoot working or you were dreaming, unless it was a ghost!" As she walks away smiling and shaking her head, I also recall a strange vision I had. It was such a clear vision but I can't make sense of that either; must be the meds?

The nurse returns soon after to tell me I'm going to be transferred to a private room this afternoon. I'm pleased; it'll make life here a lot better because I need my privacy.

12th July 2005
The Royal Free Hospital George & Mary Ward Room 9

Once moved into my private room I'm shocked to find out I've already had several operations on my right leg and as many as five on my left leg. I'm also due to have a sixth this Friday. My left leg, which is now only a stump, seems huge, but I guess it's the padding from the bandage. It feels bizarre to have been out of it for so many days, but I suppose the worst is over, so that's a blessing. The second blessing is my newly acquired wheelchair parked by the side of my bed! Now that I'm mobile again I want to make the most of it, so climb on board and go looking for anyone else who was involved in the Bombings. I need to reconnect with people that understand what I've been through, for some kind of bonding and mutual support

Exploring my new ward I find a woman covered in bandages so wheel my chair slowly towards her bed to talk to her. "Excuse me, were you involved in the Bombings?"

"Yes" she whispers faintly and nods her head. I feel sad to see a distant look in her eyes, as the saying goes, the lights are on but there's no one home. I recognise the headspace she's in and it makes me want to say something to empathise. "Yeah, I was there as well but listen, we are both still alive. I want to say we are still here for a reason. I find it's helped me to focus on the positive side whenever possible; it's helped me to stay strong and it might help you. Don't let the bombers see that they've beaten you, don't let them win!" I offer as much encouragement as I can but she doesn't say anything else. I trust the words have sunk in, and maybe I also needed to hear those words.

Just then a nurse wearing a dark blue uniform suddenly rushes over towards me looking very flustered. "Garri what you doing here?" I get the feeling I've done something wrong.

"I was just trying to offer some positive words Nurse, why shouldn't I be here?"

"No Garri, you're supposed to be in isolation, you've got an infection. That's why we moved you to your own room." She quickly wheels me back to my room shaking her head, but then she smiles at me. "It was a nice thought Garri, but please do stay in your own room now until we resolve the infection, okay?"

"Yes of course, I didn't realise. So sorry."

13th July 2005 Early Morning
The Royal Free Hospital George & Mary Ward Room 9

I'm in too much pain and can't sleep, tossing and turning trying to find a comfortable position. The air mattress I'm trying to sleep on is way too soft and isn't supporting my back at all. I ache all over and I'm sure I would be better off with a firmer mattress to lie on. Feeling irritated, frustrated and restless, I get up and slide onto the visitors' chair. The pain is relentless and makes me fidget continuously; as I touch my hair, flakes of debris fall out. As I try to brush it off, it dawns on me that I still haven't been washed. It's not a good morning, and I'm disappointed that there's no one around to help me. I sit for a while waiting for the nurses to come on their rounds with the meds trolley, but I'm so exhausted I drop into a light sleep resting back in the chair.

February 1985
Lewis Remand Centre

Exhausted yet fighting sleep, the atmosphere in this place is so frightening I can't let go. It's like being an orphan cub in a Lion's den. How do people stay safe in here? The burning thoughts in my head keep me on edge; I just can't relax or get comfortable. I lie awake thinking about my life, what's going to happen now, how will I survive, how will I get through this? How could it happen to me, that Judge and his sentencing remarks thinks he's so smart giving me hope, just to let me down again.

13th July 2005 07:00am
The Royal Free Hospital George & Mary Ward Room 9

A gentle tap on my shoulder wakes me from my uncomfortable and fitful doze. "Morning Garri."

"Hmmm." I grumble at the nurse, as I slowly come to my senses

"Here you go." She offers my medication in three little cups, two pills in each and I swallow the six tablets two at a time, washed down with several gulps of water.

"What's wrong with you Garri, why you sleeping in the chair?" The nurse looks at me quizzically.

"I feel so bad, I haven't slept all night, my bed's really uncomfortable…" It suddenly dawns on me something's gone wrong with my medication. "but wait, these are the first tablets I've had this morning, is that right?"

"What? You didn't get any since last night?" the nurse looks confused.

"No, not at all." She checks the notes and confirms that the night staff didn't give me any meds. Well that explains why I feel like shit! I'm not at all pleased, but at least when the drugs kick back in, I'll be able to cope again.

13th July 2005 10:00am
The Royal Free Hospital George & Mary Ward Room 9

My brother Hector acknowledges me through the window as he stops outside my room to clean his hands and put on a plastic apron before he can come in; there's someone with him. As he walks in, his old school mate John is right behind carrying a couple of bags that look heavy. He puts them down next to me, which makes me pay attention to his arms. I haven't seen John for at least five years and it looks as if he must have been working out, yet it's more than that, he looks so healthy he almost radiates light as he smiles and greets me.

"You ah'right Gaw?" he says in his cockney drawl.

"Yeah I'm okay, nice to see you mate, you look very well."

"Fanks, I brought you some goodies man, proper healthy food, fruit, nuts and juices, to help you heal faster. There's a blender in there as well so you can make smoothies. This is really gonna help you mate!"

"Thank you very much, but what'll I do with it all?" He hands me two small pieces of card covered in handwriting.

"It's easy, I've made some notes 'ere, 'ave a look when you're ready, you'll also find I've written some power words on this one as well. It'll help give positive energy! All you 'ave to do is keep repeating them but I'll go over it all wiv ya in a minute." He looks very enthusiastic and I'm more than curious.

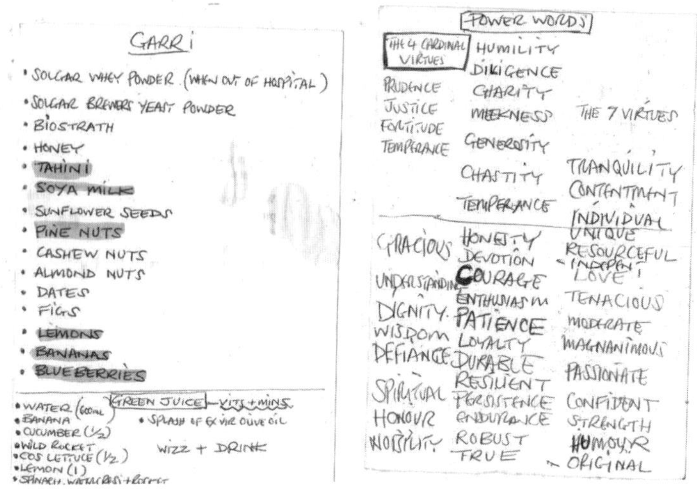

GARRI
• SOLGAR WHEY POWDER (WHEN OUT OF HOSPITAL)
• SOLGAR BREWERS YEAST POWDER
• BIOSTRATH
• HONEY
• TAHINI
• SOYA MILK
• SUNFLOWER SEEDS
• PINE NUTS
• CASHEW NUTS
• ALMOND NUTS
• DATES
• FIGS
• LEMONS
• BANANAS
• BLUEBERRIES
GREEN JUICE – VITS + MINS
• WATER
• BANANA
• CUCUMBER (½)
• WILD ROCKET
• COS LETTUCE (½)
• LEMON (1)
• SPLASH OF EX VIR OLIVE OIL
WIZZ + DRINK
POWER WORDS
THE 4 CARDINAL VIRTUES
PRUDENCE
JUSTICE
FORTITUDE
TEMPERANCE
HUMILITY
DILIGENCE
CHARITY
MEEKNESS
GENEROSITY
CHASTITY
TEMPERANCE
THE 7 VIRTUES
TRANQUILITY
CONTENTMENT
INDIVIDUAL
UNIQUE
GRACIOUS
HONESTY
DEVOTION
RESOURCEFUL
UNDERSTANDING
COURAGE
LOVE
ENTHUSIASM
TENACIOUS
DIGNITY
PATIENCE
MODERATE
WISDOM
LOYALTY
MAGNANIMOUS
DEFIANCE
DURABLE
RESILIENT
PASSIONATE
SPIRITUAL
PERSISTENCE
CONFIDENT
HONOUR
ENDURANCE
STRENGTH
ROBUST
HUMOUR
TRUE
ORIGINAL

"How you doing Bruv, sleep well?" Hector smiles, sitting down in last night's chair-bed.

"Yeah I'm better now Bruv, thanks but I had a really bad night, hardly slept at all. There was a problem with my drugs."

"What? *KMT*, you sorted it out though innit?" Hector frowns and looks concerned.

"Yeah, yeah." I nod.

"Good." He smiles, "Here, I've brought a few photos to keep you company, they told me they were gonna move you to your own room."

"Cheers Bruv." I smile too, looking through the pictures introspectively, thinking about Mum, she's on my mind a lot. "How's Mum?"

"She alright," he pauses, "she's good man, do you wanna go visit her?" He smiles anxiously.

"No, I don't want her to see me like this." Hector nods at once, he seems to understand my concerns.

"She can sense somethin' ain't right though, when I go to see her, she's looking 'round for you. I'm gonna tell her later today you've been in an accident, but that you're alright?"

"Yeah, best thing. But don't tell her how bad?" I look up at him for confirmation but he is distracted as a nurse walks in.

"Good morning Garri," she chirps.

"Good morning." I smile.

"Today my lovely, we are going to see if you can stand up." Rolling up her sleeves she approaches.

"Really? What? Now?" It's my turn to frown.

"Yes, let's do it." She insists, my Brother and John both offer encouragement as well. "Come on Garri, you can do this Bruv."

"Yeah Gaw, gwaan mate!" The nurse smiles at them and beckons me to the edge of the bed. I hesitate, but then shuffle across, dropping my legs over the side. She draws closer and with Hector on the other side they support my arms around their necks, taking my weight.

"What if I fall?" I pause, I'm unsure.

"You won't fall, we've got you." As my right foot reaches the floor, I nervously put some weight on it. Then gradually a little more weight and then a little more. Unexpectedly it's all too much, I feel weak, my leg gives way and I crumble back down onto the bed in despair. A sense of absolute failure and despondency sweeps over me, so I bury my head. I can't even look them in the eye. "Don't worry Garri, you've done so well." The nurse touches my back trying to comfort me.

"Yeah, Bruv you did well man. Don't worry." I feel their sympathy but it upsets me more, I don't want people to feel sorry for me.

After a few minutes John breaks the awkward silence, "Right Gaw, I'm guessin' you're pissed off right now, it's understandable, and you might not be able to believe this, but I'm here to tell you that what I brought you is gonna make a massive difference to your strength. I'll leave the stuff 'ere but I'll be coming back to make sure you're dealing wiv it. And listen Mate, I'm a vegan and I study health so I'm gonna share my secrets wiv ya. Maybe not today, but it's gonna happen, trus' me." I hear his kind and uplifting offer, but it doesn't make any difference at this moment. I'm inconsolable, I feel so empty and weak, and I have to escape back into my own private world.

5th May 2001 13:30pm
Stockwell Park Estate Brixton *The Endz*

My hands are covered in the soil as I plant seeds in Mum's 'garden'; she's made the balcony at the back of the flat into her own little garden with huge pots and colourful flowers. Taking pride in what I'm doing, I plant each seed an even distance apart until a row is complete. There's a few seeds left over so I discretely slip them into my jeans pocket, planning to take them home for my own garden. Mum inspects my work and thanks me; I'm glad she's happy with it. I wash my hands and she loads me up with food she cooked earlier as I get ready to leave. You just can't beat Mums cooking!

Back home I unpack the food still smiling, she's done me boiled green bananas, yellow yam, afu yam, boiled dumplings and underneath I find one… two, three, four pieces of juicy jerk chicken!

"Bless you Mum, I'm nice tonight! Mmmm." I inhale the sweet smells, rubbing my hands together in delight. I place my food on top of the cooker for later and go straight out into my garden to plant my pocketed seeds. Chuckling and feeling mischievous, I plan to tease Mum when I've finished as I know she's gonna have a laugh. I love making her laugh.

Hands still covered in earth, I find my phone and call.

"Yo, wha' ah gwan?" Her voice is strong.

"Mum! You can't answer the phone like that, it could be the Queen!" But I'm secretly cracking up; she'd change for no one!

"Who yu ah talk to? Me can talk to anybody soh, me ah pay the bill. Even if ah di Queen, me *still* ah answer like dat! Anyway weh yu waan pickni?"

I can hardly get my words out as I'm trying to stifle laughter. I accidentally let out a chuckle, "I thief some of yu seeds Mummy, they're in my garden now."

"Yu teif yu see," she kisses her teeth "Chaa! Whata way yu teif?" She's laughing heartily, just like I knew she would, I laugh too delighted my plan worked out.

13th July 2005
The Royal Free Hospital George & Mary Ward Room 9

It's been a long day and although I've requested a firmer mattress several times there's no sign anything's gonna happen any time soon. It's very frustrating to think I'm gonna spend another uncomfortable, sleepless night, so I am forced to do something. They say necessity is the mother of invention and it's true enough, so I look for something to put under my mattress to give me some support.

Could there be a loose shelf in the cupboard? No, but a small chair with a hard flat back close to my bed, might just work. I drag it towards me, and a couple of loose screws later the back comes completely away from the seat. I even surprise myself, but before I can position it under my mattress a nurse spots my crime and isn't pleased.

"Garri! What you doing? You can't do that!" She frowns shaking her head at me.

"Well I told you loads of times my back's killing me, I can't sleep in this eediot airbed and no ones doing nuffink to help me. I'm so fed up now

I don't care anymore, if I must do 'Ghetto' I can do it, trust me and I'm keeping it till they change my bed." I make eye contact and then carry on defiantly stuffing my precious bounty under the mattress. "And don't even think about sneaking in and taking it when I'm not about!" She can see that I'm upset, so she backs off at once, leaves the room, closing the door sharply behind her and legs it down the corridor! Although I know it's not her fault, I had to do something and feel more than justified 'transforming' the chair to get a better night's sleep.

Trying out the bed with the board under the mattress feels so much better. I lay back calmly feeling quietly confident that I can be independent again one day soon, after all I managed to solve the bed problem by myself. I needed that reassurance after yesterday's downer and I'm sure I can make it up with the nurse later.

14th July 2005 14:40 pm
The Royal Free Hospital

After a quiet morning, nil by mouth, it feels like I'm being wheeled back through history along dimly lit, gloomy corridors that could well be haunted by the ghosts of patients who died on the operating table still clinging on. It's horrible, so I clutch on to the Bible that Mummy gave me, and a small photo of Jesus, as I head for my sixth operation on my left leg. 'Dear God, I am about to have another operation and place myself in your hands, Amen.'

The large doors, apparently thirsty for oil, creak loudly as they wheel me through into the prep room. As they prepare me for surgery I notice the clock high up on the wall, it's three o'clock.

"Okay Garri turn over so we can give you an epidural, you may want to prepare yourself, it may hurt a bit, but try to keep still." Face down, holding my breath and as ready for the injection in the base of my spine as I can be, 'Oh My God!' Nothing could prepare me for this pain; I so need to scream out, but I use every ounce of male pride I have left to hold it in. I blow out a huge breath and inhale as much air as I can, filling my lungs to the max, while I try to Man-up. They tell me women have these all the time during childbirth, and if they can do it, so can I! Before I even get the chance to catch my breath again, they start searching for a vein in my arm to give me an anaesthetic.

Talk about torture, I feel like a dartboard as they stick in the needle and move on, stick again and move on, until at last bull's-eye, they find a vein! Finally, with oxygen mask in place they ask me to count.

"One… Two… Three… Fo… "

May 1993
Driving In My Car

It's a lovely day as we travel along Ravensdon Street towards Kennington Lane, I'm relaxed and playing my music loud. My girlfriend is next to me in the passenger seat doing shoulder moves to the tunes. As we approach the busy junction I try to brake, but the brakes don't work, the car continues at the same speed. I push the brakes again harder trying to stop, but they still don't work. Now alarmed and pumping the brakes more and more desperately as we get closer and closer to the junction, but the car still won't stop. As we veer across the busy main road, I do my best to steer around the vehicles; it's like an intense obstacle course. Buses beep, cars and vans swerve to avoid hitting us, breaks screech and lorry drivers shout abuse and scream at me through their windows. My girlfriend is screaming too, but there's nothing more I can do, we're in God's hands!

14th July 2005 20:00 pm
The Royal Free Hospital

Awake, and wondering what's happening but no one's about.

"Hello." I speak out as uneasy feelings edge in. It's not the first time I've suddenly found myself alone. I call out again a little louder this time, "Hello, anyone there?" as I try to sit up.

"Oh Hi Garri, you okay?" A member of the team approaches me from behind and calmly removes the monitors from my chest. I sigh in relief; looking up at the clock again the time shows eight o'clock. It takes a while to register that time has passed and the surgery is done, sleep is a strange thing and it makes me wonder! Then I feel the dull ache on my stump, becoming more and more painful.

"The porter will come for you in a minute Garri."

"Ah Okay, Thanks."

Once on the trolley and heading back to my room, anxiety about the little board under my mattress creeps in. I imagine that eagle-eyed nurse has stolen it while I've been away, and dreading the loss of it, I'm getting ready to make some more noise. But, as we approach my room the uplifting fragrance of flowers wafts down the ward to greet me. The aroma gets stronger as we get closer to my room, then from the doorway I see a huge bouquet of flowers sitting on the floor, and even more lying on my bed along with a stack of envelopes placed neatly in a pile. I'm overwhelmed with appreciation for the love that people send and I let go of the paranoia and anger that surged up before. Getting off the trolley and into my wheelchair, I notice a mattress lying on the floor in the corridor and realise it's the old one! I feel overjoyed they've actually changed my mattress.

I climb triumphantly onto my bed with a sense of elation and contentment. And, as if that wasn't good enough they even left my 'precious board' beside the visitor's chair. "Ha, she took heed!" Laughing and feeling stupid now to have worried that the nurse might take it, the stress is obviously getting to me.

Two Doctors in white coats approach my door, *knock knock.*

"Come in."

"Hello Garri, how are you feeling?"

"As well as can be expected thanks, my leg's sore now though."

"Yes I'm sure it is, my colleague and I just operated on your stump and we've been discussing the best ways forward for you."

"What do you mean?" I feel anxious and a bit puzzled.

"Well Garri, there isn't enough flesh and skin left to cover the bone, so we can't close the open wound. As your stump is technically shorter than the minimum required for a prosthetic limb, we want to remove more of the bone, either up to your knee joint or even above your knee." As the Doctors words assault my senses, my stomach churns, it just doesn't feel right. What shall I do now? They want to take more of my leg away, and this is the Doctor telling me to have this done! "Garri I'll leave the consent form here because we need you to sign it before we can do the surgery." I sit in sombre silence wondering how to digest this new piece of information. This is going to change my life even more; I'm not in a good place.

They leave my room door ajar, just enough for a male nurse to pop his head in. "You alright big G?" He smiles warmly.

"Not really mate." I can't even manage a grin I feel so upset.

"What's up?" He looks concerned and comes in closing the door quietly behind him. "I'm Barry, it's good to see you awake Garri." He sits down in the visitor's chair, "Tell me what's wrong, lets see if I can help." He smiles again.

"The Doctors that just left -"

"Yeah, I saw them." He listens intently.

"Well, they say the next operation they want to do is to remove more of my leg, either through my knee or above it; they've left the consent form there." Barry frowns, looking much more serious and places his hand on my shoulder supportively.

"Listen mate, it's your decision, if you don't want it done, they can't force you."

"But they're Doctors." I hear him but I feel pressured to do what they say, they must know what's best.

"Yes but it's your body mate, come on Garri." He looks me squarely in the eye and I understand him loud and clear.

"You know what, you're right, I ain't doing it." Suddenly it's like a heavy weight's been lifted off my shoulders.

"Good on you, take control and ask questions about everything that's happening to you." He smiles nodding and stands up.

"Thank you Barry, you're like a Guardian Angel mate." This time I smile back and offer him a high five, he obliges, making it a double. I feel so grateful to him.

"A'right mate, I'm glad to cheer you up."

With the consent form and bed problem resolved, the next problem to face is my bloated belly, it's as if I've been stuffed like a chicken ready for roasting. I haven't been to the toilet since I came in, just over a week ago, and something's brewing; if I don't go soon, I get a sense there'll be an explosion! Yeah too much information, I know.

Meanwhile my head's still itchy and as I have a good scratch, dirt and debris still falls out, it's a sad reminder that I haven't had a proper wash yet. I must be frowsy by now man, what I'd give for a bath. Ahhhh how good it would be to feel water on my skin, they must bathe me soon, surely? Anyway staying positive, I'm enjoying relaxing on this new bed, what a difference it makes and before long I drift off into a deep sleep, still dirty but certainly a lot happier.

15th July 2005 3:30am
The Royal Free Hospital George & Mary Ward Room 9

The desperate need to pee wakes me early and the bottle is full in no time. I'd better call a nurse for a bedpan too; I think things are on the move. I press the call buzzer and wait for a response, but no one comes. I wait about ten minutes and try again. Getting uncomfortable I lean over to look towards the staff room where I can see some of the staff watching TV. It surprises me to see they're all dressed up in fancy evening wear, Tux's and Cocktail Dresses, but their vibe tells me they're pissed off. Maybe they were called to work from a party or a ball. I guess that's a down side of their profession, emergency's wait for no man.

I press the buzzer again hoping for a response and I notice a young nurse in uniform moves away from the TV as if she's coming to me. Before she can leave a member of senior staff, all dressed up in her ball gown, calls her back and says something. I can see her face clearly and as she talks, I try to work out what she is saying. I've become quite good at lip-reading by now.

"He's always pressing the buzzer, screaming and shouting for help, just make him wait, don't go running after him so quick." I'm shocked, hurt and instantly aggrieved by what I think she said, my heart now pounding in my chest. Why is she being so nasty? The young nurse leaves the staff room shortly after heading straight to me and for sure I have some questions to ask her. I only hope I made a mistake.

"Yes Garri, how can I help?" She smiles.

"I saw what happened then, what was that all about?"

"Ah nothing Garri, just ignore her, cos I have, how can I help?" She looks embarrassed and red faced.

"No, no, come in and close the door, I wanna know what she said about me."

"She said that you keep screaming and shouting and that I shouldn't bother to come to you." I can't respond; I'm outraged to think that professional nursing staff can carry on like that. After all I've been through and what I'm still left to cope with. I really wish I could help myself, I certainly wouldn't be asking for help if I didn't need it. I wouldn't even be here if I could manage. I just need a bedpan; surely it's not too much to ask in a Hospital. I take a few deep breaths and allow my emotions to subside before I answer.

"I really haven't been screaming and shouting, but wait, even if I have, isn't it a nurses job to come and assist me if I need help, isn't that right?"

"Of course Garri, that's why I came, and I would have come sooner if she hadn't called me back. Just so you know, they were called in from a fancy Black Tie Event, so that's probably why she's so grumpy."

"That's no excuse you know, especially when I need a bedpan *Kmt!*"

15th July 2005 9:00am

The Royal Free Hospital George & Mary Ward Room 9

Mr Garlick arrives very upbeat and chipper.

"Good Morning Garri." He smiles as he approaches. I'm still feeling pissed off about the conduct of the staff in the early hours and I figure he's come to apologise for them.

"Good morning Doctor Garlick."

"Well Garri, I have some good news for you this morning."

"Hmmm, really, please carry on?" Now I'm intrigued.

"After much discussion, we have made the decision to leave your stump at the length it is, treat the infection and all being well, use a skin graft to close the wound. Your stump may remain long enough to allow you to have a Prosthetic Limb after all."

"But I thought it wasn't long enough?"

"Well, it's borderline actually, so lets hope it all works out for the best."

"Oh, that is good news, thank you, I'm very pleased I didn't sign the consent form to have more removed, I guess I must have a Guardian Angel looking out for me!"

"Indeed." He smiles and leaves to continue on his rounds.

15th July 2005 10:00am
The Royal Free Hospital George & Mary Ward Room 9

I catch Hector's eye from the corridor as he approaches my room, but he doesn't look happy to see me today, in fact he looks intense, like the weight of the world is on his shoulders.

"How you doing Garri?" His tone is low even though he's trying to put on a brave face.

"I'm okay thanks, just heard they ain't gonna take any more off my stump and I should be able to get a Prosthetic Leg. Good news innit?" It looks like what I've just said fell on deaf ears, he's not responding at all. "What's up with you Bruv?"

"Actually, it's bad news; I dunno how to say this…" He coughs to clear his throat and I wonder what's coming next.

"You need to know Mum might not make it over the weekend Bruv she's in King's College Hospital."

"What?" I feel an uncomfortable flutter deep in my belly as Hector rubs his face slowly before he continues.

"You see Bruv, what I didn't tell you before, is on the day of your accident she was also rushed into Hospital."

"What happened?" It's hard to take in what he's saying.

"It's bad Bruv, she pulled the peg feed out from her stomach. When the nursing staff tried to push it back in they split her abdomen open, the whole day was an unbelievable nightmare from start to finish. So, the big question is do you want to go and see her before its too late?" I'm stunned in silent disbelief. Hector looks at me with deep sadness in his eyes, trying to hold it together while anxiously looking for my answer. This is Mum he's talking about, our Mum.

"No," I shake my head defeated, before falling deeper into my silent cave. The feelings of sorrow cause physical pain inside my chest and a primal sense of loss rises up from deep within me, which takes every ounce of my strength to contain as it rips me apart inside. Oh God! The sense of loneliness that follows quickly escalates into despair and helplessness. So many thoughts and feelings rise up producing a giant tsunami of emotion that swells up and threatens to sweep me away.

My eyes burn as I rest back onto the bed feeling empty and deflated. All I can do is concentrate on my breathing, taking in air deeply and blowing the breath out hard, as I try to regain the part of me that now feels like it's been set adrift like a satellite stranded in space with no Mother Ship. Hector does his best to comfort me, but I'm too far away to feel anything. I can't help but wonder about the coincidence; she pulled out her feeding tube on the same day as the bombing, even though no one told her? It's uncanny we were in hospital at the same time, both in pain, both unconscious, on morphine and both facing death. Then I remember what I saw and heard when I woke up from my comma. '*Garri wake up!* 'I heard her voice calling me, but was it morphine-induced hallucinations, or somehow did her soul visit me as I lay there with my life hanging in the balance? I truly know if she realised what happened to me, nothing would have stopped her from being by my side, that's Mummy!

How can I go on now, my motivation to get through this in tatters without her, what am I gonna do? Only the thoughts of helping her gave me the motivation and strength I needed to survive underground, and now I won't ever see her again; what sick twist of fate is this?

Once again there's nothing to do but retreat into my zone and escape from this cruel world.

16th July 2005 8:00am
The Royal Free Hospital George & Mary Ward Room 9

After a rough sleepless night, one of the senior nurses comes into my room with a bathing trolley smiling.

"Have you been washed?" She asks as she approaches me.

"No! I've been here nearly two weeks, every time I touch my hair shit falls out and I stink; I feel horrible. You're asking me now, have been washed? Chaa man!" I catch sight of the nurses' face, as she steps back alarmed at my harsh outburst, making me check myself straight away. "Sorry for being abrupt, Nurse, nothing personal. I feel a bit rough at the moment as you can imagine, and I just heard yesterday my Mum's dying!"

"Oh no! I'm so sorry to hear that Garri, your apology of course is accepted… this time, but you owe me one." She smiles as she tries to lift my spirits, "you can call me Nurse Leyla."

I smile back, perhaps this is just the distraction I need this morning, and then I notice she's pretty.

Next she browses through my photos, picking up the one of my brother and I at my Niece's christening; I'm her Godfather. It's not often I like photographs of me, but it's a good one and I'm glad Hector brought it in. Having selected it, she locks me into her gaze; I notice what beautiful almond shape eyes she has, dark and mysterious with a captivating twinkle. Her smooth shiny dark hair pulled back in a ponytail showing off her charming little face smirking mischievously at me. "I want you to get back like this Garri," she points at the photo and smiles the sweetest smile.

"I'll try, Nurse Leyla!" I smile back as she approaches.

She sits on my bed and starts preparing me for my bed bath, but suddenly I'm feeling very self-conscious. She carries on dipping the flannel, into the bowl of water and carefully begins bathing my face looking into my eyes. The warm water on my skin feels amazing, and as it trickles down my chest, she moves in close with the towel. As she leans across to wash my torso, the hair from her ponytail lightly tickles my chin and it smells sweet.

"Do you have a girlfriend Garri?" She whispers and her question catches me off guard; I react quickly without even thinking,

"No I don't have a girlfriend, do you have a boyfriend?"

"No, men are all bastards!" She continues, but I sense pain, hurt and rejection.

"Hey, not all men are bastards you know, perhaps some are, but remember some woman can be a bit funny as well."

As our conversation continues I realise she must have had some bad relationships and I feel it could be helpful to offer her a more balanced view.

After finishing my bed-bath Nurse Leyla shaves my face and I feel so much better. I'm clean for the first time in two weeks and I'm getting attention from a pretty Nurse. And as if that's not enough excitement for one day, she says I'm going to be getting a massage twice a week as well, from a voluntary massage team working with the Hospital. The attention from a lovely woman and a long awaited bed bath has been the perfect distraction from yesterday's shock. Things are looking up; so let me think positively about Mum too; maybe it will help her.

17th July 2005
The Royal Free Hospital George & Mary Ward Room 9

Chilling on a Sunday morning reflecting on my life. I've had lots of visitors pop in over the past few days. It helps to know people care, but because I can't hear much of what they say, it's tiring and stressful having to lip read and watch body language to keep up with the conversation. I'm thinking of limiting my visitors for a while until I feel better.

The pain-filled sleepless nights, the worry of Mummy and also thoughts of how I'm going to live my life going forwards, is taking its toll. As I reflect I'm so glad my brothers didn't tell me about Mum before, I just wasn't strong enough to cope with it. I have to admire their strength and wisdom, but at the same time I know it's not good to bury my head in the sand. I have to take on board what's happening and deal with it, and that includes the Media attention that Hector says may come my way. Meanwhile he's asked our mate Carlton to help deal with the Media on my behalf, if and when the need arises. Carlton deals with them a lot in his work, so assures me he can do what's needed.

As the drugs trolley arrives to serve my morning cocktail of meds, Nurse Leyla comes over to my bed smiling.

"Morning Garri, we are going to change all the dressings today okay?"

"Morning Nurse Leyla." Smiling from ear to ear, so pleased to see her again. "You mean my left leg as well?" This news puts me on high alert.

"Yes Garri your left leg as well." She starts removing the bandages as gently as possible, and I feel apprehensive but at the same time as I look on the positive side it will give me an opportunity to see what's going on. I watch curiously as she undoes the bandage on my stump, whilst admiring her at the same time, until she gets to the part that's sticking to the wound. She carefully cuts the hairs on my leg that are stuck to the dressing, then she pulls at the bandage gently trying to remove it.

"Aghh that hurt!" It feels sensitive and I can see the open wound starting to show through some of the bandage.

"Oh sorry Garri, let me put some water on that crusty bit to soften it up." She's so sweet and easy on the eye, although it hurts, being distracted by her is very soothing.

Taking even more care she continues. It's all been a bit of a blur but at least this will give me the chance to take in what my body went through and remind me to have more patience with myself. I tend towards being happy go lucky, acting like nothing happened. Pushing myself too much, but now there are lots of emotional issues to deal with as well. I admit it's not easy.

After a while, the very concerned face of SJ the Senior Sister marches in.

"What's taking so long Nurse, haven't you got that dressing off yet?" she snaps.

"No, it's stuck and I'm being gentle, so I don't hurt him."

"Gentle? Do you realise leaving the wound open like this can spread infection, let me have a go at it."

Not liking the sound of that, SJ has my full attention as she grabs the dressing and firmly tugs most of it away with one quick firm pull.

"Arghhhhh!! What the …" I scream the ward down, but before I can do anything she tugs sharply again and the whole lot comes away quickly, hairs an all!

"Why the fff did you do that?" By now the pain is so intense I'm dripping in sweat and I so want to cuss a bad word.

"What, you'd rather the infection spread?" She responds quickly before disappearing out the door. Nurse Leyla pulls a sympathetic face, as she quickly continues to clean my wound. As I focus on it, I can't believe what I see, it's like a piece of raw meat in a butcher's shop, the amputated end exposing dried blood, dark brown flesh and bone. My leg is swollen to twice it's normal size, even without the bandages, and it's really a shocking sight.

After the dressing is re-applied, I calm down and spend the rest of the morning tying to recover from the stressful ordeal.

By early afternoon, SJ ventures back, peeping around the door grinning tentatively.

"You alright now Garri?" She asks brightly and without any remorse for what she did. I resist the urge to cuss a bad word, as I know she did it for my own good. I smile through clenched teeth and shake my head at her.

"Yes thank you I'm recovered somewhat." I laugh and warm to her again. We chat about what's going on and I mention the idea of reducing the amount of visitors to just family and close friends. "Although people mean well, they don't realise how much their visits drain me."

"Okay Garri, I understand." She shows empathy; ah she actually has a heart! We decide only my brothers as well as John, who's bringing me healthy food supplies and my work colleagues Anita* and Tina, both wonderful woman who have been so helpful. Anita is dealing with all my finances and I'm so grateful for that; she is now my adopted Lil' Sis.

Hector arrives late and I tell him I've decided to limit my visitors, he agrees it's a good idea. Hector is travelling to and fro between my Mum in King's College Hospital and me. I marvel at his strength, and wonder if he's getting enough sleep. After a quick chat he drops off sound asleep on the chair beside me, and looks like he's probably there for the night. It's fortunate that my company have kindly offered a car service to bring him. I must ask him to bring Tony with him as well sometimes; I miss Tony.

20th July 2005 Morning
The Royal Free Hospital George & Mary Ward Room 9

Hector asks again if he should take me to see Mum in Hospital. They say I'm stable enough to go now, but the idea makes me uneasy. Although I so want to see her, I definitely don't want her see me like this, in case it upsets her. But also I don't want my memories of her, to include an image of her dying in a Hospital. I'd rather my last memory be peacefully sleeping in the Nursing Home. It's a tough decision but it's one I've made after much thought.

After breakfast Hector is off to see Mum again.

"Give her my love and look after yourself."

"Take it easy Bruv." He leaves and although I know he's upset, he never shows it. Just puts on a brave face and gets on with life, whatever happens.

Soon after he leaves, they say I'm stable enough to go down to the gym. 'Follow the yellow line when you get to the lower ground floor' they tell me. So here I go, down in the lift on what seems like a huge adventure. I like the sense of independence and it uplifts me as I wheel myself from corridor to corridor singing ♪*follow the yellow paint line.* People are looking at me like I'm crazy, but they're smiling, so it's okay. It would be so easy to feel depressed going along these gloomy corridors. I can't help but feel a fresh lick of paint would make all the difference. Anyway, I keep following the yellow paint line until it stops at a set of double doors. All it needs is a sign that says welcome to the Wizards so I would be sure I was there. Just then the doors swing open and one of the Trainers walks through; she holds the door open for me on her way out.

"Thank you so much." I smile as I wheel through.

"You're very welcome, enjoy the Gym." She smiles back and cocks her head to one side.

Once inside I meet Judy* my Physiotherapist/Gym Trainer who signs me in for an induction. She seems friendly and very efficient. I'm glad to be here, and yet apprehensive at the same time, wondering what the hell I can do in the Gym now. As I quickly scan around I catch sight of an elderly woman with silver curly hair carefully walking on two prosthetic legs inside a set of parallel bars! Suddenly, from the depths of uncertainty, my future emerges before my eyes! She lifts my heart as if by magic; I simply can't stop staring. Her blue eyes sparkle as she beams at me, obviously enjoying the expression of respect and admiration I'm giving off; my mouth is probably hanging open. I feel like I've been injected with hope, it's so fantastic to see a way to walk again. I vow to myself that if this lovely lady can walk on two artificial legs at her age, I will definitely make it my goal to run on my new leg, this is my challenge!

Judy removes some of the bandage covering my stump as my excitement builds. She helps me place it into an air cushion, which protects the wound from pressure when I put weight on it. The PPAM-Aid device is a small metal frame that will support my left leg as I stand on it, to start walking again. Once it's on my leg, Judy stays close by my side, just in case. I clock her white trainers with a red flash; I catch myself fascinated by people's feet these days.

I'll always remember this moment, as I stand up for the first time since the Bombing, slightly wobbly on my crutches. I feel like a child who is trying so hard to balance, wants so much to do it, but feels a little uncertain. Once steady I take my first step. A monumental moment! There's a comforting familiarity about putting weight on my leg again, yet it's different, very different. Judy encourages me every step of the way as we walk along together then stop, and try a little more. I'm learning to walk all over again.

July 1990
Brixton Fashion

The loud rhythmic sound of Hip-Hop thunders out around the catwalk and the spotlights are on me as I walk down modelling an outfit from Tyrone's collection. I get halfway along then I stop to strike a pose. At the end I turn dramatically posing again, before walking back showing off the back view to the audience; the vibe is electric. Nice work if you can get it and I feel so fortunate to be here after all the rehearsals, perfecting my walk to help show off Tyrone's Collection. I really do enjoy fashion and this collection is awesome!

20th July 2005
The Royal Free Hospital

In no time at all I've done seven laps of the gym, balancing on this strange metal apparatus that I've never heard of before. I must admit it's amazing and makes me feel hopeful and much more confident about being able to walk again. Using my legs is vital of course; the exercise along with the healthy food John brings me will help to strengthen both legs. I never want to feel like I did the first time I tried to stand and collapsed; it was a devastating blow being so weak and helpless, never again!

"Come on Garri, it's time for some lower back and tummy exercises to strengthen your core, you'll need a strong core to get you up and moving again." The Physio keeps encouraging me, pushing me hard, she is determined to test me to my limits and seems to know I will respond. Each time I think I've finished a set she pushes me for more. "Just five more Garri, five more."

"Okay no pain, no gain." Once we finish I am in pain, but in a good way this time.

"Garri you made a great start, looking forward to seeing you again tomorrow!" she nods encouragingly.

"Thanks Judy, I've got a great Trainer." She smiles, blushing lightly as she removes the walking device and replaces the bandages before giving me a bed exercise program to take back to the ward. "Thank you very much." I smile as I leave the gym and really feel I've made a big step forwards today in many ways and with progress made, my spirits are lifted.

On my return to the ward another massive bunch of flowers and get-well cards greet me. I'm touched that people bother to put pen to paper and

Bed Exercise Program **-Garri Holness**

Arm exercises:

1. Theraband exercises
   - bicep curls 2 x 20
   - arm raises to roof 2 x 20
   - pulling theraband apart x 20 hold 5 sec

2. Bottom lifts in chair hold 10sec x 5

Leg exercises:

Stretches with theraband 30sec each
1. calf stretch with leg straight on bed
2. calf stretch with leg bent
3. hamstring stretch with leg straight in the air roll foot in and out
4. bend knee to chest
5. Straight leg raise 2 x 10 hold 10 sec

Lying on tummy

6. lift leg of bed straight x 10
7. bend knee x 10 hold 5sec
8. bend knee and lift leg x 10

Sidelying with theraband

9. Lift leg in the air with straight knee 2 x 10

10. Squeeze pillow between knees x 10 hold 10 sec

11. Bridging with legs on pillows x 10 hold 10 sec (fold arms)

Standing exercises with frame
12. balancing on one leg x3 best efforts
13. mini squats 2 x 10 hold frame

acknowledge me. As I read them, I am amazed that I've made such an impact on peoples lives in the ways they describe; it's overwhelming, especially as I've only known some of them for a short time. It's nice of course to be praised but I'd also like to understand why they say such things. I decide it must be because I've tried to stay positive through it all. If keeping positive portrays me as a 'bubbly character' that inspires them, I want to do it even more. I have to credit Hector for reminding me negativity brings us down, he helped me to stay calm and positive right from the start and one day I want him to know how much I value his help.

The idea of positive thinking isn't new to me, but I must admit I hadn't paid as much attention to it until I faced death. I vow to myself that I will try to be more actively positive from now on, so that I can heal quicker both mentally and physically. I also want to share this idea with others when I put my attention to the article Carlton asked me to write for the one of the Tabloids. Yeah that feels good let me spread some positive energy by writing something to uplift.

I'm hungry after the gym, so I move the gifts off my bed in readiness. While I wait for lunch I try to work out a few of the bed exercises from the sheet Judy gave me.

Lunch arrives promptly but the more aware I become of healthy food, the more it becomes obvious to me that the food here is processed. I have to eat though, even though John 'the Food-Police' wouldn't approve I can only do my best. I'm fortunate enough to make healthy smoothies like he showed me from nuts, seeds, fruits and fresh juice, especially cranberries pomegranates and blueberries. I'm so grateful for my own little fridge to keep them in as well, given to me by my lovely work colleague Tina. John says all these things are good for me and will help me get better quicker. I'm so grateful to him for the blender and the advice. I've realised how important it is to take responsibility for what we eat and drink. He said if we eat too much processed food, we simply can't be healthy. I really do feel the difference since I have been actively supplementing my Hospital diet with his suggestions, along with using the 'power words' he advised me to repeat. Everything we are subjected to has it's own quality of energy. It's either useful or it's not and we alone can choose what we take in.

After lunch the sun blazes in through the window and my room is a getting quite hot so I switch on the fans. I really prefer being in my own room. Yeah man, look at my room, people's kindness has made such a difference, I feel quite at home in here. I'm so grateful for two large fans to keep me cool, the portable TV and DVD player. Not to mention a box of unopened DVD's that I will get around to watching at some stage. My precious little radio on the window ledge, already tuned in to two-step Garage on Fresh Fm and wonderful flowers. Check me out, doing shoulder moves to the beat. I hope I'll be dancing again soon.

I overlook Pond Street and in the distance I can make out the greenery of Hampstead Heath what a great view to enjoy! People watching keeps me amused for hours especially as its summer; everyone is so carefree and happy in the sun. The thing about London is, it only takes a glimmer of sunshine and everyone strips off, whether they have the body for shorts or not! Cars drive past with their roofs down too and because this is a wealthy area, some of the sports cars are real head turners. I'm content today, gratitude is part of a positive mentality; I'm very happy to be alive!

The Masseuse arrives mid afternoon. What a lovely girl and how wonderful to volunteer her services to the Hospital, I'm so lucky. She has a caring vibe and I like her calm energy. After the initial painful knot removal from my muscles, it feels so wonderful to have them soothed by a massage and by the time she's finished I'm floating on air. "Okay Garri, you're done, I'll leave you to have a snooze now, you look so relaxed." She smiles patting me on the back and laying the sheet over me.

"Thank you." She leaves quietly and I drift off.

20th July 2005 *Dreaming*

The Royal Free Hospital George & Mary Ward Room 9

Flying through space, its dark and I don't know where I am. I'm confused yet I know I'm supposed to be here. I go with the flow, no resistance. Enjoying the sensation of flying, feeling calm, cool and connected and with an important mission to fulfil; I know exactly where I must go and what I must do. It's like I'm flying at speed through the dark tunnels of my mind, until my awareness suddenly switches as I recognise the bright lights ahead. I'm back underground on the Piccadilly line and yet strangely unaffected by the hustle bustle of the rush hour playing out around me. In the crowd I'm drawn to a man I see from behind but as I try to follow I lose sight of him, as a blonde woman walks straight towards me; I try to move out of her way but it's too late and she literally walks straight through me. What? Tingling from head to toe as our energies momentarily merge, she stops still as if she feels it too and then looks back. I am left with a full and complete sense of who she is, where she's going and also what will happen next.

20th July 2005 Late Afternoon

The Royal Free Hospital George & Mary Ward Room 9

I wake up with a start! There's a strange stillness in the room, it's like time's stood still somehow; half in and half out of my dream, the small TV in the corner catches my eye. I recognise the Oval and Stockwell tube stations on the News, as they report a further day of London Bombings! But at least this time the bombs failed to detonate. Wide-awake now, I can't believe what the World's coming to, what's this all about? Just then, two young nurses pop into my room.

"Garri are you okay?" They look concerned.

"Yeah fine thanks and you?" They both smile and look at each other, one checks my drip as the other starts to check my dressings.

"Are you sure you're okay, we were worried about you, with what's going on in the news today?"

"Oh yeah, I did see it briefly, but I'm okay thanks. I've got some magazines to distract me and I rarely pay attention, it's mostly bad news. Anyway, I'm gonna be busy writing an article for one of the big Tabloids later."

"Wow! That's great Garri, please can we read it when it's done?"

"Maybe!" I wink and smile, we all laugh.

Late afternoon turns to evening as I enjoying my creative writing, and before the nurses change shift, one of them pops in to give me my last meds for the day. "While you're here would you mind passing me that photo of my Mum please?" She smiles and hands the framed picture to me. I have the need to be close to Mummy tonight; I feel her calling me.

20th July 2005 *Dreaming*
The Royal Free Hospital George & Mary Ward Room 9

Jumping straight back into my dream I see the blonde woman standing in a daze, suddenly she shakes her head as if to reboot and rushes back along the platform. Then I catch sight of the man I came to help all dressed in blue with his sports bag. Right on queue, she pushes in front of him to board the packed train into the only available space. He taps her lightly on the shoulder and wishes her a good day, then smiles as she stares at him through the window.

I follow him onto the next train and as he turns to face me, it's like looking in the mirror! I can't help but stare, its not often you come face to face with yourself! Somehow knowing *he* is *me*, but in an earlier time line. I suddenly remember the sense of being stared at. Even though he can't see me I know he can feel me staring at him, how weird is that?

There are people everywhere squashed together and still some pushing to get in the overcrowded train. He shouts out a funny remark in answer to a man on the platform and puts his bag on the floor. I notice his trainers, chaa man they were my favourite, I'd forgotten I'd lost them! Then I remember the bead of sweat, I watch it trickle along his brow and down his face until he wipes it away, then I lean in to whisper, "*we shudda walked man,*" and I know he can hear me.

My mission is to reinforce his body with extra life-force so I can limit the damage and survive the explosion that's about to rip this train apart. As we move away from the station I merge with him and visualise surrounding his body with as much energy as I can. *Boom!* There it is, the carriage fills with ball of explosive light and searing heat, we are forces head first into the yellow handrail and knocked out.

In the darkness, I see his solitary soul still clinging to the handrail that only exists as a figment in his mind. I try to calm him with positive thoughts, as he looks around bewildered. I know exactly how he feels; he's trying desperately to understand what just happened. All he knows for sure is there's something wrong! I have to help him back into his body so we can stay alive. I whisper to him again. *"Stay focused, stay focused, you've got to stay calm, your life depends on that. It's not your time to die, get back into your body, it's on the floor. Think about Mum!"*

He seems to understand and moves towards his body on the floor of the train wreck, slowly returning to consciousness… his body moves!

Then I hear Mummy's voice behind me, I knew she wouldn't be far away!

"Garri…. Garri! Weh yu de?"

"I'm here Mum, where are you?" As she appears I rush to give her a hug. *"I did it Mum, I just saved him, I mean me! Remember my promise?"*

She cocks her head to one side, just as she used to with a half grin. *"What promise yu ah talk abou' me son?"*

"Remember when I was little I said 'Wherever you go I'll go with you, when you die, I'll die with you'? Well, I nearly did die, but now I know it isn't meant to be. But, because the promise came from my heart, part of me has to die with you. My leg Mum, I'm going to lose my leg. But don't worry I'll be okay, I can live without it. And I will cremate it and join our ashes as a bond of everlasting connection. I love you so much and I'm grateful for this opportunity to hug you and say goodbye before you go. I wish you peace for your journey to the after-life. Always remember I love you. True love never dies."

A light comes from inside her and beams out making a complete circle around us. *"A'right me son, but yu nar go lose da whole leg, just da foot me ah tek to heaven wid me. Me send yu an Angel to save your leg. Yu see from now, yu have a foot in two worlds! An' 'member me ah always watch over yu! Me lickle washbelly!"*

21st July 2005 5:50am
The Royal Free Hospital George & Mary Ward Room 9

Only half awake feeling uneasy about Mummy, a vague memory of dreaming about her surfaces as well as the nightmare of being back on the Underground. It makes me shudder, but it's time to get up and follow my morning routine. It's what keeps me grounded through all this. Bathroom by six o'clock for a wash and affirmations, using some of the power words John gave me. Then do my exercises given to me by my Trainer. I've built up three sets of twenty dips on my wheelchair as well over the past few days and although it hurts, I'm determined to get my strength back. The drugs trolley arrives with my morning tablets and then a standard hospital breakfast at eight o'clock. Nothing exciting but it keeps my body and soul together.

A flock of medical staff doing the rounds catches my attention; five or six student doctors follow closely behind Mr Garlick in a line. He's like a Father Goose leading his baby Goslings to water, and by nine o'clock he knocks on my door.

"Good morning Garri, how are you this morning?"

"Morning Doc, I'm okay you know, how are you?" The small group of his protégées wait respectfully, hovering in the doorway.

"We're busy this morning, would you mind if we all take a look at your charts together?"

"Yeah, come in, the more the merrier!" They waddle in smiling and form a semi-circle at the foot of my bed, centring their attention on me. Although they make me a little self-conscious I do understand the need for education. It's not only for them, it's even more important for me to know. I want to understand exactly what's happened and how I'm doing.

"Garri Holness was injured in the London Bombings on the 7th of July. As you can see, he has sustained multiple injuries. After being on life support for five days and receiving intensive blood transfusions, Garri is now doing remarkably well considering the extent of his injuries. His eardrums were both perforated; his hair, eyebrows, eyelashes and body hair were all badly scorched. There are burns and injuries to his face, head, neck, arms, back and both legs and he has been experiencing severe spinal pain. There is an open wound from shrapnel on his right shin. He also sustained multiple shrapnel wounds between the shin and the foot and has unfortunately suffered the loss of his lower left leg, below the knee. We had to carry out two amputations on the left leg because the first time we tried to save as much of the leg as possible, but there was simply not enough skin and flesh left to cover the protruding bone. We have managed to save his left arm that was also severely damaged by shrapnel. On arrival there was a large swelling and injury to the solar plexus area, which was badly damaged by shrapnel from the blast, this injury caused him breathing difficulties and severe constipation." The Student Doctors are no longer smiling; instead they stand staring in stunned silence as the extent of my trauma is spelled out to them in detail. I can actually feel their disbelief as they focus intently on me "But we have managed to ease his chronic discomfort somewhat, haven't we Garri?" He looks over smiling and raising an eyebrow waiting for me to confirm.

"Ah yeah…it was a bit hard. I mean soft actually but the main thing is I've been now! Thank God!" There's a flurry of giggles from the Goslings and Father Goose shakes his head chuckling, before he continues.

"His overall trauma caused swelling that made him appear to be twice his normal size. As you can imagine this jolly handsome half naked incredible hulk of a man, caused rather a stir amongst the nurses in A&E! So, any questions?"

Breaking up the severity of the report with humour, we all laugh together enjoying the lighter mood. Even so, as I hear the seemingly endless list of injuries I once again understand there is much for me to be grateful for.

I don't have much else on today, although I may get some visitors later. I will put my focus on enjoying my time at the gym, as each day passes I feel myself getting stronger and more confident. I'm determined to strengthen my core, as I need to compensate for my leg. I also need to improve my balance, as this will be my lifeline. After all I'm learning to walk all over again.

I have a feeling my brothers and a couple of friends may pop in later, but as I lie back and relax, thoughts of Mum stream into my head again, so I pick up the phone to call my brother Tony. With the Loud Speaker switched on and holding the mobile to my good ear, the ring tone sounds faint; he picks up.

"Hello… Tony? What's going on Bruv?" An awkward silence screams down the phone and I know instantly something's wrong, and I know exactly what it is. "Mummy's gone innit?" I hold my breath.

"Yeah Bruv… she passed away this morning." His words sound distant and muffled, but I hear enough to understand.

"Bloody Hell, you alright bruv?"

"Yeah, yeah." He sounds as if he's coping and that's a relief.

"Okay I'll see you later T." I hang up dazed, but absolutely certain in the core of my being that Mummy came to say goodbye last night. I tell myself she's gone to a peaceful place, no more suffering, and she's also with her family and friends. It's hard for me to shed a tear, as I feel numb and emotionally drained after everything that's happened, on this roller coaster ride I call my life.

I reflect on memories of Mum, and our closeness, which will always remain in my heart. Life is stranger than fiction; they do say you should be careful what you wish for, and I know first hand how true that is. I distinctly remember making a promise as a young boy to die with Mum when she died and at the time I meant it. Oh God we nearly did die on the same day, didn't we? Memories of my dream flood in. "Tu Rhaatid!" I recall the vivid details and I feel so grateful for that. Seeing myself flying through dark tunnels underground, trying to save myself and then hearing Mum calling me. I felt her, I saw her, and I hugged her. I know when she came to find me and say goodbye, she gave me her last breath. Leaving me certain that she'll be watching over me from now on. It wasn't my time to die; that much has been made clear. I'm so lucky to be still alive.

I ask the nurse to stop any visitors coming for me today, I need to be left alone to reason this through and commune with my spirit. Meditation!

22nd July 2005
The Royal Free Hospital George & Mary Ward Room 9

I awaken early to another morning of the same routine, but nothing will ever be the same again. I've so much to reflect on, with the loss of my Mum, it's the end of an Era! Staring into the mirror trying to do my morning affirmations. I notice my scorched eyelashes are making a bid to grow back. My hair still patchy where it was literally blown off my head, is still intermingled with debris from the wreckage. Maybe I'll shave it all off and start again. Scars landscape my whole face, my forehead, under my right eye, along the bridge of my nose and under my mouth, but still I'm glad I can breathe and I'm alive. I won't let it get me down, I must choose to get on with my life and see the positive side whenever possible. 'Easy fi say, not easy fi do' but I will attempt it.

Reminded of an appointment with the hearing centre downstairs in twenty minutes, I get ready to go regardless of how I feel; I desperately want to be able to claim back my hearing. As I arrive, a young Indian couple walking through catch my attention for some reason, and then soon after they disappear, he returns alone. As he approaches I feel the need to talk with him.

"Excuse me mate." He looks over and smiles.

"Yeah mate, you. Could I have a minute of your time please?" He comes over purposefully. "I wonder if you read the Qur'an?" "Yes I do!" He raises his eyebrows and smiles again.

"Could you please explain something to me I'm very curious what the Qur'an teaches about violence and killing in the name of Religion?" He pulls over a chair and calmly sits next to me.

"Can you speak slowly please, my hearing isn't great."

"Yes, of course. Let me explain something to you. Muslims are peaceful, we respect and help women, children and innocent people; if we are being oppressed, naturally we'll fight back, like everyone else." I watch and listen intently, partly relying on my newly acquired lip reading skill.

"I am a survivor of the recent Bombings you know." His face is full of compassion as he lowers his eyes and shakes his head.

"So sorry to hear what happened to you. I know certain groups, who despise the West have taken sections of the Qur'an and interpreted them in a most inappropriate way to brainwash the youth, as well as those who are weak minded or lost in our society. They promote such evil deeds and promise Martyrdom to those who comply. However the majority of us believe it's wrong. I believe it's wrong!"

We talk and reason together until I have to leave for my appointment, it's helpful to understand another point of view.

"Thanks for that Mate, it was really a pleasure to talk to you. Gotta go in for my appointment now, but I feel so glad you spent this time to chat." I shake his hand smiling.

"Likewise, I'm sure." He scribbles his name and email address on a piece of paper and hands it to me. "Look after yourself Garri and drop me a line when you're ready."

After examining my ears, the Doctor sadly confirms I still have perforations in both eardrums, the left side more so than the right. I knew something was wrong, although I can sometimes hear faintly, it may be just a vibration. This is not good news at all, I feel it more because music is such an important part of my life, but let's hope it's not permanent.

Heading back upstairs to my room feeling down about this latest setback, the magnitude of what's happened, hits me again, it will continue to impact my life in so many ways. Will I ever be able to hear myself sing again? The reason the guys call me Sugar is all about the voice, but can I sing if I can't hear properly? It's deeply upsetting. By the time I get to my room and see all the flowers and cards again, I'm reminded I'm loved, and once again reconnect with the feeling that I'm glad to be alive and of course the comfort that Mum is no longer in pain and discomfort.

My mobile vibrates and I answer. The voice is familiar but faint so I change the settings to speakerphone and increase the volume to max.

"Hello… hello are you there Garri it's Pippa*"

"Hello, can you speak up a little, it's not easy to hear you?"

"Garri, it's Pippa, how are you today?"

"I'm okay Pippa thanks, and you?" I put on a brave face.

"Yes I'm good thanks but listen, the BBC have been trying desperately to get hold of you, shall I give them your number?"

"No, please don't do that, it's not easy for me on the phone."

"Okay, what do you want me to say?"

"My friend Carlton Best has agreed to deal with any Media on my behalf. Hold on please while I get you his number…" I'm so glad to hand this over to Carlton, as I really need some peace.

The next few days pass quietly. I'm in mourning and my grief is intense, so much loss! During this time Carlton returns the call from the BBC and arranges an interview for me on the 26th.

26th July 2005
The Royal Free Hospital George & Mary Ward Room 9

BBC World News and BBC Radio 2 arrive and I'm ready, even though I still feel disconnected with the world as if I'm looking in on someone else's life. The interview lasts around twenty minutes and I don't really know what to say, but I do know whatever comes out of my mouth comes from my heart and not my head. Carlton gives me the thumbs up when it's done, so I figure it must be okay, but I'm glad when it's over and done with.

After the interview I sit thinking with my head in my hands and am reminded there's still debris in my hair. I really have to get this sorted out soon, so I call my brother Tony.

"Yo Bruv, what's good?"

"I'm alright you know Shuggs, what you saying." He sounds calm.

"I need a hair cut Rude Bwoy, what you doing later?"

"What you want me to cut your hair?" He laughs.

"Yeah man, I need you to shave it all off."

"Okay I'll be there later." Still laughing.

"Respect Bruv, see you soon."

27th July 2005
The Royal Free Hospital George & Mary Ward Room 9

It seems surreal this morning as I lie here seeing my name in Headlines and reading my article in the newspaper.

Almost one month ago, my life, like so many others, was changed forever by the terrorist attacks, which devastated London and left 52 people brutally murdered. I was on the Kings Cross train when one of the bombs exploded. Even though I will bear the physical scars of that awful day for the rest of my life, I want to offer a message of hope and reconciliation. I believe passionately that we should not sink into the sort of bitterness and racial hatred that has threatened to take root in the past few weeks.

The memories of what began as an ordinary working day will, of course, never go away and it's worth explaining what I, and my fellow passengers, went through on that July morning and its aftermath – not to attract pity, but to show how hope and friendship can blossom even in the shadow of terror...

Although still somewhat disconnected, I'm feeling proud and overwhelmed after seeing my efforts at writing in print. As the memories of the day flood back in, my phone vibrating is a welcome distraction. I reckon I have about 40% of my hearing back in my right ear, but the left one remains deaf, so I have to remember to answer the phone with speakerphone on, and listening with my good ear.

"Hello? Garri Holness."

"Hello Garri, this is John from BBC Radio 2, how are you?"

"Hello John, I'm as well as could be expected thanks." Surprised to hear from him, I wonder what he wants.

"Carlton gave me your number because I'm just calling to tell you that your interview has gone down really well. You've made grown men cry just listening to you." He sounds animated and pleased.

"Really?" I'm pleasantly surprised.

"I think it's the way you speak without malice or hatred in your heart, just words of wisdom and positivity, truly inspirational and I just wanted to let you know personally."

"Thanks man, that's nice to know, very touching."

"Well, good luck on your journey Garri, keep up the good work and get well soon. I'll contact Carlton if I need anything else."

"Thanks John." I hang up and start to reflect on what he said but the phone bursts into life before I can put it down."

"Garri man, it looks like overnight you have become a Celebrity. 'The Darling of the Nation' they're calling you, seems you've inspired everyone!" The excitement in his voice carries down the phone and into my room on the loudspeaker.

"Carlton Best is that you?"

"Funny, funny! Come on man, it looks like I really need to be your Agent now, right? My phone's been ringing off the hook; everybody wants to interview you. And I mean everybody from across the world as far as Japan and America, to Malta and Germany the list goes on. GMTV wants you on there as well. BBC Breakfast wants to do a documentary that follows your progress; the Nation wants to know all about you. The Tabloid Press are chomping at the bit for you. By the way I gave John at the 'Beeb' your number as he wanted to tell you the good news about the interview himself."

"Whoa, hold on, how can that happen in only a few days?"

"I've been busy innit?"

"Thanks man for all you've done, it's good news, but my main concern now is getting better and staying focused on the road of recovery anything else is really just a distraction to me. I only want to be fit and healthy enough to go back to work, I love my job and all the people I work with. They're a great crowd and they've been very supportive."

"Sugar, forget going back to work you're famous now. Rest up, talk soon."

"What?" The phone clicks off and as I put my hand to my head, I'm shocked to feel my shaved head, I'd forgotten Tony did it, it feels smooth and clean, no debris.

The next few days fly by, talking and talking, interview after interview, receiving emails, cards and messages from the public. I'm stunned to find masses of fan mail from women and even proposals of marriage! This is a huge boost to my self-esteem, which was at an all time low. I'm smiling again and my sense of humour is returning, slowly but surely, it's helping me to heal mentally. Thank God!

3rd August 2005
The Royal Free Hospital George & Mary Ward Room 9

There are cameras and microphones everywhere as I do an interview with BBC Breakfast and BBC Radio 4 together from my Hospital bed. Then the Newspapers take over, it's non-stop and seems to be the start of something quite bizarre. They want to know every little detail about the journey to work, what happened, how I feel about the Suicide Bombers and so on. My brother Hector said right from the start that I should be careful not to buy into the growing hate campaign against the Bombers and instead show compassion. Of course he's right, but I wouldn't have done that anyway, its not who I am. I just try to be frank straight to the point and clear that I'm not seeking revenge or retribution, merely trying to understand the situation and move forwards.

BBC airs my interview all day over and over, and BBC Radio 4 broadcast their interview with me twice. Each time the interviews go out I'm inundated with emails, as well as letters and cards coming in thick and fast by bike messenger via the BBC. They even call to say this is unprecedented. I have touched the hearts of a frightened Nation and it feels good to be able to be of use.

4th August 2005
The Royal Free Hospital George & Mary Ward Room 9

Late evening I'm distracted from my soul searching by a nurse.

"Garri, sorry to disturb you but a young Muslim man said he was compelled to drive from the other end of London to come here and express his sympathy after seeing you on TV; he hopes you make a speedy recovery and he left this for you." She hands me a card and as I read, tears well up.

'The wisdom in your thoughts and your strength to rise above adversity is breath-taking and I feel ashamed that a man could act in such a dishonourable way, but proud that another man can stand up taller than they could ever be. You are of great stature Sir.'

I feel moved by his words.

5th August 2005
The Royal Free Hospital George & Mary Ward Room 9

After rambling on introspectively about my life going forward, I manage to stick to my daily routine. I can't afford to be distracted, as the most important thing is my healing. Up early taking my tablets, thanking the nurse. Off my bed and into my wheelchair, gently does it. A few quick dips on the arms of my chair, exercising hard to keep my strength up; and all this before even having a wash! Talking of having a wash, into the bathroom and in front of the mirror again. As I scrutinise my face this morning I notice my eyelashes are curling up, as they gradually grow longer. I take it as a good sign that I am regenerating. I make a point while looking in the mirror, to make eye contact with myself every day and say mentally 'I will stay focused on my goal of being independent again, I will work hard to keep fit and keep my muscles strong' and that keeps me right on target.

Nurse Barry arrives to change my dressings, so I wheel myself back over to my bed and launch myself onto it playfully. It's great having him around to help me, he tells me straight what's going on and helps keep me level. I've noticed my stump is turning darker lately, which doesn't seem good. Barry brings with him an amazing portable mini V.A.C. machine today, to help fight the C-Diff infection that threatens what's left of my stump. He says there should be big changes within a week. He fits a sponge onto my stump with cling film and then a tube that fits into the pump, so I can hook it up any time I'm sitting still. As well as this Barry brings in a stash of innovative topical silver dressings, which are still at the experimental stage so not generally given out. He believes they are fantastic and will help my stump heal even quicker, reducing the risk of losing any more length. He has to battle hard with Orthopaedics to help me get through this touch-and-go phase, so I'm feeling very grateful to him.

The next person to arrive this morning is Mary with the breakfast trolley and my stomach is rumbling.

"Good morning, you timed that perfectly! I'll have two slices of toast please and one spoon of sugar in my cereal… thank you very much."

"Good morning Garri, how are you today?" Mary smiles placing the tray on the bed and fills it to my specification.

"All the better for seeing you sweetheart." I smile back and wink.

"Garri I'm a married woman, but thank you anyway dear." She giggles with her hand over her mouth as she walks away; it's good to make people laugh.

Even though normally I'm a fussy eater, I'm aware I need lots of energy to heal. I eat as much as I can, whether I like it or not, and even if I don't feel like eating. My diet definitely affects my physical well-being and my mental equilibrium. I've already noticed that the healthy food John brings me has had a positive effect on my body, and I'm pretty sure it gives me more energy in the gym. I'm excited to monitor it and the more I monitor it, the more obvious it is. We are what we eat!

May 1999
Mum's House Stockwell Park Estate Brixton

Under the weather, feeling hot and a bit clammy; my belly doesn't feel right, my body doesn't feel right, my head just doesn't feel right. Before I can ask Mummy for help I hear her footsteps quickly approaching with a sense of urgency and she hurriedly plonks a cup of Bush tea beside me with a knowing look in her eye. "Garri drink dis, me just boil it!"

The aroma rises up from the cup and distresses my whole being, it smells so strong and pungent and I really don't want to have anything to do with it. I nip my nose and make an attempt to sip it down little by little.

"Garri, move yu hand, move yu hand from yu face." She grabs my hand and pulls it away so I have to experience the full flavour of the brew.

"It taste bad yu see!" I sip it unwillingly pulling a face that shows my disgust.

"Just drink it, before me giya two box"

"Alright Mum." I surrender, nothing more I can do.

"Trus' me, yu feel better in a lickle while, ah di bitter taste ah wey ah go help yu." She nods knowingly.

"Yeah, Yeah." I'm unconvinced.

"Noh feisty wid me bwoy!" She puts me in my place and I sip again on the bitter brew as Mummy stands over me till it's all gone. As she walks away I feel a sudden sensation in my core that rises up producing a hot sweat that actually feels good. Hmm something's happening, perhaps she's right; maybe bloody old-fashioned Jamaican remedies do work!

5th August 2005
The Royal Free Hospital George & Mary Ward Room 9

Grabbing my water bottle and a towel I wheel myself to the elevator, down to basement and a few corridors later the Gyms in front of me.

"Oh Hello Garri, how are you this morning?" Judy smiles and leads me through.

"Okay thanks Judy, how are you?"

"Yeah I'm good, anyway how's it going on the ward, is there anything you need to tell me?"

"Okay so far, but funny you should ask cos they fitted a VAC on my stump this morning?"

"Yes I know, so we've got a new challenge lined up for you today; you up for it?" She looks mischievous and I wonder what's coming next.

"Yeah, I'm up for it." I can't help accepting a new challenge.

"Okay good! We'll start with some tough core exercise and after that you'll be learning to walk on crutches without the PPAM-Aid so you can continue to walk around on the ward this weekend, okay?"

"Sounds good, I'm definitely up for it, if you think I'm ready."

"Okay let's go!" Her confidence in me spurs me on.

We start with all sorts of abdominal workouts and press-ups. I'm pushed to my limits and feel the pain, but I've got to stay focused on my recovery and just deal with it. After a thirty-minute non-stop intensive workout, all the muscles in my body hurt. Sweating buckets I take a break to sip some water and wipe my brow.

Next it's time to come to terms with walking on the crutches, but first I've got to learn how to stand up. Judy shows me how to use both crutches fitted together to form a support to push up on so I can stand, man that's clever. Standing up on my right leg, which is now much stronger than the first time I tried it, I take a step using the crutches and then another, a bit wobbly at first, but readjusting my balance with each stride. Judy walks close beside me, to guide and support, just in case: I like it. My confidence grows, but suddenly as I catch sight of myself going along in the mirror the volume on my internal chatter increases. Can you do this? *Of course I can do this.* Are you sure? *Yeah I'm sure man just let me get on with it. The Trainer's here for a reason, stop making me doubt this shut up and let me get on!* But this is how I'm gonna be for the rest of my life, look in the mirror, I'm permanently disabled! *It's true I have to accept that, but I can make the best of it, just another challenge to overcome!*

6th & 7th August 2005

The Royal Free Hospital George & Mary Ward Room 9

With renewed confidence and my crutches up on the ward, the weekend passes quickly as I practice walking to the bathroom instead of using the wheelchair. Of course in-between resting my body, after the intense training on Friday, and hooked up to the portable mini V.A.C. machine, whenever possible. It certainly feels like I've turned a corner.

8th August 2005

The Royal Free Hospital George & Mary Ward Room 9

Next thing I know its Monday morning again and time to get back into that Gym for more walking! The Gym has become a central focus of my life.

I know if I work hard I'll recover quicker. We go through the same routine as Friday but the Trainer adds an extra lap or two, and I'm happy for that; I'm ready to be pushed and Judy is pushing!

Carlton is waiting for me when I get back to my room.

"Hey Sugar, where y' been?"

"I've been in the Gym downstairs, why what's up?"

"Alright, what does she look like?" He's wearing a cheeky grin.

"Don't try that Carlton, I've been working hard mate." Shaking my head and smiling, I move across onto my bed.

"Okay, I believe you, meanwhile there's been a huge response to that article you did for the newspaper and I've brought some of the letters sent in from the pubic, have a look at these." I sort myself out quickly sitting up using the pillows as a backrest and start reading some of the messages

Dear Gary,

It was good to see you on "T.V. Breakfast" this morning & to hear your views, which I endorse.

I wish you a Good & Speedy recovery, I'm sure that we shall hear of your progress on a future programme, I hope so.

Yours sincerely,

Rita Lee

04-08 05

Dear Gary

I was very tearful watching you on T.V. this morning. The terrible shock you had on the train and your courage dealing with your injury is quite astounding, I admire you so much.

I am a 91 year old R.C and like you, count my blessings that I am still fit and mobile and coping with life with the help of my wonderful family.

Wishing you every happiness, good health and good luck in everything you do.

With love to you Gary

Ellen D'Arcy

Carlton brought in. I'm reduced to tears. Already emotional about Mummy, I'm deeply moved to find out that I've touched so many people in the UK and also throughout the World. It goes way beyond belief.

Hector calls, a welcome break from the unexpected flood of emotions.

"What's up H?" I try to steady my voice as I answer.

"Garri I'm sorting out the funeral, but can I ask you to do the 'Eulogy' for Mummy?"

"Yeah no problem Bruv." I'm pleased he's asked, I'd really like to have something useful to focus on. I can be quite creative, when I'm ready and the guys at work have already offered to help, so I'll ask.

"Good, later."

"Okay Bruv, lickle bit."

I can't focus on anything but Mummy now; I just have to start work on her Eulogy so Carlton leaves me to let me get on with it. It takes me the rest of the day to design the layout and decide which photos of Mum to use. Then there's the hymns and thinking about the tributes to be included. It's taking me on a journey back through time that ends with a great sense of accomplishment, even though it still feels surreal, as if I am talking about someone else.

9th August 2005
The Royal Free Hospital George & Mary Ward Room 9

After my morning routine I have a surprise visitor. Anita pops in right on queue, to see if I need anything.

"Hi Garri, how are you today?" Her beaming smile fills the room.

"Anita, the very person I need, I'm as well as can be expected thank you, how about you treacle?" She laughs out loud and squeezes my arm.

"Oh Garri, you're so funny! I'm good thanks, so what can I do for you?"

"I've put together a rough Eulogy for my Mum's funeral, do you think it'll be okay to ask the design team if they could offer a bit of help with it. Perhaps make me a draft and then print off some copies for me?"

"Yeah, I'm sure that will be fine, in fact leave it with me, I'll deal with it as soon as I get back." We chat for a while as I bring her up to date with what's going on before she leaves. I'm left feeling so privileged to have such wonderful work colleagues.

10th August 2005 2:00pm
The Royal Free Hospital George & Mary Ward Room 9

The lovely Anita turns up with draft in hand smiling and bristling with pride as she hands it to me.

"Here you go Garri, your Mum's Eulogy."

"What already, you're quick!" I look at her in amazement!

"Of course." She nods and shrugs her shoulders as if it's nothing. I'm very impressed and extremely happy with what they've done; it's beautifully put together.

"Thank you so much Lil' Sis, you're a star." As luck would have it Hector walks in just then and seeing Anita smiles.

"Bruv perfect timing, come and have a look at this. What do you think?" He takes a moment to thoughtfully look over the draft; then his smile says it all as he nods.

"Yeah man good to go."

"I agree we are good to go, so Lil' Sis can we possibly get 300 copies printed?"

"Of course you can guys, I'll go back and sort it out now. See you soon Garri, bye Hector."

"Bye Lil'Sis thanks again." Hector hands her the draft, nods and smiles, she gives me a hug and rushes out.

As we talk, Hector tells me the Man dem from Brixton are asking after me, and wonders if I'd like to see a few of them later today. It's always good to see old mates and I'm feeling relieved after getting the Eulogy done so I agree it's a good time to lift the visitors ban and look forward to seeing them.

By late afternoon a few of my old friends arrive; we catch up until I drift off into my own introspective world, leaving them to talk amongst themselves. I find it funny how my two worlds have collided through this experience. Once this little boy from Stockwell Park Estate trying so hard to fit into society with a youth custody sentence around his neck, now in contrast, a successful professional, fitting in at work and mixing with the affluent middle classes from Private School backgrounds. Not only trusting me with their Accounts but socialising with me too. They don't have a clue about my 'Rudebwoy' past. Well at least they didn't until they met my old friends in Hospital; big black guys with swagger, gold teeth, chains and distinctive Brixton Bop. And to top all of that, my older brother Hector who is proud to offer up stories about his gangster life-style back in the day.

Yeah, I'm the first to admit I'm a product of my environment but I'd like to think it's possible to make good, no matter what start you have. The trick is not thinking about the obstacles, instead it's about focusing on how to move past them regardless. It's about digging deep and taking time to find out who you are. I managed to connect with my soul at an early age and I believe fate had a hand in that. It turns out youth custody was to play an important part in my life path, the part where I had the opportunity to find my inner strength; the emotional strength that I could draw upon, when I was underground in that nightmare. When I had to face feelings of being imprisoned, unable to move freely, being confined in a dark place and having no control over the situation, it wasn't new to me. I'd done it before and survived it, so I figured I could survive again, a blessing in disguise!

"Do you need anything Sugar?" The Man dem call me back from my 'zone out'.

"Hmmm, what?"

"Do you need anything Shuggs?"

"Oh yeah man, a blessing that's not in disguise would be good thanks." I nod and smile.

"Wha'?" They look confused.

"He looks tired man, allow him." They all smile sympathetically.

"Yeah man, mek 'im rest, we'll come back another day, glad you still wiv us man."

"Yeah likkle bit." I rest back feeling emotionally exhausted after yesterday and the intensity of creating Mummy's eulogy. As they leave it's good to feel their support and man love they truly are a fantastic group of guys.

Sleep is a big part of my healing process, yet it's an on going problem, as I can't sleep very well on my back, but I'm forced to try, as I can't even lie on my sides. Also the most irritating thing of all is getting an itch I can't scratch. It's torture! Sometimes my stump is so itchy I have to turn the radio on in the middle of the night, and hope the tunes take my mind somewhere else. I'm sure if people could see me they'd think I'm an insomniac bopping along to wicked old skool tunes in my bed in the early hours of the morning. So tonight as I often do, I turn the radio on and get involved until I drop off.

11th August 2005
The Royal Free Hospital George & Mary Ward Room 9

Morning routine feels a bit off this morning. I can't seem to get going, not sure why. Gym session is arranged for half past ten, but I'm running late, if only I could run!

I rush down and my Trainer Judy meets me at the door tapping playfully on her watch. I just smile, put my head down and go in. We start with some leg exercises on my crutches; fourteen laps around the gym, followed by some upper bodywork.

I'm totally whacked by the end of it and head back to my room for some well-earned bed rest. On my return even more cards and gifts have arrived, from all over the world. Amongst the gifts I find an Arsenal shirt signed by all the players *'The Untouchables'* and a personal message from Arsene Wenger. How fantastic is that?

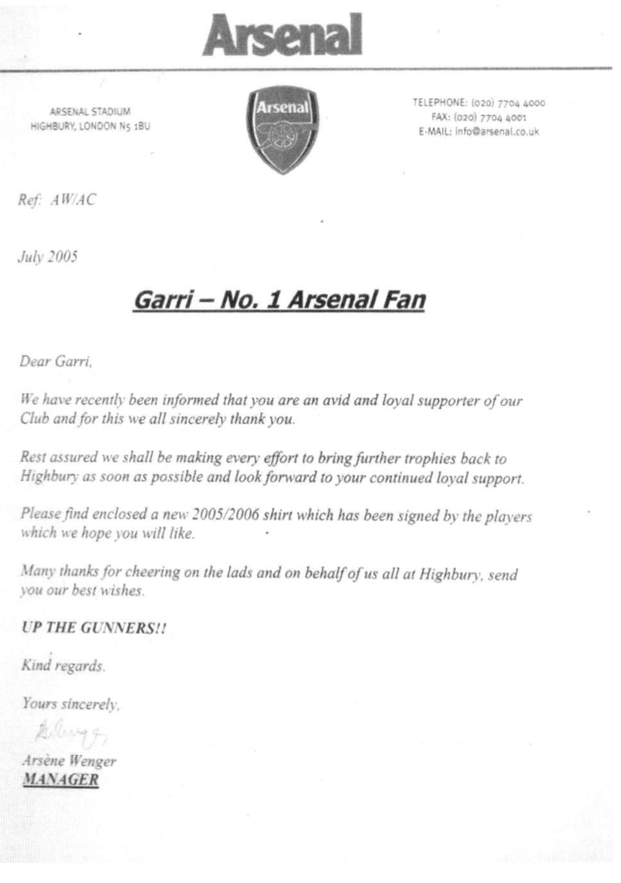

Arsenal

ARSENAL STADIUM
HIGHBURY, LONDON N5 1BU

Arsenal

TELEPHONE: (020) 7704 4000
FAX: (020) 7704 4001
E-MAIL: info@arsenal.co.uk

Ref: AW/AC

July 2005

Garri – No. 1 Arsenal Fan

Dear Garri,

We have recently been informed that you are an avid and loyal supporter of our Club and for this we all sincerely thank you.

Rest assured we shall be making every effort to bring further trophies back to Highbury as soon as possible and look forward to your continued loyal support.

Please find enclosed a new 2005/2006 shirt which has been signed by the players which we hope you will like.

Many thanks for cheering on the lads and on behalf of us all at Highbury, send you our best wishes.

UP THE GUNNERS!!

Kind regards.

Yours sincerely,

Arsène Wenger
MANAGER

There's a big smile on my face now. Interesting timing! Exactly what I needed to lift my spirits after feeling a bit off this morning.

My friends Annabel and Jim arrive just as I'm opening a gift containing some much-needed shorts from my mate Dominic. I hold them up in disbelief and Jim laughs his head off.

"Not sure that's gonna work Gazza!" As he eyes up a child like pair of shorts and Annabel smirks.

"I can't fit in these! Dom's a joker."

"Either that or he's trying to tell you something?" Annabel pipes up and we all laugh. "It's a good thing I brought you this then Garri, you can drown your sorrows." Annabel hands me a chilled can of Guinness from her bag. "Shhh!" we laugh more.

"Yeah, yeah thanks very much!" I grab it and hide it in my fridge.

As I open the last gift I am delighted to find shorts and a t-shirt from the guys on dispatch at work that will actually fit me!

"Thank God for Rusty and the crew!"

Annabel is a fantastic woman and very funny too, she's always joking with me and says I should take part in the Paralympics; it makes me smile and it keeps my spirits up. Annabel and Jim are in the Army and have experience of Soldiers being injured; my injuries are nothing new to them. They offer helpful advice as they recount war stories of men who lost limbs and how they made a good recovery. Jim also advises me how to position myself at my Mums wake. It's going to be important that I feel comfortable and not overwhelmed. He advises me to sit with my back against a wall and place chairs in front of me. Not only will it protect my leg from being knocked, but also people can sit down to talk to me and I can see their faces to lip read without cricking my neck to look up at them. He's a great guy, and full of such practical advice. By the time Jim and Annabel go, they leave me with courage and hope for the future, so very inspiring. I want to learn to help people just like they do if I can.

The Media coverage steps up becoming very intense. It seems the public really enjoy my attitude in a world that's so full of bad news. The Media say I am inspiring millions from my hospital bed by not showing any hatred towards the so called Muslim Suicide Bombers, and instead focussing on what good can happen now. I believe negativity breeds' negativity and positivity breeds' positivity and I'm not shy to say so.

My brother Tony pops in late to shave my head again ready for tomorrow. It's good to know that my hair is growing, although it's still patchy. I'll take it as a good sign and I'm getting used to having no hair on my head, I feel clean .

12th August 2005
The Royal Free Hospital Passenger Ambulance

It's Mums Funeral today, two hospital staff will accompany me. Julia, a Reporter from BBC Breakfast will also shadow me from my hospital bed to the funeral as part of an on-going Documentary. On so many levels it's going to be a challenging day outside of my 'Hospital Bubble'. I'm still hooked up to the mini V.A.C. pump so that's going to make it a bit awkward to move around, but I'll have to make it work, without it I can't go.

The TV Crew are ready and waiting by the van when we come down.

"Hello, hello Garri, good to see you." They all smile warmly.

"Hello Julia, hello everyone." I smile back and get into my seat as Julia watches me. It takes a little while to sort out all the equipment and then we are ready to go.

"Garri, do you realise you do that a lot." Julia points at my hands.

"What?" I've no idea what she means.

"You're brushing your lap, like this." She demonstrates, as if she's brushing something off her lap with the backs of both hands.

"Really? No I didn't realise, maybe I'm checking to see if both legs are still there!" I smile flippantly, but as I sit back in my seat, this time I catch myself doing it. I guess the unconscious effect on me is the most challenging to heal.

It's hard to take in the fact that I'm actually going to my Mum's Funeral today. I reflect on the last time I saw her on the 6th July at the nursing home lying peacefully in her bed. I was fit and healthy then, as I leaned over to kiss her while she slept saying *see you tomorrow* but that never happened, and now I am going to her Funeral! It's a tough burden to endure.

I've arranged to meet up with family and friends and as we arrive at Stockwell Park Estate my lovely friend Halle comes over to greet me. She stays by my side comforting me as I sit and wait in my wheel chair. Forgetting about Julia and the cameras I close my eyes and zone out unsure of how to be. As I open them, four beautiful white horses pulling a glass carriage are coming along the main road only a few hundred yards away. Inside is a white coffin and leaning against it, is a huge photo of a beautiful woman smiling right at me. My belly turns over, its Mummy's face and it brings home the painful reality of her death! I can't wheel myself over to the carriage quick enough, leaving the others behind. With salty tears pouring down my face and into my mouth, the emotions of the moment hit me so hard they take my breath away. This is the first time I've let my emotions out, as my Mum's body is about to leave Earth. In my heart I know her spirit will live on, but the pain and sorrow I feel in this moment is severe. Half-heartedly I try to wipe away the tears pouring down my face with my sleeves, but it's not important who sees me cry now, I'm burying my Mother!

We follow the carriage slowly up the road to the Church, where hundreds of people wait outside. I'm overwhelmed as they greet me with smiles, love and concern. Both my Mums generation as well as my own, have turned out in droves to pay their last respects, it's very moving to say the least. Inside the Church it's packed to the rafters. It appears Mummy was a much-loved woman and now that love is being extended to her children as well. Everywhere I go I am greeted with positive energy and encouragement. It seems funny to me that we don't know how our community feel about us until something like this happens, but it's a comforting feeling none the less.

Someone approaches from behind and slowly starts pushing my wheelchair further into the Church. As I look round I see the coffin following us down the centre aisle. Carlton finds a space for my wheelchair at the front and I put on the brakes. I'm in a daze as I try to focus on family members sitting in the front pews, then one by one we are called up to read our tributes…

Suddenly it's my turn. All eyes are on me; this is daunting *'can I do this?'* I'm unsure and anxious, feeling isolated, confined and emotional; so many thoughts and feelings bombard my head, but I have to go forward and speak! I wheel forward slowly and carefully in my chair and as I get closer to Mummy's coffin a sense of calm descends on me. It's as if Mummy is here helping, I feel her as I start to speak.

"*Vera Holness.* My Mother, My Father, I will not mourn your passing.

I will celebrate your life and remember everything you stood for. *Glamorous,* when she was ready. She had her own style and loved doing things her own way. She was beautiful inside and out, kind and generous. *Stubborn,* when she was ready. Strict, instilling discipline in us, teaching us right from wrong and to always have manners. Yes! She was a serious, smart and strong. She always stood her ground and backed her boys 100%! *Troublesome,* she was always involved in things she shouldn't have been and yet still managed to keep herself to herself! Such a character, a one-off with an amazingly strong presence, yet was really funny at times. So you see, there's no need to mourn your passing, better to celebrate your colourful life. So Yo! Me Big Darlin'!

Me know yu ah listen, peace! Can't stop loving you. Won't stop loving you. Cos as it is written, true love never dies!"

I hold it together by the skin of my teeth and I'm pleased the few Jamaican words I included especially for Mum also stirred my brethren, resulting in a rippling of hearty chuckles. After the last tribute is offered, people file past the open coffin, having a last word, smile or glance at Mummy. I feel proud and strong now. It's been such a beautiful Service and I know she's here watching the proceedings; I can still feel her. Finally we three brothers gather together on the platform, and my heart goes out to my sister Toria in Jamaica. I wonder how she must feel being the eldest child and unable to be with us on this emotional day. Hector as the eldest son and now head of the family takes the lead and wheels me close to the coffin. Then he and Tony lift me up so I can say my last goodbye. We all lean into the coffin to say what's in our hearts and I place my last kiss on her brow. I feel Mum has had a good sending off and I'm so, so grateful I was able to deliver my tribute without breaking down. Proud of my little Nieces too, they were so brave and did very well in the circumstances, it was their first experience of losing a loved one.

After the ceremony we form a procession following the Horse and Carriage through Stockwell Park Estate. My Brother's lead the procession walking side by side slowly and respectfully dressed up in their suits, hats and gloves. I should have been there too in my suit *walking* up front next to them. Although it's a miracle that I'm here at all, and for that I am both proud and very grateful. As we leave the Estate, the pace quickens and everyone piles into the cars, except for my brother Tony who spontaneously jumps up into the carriage with the horseman. What a sight to behold as he proudly sits leading the procession for Mummy on her last journey before her passage to the afterlife. I'm amazed and pleased that he stepped up, it's so out of character but very fitting. I look on him from behind filled with pride.

It seems surreal watching the many carloads of people lining up behind us and bringing Stockwell Road to an absolute standstill. The camera crew is still filming the whole scene, but I'm glad they discretely disappear before we arrive at West Norwood Crematorium.

Our last goodbye before Mummy's body is cremated. After the curtains close and the coffin disappears; the committal is complete and everyone leaves quietly and respectfully. I linger for a moment and follow on slowly in my wheel chair approaching the green, which is now covered with floral tributes. The large photo of Mummy has been placed upright and welcomes us smiling, just as I remember her.

We three brothers gather together again and are given three white Doves from a cage to release. I hold my Dove close to my face quietly whispering my message to give to Mummy.

"When you see my Mum, tell her I'm okay and I'll be okay not to worry about me. Tell her I'll always love her." My Dove starts wriggling in my hands, seemingly eager to fly up and deliver its message. So I open my hands and let go. The fluttering of freed wings liberates a cluster of soft white feathers, which float down slowly from side to side towards me as if leaving something significant behind. I manage to grab one before it reaches the ground and put it into my pocket. The doves take flight, a straight path upwards high into the blue sky and out of sight.

As I turn towards those watching with tears in their eyes, I can feel the love of my community; real love from my boys I used to play football with, old school friends and the Elders I grew up around. They all step forward to have a caring word or a silent moment with me. My Mums friends are outstanding, 'the Golden Generation' they are the awesome generation who had the strength to leave home, work hard and have family here building a better life. And they know just the right thing to say at the right time. I'm so thankful to them from the bottom of my heart.

After mingling for a while we head back to the Stockwell Park Community Centre for the wake. My medical team guide me to my Ambulance and off we go. I'm so glad I was able to make it today but it's been very long and emotionally intense, so I don't plan to stay very long.

Sitting with Halle at a table, and chatting calmly over a drink feels good. An old friend comes over to join us. It goes well until he starts getting annoyed, telling us about an old argument he was having with someone in the community. I feel a sudden dip and have to escape this angry energy straight away as I feel it pulling me down. It's such an instant reaction I don't quite understand why, but I do understand I have to act on it.

"I'll be back in a minute, I just need to get something from the car." Halle wheels me to her car and surprises me with an eight inch portable TV to take back and watch while I'm in hospital. I'm very happy to receive it and give her a hug. On the way back from the car I decide I won't go back in, I've had enough for today, so ask the Medics to take me back to the hospital instead. I slip away quietly and without a fuss.

Back at the Hospital by around four o'clock, feeling mentality and physically exhausted. I need to lie down so I can quietly digest my Mum's day. This monumental day outside of my hospital life has brought me back to the real world with a bang. Literally removing the screen of numbness the Hospital has provided since the bombing occurred. The enormity of what's happened is becoming my new reality now and I know I must take time to digest it, to get used to it, to accept it. My life has totally changed. Nothing will ever be the same again without Mum, and without my leg. Lonely and worried, it feels like me alone versus the world. The future is a daunting and a hostile prospect in this moment; it truly is the end of an Era.

13th August 2005
The Royal Free Hospital George & Mary Ward Room 9

Feeling so emotional I don't want to do anything at all. I stay in bed, in and out of sleep all day.

11th April 1981
Brixton Riots Stockwell Park Estate

"Hector, Hector? Where yu de? Yu noh 'ear me ah call yu?" No answer, after a brief silence Tony shouts out.

"He went out Mummy." I feel her deep intake of breath as her whole body tenses up as she grabs my arm and drags me along behind her through the estate and onto the streets of Brixton looking for Hector. Mummy sounds very upset and it alarms me.

I can feel her panic as she calls out looking for my brother amidst the mayhem in the streets. I hear sirens and shouts, breaking glass, banging and crashing all around. A Policeman dashes past, missing me by inches and brings a black youth to the ground with a rugby tackle. I hear the sickly thud of bones on concrete as he drops face down. The skinny youth lays unconscious oozing blood from his nose as the Policeman gets to his feet and stands over him on his radio. Mum grabs me tighter as I try to break free to have a closer look.

"Garri stay wid me, stay wid me!" Her eyes flash in my direction momentarily before she continues looking desperately around for Hector. Then we see a group of older black and white youths together near a shop with a broken window; jewellery from the display strewn about the floor. I drag behind to see what's there, as they seem to be helping themselves, but Mum is having none of it yanking me along with her iron grip. It seems like all Hells broken loose in Brixton.

14th August 2005
The Royal Free Hospital George & Mary Ward Room 9

This morning whilst washing my body and face I look in the mirror and gaze hard into my own eyes. I speak out loud as I do my normal affirmations but this morning I acknowledge out loud, "I am alive!" It goes in deep.

15th August 2005
The Royal Free Hospital George & Mary Ward Room 9

My brother Tony calls, and I sense deep sadness in his voice. I listen intently as he speaks. He goes on to say he feels left out of the family, as a photo in his local paper shows Mum and me with my older brother Hector. I understand his feelings of loss now that Mum is no longer around to advise him. He relied on her opinions and wisdom just as we all did. I have to say something, but I don't know what to say I'm not Mummy, I don't have her wisdom, so I just let it flow from my heart and my love for him. "Bruv you'll never be left out, know that, and you know what else, I'm glad you didn't get involved in the Media stuff, as they can sometimes say things that aren't positive. Just remember most people like a good gossip, so you're better off keeping your private life private, know what I mean?"

"Yeah man, you're right." I think he understands.

After the call I feel sad, so I busy myself by opening some letters before going to the Gym. I find a note attached to an email telling me that an Author who is writing a book on inspirational people would like my views and comments to include in his book, this idea inspires me. My mind races and a sense of hope floods in; they must think I have something helpful to say.

When I get back from the Gym a large package waits on my bed. It contains a stack of letters, text messages and emails from the BBC Breakfast Editor, telling me the public response to my interviews is overwhelming. I can't believe what I read and tears well up, but I manage to catch them. As the day ends I have journeyed through a varied range of emotions.

Gary's remarkable response to the bomb attacks is an inspiration to us all. I was moved to tears by the extent of his bravery and courage. An amazing person! Please do keep us updated on Gary's progress.
Dave, Newport Pagnell

Truly inspirational - and so very Christian!
Sue, Northumberland

What an absolute star this man is. His determination, his clear sense of focus, his complete lack of any histrionics - he contains all the characteristics which make me feel proud to be British.
Wendy Marshall

I was born without my lower left leg and lead a full and normal life. I know that Gary, with his remarkable attitude, will have no problem learning to walk again or doing anything he sets he mind to achieving. Good luck to him!
Sue, Battle, East Sussex

What a lovely man Gary Holness is. He is the antithesis of what the terrorists are and they must be reeling as they watch this great man's resolve. I cried as I watched. It was impossible not to. Good luck to him.
Pamela Lambert, Runcorn

16th August 2005
The Royal Free Hospital George & Mary Ward Room 9

There's a meeting planned today between Solicitors and Police regarding compensation from the Criminal Injuries Compensation Authority. (CICA) They will sort out how much, if any, compensation the survivors of the bombings can claim to help with rehabilitation. I really can't even begin to deal with that at this time, so I hand it over to my Solicitors hoping they can get me what I need to help with inevitable extra expenses of my life now. My focus is on my well-being and it's important that I continue to improve quickly as there's talk of me going home soon. I don't feel ready yet, I want to wait until I am really confident that I can manage now Mummy's gone, being home alone is not going to be easy.

17th August 2005
The Royal Free Hospital George & Mary Ward Room 9

Feeling more upbeat this morning due to some positive vibes from my visitors. The 'Main Man' at work, the Head of HR, and my Department Head have arrived all together to bring me a pile of get well cards, presents and flowers, as well as a poster size collage of the beautiful women at work, smiling and blowing kisses to me. Amongst the mail there's a letter from the Big Boss in the States. It's a thoughtful letter, and he says if there's anything I want, I just have to ask. He also tells me his next-door neighbour is my biggest fan and he encloses a card especially from her, it's very touching as well.

"That's nice thank you!" I am overwhelmed by their thoughtfulness and generosity.

"So Garri how are you really doing?" My Boss looks at me eye to eye thoughtfully and I smile.

"I'm getting there."

"There's no rush to get back to work Garri, as we've got a temp covering your position until you're ready. But we really miss your mad hats and jackets, nothing's quite the same in the office without you." I feel a sense of relief the pressure to get back to work is taken off.

"Aw thank you very much; I can feel the love."

"Yes, I bet you can Mr Holness, with all the female admirers going crazy for you."

"Really? Sounds interesting, tell me more." Robby*shakes his head laughing.

"Garri, I'm surprised some woman hasn't already come forward to say she has your love child."

"Behave Robby!" I laugh embarrassed." I didn't know I have female admirers at work, tell me who."

"Yeah, yeah, yeah." They all laugh and we chat for a while catching up on my progress.

"Anyway we've got to get going now, so nice to see you."

"Thanks for coming guys."

"Its our pleasure Garri, it's true the office is just not the same without you." They stand up to leave just as the Masseuse comes in rubbing her hands together, with a big smile on her face.

"Ah your guests are leaving Garri, just as well, cos I've got the go ahead to massage you without gloves today!"

"Ooer a gloveless massage eh? Maybe we should stay and watch Garri"

"Noooo, you were just leaving, see ya!" They leave, looking back, laughing and winking at me as the Masseuse kicks the door closed behind them, joining in with the fun. The good news apart from the glove free massage is that the infection has cleared up and I'm no longer contagious, proving I'm getting better and that's a fact. There is a huge difference in the massage today. I feel a heartfelt connection, which I just haven't felt before. I think I now understand the phrase, 'healing hands'!

After lunch I take time to sort through my mail, various bills, cards, letters and several magazines. A music magazine appeals and flicking through, I get so engrossed I don't notice the time until suddenly I'm late for the Gym. Rushing down to the Gym contemplating a mini studio in my flat like I always wanted. Wow, what an exciting prospect! And I make it just in time to get on with my workout, without any watch tapping from my trainer Judy!

After the workout is complete I'm back in my room finishing off some paperwork, just as my Housing Officer calls. She says I could be offered a more suitable home in the New Year. It suddenly dawns on me that I wont be able to manage the stairs at home and my flat is not wheel chair accessible. I wonder what will happen, and can't help feeling a bit sentimental about my flat, as I recall the first time I saw it.

December 1999
Croydon

Flat hunting and on my second viewing of the day, I look around the outside of this converted Victorian house and like the vibe here straight away, although I'd like to come back and see the area at night as well. The location is good, easy access to transport, free parking and a good-sized garden. Hmmm promising. I press the buzzer on the front door and an interesting woman in her early thirties answers.

"Miss Cross?" I ask smiling.

"Mr Holness?" She replies smiling back.

"Yes." We shake hands and she invites me in. Miss Cross has an air of calm about her and moves gracefully as she shows me around. I note the high ceilings in the hallway. The vibe in the front room is very relaxing, two large plants in opposite corners; I'm feeling it. The kitchen and bathroom are both a good size. Mmmm As she leads me into the bedroom, she continues walking around to the far side of the bed and I politely stay at the doorway just looking in.

"This has a nice vibe." It feels calm and airy.

"Yes its Feng Shui," She replies confidently.

"Oh okay, nice." I wonder what the hell Feng Shui is, but anyway she made it sound nice and I love the flat. Then she opens a door to what looks like an airing cupboard in the corner and beckons me over. "Do you want to take a look down here?"

"What is it?"

"I was going to make it into an office space, come and see."

To my surprise the door leads down some stairs, and on to another room. I don't recall seeing this room in any of the photos or plans of the property, how interesting, a secret room, it appeals to me. As I walk down the stairs all I can imagine is a mini music studio. Such a big long space and another little room at the end under the stairs for storage. I'm sold, and this is the icing on the cake! We're both smiling and its obvious we have to make a deal. After a little negotiation and a cup of tea, we agree on a price, happy days.

18th August 2005
The Royal Free Hospital George & Mary Ward Room 9

The next couple of days pass quickly as I contemplate the idea of being back at home. It's a little daunting to wonder how I'm going to cope with the stairs living alone, and not being able to get a wheelchair in at all even on the ground floor. The idea of moving to a new home that's all on one level with wheelchair access suddenly becomes very appealing. I really hope they find me a suitable place quickly.

19th August 2005
The Royal Free Hospital George & Mary Ward Room 9

Having an interview with American Public Radio, I keep it together quite well while telling my story, but the female reporter isn't doing too well at all. By the time I get to the part about Mummy I see her eyes fill up and tears run down her face; I just can't continue.

"Please don't do that." I smile at her, and she wipes the tears away quickly.

"I can't help it, it's such an emotional story." She smiles back.

"If you do that your gonna start me off." She nods.

"Okay sorry I'll try Garri, you're amazing." I do my best to continue.

20th August 2005
The Royal Free Hospital George & Mary Ward Room 9

I'm taking it easy, reminiscing about Mum's funeral, thinking how proud she would be, with her send off. I miss her.

July 2001 Brixton

I'm taking Mum shopping so I can help her carry the heavy bags when we see Hector and his daughter Leigh* coming along the other way.

We all stop in the street for a family gathering. As I chat to Hector, I notice Mummy asking my niece Leigh for her little pink skipping rope.

"What yu doing Mummy?" I watch her take the rope put down her bag and with a handle in each hand loop the rope behind her feet. My mouth falls open disbelieving what's unfolding before my eyes.

"Wha'? Yu 'tink me kyaan skip? Yu mussi t'ink ah only young people kaan skip. Well me kaan skip, me feel young!" Mummy looks at us smiling defiantly and skips over the rope, not once, but twice before she gives the rope back to my niece triumphantly. Seventy-seven years old and still strong willed enough to skip; she amazes me!

21st August 2005
The Royal Free Hospital George & Mary Ward Room 9

Today my close and beautiful friend Halle is visiting. It's so great to see her, especially in her tight white skirt, her bottom looks attractive, sexy and Phat you see, and it's a flirting day! Perhaps now the Hospital Staff will realise that I'm really not Gay. Feisty lot!! Just because I don't have a girlfriend or a photo of me with a girl, people so easily jump to conclusions!

22nd August 2005
The Royal Free Hospital George & Mary Ward Room 9

Monday morning brings my usual start to the day, then porridge, muesli, two slice of brown toast and a mountain of tablets, washed down with herbal tea. Change the dressing; the stump looks good, healing much better since the mini V.A.C. has been doing its job pulling out the infection. The swelling is reducing and the signs of healing are obvious. On the down side however, I do feel a little fluey, so holding back on the exercise this morning.

My Angel Alison, the young woman who helped save my life underground is visiting with her Mum today; its heart warming to see her and we talk non-stop for an hour. She gives me a funny get-well card, in an envelope marked Garri The Superhero! The caption says laughter is the best medicine and the words inside touch my heart. During the conversation I mention the need to have a skin graft, and she must feel my angst, so without pausing for thought, she drops her trousers to show me her skin graft at the top of her leg, in front of her Mum, what a woman!

Saved by the bell, my mobile rings! It's my Police Family Liaison Officers asking if I would like to attend one of their posh dos in April as guest of honour. Of course, I say yes. It is so nice to be asked. I've had such a good relationship with them, my 'Cagney and Lacey'! After the call Alison and her Mum get ready to leave, so I take a nap still not feeling too good.

Late afternoon Susan, one of the Doctors, pops her head around the door beaming her lovely smile. Susan often pops in to see me on her way home, but I can see in her face this evening she needs to talk. We always seem to end up discussing the dynamics of relationships. Sometimes I wonder if she thinks I'm a Relationship Guru! Tonight though I need an early night to help me fight off the flu symptoms attacking me, so I keep it short and sweet.

23rd August 2005
The Royal Free Hospital George & Mary Ward Room 9

I decide I'm staying in bed today. I slept badly and still feel tired and unwell. I really have to see Mr Garlick from plastics, I hope he can come to me.

I ask and he arrives to tell me because the infection in my stump is under control he will go ahead with the skin graft tomorrow as planned. Another step forward and reducing the likelihood of losing any more length off my leg, which is great news! Although I am pleased with my progress, I feel as if my temperature is up. I've a thumping headache along with hot and cold sweats, and I can't help thinking that Man Flu is the worst thing ever! Eventually, even though my man flu is still raging, I cool off enough to drift off into a deep sleep.

August 1983
Stockwell Park Estate Brixton

I'm heading out with my Football boys Colin, Inky, Mark, Tony, Anthony, John, and Paul. Some of them are great Footballers and I enjoy hanging with them, but because I'm the only black boy, Mum worries they might pick on me; it's not like that though, they're my good friends and have been for quite a while.

Were at Slade Gardens free-running in line following the leader; these guys are proper dare devils, especially Colin and John. One by one they take a run and leap off a roof about twenty foot high and down into Slade Gardens, but when it's my turn, I've lost my bottle, so just hang down the side and then let myself drop. I hope none of them see as I run to catch them up on the way back into the Estate.

Next to the pond in between Chute and Burrow House running along they jump across the pond onto the island in the middle. I try jumping across too, but sadly end up slipping in the water before scrambling across. I've really hurt my arm and my clothes are wet too but I've gotta put on a brave face, there's no way I'm going home with wet clothes, Mum will cuss some bad words. So enduring the pain as well as the cold wet jumper, I follow behind the others for a game of wall jumping until I dry off. We climb up onto the boundary wall that surrounds the gardens where we live. We have to run fairly fast along the narrow walls to gain enough momentum to leap over the gates that sit between the walls. On one side the drop is only about four feet into the garden, but on the other side it goes down between twelve and twenty feet, so we have to fully focus on what we're doing. A fall down there would be serious. Mum distracts me mid jump calling from the flats.

"Garrrrriiiii! Garrrriiii! I only just make it safely across!

After getting home I go to bed without saying a word about my arm. By the next morning though I can't even move my left elbow. I finally tell Mum what happened and she realises quickly it's a hospital job, she ain't happy. I broke my arm and I'm in a lot of discomfort!

24th August 2005
The Royal Free Hospital George & Mary Ward Room 9

Bunged up and still heady this morning, but after a check up by the Plastic Team they say the operation can take place between four and six this afternoon, so I'm not allowed to eat anything. The day passes slowly as I watch the clock wondering when I will be taken down to Surgery. By four-thirty I'm so hungry I can't wait much longer, so get on to one of the nurses to ask Mr Garlick's team what's happening. She assures me it's still scheduled for today.

They come for me after eight o'clock. Seems late to me, but what can I do except climb onto the trolley and lay back as they wheel me out of my room and towards the lift. We descend a few floors, to the operating suite again, and back along the old, unpleasant grey corridors of this Victorian hospital. There's definitely something spooky lingering here, I can feel it but I can't see it, as if someone's whispering to me from somewhere just out of sight. I think about all the souls that must have died in this hospital on the wards and on the operating tables over hundreds of years since the 1800's when the place first opened its doors. I can't help but wonder if their ghosts still haunt these spooky corridors and the thoughts make me shudder.

I'm elevated from my eerie imaginings by a lovely nurse as she begins to prep me for the op. She places the monitors on my chest and inserts the drip into my arm very gently, such a difference to when I felt like a human dartboard last time; and no epidural thank God!

"Can you please count from ten backwards for me Garri?"

"Okay, here we go again, ten, nine, eight… seven, six, fooour…

When I open my eyes, what seems like only minutes later, the clock shows ten past eleven. As I'm coming back to my senses I feel a lot better than I did after my last operation, with no pain to speak of, strange. Anyway I'm starving hungry now, can't wait to get back to the ward and raid my food store before bed.

25th August 2005
The Royal Free Hospital George & Mary Ward Room 9

A new pretty blonde nurse has come to see me this morning,

"Good morning Garri, I'm Lucy, I work with Mr Garlick and the Plastic Team and I'll be looking after you now." She's very upbeat with high energy.

"Good morning Lucy, nice to meet you."

"Let's have a look at your new skin graft shall we?" She smiles cheerfully.

"Yes please go ahead, lets have a look." I'm very keen to see. She undoes the bandages, looks at the results nodding and she seems delighted.

"Wow Garri, this is amazing the skin graft has already taken, its actually quite dry, I don't even think we need to put you back on the mini V.A.C. as we'd planned. Before I'll know for sure I'm going to need a second opinion on that, I'll be right back. Don't go anywhere okay?" With that she rushes out in search of a Senior Doctor.

This is the first time I've been left alone with my leg undressed so of course I'm going to have a good look. I can see where the new skin has been stapled onto the stump closing the wound and it's so interesting to see their handy work close up for a change. I can definitely see the signs of healing already too, which pleases me. As I explore the Plastic Teams excellent work, I feel absolutely in awe of what they've managed to achieve on my stump, it's quite incredible.

Lucy returns soon enough with Mr Garlick and two new Doctors, whom I've not seen before. Mr Garlick smiles as he approaches.

"Good morning Garri, do you mind I've brought a couple of my interns with me today, they are very keen to have a look too?"

"Okay then."

He takes a look, his smile broadens and he looks up at me nodding.

"Excellent result Garri, remarkable actually. It's true you don't need the V.A.C. machine anymore, your skin graft has taken perfectly, in fact you don't even need a dressing, lets allow it to have some air, leave it to it's own devices and see what happens."

I'm over the moon about this and realise that I owe a debt of gratitude to both Nurse Barry for helping me to refuse the operation to take more of my bone away, and to my super healthy friend John, who continues to bring me health foods that truly seem to aid my healing and well-being. He said right from the beginning, on the day I tried to stand when my right leg collapsed, he would help make me strong again; he was right, I'm so grateful, thank you John!

26th August 2005
The Royal Free Hospital George & Mary Ward Room 9

Cooler this morning as I get up to go for my wash as normal, the nurses still tease me about a bed bath; they uplift my mood by pretending to fight over me, and I enjoy disappointing them all by saying I can do it myself now! I look forward to another easy day relaxing in bed and focusing on healing, Doctor checks me out, and all's well.

Julia from the BBC pops in to say hi, even though she's not at work today. We have a fantastic conversation about life in general, my experiences, relationships and her, actually quite a lot about her. I find that women ask me for a male perspective on their relationships, more since my accident. Maybe facing death has mellowed me, but I also think its because I grew up with my mothers influence. Mum was such a big part of my life and she gave me an insight into women; I've always known that. I've come to believe its unfortunate today that many women become too competitive, rather than co-operative. It's probably because they need to compete to survive in the work place. I say unfortunately because it sometimes goes too far, it spills over into their relationships and they even end up in competition with their men. This of course is a recipe for disaster; healthy relationships are all about compatibility, building together and dedication, rarely about competition with each other.

A good two hours flies by as we put the world to rights and before she leaves Julia promises to bake me a cake and I pray the cake won't be a recipe for disaster! My brother arrives just as she's leaving.

"Don't forget the cake, Julia!"

"Okay Garri, you got it." She smiles nodding.

" You alright?"

"I'm alright Bruv."

"Just dropped in quick to bring this, can't stay." Hector hands me the DVD he had done of Mums Funeral, so I put it straight in the DVD player and we watch the beginning of it together.

"Well done Bruv, excellent recording, I feel proper proud Mum went off well. With so many people packed into the Church and outside, bringing in so much love." I feel happy that it's all captured on video, and when I get some 'me time', I'll totally reflect on the day. Hector doesn't hang around.

One of the night staff pops his head round the door smiling.

"Good evening Garri, I heard you like music so I brought you some music magazines."

"Cool, thanks mate, that's really thoughtful." We talk music for a while and get along well; music brings people together for sure. Turns out he has a mini studio at home and he starts showing me all the latest home studio equipment in the magazine; it's a lovely way to pass an evening.

27th August 2005
The Royal Free Hospital George & Mary Ward Room 9

The Plastic Team Doctors arrive after breakfast to check my skin graft. Again all is well and I couldn't ask for more. Carlton rings to remind me that Malta TV is coming to interview me later today; I'd completely forgotten so it's a very good thing that he called. He also has a pair of tickets for me to the Premiere of Green Street, the movie I was a feature extra in just before the bombing. Of course I'd love to attend, but sadly I can't go, I ask Carlton to give the tickets to my brother Hector. I feel he would enjoy it more than Tony.

I start preparing myself for the interview with Malta TV by doing a short meditation, and they arrive exactly on time. Two lovely ladies and a cameraman; we all chat for a while and get on well. I seem to get on better with female reporters, not sure why. I realise that women have been paying me a lot more attention recently. They tell me I have a lovely smile, so of course I smile all the more. Who wouldn't?

28th August 2005
The Royal Free Hospital George & Mary Ward Room 9

Same old morning routine but it's a beautiful day outside. The sun is shining through my window while I have my breakfast, which is always uplifting. Getting ready to watch the Football on TV, but Arsenal is losing to Chelsea. That's not good news, when you support Arsenal! Just as it's getting interesting my ex- girlfriend Lucy, walks in; she's a beautiful girl and very elegant. Seeing her brings back memories of being in a rave with her and seeing Jade Jagger close by. I was looking at Jade, then back at my girlfriend, then back at Jade, until at last they both noticed me. When they clocked each other they realised they were doppelgängers. Anyway Lucy is a very talented and creative Actress but like many of us I think she could be so much more successful if she was a bit more positive in her life in general. We start chatting about old times, but I'm still trying to watch the football match and only half listening to Lucy.

"Bloody Drogba, that was so off side." I get annoyed at the football.

"What?" She looks confused.

"Oh sorry Lucy, my Team needs me, they're losing!" I'm torn.

"I need you too, but you're ignoring me and watching the Football." She teases me with a side ways smile while shaking her head and pouting.

"No, No Toola Oola, I'm not ignoring you, I'm a man, and I can't do two things at once, right? So I can't ignore you *and* watch Football, I'm pretty much just watching Football!" We both laugh and I find salvation in my humour. Half time and now she has my full attention so we discuss Lucy's new relationship problem fully before she has to go, then I get back to my Football. It doesn't end well, I'm feeling cheated so not in a good mood, bloody Chelsea!

Uplifted again by the arrival of my lovely work colleagues Tina & Lisa, but brought down again by the simultaneous arrival of Hospital lunch looking a very sad and unappetising. Before I even have time to sulk, they produce a Salmon Salad, closely followed by Strawberries & Blackberries. Lush!! My frown turns into a smile as I eat well and thank them; my belly is full and I'm in a much better mood. We talk for quite a while, as I update them on my progress until they notice I'm getting tired; good food can do that, so they get ready to leave.

"Thank you so, so much girls, I really appreciate this. Same time tomorrow?" Smiles and laughter as they hug me before they leave.

29th August 2005
The Royal Free Hospital George & Mary Ward Room 9

Nurse Lucy is checking out my skin graft again; she has such a nice way with her. "I'm very happy with your progress Garri, you'll be pleased to know, I'm going to remove the staple from your skin graft today. Also Garri, if you don't mind there's a team of trainees waiting outside to see if you'll agree for them to come in and observe."

"Yeah alright, seeing it's you let them in." I wink and smile and she pulls a funny face.

"That's very generous of you Garri thank you!" Half a dozen students pile in to my room closely followed by Mr Garlick.

"Mr Garlick." I raise my eyebrows and nod in acknowledgement.

"Garri." he nods back. Lucy smiles at us both and begins her presentation.

"Let me give you some background information, Garri is one of the Survivors of the London Bombings and he's recently had a skin graft on the stump of his left leg. Just to remind you, the donor site must be left to settle for ten to fourteen days; once this is achieved a hard crust should appear on it. After water is added, the crust can be pulled away easily to reveal soft newly formed skin underneath."

Dr Garlick moves forward to get a closer look at my leg.

"Good, it's about 98% complete, you should be going home soon, I see no reason to keep you in Hospital any more Garri."

"Great news Doc! Thanks." I feel buoyant.

"If everyone healed like you we wouldn't need so many Hospitals." The group laughs with him before they leave to continue their rounds.

As the last one files out Alison walks in and I am so happy to see her again.

"How are you my little Angel?"

"I'm fine thanks Garri, how are you?"

"Even better for seeing you, and my skin graft is almost healed, the Doctor just said I should be going home soon."

"That's great news Garri." She looks genuinely pleased for me and we talk for ages until Dom turns up. Alison leaves me her number and wishes me well before she goes.

Dom used to work with me at the Agency and we got on really well from the start I'm very pleased to see him; it's really good to have some male company as well today.

"Dom how's it going?"

"Gazza, me old china, I'm good, so how you feeling today."

"Alison, the girl that left as you arrived, just told me that I was underground for more than hour after the explosion and I was the last one out alive from my carriage. She said it's a miracle that I'm still here at all mate. How is one supposed to feel about that?" Talking posh, Dom follows my lead slipping straight into his overdone posh accent! He reminds me so much of Jim Carey the actor and is very funny and bubbly just like him.

"Bloody hell old chap, one is jolly lucky to be alive!" I laugh, we carry on.

"Indeedy! So Dom me old mucker, I do hope you managed to procure some adequate shorts this time, the previous pair you were kind enough to send, nigh on strangled me. I simply couldn't get into them, what, what, what!"

"Yes of course my good man," Dom keeps a straight face, "I surely do understand your predicament. However don't fear here you go, I think you'll find these will cover your needs more than adequately, what, what, what!" He winks and hands me a pair of shorts that look like they'll actually fit me this time. We continue joking and laughing well into the evening!

30th August 2005
The Royal Free Hospital George & Mary Ward Room 9

I'm slightly surprised, to see myself on TV this morning, the commentary is complimentary. I feel proud and heart warmed as they mention how positive I'm keeping after all I've been through. It suddenly jolts my memory that the BBC and the News Of The World, will come back to interview me again today. Ah great maybe Julia will bring my cake; I can't wait!

They arrive, but sadly there's no cake, all that sweet-talking for nothing. Chaa! The interview however seems to go well and I'm determined to remain positive. It's scheduled to be shown on Friday and they mention that people have been responding very positively to me so far. They say I've become the Hero of the Nation just because I haven't been revengeful about the Bombers; it's a very interesting situation.

Next up, the News of The World is here to update an on-going exclusive arranged by the editor, Andy Coulson, who seems to be a cool guy. They are covering my first steps learning to walk again. They take loads of photos for their Sunday issue and as we look back through them, they let me select the ones I like best. The interview goes so well that they ask to come back and see me again later in the week, I agree. They too refer to me as a Hero.

It feels good to rest a little after they leave, before my visitors arrive later. But, I can't help wondering what I did to become a 'Hero'.

31st August 2005
The Royal Free Hospital George & Mary Ward Room 9

Stripped to the waist and heading for the bathroom, I get a sense of being watched and as I turn around a small group of male and female nurses are standing watching me. I don't understand what's going on, so I smile, and they smile back but continue staring without saying anything.

"What's up?" I shrug my shoulders

One of the female nurses comes over and whispers in my ear.

"Wow Garri, look at those biceps, you must have been working out a lot, muscle man!" The penny drops, and I feel flattered to have this little ego boost at this sensitive point in my life, especially as I'm covered in scars.

"Thank you, how nice of you to say that." I smile and feel proud they all notice the improvement. I've been working hard almost every day to get fit again and it's so nice to be acknowledged.

Back in my room, just in time to see BBC Breakfast, I take a minute to watch. I'm pleased that I manage to hold it together in the circumstances. Then Doctor Garlick walks in.

"You alright there Garri?"

"I'm good Dr Garlick, thank you very much." I turn off the TV.

"Well, I've got some good news, you can go home whenever you're ready." He looks triumphant.

"Really? That is good news, but I've been wondering, could I stay another week, to be on the safe side; is that okay?"

"Well it's totally up to you, but make sure you get some fresh air over this weekend."

"Okay great, I will, and thanks." Now I have mixed feelings; on the one hand I'm feeling rather anxious about leaving the safety of the Hospital, but on the other hand I know I am out of danger and need to start getting on with the rest of my life.

I distract myself with a stack of mail, that's been piling up over the past weeks. I'm receiving so many get-well cards notes and flowers as well as some saucy photos of women with proposals of marriage. Unbelievable! Although I don't really understand it, I must say it feels good! I even got a letter from long lost distant cousin, wanting to connect; that's nice and the support makes me feel so much better.

Back to the Gym, and my super productive trainer is really pushing me to work hard. I like the results; especially after the ego boost I got this morning. We work biceps, triceps, chests, shoulders, abs, thighs, and my remaining calf! Aw, it's not funny, perhaps I shouldn't be so flippant, I know it's a challenge. I've been given a second chance at life, and I just have to deal with it, the best way I can. And the best way for me at the moment is to work hard in the gym, bring myself to be the fittest I can be and stay cheerful as possible.

Returning from the gym I have an enlightening encounter with a couple of Yoga Teachers, they suggest I need to relax more, and learn to take control of my mind. Food for thought indeed, meditation does help me when I can remember to do it!

Jean* from work arrives and we decide to go out for a drink, I haven't been out for a drink in ages, it feels like a lifetime ago, and maybe it was; I'm feeling keen and excited. We decide to go to 'The Roebuck' wine bar across the way from the Hospital. Dr Garlick did say I should get out for some fresh air, so I'm just following Doctor's Orders! Out of my bed in a second and into the wheelchair with a big smile on my face.

"Do you need help, shall I push you Garri?"

"Hmmm, no thanks Jean, I'll do the pushing Babe!" I'm determined to show her I can manage.

"Garri!" Laughing and wheeling myself quickly towards the lift, she has to run to catch up. I continue teasing her all the way to The Roebuck and we can't stop laughing.

It's around five-thirty as I lead her through the gate and around the back of the Pub to the beer garden. It's important for me to take the lead these days whenever I can, so I ask Jean what she'd like before the waiter approaches.

I order a large glass of red wine for Jean and chicken skewers with home-made chips for me, along with a Bud to wash it down. It feels really good sitting in this beer garden, on a lovely warm evening with such an interesting person. I imagine an okay life in the future after all. The food arrives and I'm ready to eat, but so is Jean, and she manages to help herself to more than her fair share of my chips and three glasses of wine. Damn!

"Time flies when you're having fun, it's nearly ten already Garri!!" "Where's the time gone, I must say Jean I've really enjoyed being out, especially in such great company, but I suppose its time to head back to the Hospital now. I've got to take my tablets and wind down." She leans in and kisses me, which is a lovely surprise and I wheel away grinning.

"See you soon Garri."

"Yeah bye for now Jean."

What an enjoyable evening that was, Jean is a beautiful lady inside and out, and it's always good to be around beautiful people.

1st September 2005
The Royal Free Hospital George & Mary Ward Room 9

The morning passes quickly but when the lunch trolley arrives at the door I'm exhausted. I start eating and close my eyes, but when I look again it's two o'clock and my lunch is gone, whoa! What happened? Next thing I know Halle and her niece walk through the door.

"Hello Garri, how are you?" She smiles a warm smile as she sits down.

"Oh hello Halle I've just woken up, but I'm okay thanks… what a nice surprise, how are you?"

"I'm well thank you, and I've brought my niece with me, this is Krystal*." The young woman with Halle steps towards me.

"Hello Krystal, it's nice to meet you." I smile.

"Hi Garri, I've heard so much about you, and told my Aunt I want to come and meet you."

"Really?" She nods and smiles shyly.

"Okay, can you please excuse me for a minute ladies, I need to freshen up."

"Yeah okay we'll be right here." I make my way to the bathroom on my crutches and return as quickly as I can.

"Okay that's better, shall we go out for lunch ladies? I think I'll take you to the beer garden at the Garden Gate."

"Okay Garri that would be very nice, I didn't realise you could go out, shall I get your wheelchair?"

"No thanks it's okay I can manage; come on let's go." I leap across the bed and land in my wheelchair, showing how well I can manage, then wheel myself playfully out towards the lift, with the ladies hurrying to catch up with me. They both look amazed at my behaviour and it makes me feel great, I'm even more determined to be independent. I really am becoming so much more confident of late.

After a couple of glasses of wine, we decide to go in search of lunch. Unbelievably Garden Gate have actually run out of food, and we're so hungry! We find a pizza place on the corner. As we enter the owner of the restaurant does an obvious double take and then rushes over. "Hello and welcome, you're the guy from the bombing aren't you?" He smiles excitedly.

"Yep, that's me." I'm surprised.

"Please take a seat Sir, and allow me to offer you Pizza on the house."

"Wow, thanks very much." I feel like a VIP!

"You're famous Uncle Garri!" Krystal giggles.

"I'm Uncle already, am I Krystal?" I laugh and raise my eyebrows at her.

"Yeah, gimme your autograph Garri." Halle joins in teasing me and extending her arms for a hug.

"Behave Halle!" *KMT,* but with a smile on my face, I'm amused by it all and hug her warmly. Both Halle and Krystal are laughing as we all follow the manager who leads us to his best table.

We sit enjoying a lovely meal with wine and lively conversation. We chat for ages before the girls decide it must be time for me to go back to the Hospital, but I'm having none of it! I'm feeling so good to be out, enjoying their company and I must admit to being a little wine merry. I string it out for another hour or so, changing the subject until they firmly take the lead back.

"Garri because you've been drinking we aren't gonna let you drive."

"Really?" I don't have enough coordination to say no, so I sit back and enjoy the ride!

"Thank you for lunch Garri. I can't believe how well, you're doing, such a wonderful surprise."

"Thanks and see you soon Babes." Halle and Krystal both give me warm hugs and I feel happy. Another fantastic day out in the world, I'm so grateful to be alive.

2nd September 2005
The Royal Free Hospital George & Mary Ward Room 9

Up at seven, and I've decided to start a video diary today. I've been given a camcorder as a gift with the suggestion I should use it to record my progress. So it's time to play with it, to find out how it works and make a start. It can't be that hard and anyway if all else fails there's always the manual! Several hours pass as I play with my new toy.

Having a wash and brush up, I want to look my best for an appointment at two o'clock for lunch with another friend from work, well what can I say; I have to focus on the up side!

Today we venture a little further down the road, but an Ambulance comes flying past with its siren blaring and I freeze. It throws my thoughts right back into the day of the Bombing and I have the sinking realisation that all is far from well with me; I still have much healing to do. Meanwhile I force a smile and try to carry on to the wine bar.

After a couple of glasses of wine, and some great food, I manage to relax.

The wine numbs me and I start enjoying being out again. I can't believe how many empty glasses are sitting on our table.

I become aware of a man staring at us from inside the wine bar, soon after he comes out. "Hey you're that guy from the Bombings aren't you?"

"Yes I was in the Bombings Sir." He moves closer with his hand outstretched; we shake hands.

"I'm really happy to meet you young man, and your food and drinks are on the house! Let me treat you."

"Thank you Sir, that's very generous!" We smile enjoying the treat and he seems happy I accepted his hospitality.

At six-thirty we head back up the hill to the Hospital and my friend leaves me in the hospital car park with a big smile on my face. Getting out and about is great for my morale.

3rd September 2005
The Royal Free Hospital George & Mary Ward Room 9

Same old routine; wash, tablets and breakfast then sort out the dressing on both legs. This time I have my video camera to play with too.

My phone rings, its Tina calling from her car, she's looking for a parking space as she's kindly offered to take me out. We've planned to go for a little spin around London and aim to have lunch near London Bridge. Tina is such a laugh and uplifting to be around.

Tina calls shortly after to say she's outside, so I go down to meet her. It really feels good going through the streets of South London on this bright sunny day.

I'm feeling relaxed and more like my old self, sitting down on a bench outside in the beer garden and lunch is absolutely wonderful! The sun is shining, people are mulling around and it feels like normality is returning. When it's time to go, I get up to walk towards my wheelchair, forgetting just for a crucial moment that I've lost part of my leg. As I step forward onto my missing foot it feels like I've stepped off the edge of a cliff in slow motion. For a split second I'm unsure of what's happening, my hands automatically reaching out to save myself, but the cobbled pavement rushes up to meet me too quickly, and I smash heavily downward, full weight on my stump!

"Argh!" I'm in serious trouble; excruciating agony shoots up my leg and course's throughout my whole body. My pain threshold is tested brutally to its limit as I experience pain like never before and I just don't know what to do.

"Oh no Garri! What have you done, are you alright?" Tina cries out but I can't even answer, the pain is much too intense, both physically and mentally. Furious with myself, I just can't believe how stupid I feel. Sweat dripping down my brow, burning pain and icy cold shivers run up and down my spine. Shooting pain surges up from the stump and as I grab hold of it, I can actually feel it throbbing and swelling up already. My male pride is totally in shreds as my mind drives through a wild dialogue of panic and confusion.

'Oh No! Have I seriously damaged my leg? Will it be okay; is it broken? What am I gonna do? Shall I tell them in hospital, but they might stop me going home. What about the casting appointment for my new leg on Monday, Bloody Hell! Oh man to think I was doing so well. What if they can't do it now? Have I come this far only to ruin my chances of getting a prosthetic leg in this Pub Garden, why did I ever come out? Is this a sign of what's to come, stuck to a wheelchair forever, depending on other people?'

As my mood drops through the bottom of the bottomless pit, I suddenly become aware of Tina. She's visibly shaken and in tears, so of course I have to try to put on a brave face. Male pride is a powerful thing, and thank God for that!

"I'm alright, don't worry, I have to go through things like this. It's gonna happen sooner or later, so I better get used to falling over. It's my own fault, don't worry, I'll be okay."

She visibly relaxes as my words sink in and I almost convince myself…

In the car, I have to get this pain under control some how, so I close my eyes to meditate… We arrive back at the Hospital at five o'clock and I feel sick to my stomach. Tina leaves me at the door, instructing me to let the Doctors check me out. I produce one last smile to cover the agony, and reassure her with a hug as we say goodbye. It's good she leaves quickly, because I'm desperate to have a good look at the damage I've done to my stump.

Rushing back to my room I can't wait to undo the dressing before anyone sees me. Trying to assess the extent of the damage and explore the swollen areas, I feel vulnerable and alone. My eyes well up as thoughts of Mummy surface and I try to soothe my stump by massaging it, but it's throbbing more and more. So worried now I cant decide what to do next, so I turn my attention to a magazine and then the paper, then a book, then the TV, then I settle for Freak FM on the radio, but nothing really distracts me, so I check my stump again. This time I have a closer look, to see if I have broken or chipped anything. There's no way I can afford to lose anymore of my leg, It's only just long enough to have the prosthetic leg fitted as it is. Any more and I would not be able to use my knee and that would make walking so much more difficult. Finally I force myself to think positively and relax. I know I have to believe that it's okay, that it's just swollen and painful. I know positive thinking makes a difference but this is a huge test for me. After many attempts I finally manage to visualise the Doctor saying it's okay just a bit swollen, and I visualise it over and over until I can actually believe it. I end the day distracting myself by catching up with the mail and answering any that I can. Tomorrow is a new day.

4th September 2005
The Royal Free Hospital George & Mary Ward Room 9

Up early as usual, but still in agony and concerned about my stump. As we get ready to change my dressing, I tell the nurse that I knocked it on the side of the bed last night, and it really hurt. I have to tell a little black lie because I don't want them to stop me going out or going home soon. She calls the Doctor, who checks my leg thoroughly and confirms there are no broken bones, it's just a bit swollen, however he says the swelling could interfere with the casting appointment tomorrow. Feeling better about it now, I do a quick video of the swelling! One day I'll look back on this video knowing it didn't cause a problem and I look forward to that day.

As much as I keep thinking positively, my leg just doesn't feel right after the fall so I decide it'll be a good idea to get a second opinion at my fitting appointment at Roehampton tomorrow, best safe than sorry. Lesson learned I doubt very much that I will forget I've lost my foot again!

5th September 2005
The Royal Free Hospital George & Mary Ward Room 9

I wake up still feeling pissed off with myself for falling over, but there's no time to dwell on that I've got to get ready, as the transport to go to Roehampton is due soon. Even though my stump is swollen, I'm hopeful it'll be okay so I quickly down my breakfast and make my way down to the ground floor.

The transport arrives to pick me up, and as we set off it soon becomes obvious the Driver doesn't know where the hell he is going. The regular passengers are trying to direct him, but he's not listening. Two and a half hours, several pick ups and lots of moaning and huffing later, we eventually arrive via the scenic route. What a commotion! Still it's fun to be out and about and away from my hospital bed. Glad I remembered my video recorder too, I'll get some good footage of the first phase of my new leg, can't wait!

Roehampton Walking School is part of Queen Mary's Hospital and it is a real eye opener. People walk past me all shape and sizes wearing prosthetic limbs it's an encouraging and inspirational place. A smartly dressed man glides past on two prosthetic legs, and I just can't take my eyes off him as he walks so effortlessly and heads into the car park. I continue to watch as he gets into a Land Cruiser and drives off. Bloody Hell! Amazing! I want to be able to do just that, I feel totally inspired and uplifted now.

Then I catch sight of Carlton and the News Of The World team, they're here to do an interview on my progress and I feel more than hopeful after seeing that man drive off in his car. The interview goes well, although I'm not my usual bubbly self. After they leave I see one of the Doctors and the Prosthetic Specialist, but unfortunately they can't do anything until the swelling goes down. This jars me, but I half expected it and what's more it's my own fault. Oh well, they confirmed no serious damage done and now I can look forward to the two and a half hour trek back to the Hospital!

On the mini bus I find that my wheelchair position doesn't have a seat belt, so I move onto the seat in front as I don't want to risk any more accidents. I remove the armrests and footrests from my wheelchair, and fold it in, so it can be stored behind my seat. When we arrive back at The Royal Free Hospital I reassemble it and make my way in, only to find when going up in the lift I've forgotten my foot rest on the mini bus. Chaa man! I have to learn to slow down and be more careful with everything.

6th September 2005
The Royal Free Hospital George & Mary Ward Room 9

Still pissed off with myself, knowing I caused a delay on my fitting, but I do realise I have to regard it as a learning curve. After breakfast, Nurse Barry pays me a visit, it's always good to see him, if it wasn't for him I may have lost my left knee completely. It only takes a brief discussion before he's uplifted my spirits again; the man is a Godsend!

As I lie on my bed going through another pile of letters, I can't believe the post is still arriving thick and fast. I get a vibe of the enormous impact this bombing, my survival and my positive attitude is having on people. I guess the fear around the attack has really hit home in the eyes of the public. They tell me it's unusual that a victim doesn't seek revenge. But I don't think of myself as a victim, I'm a survivor and I'm being real; I feel lucky to be alive. Why would I want someone else to die, it makes no sense at all to me, it's not Heroic, its common sense!

After a good work out at the Gym, a stream of Doctors and Nurses pop in to see me, they heard that I'm getting ready to go home. They tell me they're really going to miss me. They say lovely things and many of them ask for a contact number to keep in touch! I'm very happy about that.

During a moment of 'me time', I'm reminded of my Mum and what she went through after she had her first stroke; the injections, tubes, tablets and the uncanny coincidence that the problem was on her left side, just like it is with me. The comparisons are freaky. I try to make some kind of sense out of it, but it goes way beyond words, perhaps some kind of puzzling spiritual message.

Liz my Housing Officer gets my attention as she walks in smiling.

"Hi Garri, how are you?"

"Hello Liz, what a nice surprise, I'm okay thanks, and you?"

"Yeah good thanks, I've got some news that could make you feel a lot better Garri." She takes some papers out of her bag.

"Fantastic fire away." I feel hopeful.

"Well, it looks as if we will be able to offer you a new home because of your circumstances."

"Yeah! That's great news Liz, I hope it's a house." I'm feeling excited at the prospect of a suitable home.

"Well there's a new build coming up, so we'll send you the plans to have a look at and see if you like it."

"Where is it?"

"It's in Peckham and I've brought these forms for you to sign, is that okay?" She offers me the forms.

"Okay, leave them there and I'll have a look later."

"Okay, got to dash now, lovely to see you and take care Garri." Leaving the forms on my bedside table, she rushes out.

"Thanks Liz, see you soon."

Next through the door are several of my old work colleagues and they arrive bearing gifts and broad smiles. It must be lunchtime!

"Hello Garri, how are you?" And before I have time to answer, gifts are deposited next to me on the bed, along with another stack of cards.

"I'm okay thanks, all the better for seeing you guys."

"That's what we like to hear, what, what, what! " Nicholas Peacock* is such a funny guy; he is the originator of the 'what, what, what' phrase that Dom and I play with a lot. On top of that he went to school with Prince Charles so naturally talks with a public school accent, with a plum in his mouth, as some may say. "So where's all the hot Nurses, and which ones are you chatting up now?"

"Behave!" I shake my head smiling.

"*Us behave!* Right, you must think we're as mad as a box of frogs!" All laughing we turn our attention towards to the gifts and cards they brought. I'm now the proud owner of a brand new portable TV with inbuilt DVD player and several box sets of DVD's. How very generous!

We catch up for a good while and Dominic purposefully hangs back when the others leave. "Garri I've been thinking I want to do a Benefit Gig for you to raise some cash, it may help you when you get home. I know that after care can be expensive, as well as those big-boy shorts you need! What do you think?"

"Wow, that's a generous gesture, and I do still think about the first pair of shorts you got me Dom, what were you thinking?" I laugh, "But seriously the Gig, wow! I don't know what to say." I feel so overwhelmed by his generosity I can't find words so I just keep nodding in agreement as he explains in more detail what he envisages.

Two Police officers show up after lunch, to question me about the day of the bombings. They need my statement to add to their body of evidence in order to build the complete picture of what happened. I'm glad to get it out of the way, one less thing to think about.

Next on the agenda for the day is an interview with Social Services. They help me with all the information I'm going to need to get myself sorted out when I get home. We apply for my blue badge, if and when I can ever drive again, and look at grants available to adapt my house for my disability.

After they leave I decide to take the forms downstairs to post straight away and it's such a beautiful day, I stay outside to catch a few rays. Dinner at five-thirty, then time to rest for a while, what a full on day, but thankfully I'm in a different headspace now!

7th September 2005
The Royal Free Hospital George & Mary Ward Room 9

Same routine in the morning but today is a very special day, I have a home visit, I'm going home for a few hours. It'll be good to familiarise myself with my old surroundings before I move in. If I remember correctly, I may have left some tidying up to do. Mummy always said 'clean up *before* you go to bed, as you never know where sickness is.' Hmm Mummy you were right!

7th September 2005
Hospital Minibus en route to Home

My head is full of thoughts about how it will be; I hope Hector is there to meet me as arranged. Anxiety and excitement mix together to cause an adrenalin rush, as we pass through the streets of London and over Vauxhall Bridge on my way home.

7th September 2005
Croydon Home

As I approach my unkempt garden I'm sad, I always kept it neat and tidy. I knock on the window, and my brother Hector comes to the door to greet me.

"Alright Bruv?" I nod but remain silent as he steps aside to let me in for the first time since the bombing. It's a daunting feeling being back here now on crutches. Although so familiar, it has an eerie and uncomfortable feel, no atmosphere just cold, like someone died and nobody lives here any more, a bit spooky in fact. I guess part of me did die though.

The door buzzer rings. Snapped back into reality by a woman from the local Occupational Therapy Team. She's here to go through some of the modifications I'll need in my flat to help me cope. I'm actually coming home tomorrow; the reality of it starts to sink in!

7th September 2005
The Royal Free Hospital George & Mary Ward Room 9

My last night in Hospital and what a journey it's been. As I look back at the ups and downs I'm grateful to all those who helped me get back on track, so many amazing people, and of course my brothers; each one special in his own way but different from each other. After some last minute packing and many goodbyes later it's off to The Roebuck for a drink with one of my favourite Nurses, say no more!

8th September 2005 8:30am
The Royal Free Hospital George & Mary Ward Room 9

Exactly two months and one day after the terrorist attacks, I'm all packed and ready to go, bwoy! Although apprehensive, I'm also determined to move on with the next stage of my life. Visiting home yesterday was emotional, like visiting a long lost friend, but today it should be easier. I didn't like seeing my flat grey and dull and my garden so out of sorts, but still I can't wait to get home.

As I rub eyes my face feels dry, eh, eh, where's my cream? I delve into one of my bags to get my coconut oil and apply it. As I check in the mirror one last time I am very happy to notice my eyelashes have almost completely grown back. It seems like such a little thing, in the scheme of things, but I can't express how much it means to me. It's as if I've made them my barometer towards healing.

One of the lovely nurses gives me my last jabs to keep my blood thin, along with a bag full of painkillers to take home. I've been taking these drugs since I got here and I look forward to stopping them altogether very soon. Finally they say if I have any problems I should return to A & E and ask for Mr Garlick, telling them I'm a patient from the 7/7 Bombings.

Media camera crews show up and wait by the door; there's so much going on in my mind, I'd forgotten that during the course of the last few days Carlton arranged for the Media to come along and cover the headline; *'Garri Holness 7/7 Survivor Leaves Hospital'*. Such a fuss, I can't help but laugh to myself, yet it feels nice that people care how I'm getting on.

Transport arrives just on time but it's very emotional saying goodbye to all the wonderful Doctors and Nurses who have looked after me with so much care and attention; I've built up quite a good relationship with several of them. The flowers and thank you cards I sent for each department arrived as many of them have turned out to see me off, thank me and wish me well. It's quite an occasion with everyone lining up along with the camera crews. Tears are shed as I leave the Hospital to get into the minibus, and I could easily let go and join in, it's so emotional. I'll never forget this moment, the praise, the love and the positive energy I'm getting from these guys, will sustain me for a very long time. What an amazing start to the next chapter of my life.

I know more challenges lay ahead; it's not so much about coming to terms with what happened any more, it's all about accepting it and dealing with the lasting effects. Life without a leg is going to be a challenge, that's for sure, but it seems manageable when you take into account 27 people died around me, and 56 who died in total. Considering how close I was to the Bomber I certainly feel privileged to still be alive to continue my journey. There's a massive mountain to climb, so to speak but this is where my independent life begins. As long as I stay strong, positive and motivated, I know I can get through. Come rain or shine, it doesn't matter, I am grateful for each day, as I'm alive to witness it. Through the grace of God, I am still here and can't help wondering if I have a purpose, a reason why I survived..

8th September 2005
Hospital Minibus Going Home

On my way home, Hector calls, he tries to convince me that I should go to stay with him for a few days before I go home alone, but I assure him I'm okay and feel the need to be within my own walls. Although he clearly isn't happy about that, I'm strong about this decision, as I want my independence as soon as possible. I can't allow myself to doubt that I'm capable and I keep reaffirming that I will be okay. Ever since we were young Mummy instilled in all of us not to depend on anyone, she insisted we should be able to cook, clean, iron and look after ourselves. '*Don't depend pon no woman*,' she said and I won't Mum!

8th September 2005 Mid Afternoon
Croydon Home

I arrive home on crutches, as there's no wheelchair access to my flat. The Hospital assistants help me in with all my things. There's a pile of Mummy's stuff, including the urn containing her ashes, left in the middle of my lounge that wasn't there yesterday. I can't quite believe it, perhaps there was nowhere else to store it, or maybe my brothers thought I would find it comforting. Either way I can't deal with it now, so I just put my stuff next to it and call my brother Tony. I need his help to take me to get some proper Yard Food and general supplies.

After shopping we spend some time hanging out and going through Mummy's stuff together, ending up reminiscing over happier times. It turns out well that Mum's stuff is here; it's comforting. Tony picks up my small electric shears and looks at me just smiling and I know exactly what he wants!

"Garri do me a favour, cut my hair." He looks at me with optimism in his eyes.

"Tony gimme a break, I just got out of hospital mate." It's the last thing I feel like doing.

"Just cut my hair for me man, it won't take yu long, I'm going out later on, I beg yu just cut it please." He smiles.

"Chaa man, yu troublesome yu see." I shake my head but can't help laughing with him.

"Just kool man, just kool, give yu somethin' to do, innit?" He wins me over.

"Alright bruv, but not with that shaver, let me get the proper barber shears that I use for my head." After a quick trim, and one of my creative designs at the back, he's on his way in a cheerful mood. I feel close to him and enjoyed being creative with his hair.

Once alone thoughts of spending my first night here trigger strange and deep feelings of vulnerability, loneliness and grief, as well as sheer frustration. After aimlessly wandering around my flat I end up in the bedroom sitting on my bed. As I bend my left knee and place it stump down onto the bed; it looks astonishing! If anyone could see me now, it looks as if I magically put my foot straight through the bed! I chuckle as I hear what Mum would have said *'Sometimes yu fi tek bad tings n turn 'em into joke!'* I'm amused, amazed and freaked out all at the same time. And for my next trick!

It's weird being home and not being able to hear as well as I could before. I have to come to terms with an almost silent world. What used to be loud and clear is now muffled and distant and I wonder if I will ever be able to appreciate the sweet sound of music again. When I lay down on my right side, I can't hear anything at all, not even the faint sounds that filter in through my right ear. Still, I have to be thankful that I can still hear something on one side. I'm comforted by the thought that I have an appointment arranged for an operation on my left ear at the Royal Free Hospital with one of the top Surgeons. Maybe he can help me get back some of my lost hearing and maybe not, time will tell, but there's hope!

Kicking back to relax under the covers of my own king-size bed, I'm glad to be here on my firm mattress at last and I drop off into a light sleep.

April 2005
London Carlton's Recording Studio

Carlton smiles and gives me the thumbs up, I can see his mouth moving but I can't hear him. He gestures for me to take the headphones off cos he's playing the track through the speakers. With the headphones off, I can hear what we've just recorded and it sounds wicked!

"That was a great take Sugar, yeah man, the tunes coming on good, we gonna use that."

"Yeah man, let's do this!"

8th September 2005 Early Morning
Croydon Home

I wake up hot and sweaty and try to kick off the covers, but the left side of the cover stays put, and I'm reminded in my half-sleep state that I've lost my foot. The last time I slept in this bed I had both feet firmly attached to the ends of my legs! Another painful reminder things will never be the same again, so I reach over to my bookshelf, take up the bible and it falls open on Psalms 23, so I read it out loud.

"The Lord is my Shepherd, I shall not want..." While reading the Psalm each word resonates through my body and it seems to echo throughout the flat. This Psalm connects within me, as if it was written for me, a message suitable for this challenging time. Thank God for that! I just have to come to terms with being how I am now it's not going to change. I have to acknowledge it and do the best I can. I feel inspired to get back into my music and I think my emotions can actually help me write with a depth and passion like I've never known before and that's good!

November 2003
London Carlton's Recording Studio

"Sugar listen to this, tell me what you think." Carlton plays me an advert he's working on for the Green Party; I think they're already one of his clients. I listen carefully and it sounds good, but I can hear a synthesised sound in the mid range that's slightly off. "You hear that Euro kinda beat underneath, can you mute it for a minute?"

"What do you mean, Euro kinda beat?" He looks puzzled and plays the track again.

"You know that tinny synthesised sound, listen… there right now! Stop!"

He finds it and mutes the track, we listen again and the tune flows much better without it.

"Ah yeah, I see what you're saying Sugar, much better, glad you passed by."

"It's nothing man, I was already at the Nursing Home on the corner looking after Mum innit, plus you're helping me take my mind off worrying about her."

"So lets build a tune together?" He looks at me smiling and I feel excited at the thought of singing again.

"Yeah man, build it yes" I smile and nod my approval.

"Yes Sugar!" He seems very pleased.

"A long time me an the mic don't talk, yu get me!" Excitement builds and I can't wait to make a start.

9th September 2005
Croydon Home

I wake up early, the hospital routine is still very much part of me. Being at home though is like a new adventure, and as I settle in I really want to keep up a healthy routine so I can continue to improve. I've got to make sure I eat regularly and exercise too, as I must keep my strength up, I can't afford to let my leg waste away. Although Tony my big brother says he can help if I need to go out for anything, I'm trying so hard to be independent. The buzzer rings, and thinking it must be Tony I answer the intercom. "Hello."

"Hello Garri its Jennifer from upstairs."

I open the door, "Hi Jennifer, I was expecting my Brother, what a nice surprise."

"Garri, I don't want to disturb you as you just got back, but I wanted to let you know if you need anything I'm just upstairs, food, help with something, washing, whatever, just call and I'll be there." She sounds so caring.

"Thank you ever so much Jennifer, I really appreciate that." It's comforting to know someone is there close at hand if need be. Mmmm and Jamaican food too!

I fancy a cuppa so put the kettle on. *Knock, knock… knock, knock* on the inner door. Ah that might be Lisa with my post. As I open the door, I'm a little surprised to see Hyacinth, my neighbour from down the hall. "Oh hello Hyacinth-" but before I can say anything else, she cuts in, talking at full speed, "Oh Garri, I'm so sorry to hear what happened to you even my little son cried over you, do you need anything? If there's anything I can do you must ask me. If you need food or anything like that feel free to ask me doesn't matter what time of day or night,"she doesn't even pause for breath!

"Oh okay thank you very much, I will, thank you." Again a sense of being cared for feels comforting and now Indian food is on the menu as well. I laugh delighted as my food options increase!

The kettle boils and just as I sit down to drink my tea, there's another knock on the inner door and this time it is Lisa with my post. "Hello Garri, lovely to have you back, here's your mail." She reaches up to give me a quick hug, hands me a stack of letters and then I point her through into the lounge, following her on my crutches. I'd forgotten how tiny she is, around 5'1".

"Alright treacle?"

She smiles, "Yeah I'm fine Babe, more to the point how are you?"

"I'm alright Lisa I'm coping, gotta thank God I'm still alive." She nods and for a moment looks me in the eye without blinking as if she's looking at my soul. "Well, you know where I am if you need anything, food, cleaning, shopping, and because you're a single guy, a saucy little snog!" She bursts out laughing.

English food as well! I can't believe my luck today; at this rate I'll be able to open a multi cultural restaurant! But wait, what else did she say? "Sorry what did you say, a saucy little what? You're a naughty girl!"

"Naughty, but nice." We both laugh and the buzzer goes again.

"Whoa, its like Piccadilly Circus in here today."

Tony arrives and Lisa politely leaves. "Remember Garri if you need anything I'm only upstairs." She hugs me then smiles at Tony on her way out.

"Ah, so yu ah gwaan Sugar." He's glued to the sight of Lisa's backside disappearing up the stairs.

"Kool noh Big Bredda." I shepherd him into my flat and he brings in the delicious smell of yard food. Suddenly it's nearly one o'clock and I'm aware how hungry I am. We eat together, smoke together and start putting away the rest of Mummy's things. It feels good to be with family.

I catch a glimpse of Carlton from the corner of my eye, coming along the garden path. "I beg yu open the door fi Carlton Bruv." Tony opens the door and Carlton joins the party. We carry on smoking, drinking tea and chatting all afternoon. I'm excited and surprised to learn that 'Richard and Judy', 'This Morning' and several other TV and Radio Shows are chasing me for interviews as well. Finally the guys leave and I fall into a deep contented sleep in my own bed.

10th September 2005
Croydon Home

Getting used to my flat again, the morning starts well after a good night's sleep. I switch on the TV for company without choosing anything particular as I start tidying up. I'm expecting Halle to pop in, so I want the place to look clean and tidy but Football catches my attention. I just have to sit down and watch; me an' football eh, I can't resist.

Before long, here she is nice and neatly! "Hello Garri."

"Hello Babe, come in." Wearing a beautiful smile and carrying several bags of what smells like delicious Caribbean food, I lead her straight into the kitchen. As we unpack the food, I'm so happy she's brought yam, green banana, sweet potato and I swear I can also smell fried snapper escaping from the bag!

"Mmmm, Halle you're a good cook, it smells nice yu see." We open a bottle of wine, and share the food. It's beautiful being with such a wonderful woman all cosy and cuddled up on the sofa. The simple things in life, good food, a little wine and the attention of a beautiful woman what more could a man want? When's the football starting?

11th September 2005
Croydon Home

I wake up feeling great this morning, after such a lovely evening with Halle. I definitely notice how well I feel after I eat good home cooked food. Just like the '*ital* food that Mummy cooked, fresh whole food that offers us vital information straight from mother nature, not chemical laden processed food. I really miss my Mums cooking. I remember the days Mum used to wake me up early in the morning on Sunday to pick out the black bits from the rice and wash it. To sharpen the knife and pluck any left over feathers out of the chicken before cutting it up into pieces, then grate carrots and make carrot juice. It was an amazing feeling of accomplishment when we sat down in the evening to eat together. My Mum was clever, she taught me to be independent at a young age. That's part of the legacy she left behind and I will become independent again soon, but for now I'm grateful for all the help I can get.

12th September 2005
Home Croydon

I wake up thinking thank God for Roehampton Walking School where

I, and so many other people who have lost their ability to walk, regain confidence using different walking aids. Such an awesome place, it makes me feel so lucky! I'm looking forward to going back there today to start training regularly. I need to get back on that PPAM-Aid like I did in Hospital. I'm really looking forward to the challenge of it. I'll be going three times a week so that when I get my new leg I'll be prepared and ready to walk on it. I can't wait for that day! I'm a quick learner, fairly athletic and very determined, so it's my goal to progress as fast as possible. I really want to start walking and even running as soon as I can. It'll feel like a victory and I can almost taste it already!

12th September 2005
Roehampton Walking School

We finally arrive in the mini bus after picking up around eight people on the way, the journey was long and slow, but I remind myself to be grateful to be here at all. I'll be picked up every other morning from home by the mini bus to come here until I can walk. Fast-forwarding though, I'm looking forward to the day when I can drive here myself, like the man I saw the first time I came. He is my inspiration!!

They say we'll start our workouts around ten o'clock, and I'm keen to get going. Looking around the other people here look middle-aged, elderly and frail, very few younger people. Then I notice a familiar face in the hallway, our eyes meet and we exchange a smile. I recognise Martine from her photo in the Newspapers, she's also a 7/7 survivor who lost both legs. I wheel over to her at once and start chatting, we have a common bond, we went through something that only another survivor can appreciate.

Martine is sitting in her wheelchair next to a black girl who has also lost both legs as well as an arm; she introduces me to Jenny. My heart goes out to her, she seems emotionally fragile and I don't want to evoke any discomfort by asking what happened, instead I keep the conversation upbeat and light-hearted. Martine has a great sense of humour, so the banter flows between us and Jenny smiles. I so relate with how Martine deals with what she's been through. We're like two peas in a pod in that we both do flippant very well, and I have come to realise sometimes it's the only way to get through the day.

Our attention is grabbed as the Trainers arrive. "Come on you lot, boys this side and girls stay there." I leave the girls and join my group, we are divided up again and I'm put into the group going upstairs to the gym.

As I look down through the window one of the female Trainers with the group downstairs catches my attention. I notice how she carries herself, ever since the accident I've been much more aware of how people walk, their feet, calves and even their shoes. Anyway I notice there's a very slight unevenness in her stride, seems as if she has a prosthetic leg. I watch how gracefully she moves on it. I'd like to talk to this woman and find out more, why isn't she leading my group? I'm really disappointed, damn! Oh well, I'm sure I'll bump into her when the times right, maybe at lunch time today. For now though my focus is to walk and strengthen my body, it's a challenge that I must face and unbeknown to the mystery woman, she has thrown down the gauntlet for me to be able to walk without people realising I've lost a foot, and I will rise to the challenge.

After lunch I'm straight back downstairs, but much to my disappointment the inspirational woman has vanished. Still, I have a mission now and I'll focus on that. 'We can rebuild him!' Six Million Dollar Man fi sit down, it's my turn now and I know Mum's watching me and I'm gonna do her proud.

16th September 2005
Roehampton Walking School

After a week of intense training, my core muscles ache, but on the positive side my walking has improved already. I have to do well on the PPAM- Aid, I give myself no other choice, I'm so determined I'm gonna walk again as normally as possible!

Although it's sad to see people who are facing major physical challenges, it's also uplifting to see how fantastic the staff here are, the way they encourage and support us as well as everything else that they do; they are outstanding. I'm embracing this part of my journey, I have a clear goal and I'm enjoying building good relationships with the staff and other amputees. Deep inside however I sometimes doubt if I can really overcome what's happened to me. I know it's a doubt I can't afford to dwell on though. It helps when one of the other Amputees, an older man who lost his leg in a motorcycle accident, says that I'm his role model, it pushes me to do better when he watches me walk, then tries to copy me. The feeling of accomplishment is very satisfying.

It's also heart-warming when people walk up to me, hug me, shake my hand, and tell me how I've inspired them, it helps me to feel worthwhile. It gives me Goosebumps, as it's not easy to believe they are talking about me, but as I take a more thoughtful look around me, it does feel like I'm meant to be here, perhaps by going through this I could help others who haven't found the motivation to focus on moving forward yet. It's obvious that some amputees can relate to me because I've also lost a limb, I'm one of them.

I have a strong need to succeed, to show the Bombers they didn't beat me, that I'm not broken. I'm still an independent man, with a worthwhile future ahead of me. A feeling of awe rises up inside my chest as if my new path in life is being born in this moment and I simply can't contain it. What if I've been given this second chance at life to motivate others? Could that be true?

18th September 2005
Home Croydon

After breakfast I start my household chores and food prep for later. The intercom buzzes, its midday and I'm not expecting anyone. I get my crutches and make my way to answer it.

"Hello?"

"Hello, is that Garri Holness?"

"Who's this?"

"It's the Evening Standard Newspaper, is it okay if we have a quick word with you?" I'm a little taken aback.

"On a Sunday, are you joking?" I laugh.

"Sorry we've got deadlines."

"Okay just a quick word, you're lucky you've caught me in a good mood!" I laugh again and press the buzzer to let them in.

"Thanks for seeing us today Garri, sorry to intrude on a Sunday, but we really need an update on your progress for tomorrows front page."

"Before we start, can I just ask where you got my address from?"

"The electoral register, actually." He looks a bit embarrassed; after all it's not fair to intrude on peoples privacy unannounced, especially on a Sunday.

"Hmmm the electoral register eh? "He moves quickly on with a few questions, asks for a photo and they're gone within twenty minutes. Actually it was quite a pleasant interview so I don't mind too much as it feels good to think people might be curious about how I'm getting on at home. However I do think using the electoral register to find me is crossing the line, he should have called Carlton to ask first. Anyway, back to my space to unwind!

19th September 2005
Queen Mary Hospital Roehampton

Today I'll be measured up for my new leg and I'm feeling slightly apprehensive, but very excited. The minibus drops me off at the walking school as normal but this time I head for the Prosthetics Team.

"Good morning, I'm Garri Holness and I have an appointment with Lawrence." I feel cheerful and the receptionist greets me warmly. "Okay Garri, please wait in room one, I'll let him know you're here." After a few minutes Lawrence comes over to greet me. Tall and slim in his all whites, he looks more like he's gonna play cricket. "Hello Garri, welcome back."

"Hello Lawrence, I hope we can move forwards this time as I'm really looking forward to getting my new leg."

"Yes, I'm sure you are, it should have sorted itself out by now I would think, come through and let's have a look." I follow him through, roll up my tracksuit leg quickly and climb up on a high stool so he can inspect my stump. I've learned it's better to wear clothes that allow easy access to my leg these days. It's a pain to undress every time. I'm actually thinking that someone should design a range of clothing for amputees, with zip off legs and arms or even Velcro. There're lots of young soldiers that would benefit. Maybe I'll just have to do that one of these days. Ozwald Boateng at house of Gucci you may have to sit down!

Lawrence is pleased. "Great, the swellings gone right down, it's looking good. We can go ahead with the cast today Garri and you should have the leg by next week." Music to my ears!

"Fantastic, lets do this." Lawrence covers my stump with a gel, and then wraps it in cling film. I watch, totally amused, as he smooth's out all the air bubbles until it is neat and tightly wrapped. Next he reaches into a bucket and brings out strips of white Plaster-Of-Paris in his hands, which he applies layer upon layer until he's created a virtual masterpiece.

"What you doing now Lawrence?" I ask as he continues to work on the creation, pushing in with his fingers at different areas.

"I'm trying to make an exact copy of the contours of your remaining muscles"

"Ah, I see."

"This way you shouldn't experience any discomfort, remember you have to walk on this. It's like a shoe fitting and we don't want it rubbing, pinching or irritating you otherwise you'll get blisters or callouses and it'll be sore, and we don't want that do we?"

"No, you're right there." He gets a marker pen and starts marking the back, front and sides with black lines and dots when suddenly I freeze, it's feels like something hit me in the stomach as a deeply hidden memory unexpectedly surfaces.

28th June 2005
Home In Bed Dreaming

I'm carefully drawing lines and dots across my left thigh with a black marker pen, then I try to wipe it off because I don't like it, weirdly my hands sink into the line and through my flesh, it's a nightmare....

I wake up and turn over in bed trying to escape the disturbing dream. But the next thing I know I'm hopping on one leg down Aytoun Road, distraught and calling out for help but no one's around. An area that's normally bustling with people is dark and deserted like a ghost town. Suddenly I see my mate Patrick approaching. "Patrick help me, help me!"

"Garri, what's up man, you okay?"

"Nah, look!" I point to my leg and he grabs me tight helping me to sit on the back seat of a nearby car. My left leg's gone and I'm bleeding like crazy. I wake up again in a panic and kick the covers off to check my legs, phew its okay, I let out a sigh of relief, it's only a dream!

19th September 2005
Roehampton Walking School

"Garri, are you okay?" I'm stunned as I try to digest what just happened. Was it a premonition? "Patrick?" I'm still confused.

"No Garri, my names Lawrence, but some people say I do look like Patrick Viera, you know the black guy, plays football?" He jokes.

"Oh... Patrick Viera, yeah, yeah of course I know him, I'm an Arsenal supporter, yeah man you do look like him, I agree." I try to rebalance as Lawrence continues working on the cast. I can't believe what just happened, did I have a precognitive dream just a few days before the bombing? That's crazy?! I just can't take it in right now, so I slip the experience to the back of my mind and try to carry on. Lawrence has split the back of the cast enough for me to get my stump out, so I oblige.

"Okay, we're done here for today. You can get on with your exercises now and I'll see you next week for the first trial. You sure you're feeling all right Garri? "

"Yeah, yeah I'm okay I'm good man; sometimes I just zone out." Still in a bit of a daze I spend the afternoon at the walking school fully focussed on practicing in the PPAM- Aid making sure I'll be more able to walk next week when I get my new leg. The disturbing memory of my pre-cognitive dream fades away.

21st September 2005
Roehampton Walking School

I hand my Motown CD over to a nurse to play as background music while we're walking and exercising. It creates a great vibe and both staff and the patients approve! The nurses tell me another Survivor from the Bombing will be coming in soon. I wonder how many of us will end up here. It would be great to know how everyone is doing.

On my way out, a man outside waves his arm trying to get my attention; he approaches smiling. "Garri isn't it?"

"Yeah."

"I've been watching you on TV and I think you're a great guy; very positive and upbeat and I'd really appreciate it if you could speak to my son. He was involved in the Bombings as well, but he's finding it hard to cope with his severe injuries." The man looks hopeful at me.

"Of course I will Sir, next time I'm here I'll have a word; if there's anything else I can do to help, feel free to ask. I'm really happy to help if I can."

"Thanks very much Garri, and keep up the good work." He smiles and talks to himself as he walks away, as I realise how hard it must be to watch your child suffer.

Wheeling my chair towards the minibus, I'm satisfied that I've made more progress today and now look forward to staying at home for a few days to get my house in order. There's so much paper work that I've been putting off. It's time to get my head around all the application forms for things that I'm gonna need.

As the days pass, I get on with my chores. I'd no idea how complicated and confusing the application forms are, and it's certainly trying my patience. I've great empathy for people less able to cope with forms and therefore miss out on some of the much-needed benefits on offer. I guess we all have to manage as best we can.

26th September 2005
Roehampton Walking School

The day has finally arrived to get my new leg and of course I'm so excited. While waiting in the main hall for Lawrence I sit people watching, it's very interesting. After around fifteen minutes I see him approach walking towards me with a spring in his step this morning. "You ready Garri?" I smile and he smiles back looking almost as pleased as me.

"Yeah I'm ready, come we go." I'm excited to think my first steps towards independence are so very close now. Lawrence leads me through to the fitting room, where he leaves me to wait while he brings my new leg through. The anticipation makes me smile till my face aches. It's not every day you get a new leg!

When he returns I'm surprised to see the top section of the Prosthetic leg is see-through rather than black like others I've seen. "Why's the top part of my leg clear Lawrence, is it cos I is black?" He looks surprised for a second, and then we both crack up laughing. "Garri, you are funny."

"You might think I'm funny Lawrence, but it's already got a white foot, what's a black man gonna do with a white foot. Imagine me walking along with one white foot and one black foot especially in sandals, I bet I'll get some funny looks mate!" Lawrence splutters now he just can't contain his laughter.

"I do understand, trust me," still laughing, "but this is only a prototype, we need to be able to see through the top so it shows us how your stump interacts with the socket. Often we have to make slight adjustments until we get it perfect."

"Oh okay, that makes sense."

"We will make your actual leg according to your colour spec, you can have blue if you like, or even green!" Now my turn to laugh!

Having calmed down, Lawrence gives me a silicone sock to fit onto my stump and then a thick woollen sock to go over the top, which acts as padding to make a snug fit. I put my stump into the polystyrene mould, and then carefully place it into the new leg. I quickly buckle the straps, Oh my God, the leg is on it feels like an epic moment!

"Stand up then Garri." I pause, but before any doubt filters through, my positive internal dialogue kicks in. *'Ain't no Terrorist getting the better of me, no way; you see I'm gonna walk again right now!'* I stand slowly and carefully, however my balance is surprisingly steady. Looking in the mirror, I take my first step; such a deep sense of satisfaction rises up as I see myself actually walking.

It feels a bit weird on the left side and I don't put too much weight on it at first, but it seems okay. I add a little more weight and a little more as I get used to it. Wow, it feels so good my inner voice gets carried away. *'You see, I can do it; I know Mummy would be so proud of me. Dads got a metal plate in his foot and he managed to be okay, so I must too, I can do this'*

Then Lawrence interrupts the chatter. "Stop there Garri, let me just adjust this, how does it feel now."

"Feels like I'm walking on the side of the foot."

"Right I'll adjust that, try again."

"Ah, that's much better." I'm getting more confident with each step I take.

"Right, see if you can walk a bit faster…Good job, slow down now, good, turn around and come back. Well done that's extremely good for a first attempt Garri, you should be proud of yourself, at this rate you'll be running the Marathon by next month!" I feel inspired!

26th September 2005
Croydon Home

I actually walked unaided today, I've made progress and it's good, but there's a long way to go yet. How will it be when I can actually walk outside on my new leg? There's still a niggling doubt in the back of my mind about how I'll fit back into society, I feel like a little bird in a nest getting ready to fly, I so want to, yet part of me wonders if I can, and then how people will accept me. I'm different now I have a disability. Then, I remember seeing that guy walking confidently on two prosthetic legs to his car and at the time I wondered how he must feel, well now I know how it feels to walk!

There's a mounting sense of excitement as I remember the BBC are coming to Roehampton to film my first steps tomorrow. The new leg will be ready by then, so I'll be walking on it for the first time instead of the prototype that I used today. I try to stay calm and relaxed, I've got to be up at five in the morning, but I can't get comfortable, wrestling with my pillows and turning over and over, sleep is impossible at the moment, I'm far too excited! I get up and make a hot drink, switching on the TV as I get back into bed. I start surfing the channels and end up watching Athletics. By the time I've finished the drink my eyelids feel heavy so I settle back down to sleep.

June 1988
Aylesbury Youth Custody Sports Day

I'm outside in the yard, up close and personal with the high jump bar, analysing the situation. There's no breeze and I'm feeling good as I've just cleared my personal best by miles. Now I'm gonna take a shot at the long standing Brixtonian champions high jump record.

"Shuggs you ain't gonna get over that height." The guys taunt me.

"Yu ain't beating that record, da Rasta's been unbeaten for years man." They are so condescending and smug.

"Trust me, I'm doing this, don't try an' put me off, just watch me!" I feel strong.

"There's no way yu can break his record, I'm tellin' yu." Just then The Rasta himself walks over.

"Whaa Shugga! You *think* you can break my record?" He leans into my face smirking arrogantly.

"Just kool Ras, its gonna happen, trus' me." I stay calm.

"You know how much man, tried an' failed? So you Shugga, ain't breaking my record!" He's full on in my face laughing, provoking me, and trying to put me off.

"We'll see." I'm still calm, cool, confident and smiling right back eye to eye. Everyone's watching, so I shut him out of my mind, take my time and prepare by running through the jump in my head, seeing myself clear it and knowing it's gonna happen.

"Okay go!" I run the planned curve with high energy and approach the big jump sideways with sheer determination. I'm really gonna break the record. I hit the perfect stride to take off powerfully from my left leg, gain maximum lift as I launch my body up into the air. As my back flips easily over the bar I land shoulders first on the mat with a cushioned thud. Pure joy rises up my body as I realise I'm clear and the shouts go up!

"Brap brap brap, brap brap! Gwaan Shugga! "

"Rah Shugga, you broke my record!" The Rasta looks astounded!

I get back to my feet, "I told yu I could do it; simple 'tings Rasta!" Laughing all over my face, I join the others guys who are all laughing as well. They slap me hard on the back. I did it!

I shout over to him, "Nuh get vex Ras, still Brixton man 'ave di record!" As I swagger towards the jump enjoying my newfound rise in status. "Shugga man, yu a Gangster, yu a G!"

The Rasta is vexed. "*KMT* go away from me man." He looks defeated! I smile a broad smile looking at him, calling out confidently. "Put up the bar man!"

27th September 2005 5:00am
Croydon Home

Eyes open and smiling as the residue of my dream lingers on, leaving me upbeat. As I wash and fix myself up, I dwell on the dream. I wonder if my record still stands. The Taxi rings the buzzer and I'm getting butterflies as I walk out on my crutches to meet him, just think by the time I get back home, I'll have my new leg on! Whoop!

27th September 2005 7:00am
Outside Roehampton Walking School

I see Carlton amongst a group of Journalists milling around as I approach. The Press Team from Roehampton are coordinating with the BBC breakfast team, News Of The World, BBC Radio 4, German TV, Malta TV. They see me approach and all look so pleased to see me.

"Good Morning all."

"Morning Garri, are you okay?" Already the cameras start rolling.

"Yeah, I'm very well thanks, a bit tired with the early starts, mind you, but I'm very much looking forward to today."

"Yeah it's a big day for you, 'Garri Holness takes his first step on his new prosthetic leg'."

"True that, right I'm just going through to get my leg, I'll give you a shout when we're ready."

27th September 2005 7:30am
Roehampton Walking School

Having left Carlton outside with all the Journalist and Cameramen, I see Lawrence appear right on queue with my new leg. "Morning Garri, how are you today?"

"Morning Lawrence, I'm well, very well and yourself?"

"Yes I'm okay thank you. Big crowd of press out there isn't it?" he laughs.

"Yeah looks like it, it's a big day Lawrence."

"Okay Garri here's your leg, remember to put these over your stump, just like we did yesterday, okay." He hands me all the things I need and oversees to make sure I'm doing it right. Slowly I rise to my *feet*, looking in the mirror and after taking a few steps using the walking frame, just to make sure everything is working okay, I take a deep breath and call Carlton to bring the journalists in.

The camera crews rush through, already starting to take pictures and filming as Julia begins her intro.

"Good morning, this is BBC Breakfast Live from Roehampton Walking School, this morning we are following up on Garri Holness, our 7/7 Survivor who is about to take his first steps, since the attack. So Garri how does it feel to walk again?" She smiles and pushes the mic under my chin.

"It feels great actually, it's another step towards my independence; and I can feel my Mum watching over me, each step I take, so that's great."

"And for those of you who don't know, Garri Holness tragically lost his mother while he was in Hospital and never got the opportunity to say goodbye. We're so sorry for your loss Garri." She frowns showing empathy.

"Thank you, I appreciate that." I take a few more steps along the handrail and Lawrence makes some adjustments to the leg, explaining on camera exactly what he's doing. It's intense, the cameras *click, click, flash, flash* at every turn.

"So now we hand you back to Natasha in the studio where she has an update of all the emails and text messages that are coming in thick and fast, from well wishers all over the world! Garri you certainly inspired us with your positive attitude." I can't help but smile as Natasha reads out some of the messages…

27th September 2005
Home Croydon

A big day on the calendar, I'm so excited to *walk* into my home. It feels amazing to actually come through my door, put the crutches down and still be able to walk through to the kitchen. Even though my leg is pinching my stump a little, I don't care, I'll get used to it. I simply can't express how it feels to stand in the kitchen and prepare food. It may seem like such a simple thing to many people, but it's a *huge* thing to me in this moment, and I will always remember it; I've got my independence back.

After I've cooked I sit down to eat and relax. I can't help looking at my new leg, my new 'toy' and I inspect every inch of it so I know exactly how it works and how it's put together, and especially how to adjust it, although I'm not supposed to do it myself. Next I wonder if I can go downstairs to my dressing room, this will be a massive adventure, I feel a little challenged but also excited. I have to find some clean shorts and I know I've got a couple of pairs of trousers with zip off legs somewhere. I've not been downstairs since the Bombing. I can't wait to see my clothes. That's it, decision made I'm going down!

Leaving my crutches in my bedroom at the top of the stairs, I venture through the doorway, carefully, and very slow one step at a time down the stairs. The steps are narrower than I remember, but maybe because I'm focused 100% on them right now and not just rushing up and down. Once at the bottom I feel a great sense of accomplishment. I'm so happy to have made it easily and then I catch sight of my shoe rack. The designer shoes call to me, changing my mood as I realise those days are over. I can't afford to let myself sink down though over shoes so I move on and start looking through my clothes. Deciding what I can still wear and what I have to say goodbye to.

28th September 2005
Croydon Home

Today I'm following the advice of the Doctors taking a short break from the walking school, but I'll go back Friday and I'm looking forward to it. Today is for sitting back and reflecting on my life, the many challenges that lay ahead of me; a little self-doubt creeps in. I wonder how I'll cope with walking outside alone; can I run, what will it be like at a gym? How will it be at work, travelling on the Tube? Will I ever be able to hear properly again? What about buying shoes and trousers; actually shopping in general. Can I drive; will I have to change my car to automatic? What about dancing, relationships and intimacy! How will women cope with my stump and my scars, will it put them off? Oh man, it really is all going to be different now!

29th September 2005 10:00am
London Carlton's Studio

Today German TV are filming, they want to know more about me, and what I did before the Bombings. We decide to let them in on our music so I sing the song we are working on, and it seems to go down well. They make a recording of me singing over the backing track we already put down, to broadcast on German TV. I feel so lucky working with Carlton; he's a talented pianist and producer and he really does encourage me. Then I get a buzz when I realise hearing out of one ear only is actually an advantage for a singer; ha ha I don't have to cover one ear. True positivity despite adversity!

It's been a great couple of days; yesterday I walked and today I'm singing for a fantastic Production Team; two reporters and a cameraman who seem very genuine. I can feel their sincere support and care.

29th September 2005 3:00pm
Croydon Home

Feeling good about singing, I take a little time to relax and read through more get-well cards I've received via the BBC. Interrupted by the buzzer, I look out to see a courier with a package to sign for.

Ripping it open I find a DVD of the Movie 'Green Street' from Vicki at work and wonder how she managed to get hold of it so soon. Anyway I can't believe my luck, it's so thoughtful of her as she knows I missed the Premiere while I was in Hospital. Gotta phone to thank her straight away.

Obviously this is my 'must see' viewing for this evening, remote control, "weh yu dey?" I get comfortable on my sofa and watch closely as the scenes play; I remember what it was like to be on the set, it all comes rushing back. What we did, the people I met and how well we all got along, even though I was only an extra.

April 2005
The O2 Dome London, film set for Green Street

I'm about to kick back and chill after lunch with some of the cast, the production team, make up artists and the other extras. Several of the main actors GSE (Green Street Elite) are playing football just behind us, and Elijah Wood is in goal.

"Oi oi, oi oi!" Someone holla's from behind; I turn just in time to see the ball bouncing straight towards me. Being a *'baller'* that's an open invitation to join in! I get the ball under control, showing off a bit, and holla back!

"Who wants 'im eh, who wants him?"

"On me 'ead son," Leo shouts over at me.

"On your 'ead?"

"Yeah mate on me 'ead."

"Alwright mate." Taking five quick steps back, I line it up, run forward and *Pow*! The cross is beautiful, if I say so myself, but he doesn't score and the others respond by mocking him.

"You bloody Muppet, great cross like that and you end up flopping it!" They put a smile on my face, and send the ball back to me again for another go.

"Alwright! Who want it naw?"

"Send it to me."

"Nah mate, give it to me I'll score" A bit of rivalry is evident.

"Send it in mate, on me 'ead." I send it in again, another inch perfect cross; this time it ends in a great bloody header. Eruptions of joy and hive fives follow, but it seems Elijah doesn't like being in goal any more! I try to make him feel better.

"Just cool Elijah you're good man, you nearly saved it." He half smiles briefly, but still doesn't look too happy. The ball goes to Leo, he crosses the ball and although there's a bit of competition going on, there's still a nice sense of bonding and mutual respect between us.

"Ok mate you have had your fun, give the ball back to G so we can get some quality crosses in." The others taunt him again but at that moment Leo swings in a peach of a cross right at me, which falls perfect for my left foot; natural instincts take over, and a connection of sheer class, as the ball swerves into the corner of the goal. Pure noise! I didn't play semi-professional football for nuffink!

30th September 2005
Roehampton Walking School Gym

Bench-pressing again, and although I'm coping quite well these days, I'm determined to get stronger. Fully focussed on my mission and lost in my own world, a man in his early fifties startles me as he taps me on the shoulder.

"Well done mate." I look at him knowing the weights aren't that heavy. "What for, these weights?"

"No, not that, I'm impressed with you, I've been following your story in the Media, and everything you've said has been spot on. What a total inspiration you are! Can I shake your hand, as I really do admire you?" Somewhat taken aback, we shake hands.

"You've touched so many hearts and I've seen people cry after hearing your interviews."

"Thank you very much, I don't know what to say." He walks off happy as quickly as he arrived.

Focus lost, I have to take a moment to digest what just happened. I'm not trying to impress anyone, I just wanna get back to some kind of normality, to learn how to cope without my leg and live life as best I can. The only way to do that is to count my blessings rather than my problems. But, the more I sit and think, the more it starts to sink in what's happening to me; the degree to which people across the world have been affected by seeing me try to be positive. It may be a simple thing, yet it seems to have a huge impact. Imagine that, little old me from Stockwell Park Estate, Brixton, helping people without knowing. If that's true, I want to embrace this situation so I can deliberately start helping even more people.

Other than the valuable insight I received, it's a regular day at the gym and walking school. Getting used to my walking routine and general exercises. Minibus picks me up and brings me back home. Same old routine but it's good to be out and about and see how the world looks out there. I'm so thankful for my blessings.

3rd October 2005
Home Croydon

It's my birthday but waking brings feelings of 'empty' joy this morning; I miss Mum today more than ever, but just think, I might not have even been here at all. A shiver goes through me, as I contemplate being alive! I may never have seen this birthday and as it is, I'm seeing it as a different person, a changed person. Inspecting my scars, my war wounds, I just have to thank God I pulled through.

Although I've not followed the strict Roman Catholic tradition I was born into, I feel very connected to my Spirituality and to God especially after facing death. I guess looking in the face of death can amplify the meaning of life! So who or what is God? What shall I believe? We have to question if the so called 'Terrorists' responsible for this horrendous bombing, think they are Martyrs in the name of God, what kind of God is that? Can they believe he wants them to commit murder in his name? I can't believe that. Surely God is Love and would want his people uplifted, wouldn't he? Thinking again about what the Muslim man I met in hospital told me, I have to look for myself what it actually says in the Qu'ran, rather than take someone else's word for it. I find my version with English translation that was given to me by a Muslim friend of mine. I'm confused by the El-Tawbah, Surah 9:29 and 9:5.

The phone rings and rescues me from the reasoning that could potentially drive me crazy. It's Halle to wish me Happy Birthday, and we arrange to catch up later over a bottle of wine. I plod on during the day doing my chores, and also receive cards in the post, which creates a beautiful display in my front room; I've never had so many messages and cards before, it feels nice to be loved. The afternoon becomes evening very quickly; before I know it, it's time to tidy up my place, set a romantic scene and 'hold a fresh,' speedily before Halle get's here, say no more!

5th October 2005
Roehampton Walking School

A young man walks over, as I'm fitting my prosthetic leg. When I look up, I notice his right arm is amputated to the elbow. He smiles and I feel a surge of his emotion before he even speaks, as his eyes fill up with tears.

"Excuse me Garri, I just had to come over and say something."

"Really? What's up?" I smile and look into his eyes.

"I was watching you on TV and the other day and when I was feeling really down about my Cancer, I suddenly remembered something you said and it made me feel good, in fact it really inspired me. So thank you, okay, thank you very much Garri."

"Aw my pleasure mate, I'm glad if I could help you."

He walks away smiling and I feel a tingle run down my spine; it's such a joy and privilege to find out I've helped someone, especially a young man, with his whole life ahead of him. It seems positivity is almost like a type of healing power in itself, can I dare to believe that? The thought puts me on a high!

My training has become more intense now including going up and down stairs and tackling uneven surfaces. My knee sometimes gives way and I lose my balance but I'm learning to cope. I can really relate to how women must feel when I see them walk over cobblestones in their high-heeled shoes. Anyway I'm moving in the right direction, and fortunately for me I'm picking up new things quite quickly. Practice makes perfect and it feels like I'm reprogramming my mind as to what's possible and how to cope with what comes my way, well at least most things that come my way.

10th October 2005
Roehampton Walking School

So, surprise, surprise! Today I'm being discharged, as apparently I'm a good student! All the Doctors and Nurses say I should be proud of myself, telling me to just look how far I've come in such a short time. I realise this is my last day, but I also know this is when all the real work and challenges will begin. I'm on my own now! Stabilisers are coming off, daunting!

11th October 2005
Home Croydon

Up and at it straight away, busy, busy all day long, autopilot on, hardly time to stop and think…

I'm looking for an automatic car, so I can actually drive again; and it goes without saying how amazing it feels to think about being mobile. My current BMW is manual, and I can't drive it anymore so it's found a good home with my brother Tony. Meanwhile it's not easy to find the right car for me. I've been all over the Internet looking, but finally managed to find a X3 Four-Wheel-Drive in 'Graphite Grey' with only one previous owner and low mileage available at BMW Park Lane.

It's ten o'clock at night already! It's been a very productive day, I made quite a few calls and I've also sorted out most of my paperwork, now all filed away, what a relief. It's good to get my brain working again after so long and its left me with a sense of job satisfaction. Now I know where to find everything and I've booked a test drive for tomorrow. I'll sleep well tonight!

12th October 2005
Home Croydon

I'm wide-awake early this morning, an exciting and busy day ahead. I have to be at BMW Park Lane at two thirty to test drive the car I found, that'll be exciting and then straight off to the Royal Free Hospital for a check up. Tony is coming with me and it's great to have his support. The buzzer rings right on queue! Tony drives us away in my old manual BMW; as we turn at the end of my road my mobile rings

"Mr Holness this is BMW Park Lane."

"Alright mate."

"The X3 you would like to view is currently positioned in the Marius Street service department, so I wonder if you can kindly go straight to them as they are expecting you."

"Okay will do, thank you, who shall I ask for?"

"Oh yes, of course, Graham will take care you, have a nice test drive Mr Holness."

"Thank you." So we head towards Marius Street instead. When we arrive, they tell us the car has been washed and returned to the showrooms at Park Lane. What a palaver, so we have to go there after all, but actually I'm happy to go shopping for a car in The Park Lane Showroom, it feels special.

"Good afternoon Mr Holness how are you?" Greeted by name at the door, that's a nice touch.

"Yeah good thanks, but I haven't got a lot of time now, as I have to be in

Hampstead just after three o'clock."

"Okay then, are you ready for a test drive straight away?" He smiles rubbing his hands together.

"For sure." Tony in the back and Graham next to me, I try to take the new experience in my stride, driving down through Hyde Park Corner up to Marble Arch and back again. The car drives smooth and makes me feel safe and comfortable, just the right height and position, really brilliant to drive, especially as I haven't driven for months and never before without my left foot! I decide just then this is definitely the one for me.

After returning to the showroom we're given the hospitality on offer. Tony takes his coffee with him to look around the show room, as a Mechanic of course he's probably excited to see what's here, maybe he's dream building too. Graham and I talk numbers, and just before signing I look up to see Tony checking out the engine of the X3. Thumbs up from him and I sign on the dotted line! That's it, the deal's done, and I'm now the proud owner of a Graphite Grey, automatic X3m Sport Limited Edition BMW. Big tings, ah gwaan! I'm another step closer to my independence!

Back in Tony's car we fight our way through the London traffic to get to the Royal Free Hospital in Hampstead, in time for my check-up. Tony's taking all the back routes he knows to avoid most of the traffic and ensure I make it. Talk about cutting it fine, we breeze in at fourteen minutes past three!

I walk straight through without having to wait a minute. The Doctor's say everything's going well, they seem very pleased with my progress. I'm more than happy with that, the icing on the cake of a perfect day!

On the way home we stop off at Camden Market, it's been a while since I've been here. We park up and walk slowly through, browsing around, I love the quirkiness of Camden Town, its enjoyable just to be here and have Tony with me. The home-ware furnishings are so different and I'm making mental notes of the things I'd like for my Flat, as well as clothing ideas to create a range of clothing especially for those who have lost limbs. On top of all that I'm still buzzing from the feeling of driving again!

Finally on the way back to Tony's house, we pick up some Yard Food from a local Caribbean restaurant. It's been great sharing this day with Tony; he's such fun and light relief as we remember our childhood together after such a full on day. It's good to chillax, eat some food, and listen to Old Skool music, on his homemade sound system as I digest my day. And what a day it's been!

13th October 2005
Home Croydon

I'm working on my compensation form at home, dealing with queries from my Solicitor and realising there are so many questions that need to be answered in depth that sometimes take me to a place I'm not ready to visit just yet. I go as far as I can, and shelve the rest for another day.

14th October 2005
Home Croydon

Today is the big day! I give Tony a shout to remind him to take me to pick up my ride. "Yo big brother, we on a move, link up!" He remembered of course. "Soon come!" Within twenty minutes Tony's blowing his horn outside and I'm all ready to go. He seems just as excited as me! We drive back to Tony's, deciding to leave his car there so he can sit with me when I drive my car home for the very first time. I feel a closer bond building between us and we create a great vibe on the way. I think he's proud of his little brother, and I am so grateful to him.

From Tony's we take a cab up to Park Lane. As we approach from the opposite carriageway I spot the X3 from the cab window waiting outside the showroom. It looks sparkly clean, mean, and ready to roll. The anticipation creates butterflies in my stomach and I can't take my eyes off it as we circle around the one-way system and come back down towards it on the same side of Park Lane.

Papers signed, logbook in hand, I have the keys and can't wait to get in and go! Once outside I find Tony, standing waiting next to the car looking proud.

"Here Tony, you drive!" I throw him the keys and he looks shocked! "Wha?"

"Drive the car, man." I nod to encourage him and smile.

"You sure? It's your new car man!"

"Jus' drive da ting."

It's a joy to see his broad smile, surprise and enthusiasm as he gets in the drivers side, starts the engine and buckles up. I'm so pleased to let him drive back to the Endz, he seems so thrilled, and common sense tells me, it's a good idea to get accustomed to the car before I drive it.

He drives with great care and confidence, that's my brother and I'm proud of him! Actually he's always been a calm, safe driver, I remember Mum would prefer him to drive her anywhere, rather than either Hector or me. Hmmm I can't think why! Thinking of Mum, I also have a plan to change the number plates, I want to fulfil a dream she once shared with me. She told me she wanted a car with a special registration plate with her name or initials on it, so when she looks down on me from heaven, she knows I remembered her dream.

Homeward bound as I drive from Tony's it feels better than I remembered; I'm appreciating the quality of the car; the smooth drive, and the solid frame around me. Can't help playing with the music player, which sounds great coming through the speakers, but I add a little more bass, perfect! Looking back in the rear view mirror I notice a familiar car following me. Aw man that's my big brother Tony being protective and I'm really touched. After around ten minutes or so, I flash my hazards to indicate I'm okay, so he turns off to go home. How nice is that?

I hardly want to go inside and leave my car, and when I do I can't help but look out of the window every so often. A final cuppa and one more peep out of the window at my ride before I settle down for the night. As I pull back the curtain a group of youths are standing around my car and I wonder what they're up to, I feel anxious and protective, so I watch silently for a while from behind the curtain. Pretty soon I'm relieved to discover they seem only to be admiring it. My concern gives way to pride and I go to my bed with renewed positivity and happiness.

August 2000
London Notting Hill Carnival

A group of youths are acting suspiciously. One of them gets in too close to a woman I recognise from one of the stalls. I'm sure she's a friend of my Mums and I see him reach into her open bag and lift something out, I'm too far away to see what it is, so I try to get closer. He backs off slowly looking around as if he is trying to find someone. The woman looks at him and he smiles innocently, as he dances away; she goes back to her stall unaware of what happened.

As I get closer, I shout "Oi, oi!" trying to get his attention, he sees me and runs off with another boy, but I can't get through the crowds, there's nothing I can do, there are just too many people. A little later I see them again they have joined up with four other boys in a doorway and I see them all laughing and joking as they share out some money. I approach them quietly from the side cutting off their escape route.

"Bredrin, yu think I didn't see what you done. It's my Mums friend. Yu fi give back the woman her tings. How would you feel if dat was your Mum?"

"It weren't me." He says defiantly.

"Don't tek me for no eidiot, and mind I don't go an' call her big son's, dem ah Frontline Man." The others laugh and make fun of him, so I turn to them.

"Wot? Wot's funny, dis your Breddrin?"

"Yeah, so" They answer flippantly.

"So you know that makes you as guilty as him innit? It's called Joint Enterprise, you're all thieving together, and I saw you counting out your share."

"What yu talkin' about, I've done nuffink?"

"But I see you there as well. And furthermore lickle man, when her big son dem come down yu think they gonna ask which one of you took it, nah, you're all getting it, so do the right ting, give it back Rudebwoy!

15th October 2005
Home Croydon

As I wake up I instantly remember my car and get excited all over again. I go to the window and the group of youths that were admiring it last night spring to mind; they remind me of my dream too. Huh, bloody Joint Enterprise even haunts me when I'm sleeping.

Door buzzer sounds early, but I'm not expecting anyone.

"Yeah, who's that?"

"Morning Garri, it's the Press again. Sorry to trouble you, but we need to do an update piece on you for tomorrow morning, any chance?"

"Yeah okay, bear with me." I get myself together and go out into the hallway to see them. It was short and sweet with a quick picture and then I'm back to my big task of the day. I'm about to order my special number plate for my car. Gonna have my Mum's initials in it, just as she dreamed.

16th October 2005
Carlton Best's Home

I ring the bell and wait for Carlton to open the door.

"Yes Golden Child." He laughs.

"Behave Carlton!" I shake my head and smirk.

"How you get here Shuggs?" I raise an eyebrow and point my mouth towards my ride.

"There's my ride over there." Carlton's eyes light up with approval as he quickly moves towards my car.

"That's a very pretty car Sugar, well done; the girls are gonna be on you man."

"Leave me alone man, lets focus." I unlock and let him inspect the interior. After the seal of approval's given we go back inside.

Carlton has been talking with the Chief Executives and the Editor at the News of the World about the ten-thousand-name petition, 'Fighting For Better Compensation', for those involved in Terrorist Attacks. They've decided that I should be the one to knock on the door of Number 10 to hand in this petition and also give an interview to the Media. I'm actually not sure I am comfortable being that figurehead, but the arrangements have already been made and I don't want to let them down. I don't fully understand what's happening with the compensation as my solicitors are dealing with the claim for me, so many complicated forms to fill in. All I know is they are trying to achieve a fair amount for the people most affected by the bombings. I've got to be back at Carlton's by nine thirty in the morning to travel up to the News of the World headquarters and then on to Downing Street. Big day tomorrow, I hope they know what they are doing.

17th October 2005 9:15am
Carlton Best's Home South London

Feeling pleased that I'm independent again I pick Carlton up to travel to Wapping. The X3 is such an easy drive and I'm getting used to it already even though I've never actually owned an automatic before.

As we arrive at the News Of The World headquarters, in Wapping, the first person I bump into is Lauren a former work colleague. After a hug, air kiss and quick chat, I rush through to the meeting. The Executives and Editors of both 'News Of The World' and 'The Sun' are already discussing the best way forward with a small group of Survivors. After the short meeting we all head towards the coach that will take us to 10 Downing Street.

17th October 2005 10:00am
London Downing Street

As the bus pulls up there's a large group of Press, Media and onlookers already gathered around the entrance. Once through the barrier, we proceed towards Number 10 together. They direct me to stand in the middle of the group, while photos are taken and then I have to knock on the door and hand in the petition. Although I'm feeling anxious, there's also a feeling of pride that I have been chosen for such an important task. After I knock, the door opens slightly ajar, an unknown face appears in the narrow gap without saying a word. His hand enclosed in a pristine white glove, reaches out, sharply takes the petition from me and promptly closes the door again. Well, that's it, job done or so I think until I turn to walk away. To my surprise one of the other Survivors steps forward and knocks loudly on the door. Determined to make her point, she obviously decides that she will stop at nothing to get inside Number 10 and speak to Tony Blair face-to-face. I keep walking away, but when I turn again to see how's she's getting on I can't quite believe my eyes, she's disappeared. I'm forced to conclude -

a. Aliens have abducted her

b. Something else unlikely happened

c. She actually got inside

I think a or b is the most probable after what I experienced! Anyway I slowly make my way to the barrier and take a seat on it while we wait to see how far she gets; I'm amused and can't believe she actually got in. The guys from the Press call over to me for an interview and I'm happy to chat with various radio stations while I'm waiting outside; the BBC is also broadcasting Live. Within five minutes she reappears, but she isn't a happy woman, seems they palmed her off with Mr Blair's aide. Still, lets give credit to her for making a stand; she got further in than I did.

Meanwhile my phone starts ringing, one call after another and a string of text messages. The interview I did on Saturday with the Press hit the streets. They loved it and to be honest I really enjoyed doing that particular interview as it gave me the chance to credit all the people at the Royal Free Hospital and Roehampton who had helped me on my road to recovery. I felt the need to show appreciation, love and respect. I'm really grateful for their hard work and continuing support.

18th October 7:00am
Home

Up at silly o'clock to have a live interview with Nick Ferrari at LBC radio, on the phone. He interviews me about the Bombing and my way forward. This man is on the button, great guy. I like his vibe. "Garri I hear that you sing and you've got a song you're working on, can I be the first to play it when you've finished it?"

"Oh yeah, of course you can."

"It could be a future Number One." He voice is warm and encouraging.

"That would be nice." His lovely gesture makes me smile as I hang up the phone.

After breakfast I decide to visit Tony. What a great coincidence, when I get there he has an amp and mixer to give me, so that I can create some music at home. Now I'm excited, especially after what Nick Ferrari said about my song earlier, this means I can actually get back into my music, which will help take my mind off less positive things. Nice!

19th October 2005
Richard & Judy TV Studio Kennington

Live on Richard & Judy, it seems to be going well. Richard introduces me as 'The Iconic Figure of 7/7' and I'm both surprised and flattered. After the interview both Richard & Judy are pleased and happy with how it went.

"Well, Garri you seem comfortable with the camera, really liked some of your answers, you're a natural, for you it's like water off a ducks back." The Production Team join in as well.

"The camera loves you Garri, you're so easy on the eye."

"Thank you." It's all a bit embarrassing and I guess they are just trying to be pleasant, so I go with it. As we head for the seating area, Judy sits down with a bottle of wine, I take a seat opposite and then Richard joins us a minute or two later.

"You chatting up my missus?" He jokes with me winking.

"No, no!" I bite my lip and an awkward silence follows.

Anyway I'm not a big drinker and this type of environment feels uncomfortable, so I leave pretty sharpish. On my way out, but before I get to my car, I switch my phone back on and it instantly bursts into life with text messages, missed calls and even more voice messages. All my friends offer great feedback about the interview even before I've even left the studio. It's really boosting my self-confidence. My phone simply hasn't stop ringing, so positive and encouraging. I'm feeling a buzz.

Above
Hector, Me, Mummy & Tony,
Brixton, 1969

Left
Dad in 1961

Right
Tony, Me, Hector, 1972

ABOVE - Stockwell Primary Football Team, 1976
BELOW - Beaufoy Secondary School Football Team, 1983

Above - Mum outside church in the early eighties
Below - Dad in the nineties, the original Usain Bolt pose

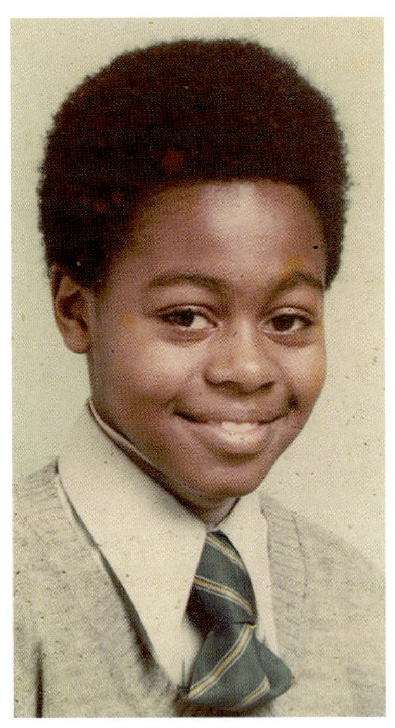

Left -	My first year Beaufoy Secondary School picture, 1979
Right -	Larking around in a photobooth, the original selfie, 1984
Below -	Mum and I after a shopping trip to Brixton Market, 1992

20th October 2005
Home Croydon

Up early and straight to the window, I still can't take my eyes of my ride; let me see if I can give it a 'one wash'. Where's my CD collection, all right! 'Stush' at Chelsea banqueting suite – DJ Karl 'Tuff Enough' Brown! You know how we do! Music found, time to find the bucket, check, wash and wax, check, sponge and water, check. Come we go! Wow, check me out, I'm washing my car. Although carefully moving round it pretty neatly, the challenges begin soon enough, I lose my balance for a moment, but then music blaring, I style it into a dance move! Must remember that move, good recovery, might have to use it again. The music is motivating me, so let's turn up the volume a little more; another little two step dance move around the car and it's done! Yeah I'm feeling it! Today is a good day I washed my car man! Me, I did it myself!

21st October 2005
Croydon Town Centre

In Croydon with Tony, as we walk along I notice when I catch someone's eyes, there is a nod, a smile or some sort of acknowledgement. I can feel a warm energy around me. I smile at everyone who smiles at me, and carry on as normal, occasionally people stop wanting to hug me or wanting to take photos. This is surreal. A woman shouts out from the other side of the precinct, "Keep up the good work you're a true inspiration!" This draws my attention to a young black guy behind her, walking into a shop talking on his mobile; when he clocks me he walks back out quickly ends his call and comes over. "Your from Brixton innit?"

"Yeah."

'You're a Soldier, real life Soldier, nuff man I know, know you, and respect you from back in the day; you're an inspiration, trust me. Man in jail's got your photos from the newspaper and stuck them on their wall, in acknowledgement and respect for what you've been through, where you're coming from and how you managed to bounce back!"

I'm speechless, but Tony just thinks it's too funny and can't stop laughing!

25th October 2005
Home Croydon

I've set up a sound system with the amps and mixer Tony gave me. I feel creative and in my element now as my old song lyrics start to flow. I want to update the lyrics adding some of what I've been through into my songs.

I don't know if I'm ready to write yet as my emotions are still raw, but feeling uplifted by the public response to me, so let me just record something to practice with, singing the old lyrics and freestyle a bit for now, *"♪I was boooorn by the river, Ohhhh…"* Although my hearing is not great, I'm listening back to what I've just put down; it sounds okay to me although there's room for improvement.

26th October 2005
Home Croydon

As I curiously open an official looking letter, I'm pleased to find the official invitation from the Metropolitan Police inviting me to view the carriage I travelled in on the 7th July. It's been kept hush, hush, as they don't want lots of Media buzzing around. I decide it's a must to go and see my carriage tomorrow; they confirm my appointment is at eleven forty-five. I'm very curious to see the carriage so I can actually acknowledge what happened and see where I was standing with my own eyes. It's one thing someone telling me about it, but seeing it for myself will be a different matter. Somehow I need this to complete the puzzle that's in my head, so I can have some kind of closure. Can't really explain it, but I know I need to see it.

Anyway to take my mind off it today, I've agreed to babysit my little Niece Leigh* and I'm looking forward to playing my role as Uncle Garri and Godfather for the day. I've got a few things that need to be dealt with up in London later on, so we'll have a little trip out together as well. After finishing a few chores in the house, we set off for London and end up in Holborn near my work place. I park nearby and take my Niece in to introduce her to the girls on reception. Then of course we have to do the grand tour, it's great to get reacquainted with my old surroundings. Leigh finds it all exciting, including the many conversations with my colleagues dotted around the building. I of course want to thank them for their support. It's a beautiful feeling being back at work, its like visiting normality. And it's just what I need, a bit of normality in my life right now.

The day's flies past and it's already time to pick up Leigh's big sister Nellie* from work then drop the two girls home to their Mum. It's a fantastic feeling being mobile, independent and even able to manage added responsibility. All in all it's been a really good day although my stump feels sore but, if you walk a lot, your feet are gonna get sore innit?

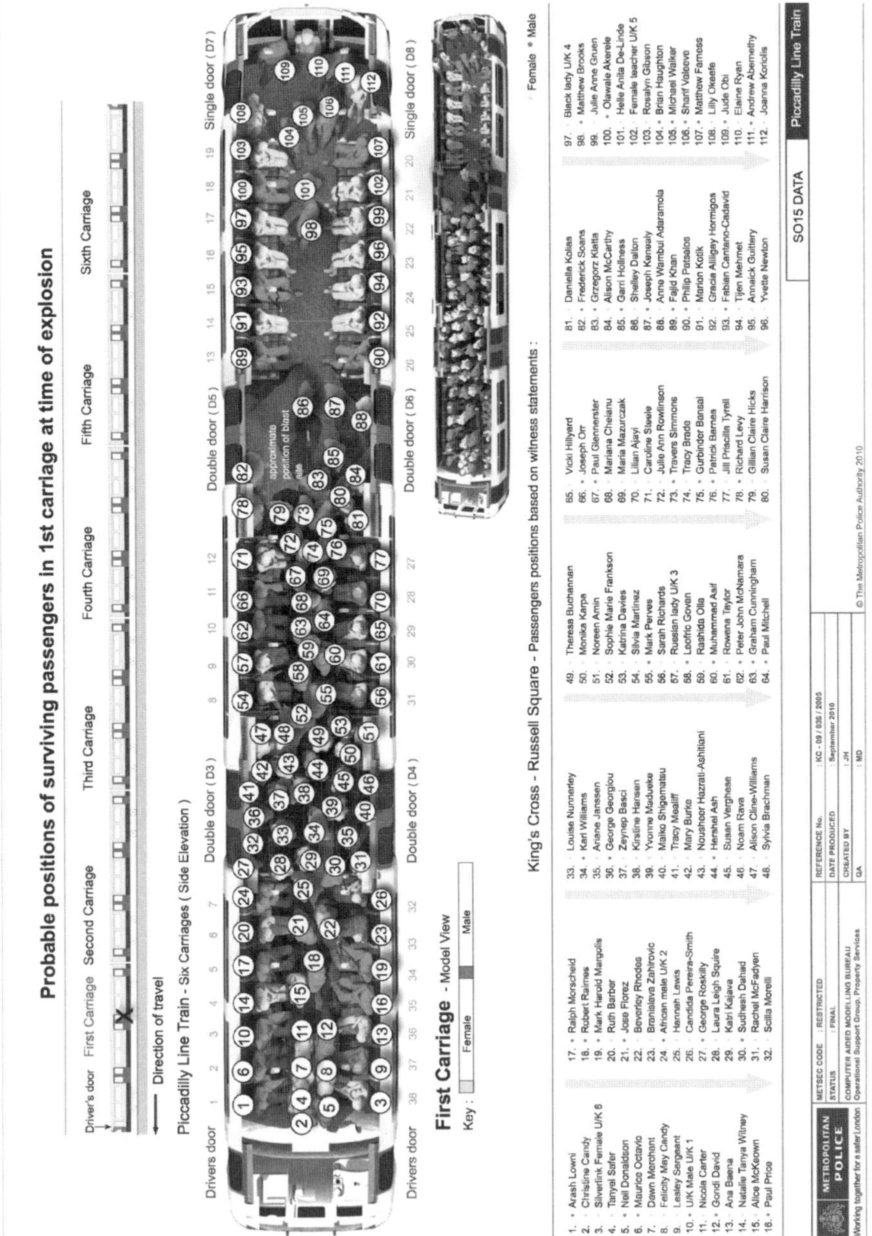

27th October 2005
Central London

Visiting the carriage from that fateful day generates solemn vibes that are hard to shake off. It's as if I'm engulfed by the time and space of that disastrous moment. To see exactly where I was standing as the bomb exploded is beyond expectation as I discover there was only one person between the bomb and me, and that person didn't make it.

It's incredible that I survived as I look around and acknowledge so many innocent people next to me didn't make it. It's not easy taking in the brutality of the situation as I stare silently at the hole in the floor where I was standing. Not a sign of the yellow handrail I was holding, it must have disintegrated. What's left of the carriage is reduced to wreckage, looking more like a scene from an apocalyptic movie than a passenger train. I feel strange as I study the row of seats where I sat up. They had been my sanctuary while I waited for rescue after dragging myself along the floor. Slowly but surely the pieces link together in my head and appease my desperate need to reconcile what happened.

The brightest thing about being here is the wonderful feeling I get meeting and talking with other survivors. Especially the ones that were in my carriage, I'll always remember Gill Hicks, she was the first voice I heard, shouting out 'I've lost my legs! It's good to finally put a face to the voice, I remember shouting back in an effort to comfort her.

A woman I don't remember approaches to tell me she held my hand in the carriage, and says that I told her I knew I'd lost my leg but that I'd be okay. As she holds my hand again just like she did on that fateful day, it comes flooding back; she's actually helping me to piece together some lost memories.

Yet another woman that I don't remember approaches, "Hello Garri, I'll always remember you." She seems bright and cheerful.

"Really, why's that?"

"I was behind you when the train before ours came in and I remember you were just about to board, when a woman pushed in front of you. All you did was tap her on the shoulder and say 'have a nice day love.' I thought to myself what a Gentleman, in contrast to some men who can be very aggressive."

"Aw yeah, I do remember that now, thank you," oh yeah she slipped my mind. That woman's lucky, but wait that's the same woman from my weird dream, who I collided with on the platform, bloody hell!

After seeing the train, I realise even more clearly how lucky I am to be alive. We were in the narrowest and the deepest tunnel! Out of the 52 innocent people that died, 26 of those fatalities were around me. My carriage was the worst hit of all four sites that were bombed, that's a scary thought.

28th October 2005
Carlton's House

After we finish another quick early morning interview with the Press, followed by an interview with Sky News, I'm sitting back talking to Carlton over a cuppa. "Carlton, I don't want to keep doing so many interviews, it needs to slow down. What d'you think?"

"I agree Sugar, it's how you feel, if you need to slow it down, its totally up to you, I'll support that."

"Yeah cos I feel the need to be in control of my life again; as great as the interviews are, it's very draining to keep going over and over the past. I need to concentrate more on my health and fitness now as well as looking forward into the future."

"Yeah, yeah, Sugar I understand you perfectly man."

31st October 2005
Home Croydon

There's a Memorial for the 7/7 victims tomorrow and I'm trying to prepare myself for what I'm certain will be an emotional day. I will start at GMTV Studio with an interview at seven o'clock in the morning, then I'll go to the Memorial at St. Paul's Cathedral. I can't stop wondering what it's gonna be like being there, I've never been into the Cathedral before. It's all uncharted terrain for me so I must make sure I'm mentally and physically okay. It's going to be a long, energy-sapping day, so I have to decide what to wear that's comfortable and sort out which route to take. I'll take a little time quietly contemplating and eat a good wholesome meal to keep my strength up. I intend to have an early night to ensure I have enough rest.

1st November 2005
GMTV Studios

Feeling a little nervous but surprisingly okay, I'm glad to be here in plenty of time for the interview, even though there were a few traffic issues on the way. Fiona Phillips and Andrew Castle, the Presenters, call me through from the Green Room and we're live on air from the Studio.

As Andrew starts asking question relevant to the day, I notice Fiona's just looking at me with a mischievous smirk, then she interrupts the flow of conversation, mid sentence.

"Garri, have you got a girlfriend?" I'm taken by surprise.

"Err, what?" I break out into an embarrassed laugh, as underneath all my boldness, I'm really quite shy.

"You've got such a wonderful smile." Getting more and more embarrassed and uncomfortable as I realise she's flirting with me, live on national TV, wow! I'm really not sure what to do next, so I just laugh, its a little light relief from all the questions about the tragedy. After the interview, there's a little time to relax, I wipe the sweat from my brow and grab a quick cuppa in the Green Room before I head home.

As I cruise back home to prepare for the next part of my day, I'm feeling nervous again. I phone Hector to let him know I'll be passing soon to pick him up. It's going to be such moving day I believe I'll need his support. I start wondering who may be at the Memorial Service; I'm guessing a few Dignitaries' will probably attend out of respect.

1st November 2005
St. Paul's Cathedral

The Cathedral is very grand and it's obvious a lot of time and effort has gone into organising the Memorial, it's packed to the rafters; there must be around 2000 people here at least. Looking around I take in the vibe, the dome above is covered in magnificent colourful paintings and I keep looking up at it. The painting of Saint Luke catches my eye and I notice a bull by the side of him. The black and white checked tiles underfoot and a large circle at the centre are topped with rows and rows of neatly aligned seats, secured together in three's. There's a serene atmosphere and it makes me feel peaceful. The Organ strikes up with rich deep chords that fill the building and the Queen dressed in a black suit and hat, leads the congregation. It's a beautiful service with 'Candles of Hope' being lit by a 15-year-old Sikh, an 11-year-old Buddhist, a 15-year-old Jew, a 12-year-old Hindu, a 14-year-old Muslim and an 18-year-old Christian. It's very moving as the multi-cultural nature of the service honours all affected. Several times during the service intense memories about the 7th July surface unexpectedly, so I'm glad I have Hector's support.

Afterwards everyone mingles in a large marque outside. My Family Liaison officer approaches to tell me a French man whose son was killed right next to me on the underground, would like to meet me and I agree. The man greets me with a warm embrace, I lean down slightly to respond; no words are needed his hug tells me everything. We are both overcome with emotion. During the tearful embrace I feel his pain and I can also feel him trembling in my arms, as I try my best to comfort him. After around five minutes, it's a long time, he steps back and thanks me. I need a moment to compose myself before I can carry on.

Looking around for Tony Blair, I'm suddenly faced with Michael Howard, the leader of the opposition. "I've been looking for you Garri, I've wanted to meet you ever since I've been reading about you." I'm already surprised and speechless but he goes on.

"You are so uplifting and inspirational I'm taking full responsibility for nominating you for an award in a New Year's Honours list." I'm lost for words so my brother Hector steps in to answer. "Why, what's he done?"

"Your brother is such an inspiration, I've been following his story."

"Really, what did he say that inspired you?" He repeats word for word one of the interviews he's heard. Even Hector is speechless now, so I find my own voice again.

"You have been listening haven't you, thanks for the nomination, but it's okay really, I'm just being me and doing my best to recover, if I help others as well that's great." Just then I catch sight of Tony Blair across the other side. "Excuse me Mr Howard, I need to have a word with Mr Blair."

After dancing around a few people to catch up with him, Mr Blair see's me coming. "Hello Garri, how are you keeping?"

"Hello Mr Blair," I'm a little taken aback that he addresses me by my first name, "As well as can be expected thanks, but you'll have to excuse me, I know this is probably not appropriate, but can I ask you about the compensation. It's not making any of the survivors feel great, in fact that's our biggest downer at the moment and we really need some help." He replies using some very encouraging words and goes as far to say 'if there's anything I need, I only have to ask.' But I'm wondering how much he intends to do, and how much he can actually do. I don't understand politics, but what I do know is that politicians seem to be very diplomatic. Anyway, I tried my best so it's time to move on.

I see several more people in the crowd that I recognise and as I mingle in, a Detective Inspector from the newly formed SO15 Anti Terrorist Branch comes over. During my time in Hospital we became friendly, as it was his job to keep me updated on the investigations. Seeing him here is a pleasant surprise, he's a proper geezer; reminds me of Jack Regan from the TV show The Sweeney! I shake his hand then we embrace; once again no words needed.

It's also very sobering to see real people here with injuries from the Bombings; it brings home the reality of what this Memorial is all about. Amongst all this grandeur, pomp and ceremony, we must remember real people have had life changing experiences and unfortunately the Government can't or won't offer adequate compensation. I'm told some of the Survivors actually boycotted the Memorial, too upset about the level of compensation they were offered to even bother coming. This is a shame in my view, as I feel we would do better if we pull in the same direction. Together we are stronger.

Anyway as I grow weary, my thoughts turn to home; at least I've done my bit. Turning my phone back on, it instantly jumps to life. Missed calls and text messages flood in again. As I go through them I find a little light relief from the pressures of keeping it together at this intense event. I'm more than ready to head for the sanctuary of home.

3rd November 2005 2:30pm
In My Car

I'm on my way to work to visit my colleagues and then on to Anita's leaving party. The first person I bump into is Gemma, her dad Jack is a chauffeur for the company, and he's a diamond geezer, very genuine and down to Earth. I hope he comes along tonight. Next I see a few of the usual suspects, Rusty and the Man dem. I won't get too involved with them though, as I'm here to support Lil' Sis, she's been so great to me, words can't express my gratitude.

Reception tells me Anita's out having a long lunch with the sales team, so I'm gonna hang around for a while until they get back. Within ten minutes the team starts filtering in, two or three at a time in a merry old state; it's so funny to watch them and then Anita arrives. We hug and sit down for a chat, which turns into a real heart to heart. It takes me back as I would confide in her from time to time and she would confide in me. I've missed her quite a lot. I'll never forget all the hard work she did for me whilst I was in hospital and even before that. We've had a good working relationship as well as friendship; pretty sure she's for real. It's such a shame she's leaving and I'm sad to see her go.

After talking with Lil' Sis I go for a walk around the building, one day I expect to be back here working again. Time flies and all those involved in Anita's send off, are moving on to Callaghan's for drinks. A few of them are so surprised when they see that I'm walking without crutches or sticks.

I've even rescued my 'Brixton Bounce' as I walk along these days! It's been a long and very enjoyable day, but its half past ten already; time to go. Jean asks if I can drop her at the tube station, she jumps in my X3 and off we go. It's wonderful being able to help others again. I love regaining the independence that I'd lost for a while. Finally time to cruise home with some 'banging tunes' on my music player.

4th November 2005
Home Croydon

My Family Liaison Officers arrive early to give me another update on the on going investigation. After exchanging pleasantries the mood suddenly gets intense.

"So Garri, we were wondering what you'd like to do with your amputated foot?"

"What? What did you say?" Caught off guard, I can't speak; it's not your every day question after all!

"Garri the forensic team have finished with your foot, so what would you prefer us to do with it? If you don't want it, no trouble, they can just put it the furnace with everyone else's limbs."

"No! Don't do that, I want it back, please."

"Why? What you gonna do with it Garri?"

"I'm gonna give it to my Mum to look after!"

"Whoa!" They look stunned and slightly uneasy.

"Yeah, I mean it, I'll have it cremated and put it with my Mum's ashes, which will end up in Jamaica, when I am ready to take them." There's a long pause before one of them breaks the silence. "I've got goosebumps!" Lacey says rubbing her arms.

"Aw Garri, what an amazing idea, you really are a special man."

"Yes Garri I agree, and if you like we can actually send it to the funeral parlour direct for you?"

"Yes please ladies, that would be perfect, I'll speak to them and then let you have their details."

"Well Garri you certainly took me by surprise today! But now I have something special to ask you to do for us as well."

"Fire away Cagney." She laughs.

"We've got a big Sports Day coming up at the Met, and we want to invite you to be our guest of honour and hand out the awards."

"Hmmm, let me just check my busy diary first, what date was that?" I smile as I'm joking around.

"Oh Garri, you are funny."

"So, I'll get my people to speak to your people, but it's definitely on!"

We all laugh.

"Okay we must go, but it's a pleasure as always to see you."

"And you too Cagney and Lacey."

"Take care Garri, keep smiling and we'll keep you posted when your foot is ready to be sent."

"Thank you, and have a great day." I'm left wondering how that all happened so easily and with the feeling that I have just fulfilled something very important, as if I was guided to keep a promise to my Mum.

7th November 2005
Home Croydon

Up early for my appointment at Roehampton. I have to be there at 11 o'clock and I'm so pleased to be able to drive there myself for the first time! I've looked forward to this day ever since I first went to Roehampton in the minibus. I just have to get the route down on the Sat Nav, shower and eat some breakfast. Then its time to put on my bionic leg and finally drive myself to Roehampton; it's great to feel the progress!

During my appointment with the Dr Shukri, he measures my stump to discover it's shrunk, so a new casting will have to be done. Apparently this is normal and to be expected. He explains that the body creates new routes for the blood to circulate up and down the stump as it heals. Obviously it will take time to stabilise itself and its good to know, I'm learning as I go along. Dr Shukri gives me a letter for my GP to update my medical records.

7th November 2005
Brixton GP Surgery

I drop in to see my GP briefly and leave the letter. Afterwards I decide to go into Brixton Footlocker to get a new pair of trainers. I need a white pair to match my funky white dungarees. I quickly find a pair I like and look for an assistant to help me

"Excuse me mate do you have this in a size eight."

"I'll be with you in a minute, just let me go check." He comes back with a couple of boxes under his arm, opens one, and hands me the left trainer. I smile as I look up at him, tapping my left leg so he can hear it's bionic!

"Could I just try the right foot please?"

"Oh, sorry, yes of course, I'm so sorry." He looks embarrassed.

"Don't worry man, just cool, you're not to know, and I'm glad you can't tell. I lost it in the London bombing."

"Aw man, you're the guy I saw on TV, wow! I thought you looked familiar."

I try the shoe on. "It fits good, I'll have these. By the way, if I have any problems with the left foot can I bring it back mate?" Having lightened the mood, we both laugh.

"Yeah, yeah definitely man, any problems you bring it back and we'll sort it out. I'll remember you!"

After thanking him I go to the cashier to pay for my new trainers.

7th November 2005
Home Croydon

Without giving it a second thought I change into my white dungarees and the new trainers, perfect match! Refreshed to feel a sense of normality returning to my life, I can still be as fashion conscious as I was before.

Although I notice an uncomfortable sensation on my stump during the day, I pay no attention to it, assuming it's all part and parcel of getting accustomed to the prosthetic leg. As the day passes, the idea of designing a range of clothing suitable for people that have lost limbs comes up yet again. It would be so great to have fashionable trousers with legs that can be removed and cool jackets with sleeves that undo, so disabled people could adjust the limb without stripping off completely.

Finally, after a busy day it's time to take my leg off to go to bed, but my stump feels so sore tonight. When I explore, there's a dark blister forming on the tip, and it's right on the skin graft. My mood dips because it had been healing so well, I wonder what happened; I decide to go to Queen Mary's in the morning to show my Doctor. Nothing more I can do tonight, so I try not to let it bring me down.

8th November 2005
Queen Mary's Hospital Roehampton

I think about what I did yesterday that was different and wonder if my new trainers had anything to do with the blister. When I mention it to the Doctor, he clarifies that the trainers could well have caused the blister, simply because the heel is a different height. Even though the difference may only be millimetres, it changes the angle of the fitting. I had no idea! The leg was originally adjusted to wear with specific trainers but because I switched brand in the name of fashion, it's caused the problem. So the rule is anytime I change footwear, I *must* have the leg adjusted to fit the new shoe at Roehampton. Painful lesson learnt!

Next up White City for an appointment with the BBC about compensation. The topic for today's meeting is what MP Charles Clark, said about introducing 'special circumstances' for Terrorist attacks. I'm not really into Politics, I just want to get on with life, the best way I can, but it seems I have unwittingly become the figurehead, and they're trying to make me into some kind of spokesperson for the whole compensation thing. I'm not really sure I want to get involved in this, but common sense tells me this idea sounds contradictory. As I understand it, they want to push through a white paper to say Terrorist attacks must be treated, as a 'special case' so they can hold suspects for 90 days without charges, but Compensation for the Survivors of Terrorist attacks is not regarded as a 'special case'. Surely the two must go hand-in-hand, either a Terrorist attack is regarded as a special case or it's not?" Perhaps this is what they call Politricks?

I arrive back home to collect Mum's ashes, at exactly 3:33pm, it seems significant for the meaningful task afoot, no pun intended. What I'm about to do now, will make me feel forever entwined with my Mum; our bond can never be broken, from now on I have one foot in the spiritual realm with her, and one foot in the physical realm. In a sense I'll have a foot in two 'worlds'. I jump back into my car, and as I drive to the funeral parlour in Brixton I laugh to myself, it's certainly an unusual task collecting the ashes of my amputated foot.

As I drive Mum's presence fills the whole car. It's as if she's kicking back on the seat behind with her feet up, chatting to me.

"Garri, tek time drive, 'member you only 'ave one foot, but how yu manage fi ah drive?"

"It's automatic Mummy." I chuckle at the comedy of the scene.

"Ohhh ah automatic, but tek time drive anyway!" I'm laughing hard now and anyone watching probably thinks I'm mad, and talking to myself but I don't care and I slow down.

"Garri what ah way yu crookified ehh? Imagine me ask you fi come help me plant some seed inna fi me garden and yu plant dem and yu water dem good. Den when yu reach ah fi yu house, yu call me a tell me sey yu teif sum ah da seeds dem, fi fi yu garden. Listen noh, any time yu come ah fi me yard, yu have to empty yu pockets before yu leave! You too teif!"

"Teif it yes Mummy, only after yu had too much seed an' I want my garden to be as nice as yours."

"Den yu couldn't buy yu own seed?"

"Kool noh Mummy."

"Kool noh, me did tell yu say me Hot!"

"Mummy, you know I'm joking with you but listen nuh, this is important." I look through the rear view mirror expecting to see her sitting in the back seat, but she's not there so I pause; then she answers again! *"Okay, me son me ah listen."* So I continue.

"Me ah go fi me ashes now and me want yu fi look after me foot 'til we meet again, take good care of it, seen? Life's strange, eei Mummy? You know I was on life support and lost so much blood I had to have blood transfusions, I even had a heart attack and died on the operating table, but I still came back. I felt your spirit over me, helping me, encouraging me. Den me hear yu sey 'Garri wake up, Garri get up, Garri!' I knew then that I would be okay. Was it really you that woke me from my coma Mum?"

"How yu mean, yu me lickle washbelly, me 'ave fi come."

"I knew it, I love you and I know you're still here, not physically but your soul is here for sure. I'm so grateful for all you done an' still do fi me. So now I want part of me to always be with you as I mix my ashes with your ashes, so I can walk with you on the other side." It's a powerful moment!

8th November 2005
Home Croydon

I place the ashes together in a safe place until I can take them back to Jamaica, then I try to get back into my music. The mini studio system in my bedroom is giving me a few teething problems, but I'm mastering it. Having just sat down my mobile rings somewhere in the flat. When I find it, it's my Housing Officer who says because I'm now registered as disabled, I can view the wheelchair accessible property she mentioned while I was in hospital. The down side is that it's in Peckham and I'm disappointed. No disrespect to Peckham, but I'm from Brixton, why would I go back to more of the same busy town environment after I moved away once? I moved outside the City to get some peace and quiet, and now I need that in my life more than ever. No drama, no circus, just tranquillity and I don't think Peckham will give me that; still I owe it to them to have a look, maybe it'll be okay, before I assume, let me look at it.

9th November 2005
Peckham London

Early morning finds me visiting the property in Peckham; it's a new build that's nice, but it's really small and very close to the market with its hustle and bustle. I'm not feeling it, so I leave there pretty sharpish to continue my day. Next I have my check up at the Royal Free Hospital in Hampstead and on the way I pass work, so may as well drop in to see Robby Richie in HR.

I knock on his office door and pop my head in. "Alright Robby?"

"Oh Garri, how nice to see you, how the hell are you?"

"I'm very well thank you Robby, I just dropped in to keep you up to speed on my progress."

"That's good, come in. I've been watching you in the press; you've done some really good interviews but I'm waiting for the papers to come up with a hidden 'Love Child' back story or something!" He laughs.

"You're funny Robby, I got no love child mate, for real." Shaking my head, he has no idea that's not who I am!

"Oh come on, a good looking man like you, with all the women chasing you, I've seen you in the Hospital and even the nurses swoon over you; pull the other one!"

"I'm really not a bed hopper mate, so you're never gonna get that story, unless they just make it up."

"Yeah well, I wouldn't put that past them, eh?"

"Hmmm."

As I drive on to my appointment at the Royal Free, I'm feeling so grateful to be able to drive myself, without having to go back on the Tube. Thank God, I don't have to use the Tube anymore!

The Doctors are pleased with my progress and that's always great. After my appointment I take a walk around the Hospital and have some lovely exchanges with a few of the nurses as well as a great conversation with Dr Garlick before leaving. On the way home, again I pass by Work as I've arranged to pick up Lil' Sis and drop her home to Stockwell, it's the least I can do, after everything she has done for me. We have a lovely chat. As I'm in Stockwell I pay a quick visit to Tony to bring him up to date with my events, and then check in with Carlton at his home as well, so we can go over any outstanding business.

Driving home my mobile rings. I have to pull up and park, as I can't answer the phone while I'm driving, something about men not being able to multi-task, innit? "Hello."

"Gazza!"

"Dom me old mate, what's going on?"

"I got a surprise for you Gaz, I've organised that fundraiser for you tomorrow as promised, old chap."

"What, what, what a surprise! Wow, I don't know what to say, other than thank you Sir, you're a Diamond Geezer."

"You deserve it mate, just make sure you're there tomorrow, I'll text you the details."

Once again I'm left to count my blessings!

10th November 2005 Late Evening
Uptown London

So here I am in the West End for 'The Garri Holness Fund Raiser' organised by my good friend Dominic. Carlton is escorting me and as we arrive we catch sight of Dominic waiting outside the front. "Alright Dom, great to see you mate."

"Likewise Gazza." Big *'man hug'*, as we do!

I introduce Carlton and Dom and then Dom leads us downstairs into the club. Wow what a big turnout, this has the potential for being a really good night. I see ex work colleagues along with a few other friends from different advertising agencies. The vibe is electric and as people notice me, they make a beeline to wish me well, so much hand shaking and hugging, it's full on and somewhat surreal. I've even got video camera's following me.

"You look sexy in black" a woman whispers' in my ear, I smile, but won't allow myself to be distracted. I have to totally focus on walking. I'm still not fully comfortable with my leg yet, and in a club with hidden steps and dim lighting, I'd really hate to fall over in front of all these people!

Only a few steps down to the dance floor, so I'm gonna take a chance; so far so good, but wait, check me out dancing up the place, "Play tune, Selector!"

"Garri come and dance with me." As I dance people are tugging at me, left, right and centre; it seems everyone wants a piece of me. Camera's flashing and even squabbles between women.

"Garri my friend thinks you're not paying her enough attention."

"You know we love you don't you!"

"Garri! Dance with me."

"This way Garri."

"I love your energy Garri, you're so positive and bubbly."

"You're a Diamond geezer." Voices keep coming at me from all around

with lots of compliments and encouragement.
"You've got a great smile."
"What you doing later Garri?"
"Can I have the last dance?"

I'm so 'whelmed over' I try to zone out but they even follow me to the toilet! It's getting rather uncomfortable so I step back into myself looking for escape and manage to find a table away from the centre. I zone out and look around reflectively; it's good to realise that amongst the commotion and the pouting camera diva's I've got some sincere friends here, with some genuine love for me. I'm both touched and grateful, especially as I'm still trying to come to terms with this major change in my life. Money can't buy the love and the warmth I'm feeling right now is priceless.

It's gone midnight, time to slip out neatly, without a fuss before I turn into a pumpkin!

14th November 2005
Home Croydon

The Press who had championed me because of my positive and uplifting conduct after the bombing are now on my doorstep demanding I tell them about a conviction that I served time for over twenty years ago. I'm shocked and refuse to talk to them; I can't see what that has to do with what's going on now. Once again I have to dig deep to survive as my past comes back to haunt me. Robby Ritchie alerted me that the papers may be looking to find an interesting back-story, but it isn't a love child, as he suggested, it's a bloody nightmare!

15th November 2005
Home Croydon

Two of the main Tabloids continue to hound me wanting me to answer to the story about my past. I'm nervous and agitated at the thought of losing my support structure, which has helped heal me through this first stage of my recovery, is freaking me out. I feel physically sick and totally alone. I just keep wondering what the past has got to do with now? And why would someone do this to another person?

Anyway, I'm not going to talk to them. I won't give either paper the story they crave, because I believe it will only drag out the situation even more.

17th November 2005
Home Croydon

The Reporters come back to my house, again and again demanding I give them my side of the story, threatening to print what they have been told! I feel alone and am more than aware I'm still suffering mentally and physically from the after affects of the Bombing and the loss of my Mum. I'm not in a good place and can't take much more of this pressure.

Finally I buckle and let them in. "Sorry Garri, I can't see the relevance of this story, I really can't, but my Editor has forced me to come here and get your side of the story, otherwise we will just have to print what we have been told." I can't believe it, he forced her to come, wow! I can see she's only trying to do her job, and really doesn't want to do the story. I'm picking it up in her vibes; it's in her eyes and her demeanour. However the other reporter seems to be getting a buzz from it. I can't feel any compassion from her at all, she seems empty, cold and switched off emotionally.

I end up admitting I was in youth custody, but won't give any details out of respect for the victims and my co-defendants. As the reporters get up to leave, obviously unhappy that I won't open up, I have a knee jerk reaction to say something else.

"I didn't assault the girls you know, and my solicitor even made an appeal." The first reporter seems relieved and jumps straight on it.

"He did?" I nod, she smiles.

"Oh okay! If that's the case, you've got nothing to worry about Garri. The article will probably end up tucked away inside the paper." Although she seems very pleased, the other Reporter doesn't look at all happy; she looks deflated! I try to understand what's going on with her, but I'm at a loss.

"Anything else Garri?" She asks. I just want to get them off my back, so I shake my head, but then a knee-jerk reaction comes over me, I have to protest my innocence to save my reputation.

"Listen, I was convicted, but none of the forensic evidence matched with my DNA, I was the one who stopped it, I'm not a rapist, and I never will be; you need to remember that." She smiles on the way out and behind the closed door I'm left alone to deal with what seems like way too much to cope with. My heart goes out to the two girls. I don't want to bring up the past for them either, or for my co-accused. Why did this have to come out, when I'm at such a vulnerable stage in my life…

20th November 1985 11:00am
London The Old Bailey Courtroom One

The Judge addresses me by my father's surname.

"Mr Linton stand-up." He pauses to clear his throat and glances up at me over his half-rimmed reading glasses with an intense glare before continuing. "You have no previous convictions. I believe you may not have raped or assaulted these girls." He pauses for breath; I feel relieved and start to believe I can go home soon. "But, as one of the older boys, you must take some responsibility. Yes you did stop the assault, albeit belatedly, but you could have, and should have, stopped it sooner." He looks at me again with a serious frown and as he shakes his head a sense of dread grips me. He continues, "These are not mitigating circumstances, and therefore this court finds you guilty of rape through 'Joint Enterprise', which means that you had prior knowledge of what was going to occur. The Crown's case against you has been proven, therefore I sentence you to seven years youth custody." As the Judge brings down his gavel with an authoritative *thud,* my blood runs cold; his words will stay with me for the rest of my life!

19th November 2005
Home Croydon

A day passes without hassle but its too good to last, The Press are on me again; they say the person who originally went to them about my case read the articles and now tells them that I lost my appeal and that I have misled them. Although I didn't spell out that I lost my appeal, I did tell them I went to youth custody. I was keen to let them know I had grounds for an appeal, because I'm not a rapist, but it's actually made matters much worse. How did this get so messed up. The Press aren't listening to anything I have to say. It seems all they want now is drag up my past, headline it and say I misled them!

The shit hits the fan! They print their story headlining me as a rapist and I go from Hero to Zero overnight! It makes me wonder if their initial interest and caring was just a façade? I wonder if they even remember I'm going through a major healing process. Or perhaps they simply don't care?

I have to get away from the Media intrusion that follows, so I flee to a flat in Southwark that belongs to a friend who's away on holiday. I feel so vulnerable and Mums' not here to comfort me, but at least being away will give me some time and space to reflect. This ain't right y'know, but God nar sleep 'im have one eye open!

21st November 2005
Southwark In Hiding

Nearly all the press jump on the bandwagon and focus on what happened two decades ago. How can they judge me again on my past? As I try to understand my sentence as an adult, I can't comprehend how a boy unknown to Police, with no previous convictions pleading not guilty and with no forensic evidence connecting his DNA to the assault, can be found guilty of rape. And get seven years. This joint enterprise law is difficult to understand!

If however I look behind the scenes, there are signs of why the sentence may have been so severe. The trial finally took place around nine months after the offence. The timing could not have been worse for me, just two weeks after my eighteenth birthday, and only a matter of weeks after the Brixton riots, I have to wonder if the trial was deliberately timed, or simply fate dealing me a bad hand. I guess I'll never really know the truth of it, but the upshot was that I, along with five other younger schoolboys were accused of rape and assault along with several other lesser charges, which were dropped half way through the court case at the Old Bailey.

Contrary to what the Tabloids have written I have never admitted assault and there's always been something that troubled me about why they wrote that. I, for one, was roughed up in a cell and forced to sign a fabricated statement, admitting things I never did. It was duly thrown out of Court during the hearing.

I guess the Police and then the Press must have exaggerated the original information given by the girls. They said a knife was used to kidnap the white girls and take them to garages. That there were twelve to sixteen black boys in the gang, which it said concluded in one girl being raped fifteen times and the other thirty times. Although I don't know all the details of exactly what happened as I wasn't present throughout the crime, what I do know is this wasn't possible. Six boys were actually arrested not sixteen, I certainly wasn't aware of a knife, and kidnapping was not even one of the many charges. We had all walked along the streets together chatting and singing a Smiley Culture song, and I believe at least one of the girls lived locally.

I wonder if the report was purposely exaggerated to satisfy the need to show law and order in this particular area, at this particular time. A time that saw the unfortunate shooting of a black woman in her home in Brixton by Police, which triggered civil unrest in the Black Community and led to the Brixton riots. During this stage of unrest an MP's daughter was raped during a burglary in Stockwell, which caused a major outcry from MP's. Then there was the killing of a white Policeman in Tottenham. All terrible situations and I feel compassion for all the victims and their families. None of this however had anything to do with me, but I can't help thinking it may have implicitly affected the attitude of the Judge, the Jury and of course the Newspapers during this time.

I remain convinced my sentencing was more to do with the state of society, especially in Brixton after two riots and the rape in Stockwell. The public outcry from the MPs saying 'Rape shouldn't be going on in our society and the perpetrators when found should be punished severely.' They're absolutely right, I agree with their statement. So, no matter what happened here, this Judge and Jury must have been under pressure to set an example, for the sake of society and to satisfy the MP's. It could be that my case was being scrutinised on many levels. And for that I feel compassion for them being in a difficult situation.

I was told there were sufficient grounds for an appeal, although it was unsuccessful. I believe social pressure, unfortunate timing, and inadequate direction from the Judge all had a part to play in this as well. The Jury asked for direction in my case, because they couldn't come to a majority verdict after much deliberation. Having stated previously in his summing up, the case was not premeditated, he directed the Jury to think about a gang of pickpockets out to thieve, but only one or two steal something, is the whole gang guilty? I'm pretty sure going out, as part of a pickpocket gang must show premeditation to steal. I believe what the Judge said was neither clear nor fair, but using this metaphor along with the controversial Law of Joint Enterprise I had to accept the punishment of guilty through association and take it on the chin.

I remain deeply and truthfully compassionate about any harm caused on that fateful evening to those girls. I really wish I could have stopped it sooner.

November 2005
Southwark In Hiding

There's a rumour the newspapers were given the story about me from within my own community because of jealousy. Hmmm, how could anyone be jealous of what happened to me? Was I getting too much love and attention perhaps, or maybe spreading too much positive energy, so someone wants to knock me down? Or is it all about the money? It would be painful to believe that somebody in my own community wants to gain money from my pain and suffering. Of course the Tabloids will naturally take full advantage, I suppose Newspapers thrive on a scandal! I wonder though if this rumour is simply a set up to turn me against my community and cause inner discord. So I aim to be aware, not to jump to any conclusions and remain reasonable.

As a reasonable man, I try to give back when I can, even in Hospital on my sick-bed, I tried to be positive and give out messages of hope, why can't they focus on that, rather than on the past for which I've done my time? I'm a survivor of a serious crime, which they seem to have forgotten. Have I not gone through enough already? It's hard to know what to do or say now, so I decide to call Carlton to talk about the situation; I need a balanced view, I'm just too emotional.

Carlton can't really help, he's also emotionally invested and taken aback by the shock of it all. He leaves me with some wise words though. *'Don't take it personally mate, as they just want to sell Newspapers and make money.'* It starts to sink in… like it or not the bubble has burst!

Day after day the Newspapers step up another gear and absolutely tear me to shreds, sensationalising my past without regard. They say the 1985 stories are in the public domain and unfortunately there is no Governing Body to restrain them. I'm devastated yet I know in my soul I have to look for the positive to find something to cling to. Let me just try to focus on how glad I still am to be alive! I know the truth and I know myself and that's really all that matters. If the Terrorists can't beat me, I must not crumble over this. I will not crumble! Positive thinking in the face of adversity is my motto and I shall follow it.

Soon after the revelations die down several other Media agencies contact me wanting to help me give my side of the story. It's uncanny to see that as soon as my energy shifts from anger and defence to gratitude and positivity, their attitude changes also. I guess this is what they call the Law of Attraction? Even so I refuse to get involved again as I simply don't trust the nature of the Media. Could it be that whatever I say, may be taken out of context and used against me, that's how it seems to go, so I decide it's safer to stay quiet, at least for now.

Eventually I even get a very pleasant call from the senior reporter of a well-known London Tabloid, who appears different from the others. "Garri, the Media are portraying you all wrong, I've looked through our archives into your past and found that it's not the way it was reported, let us redress the balance for you, it's unfair and it's not right." I feel pleased although a little surprised, but still can't help remaining somewhat suspicious.

November 2005
Somewhere In Between The Shit Hitting The Fan And The Inevitable Toilet Paper!

I've received a lot of support from friends who read the condemning articles, in various newspapers but don't buy into them. Not even for toilet paper!

I decide I should call my workplace to tell them exactly what's happening, but just then my mobile rings. "Hello, hello Garri are you ok?" amazingly it is one of the girls from work.

"Oh Hello Sam, I was just thinking about calling HR."

"So how are you?"

"Not great, as you can imagine, but I'll get over it, I've been through worse."

"I know you Garri, and I'm not listening to what the press has said. Let's meet up in Clapham later for a drink if you fancy it?"

"Thanks honey, that would be nice." My spirits lift slightly.

Late November 2005
The Sun Pub Clapham

It's good being out with Sam, she's helping me restore some confidence that people will accept me again, and I'm having a great time, which is quite unexpected. It's a much-needed distraction. Several people do glance over at us, but nothing out of the ordinary, nothing as horrible as I expected, so I'm feeling a lot more comfortable about being out in the world again.

It's starting to get late, the pub is closing soon and as I'm driving, I think I'll do the gentlemanly thing and drop Sam home safe. She invites me in, so I agree and we talk for another twenty minutes or so before I go. I'm sure it was her way of showing that she trusts me, and I really do appreciate it. I give her a peck on the cheek and wish her a good night; she has such a beautiful soul.

Destination Southwark, and thinking deeply about something Sam said; I'm starting to see people's true colours. Like I said, in my very first Tabloid interview, I'm here but through the grace of God, my Judgment Day was underground. God saved me and he restored my soul; I must remember I'm here for a purpose. I've got to focus on that, there's still much for me to do in this lifetime, and maybe this is just my cleansing period. Maybe I need to see people's true light, so that I can surround myself with like-minded people rather than those only interested in money and fame. Maybe I'm not supposed to be interested in lots of money and fame, it certainly makes sense.

As the haze starts to clear in my mind I realise it's Thursday already and I am still in hiding. I need to focus; I need to go home.

1st December 2005
Home Croydon

I think I'm ready to face the world, but I'm on the front-page of the well known tabloids again. The Editor of the Evening Standard in their comments section on page six is still referring to me as a Hero. It's nice to know he still holds this view.

Listening to a debate on LBC, then BBC Radio 2 discussing me. It's about my past and the pending compensation, should I get my compensation or not. It's always about money; it seems the general public are divided 50-50. Some say the victims of rape get less compensation therefore I should hand over my compensation to them. Other's say guilty or not, I've already done my time and it was so long ago that I should be allowed to live my life in peace now and move on. While listening to the radio, lots of messages from work colleagues arrive sending me their support. I must admit some of the texts I've received have caught me by surprise, as I didn't expect some to be so caring and compassionate; it truly is a Godsend and a lovely gesture. Thank you to these people you know exactly who you are and I'm so grateful to have you in my life!

For someone like me, brought up in the 80's in Brixton, who has done time, people say I'm an example of someone who has turned his life around, going from strength to strength, learning from past mistakes and keeping out of trouble. I can't say I was actually rehabilitated, because I was never really the bad boy they made me out to be. My Jamaican parents were all the rehabilitation I needed! Especially my Mum, and whoever knew my Mum would know exactly what I'm talking about, one look alone, and you know! My mobile rings interrupting my musings.

"Garri it's Barry!"

"Barry? Barry who?" laughter follows.

"I've only been looking after you in Hospital for the past few months, did you forget me already?" More laughter!

"Oh Nurse Barry! Sorry mate I've got a lot on my mind! You ah'right Geezer?"

"Yeah, not bad, but how are you Garri?"

"Yeah, I'm okay."

" I see what's going on but keep your head up, you've been through a lot worse mate, remember you're a Survivor and what they're talking about happened twenty years ago. You've moved on, so they should remember you are a massive inspiration to many across the globe, don't you ever forget that."

"Aw thanks for that Barry, I really appreciate you calling and I hope you're right, I just have to keep that at the fore-front of my mind,"

"Trust me Garri, it'll all blow over soon enough."

"But so much is happening."

"Remember Garri, I'm only a phone call away."

"You're a diamond mate, thanks." I come off the phone so much better than I when I answered it.

He's right I have to remember how people responded to me straight after the Bombings. How they called me 'Darling of the Nation'.

I decide to watch a few videos of the interviews I did, looking for inspiration. As I watch myself on the BBC, it seems surreal, and I actually realise I had become a popular figure over such a short period of time. On the bright side, I'm pleased with the way I came across, I've got to keep my head up and remember who I am and where I came from. I'm not going to be disillusioned by what the Media is saying. I'm not their puppet and I cannot live up to their squeaky clean expectations. I'm Brixtonian and proud of it!

2nd December 2005
Home Croydon

Head of HR Department Robby Riches calls and I feel heavy after the conversation. He wants me to come into the office and discuss the whole event regarding the revelation in the newspapers. He asks me to go in next week, but I can't say I am looking forward to it. Here we go again, why does it seem like I've got to fight for everything? It was only a few months ago I was blown up and I'm lucky to be alive, really lucky. I just need to focus on that, regardless of anything else.

Anyway, let's see what happens when the dust settles, it's very likely I may have lost my hard earned job as well as everything else. Horrible month this is turning out to be. Many wonderful things that happened before are now being snatched away. Lambeth Council had asked if I could switch on their Christmas lights, an offer for a book on my life story was being negotiated. I was planning to release a few songs that I'd been working on, and a work colleague had even asked if I could feature in a Barclaycard advert for them. So much was in the pipeline, but because of the Media, it's all collapsed, and all this because of something that happened two decade ago. It's enough to make me want to roll over and give up.

I must try to remember though, it could be worse, I may not even be here at all, so I've gotta keep the faith. I have to believe that this is the challenging road I must travel to get where I'm going. I mustn't dwell on the past, merely use it as a reference point to see where I am now and how far I've come. God has kept me here for a reason, I strongly believe that, so I've gotta keep looking forward, following his lead. Even though looking forward at this moment in time isn't easy as everything crumbles around me, I will survive and one day I will thrive, God willing!

4th December 2005
Home Croydon

My brother Tony and I are chatting over a cuppa. "To tell you the truth, when I saw you laying on the hospital bed, I didn't think you were going to make it Bruv!"

"Really Tony?"

"You looked really bad, so weak and relying on a life-support machine. Your body was full of plasters and bandages, blood transfusions, tubes and drips everywhere, not a sign of a smile and you're always smiling, I couldn't believe it you looked terrible. I've never seen anyone as bad as that and your eyes were closed, no movement at all, it was a scary sight Bruv."

Taking in what Tony says, makes me realise again, how close I was to death. In fact I'm sure I saw 'The White Light' calling me and I was going towards it but something prevented it from happening. Then, I remember a Doctor telling me I had a heart attack during one of my many operations. Bloody hell, I died on the operating table, but they brought me back. I'm so grateful, to be given so many chances by the powers that be. Tony is now the fourth person to tell me he didn't think I would make it. I admire him for his honesty and it's made me remember again how lucky I am.

I have to take a break from writing my diary for a couple of weeks. The days roll into weeks. I need to recharge my batteries and re-evaluate my life and also reflect on everything that's happened so far. I feel drained and in need of peace and quiet. Although the worst is over, and things are becoming more tolerable, I still feel broken inside. Wherever I go I'm recognised and most people wish me well, which makes me remember that there are decent people in the world who can think for themselves, and remain unaffected by the Headlines; some of them even approach me with comforting words. It's a mixed bag, but I'm grateful for any kindness shown.

December 2005
Croydon Town Centre

A woman shouts out to me, "Keep your head up mate; don't worry about what's in the nasty press. It will be chip paper in the morning." and I smile.

"You are an amazing individual and you still have a lot to give."

"Thank you." Hearing people's encouraging comments touches me, I'm realising that underneath I'm a sensitive soul. Knowing that there are actually people out there who really care for me and wish me well fills me with hope for the future. I want to mix with people who are unaffected by the Media, whose thoughts manifest from love and compassion, not from fear, jealousy and anger. My awareness is growing deeper.

December 2005
Camden Market

I'm venturing out again and it's very therapeutic being in the hustle and bustle of Camden, doing some Xmas shopping with Nellie, my niece. It's great being amongst people, getting back to normality is just what I need. Shopping complete we head home, I put one of the soulful house CD's, which I just bought in the market in the player. On the way we pass a toy-shop, so I pull over and leave Nellie in the car. I'm looking for a PS2 Play Station for Leigh my other niece as a Christmas present and I'm delighted to find one. I know she'll be over the moon with it, as she's always asking to borrow her cousins'.

25th December 2005
Home Croydon

Christmas Day and I am forever grateful to be alive but I'm feeling isolated, lonely and sad. Mum's been playing on my mind so much, this is my first Christmas without her. I can still visualise her clearly; today I can feel her presence around me more than ever.

25th December 2005
Stockwell Park Estate

I've been invited to Hector's in-laws for Christmas Lunch and festivities. It's fun watching the kids open their presents with such excitement and joy. Leigh loved her PlayStation and Nellie was delighted with her bracelet. Although I'm happy for them, I'm still a little disconnected. I watch the kids and also listen in to the adult conversations from a distant space, that's until someone says something directly to me; I snap back to attention and do my best to answer. I still feel alone, empty inside, although the food was good, I've got a lot going on in my mind. I'm here, but I'm not here.

By five-thirty I'm ready to visit Tony who's just round the corner. I say my thank you and goodbyes. Approaching Tony's I can hear music from the street. He seems to be okay, although he's older than me, Mum's always said if anything should happen to her, I should look out for him. Goes without saying though, its family.

Now that I know Tony's okay I take a slow drive back home to my own little world. It's a therapeutic drive, quiet, no distractions, no need to listen to people or try to find answers to their questions. The roads are empty and it's easy driving. I park up, walk up to my house in a daze, put the key in the door, and go in. Once inside I wander from room to room, walking around my flat helps me to clear my mind. It's the first Christmas without Mummy and the sense of loss is intense, such a surreal feeling. I won't be able to pass by her house to pick up my Rum Christmas Cake her friend Janice would make for me. Janice also passed away earlier this year, God rest her Soul. I feel sad saying goodbye to those happy days.

I end up in the bedroom, take off my bionic leg, lie down on my bed and begin to reflect on the rollercoaster ride I had this year, me, myself and I! I think depression may be kicking in, as my mind wanders back.

August 2005
Royal Free Hospital Hampstead

One of the nurses approaches me on the way back from the canteen. "At this moment Garri everybody is listening to your every word and gaining strength and courage from you, which will inevitably drain you. When your back's against the wall, will any of these people be there for you? Think on that!"

25th December 2005
Home Croydon

I recall the nurse's words and realise I didn't understand her back then, but now I lie here, reflecting, I fully appreciate her wise, powerful words. Could this have been a warning from Mum or could this nurse see into the future?

As I look around my bedroom there are boxes and boxes full of letters from all over the world from people wishing me well; some still unopened. So I plunge my hands into one of the boxes and pull out a random unopened envelope, it contains a card with a letter inside. A ninety-two-year-old woman, who has lived through two world wars, has written the letter. She speaks of the dignity, strength and fortitude that I showed during my interviews. Reading this letter gives me a boost, but also brings me to tears. In this moment I make a plan, I decide whenever I feel lost, like I'm floating, isolated or overcome by depression, I'll just reach into one of these boxes for the inspiration and strength I need to continue. I'm so thankful to all the amazing people who bothered to put pen to paper to send me their loving energy and even to the gorgeous ladies who sent photos and proposed marriage! Please know if I didn't answer you yet, I love you all!

1st Jan 2006
Home Croydon

The New Year is here and I'm spending it with my very beautiful and lovely lady friend Halle who is taking my mind off the fans and the shit! Happier New Year!

6th Jan 2006
In my X3

Driving to Royal Free Hospital for a check-up on my ears, there's a possibility that I could have a surgery to restore my hearing; the musician inside me is excited and very hopeful.

6th Jan 2006
Royal Free Hospital

The Receptionist chats away merrily at high speed, she's funny too. It's not long before I am ushered through. After doing the test, the Doctor goes over the results with me. Although both sides have healed well, the tests show the bones have been completely blown out of my left ear leaving me totally deaf on that side. They need to do a CT scan to access the extent of the damage, which is duly booked for 14th February. If the scan is favourable, then keyhole surgery is on the agenda to attempt to restore my hearing by replacing the bones, it sounds impressive if they can do that!

7th January 2006 11:30am
Brixton Underground Station

Standing underground for the first time since the Bombings feeling apprehensive, but I'm determined to overcome my fears and make this journey. The Train pulls in and I board fully focused on completing my mission. I feel like I'm looking in from a distant place as I take a seat reflecting on what I'm about to do. But before I know it we pull into King's Cross station where I get off following the signs towards the Piccadilly Line. My heart pounds as I stand on the platform, but I'm determined to retrace my steps by boarding the carriage at the same place as I did on the 7th July. Looking around me I sense an eerie feeling, as I think about what happened here just six months ago, all those Souls! As the train leaves the platform and rolls into the mouth of the tunnel, claustrophobia forces me along the carriage to the door that divides the carriages, I open the window to let in some air. I manage to keep it together with every ounce of my will power as I inhale and exhale deeply in a deliberate rhythm. I almost build a tune in my head as I breath, and it's that alone that keeps me level.

7th January 2006 2:00pm
Home Croydon

Mission completed I did it! It's so important to face my fears and not allow myself to be beaten into submission.

12th January 2006
Home Croydon

The Guardian is dangling a carrot; they want to do an article about me. They think it's very unfair the way I have been treated by some sections of the Media, and they want to put it right. They're into social injustice and my situation falls right into their camp. As charming as they sound, I'm still very suspicious. When a group of people shoot you once, where's the sense in reloading the gun and giving it back to one of them for another go? I still have much healing to do.

Robby Ritches from the HR department calls to inform me that there will be an internal investigation with regards to the Media stories. What a great way to start the New Year, not!

15th January 2006
Croydon Home

I notice this morning my stump has shrunk so much that I think I need a new lining. My leg is slipping around so much these days, which could be why I've been tripping up recently. I decide to add another sock to help secure it for now, but note that I should go to Roehampton for a check-up soon.

19th January 2006
Croydon Home

I've been pondering telling my story in a book, and I would very much like to quote the Judges sentencing report word for word, when he sentenced me. Even though it's etched on my brain forever, maybe people would be interested to know exactly what he said in 1985.

23rd January 2006
Restaurant In Hampstead

Fate is a funny thing, while talking to a friend of a friend it turns out she knows my Solicitor from twenty years ago, unbelievably she works in Chambers side by side with him. So by a quirk of fate I actually manage to speak to him on her phone. He says he will try to find the original sentencing report for me, but that it may prove difficult because it was such a long time ago. However as we talk, he also remembers the important points.

I'm amazed at how this unfolded. Dare I wonder if my luck is changing, if the Universe is conspiring to help me now, or if someone up there is guiding me? Anyway I need to get my mind on something different, like this lovely lunch! I can't focus or dwell too much on the past. I don't live there anymore.

23rd January 2006
Home Croydon

Let me get my studio things up and running again, I think I can do it myself, seems straightforward enough. Alright! So far, so good, in fact this is great fun. Just the last little bits, now to power up and see if everything's working. Mic, check! Volume, check! Speakers, check! Track one, check the input; level okay, output level okay. Right now tings ah gwaan!

12th February 2006
Home Croydon

I get the sense I am drifting along aimlessly, but trying to put on a brave face. Days turn into weeks as I try to reboot. I've got a constant nagging pain in my stump, that blister is taking its time to heal. But on the positive side at least it can heal now the problem was brought to light.

14th February 2006
Royal Free Hospital

It's a big day for moving forward with my health and well being, the CT scan on my ear is done and the good news is, I've got the okay for the Operation. I feel ecstatic, okay I've lost my foot I have to accept that, but the possibility that I can regain my hearing gives me something to look forward to, this is huge! All I need now is a date. They can indeed rebuild him, Garri Holness The Seven-Million-Dollar Man, the thought makes me smile inside!

Leaving the hospital I drive past my workplace as usual; I see Hannah leaving the building so I stop and get out, after a brief word, I bump into Pippa."What's happening with HR Gaz, I still haven't heard anything from Robby, are there any updates?"

"No update yet Babe, but I'll keep you posted." I've come to understand the reason I keep calling in to my work place, is that it gives me a sense of normality. It's become like my anchor on a stormy sea; familiar things are my comfort, my solace. As I walk to the shops nearby, I notice that my walking is becoming more effortless, much more fluid than before. The only downside is the blister on my stump, but maybe it's a blessing in disguise to slow me down. Sometimes I actually forget about my leg! How weird is that, just because I can walk again, it seems as if everything is back to normal, but of course it's not; far from it!

Back to the X3, the parking tickets that's stuck on the windscreen is a reminder that I mustn't forget to put my Blue Disability Badge on my dashboard. Oh man! *KMT.*

As I'm passing Euston Station, I quickly pop in to the Network Rail building to see my mate Mandy who works there; she'll cheer me up for sure. Mandy is a beautiful, fantastic and fun loving woman and we even have funny pet names for each other. *CD = Chocolate Drop* DD = *'Dodgy Downey** 'I need to be around positive, funny people like her at the moment. I give her a call to let her know I'm in the building.

We spent a lot of time commuting on the same train to or from work, and we had such fun and great banter. It all started when I rescued her from a guy who was pestering her on a train one evening, she never forgot and looked out for me ever since.

She arrives in the elevator, arms outstretched to greet me, I notice she's heavily pregnant I'd no idea! We hug it's so good to see her. "CD me old China, how you doing? You've lost weight." She looks me up and down.

"And you've gained weight!" I say pointing at her bump and laughing. She's with a friend who she introduces to me. They say birds of a feather flock together; it's so true, she's as mad as DD, which lifts my spirits even more. Her friend treats me warmly, which boosts my confidence. They're so kind about the bad press; these girls know what time it is! What a relief and pleasant surprise to meet people who can read between the lies! My brief visit ends, with a peck on the cheek from each lovely lady in turn; they tease me about Valentines Day as we say goodbye. I continue my journey south with Halle and Valentines Day thoughts on my mind…

Mid February 2006
Home Croydon

I've been doing a light workout to keep myself fit. It's time to step it up a bit though, to change the exercise routine. I'm beginning to feel stronger from within, so I want to reflect that outward.

February 2006
Home Croydon

Post arrives; a letter from Chief Commander Sir Ian Blair of the MET, informing us that the Police officers involved in 7/7 Bombings will be recommended for a Bravery Award. He thought he should inform us, as there will be lots of Media coverage.

Later in the day as I watch some of the coverage, they speak about courage, bravery, strength, dignity, compassion, it reminds me of what they said about me in the four months after the Bombings. I also notice anyone and everyone who helped in any way during 7/7 have been recognise in some way with a positive accolade, regardless of their personal history. They even award the dogs that helped in 7/7; the dogs you know!

What's happening right now is really a gift though, making me see things and people in a different light. It's as if I have to delete everything I've been taught and re program my mind with things that feel comfortable to my soul. I am awake! Fully focused on my awareness and my place in the system that overrules. I will forever stay focused on my freedom, my strength and my well-being!

February 2006
Brixton Town Centre

Various people in my Community tell me over and over again, it wasn't my time to die, that I'm here for a purpose. This keeps echoing in my head; I have a second chance. I have to wonder what God's plan is for me. But as I slowly de-program myself from the indoctrination I know the only way out, is to go within. God is a frequency; I must learn to tune in and the tuning tool is meditation!

Late February 2006
Home Croydon

Sitting in my front room alone contemplating I notice spheres of light at the corner of my eye. It's happened before several times, but I've been ignoring them, thinking they are a symptom of eye damage in the explosion. This time however I sense my frequency has shifted, it's been changing for a little while and I'm realising these orb type things could be some kind of phenomena. I see them mostly late evening into the night; I wonder if it's anything to do with Mummy Holness! I call out to her, "Mummy, wha'ah gwaan? Because me kno' sey ah only yu could waan come visit me at dis time, fi come gimme some strength." I smile to myself walking into the bedroom; if anyone were watching for real, they'd think I'm nuts!

March 2006
Croydon At Home

I've finally bought a workout machine online and it just arrived. It's very straightforward to put together and well worth the money. I can do some proper exercise now and in my own comfortable surroundings, this should keep me going for a while.

The X3 needs a wash as well, but I wonder if I'm going over the top doing everything myself, and not asking anyone for help? I know that life will be a challenge from now on, so I need to get ready for it. I feel that I have to clear my mind of fear and anger so I can focus and find an inner resolve! Meditation is key to finding subconscious wisdom, so let me meditate before washing the X3!

Before I know it, the X3 is washed and I'm beginning to prune and weed the garden. Various neighbours ask if I need help, but I decline their kind offers and get it done myself. I feel good after my meditation and I plan to make the most of it.

After all my hard work I'm looking forward to a nice soak in the bath. It's still a bit difficult getting in and out of the bath tub, but I'm getting used to it. Cream up my skin, put on some clothes and go into 'music mode'.

March 2006
Home Croydon

I'm working my upper body really well in the mini-gym at home. I can't wait until I get the high tech leg so I can do the leg exercises and running as well, it's funny *'yu never miss da water till da well runs dry.'* It's an old Jamaican saying.

I see the Postman outside coming down my path; he brings the dreaded letter from work, requesting a meeting with HR on the 20th March. Let me schedule that into my diary, I don't want to forget this date.

A visit to my local garden centre cheers me up and I decide to buy a new tree. I name it Marley after Bob, as it looks like its got long locks. As soon as I get home I'm out in the garden to plant it, I really do like being at one with nature, but my Marley tree is getting mixed reactions from my neighbours. Ha ha!

13th March 2006
Queen Mary's Hospital Roehampton

I've finally managed to get here to have my new casting done. It's been on the cards for quite a while, but I didn't feel like coming before. The Doctor said my leg would probably change shape once it settles down and I've been noticing the difference. It's always nice coming to Roehampton as I always get a good reception. Everyone tells me I'm always smiling when I'm here; maybe that's why they all respond well to me. I suppose they get used to patients feeling miserable and antisocial. I'm also relieved the Media Frenzy hasn't clouded their opinion of me.

Martine catches my eye through the window in the rehab gym, she's looking well, really well on her high-tech legs walking along the bars, I'm happy for her she's come a long way. I regard everybody injured in the 7/7 attacks as my extended family now, as we share the same horrific story and only we can truly understand how it was to live through that day and the days that followed.

As I'm here I must have a word so I pop my head in, "Hello Martine, you alright?"

She looks up from the bar work and smiles, "Ah hello Garri yes thanks, how are you?"

"I'm good, I've just come to have a new casting, my stumps shrunk and in need of a refit. Anyway what about you, looks like you're doing really well."

"Thank you, and yeah I'm doing okay." She continues to walk along on her bionic legs fully focused.

"Very good, well done. Keep up the good work and look after yourself."

"I will, and you take good care of yourself Garri, hopefully we'll bump into each other again soon."

"Will do." I salute her as I leave and head back towards the waiting area to see Dr Lawrence.

Perfect timing just as I arrive in the waiting room Dr Lawrence walks in as well. "You okay Garri, good weekend?"

"Fantastic, and all the better for seeing you." I'm excited at the prospect of getting a new High-Tech prosthetic leg myself. The one I've been using for the past few months is basic, so the High-Tech one is going to be a real step up for me.

I'm thrilled to hear about the different types of legs I can get now; they include a shock absorber for high impact use, which sounds perfect for sport, a waterproof leg for swimming and showering and a blade for running. I would like to be able to run again and even perhaps take part in the London Marathon if it works out.

After the new casting is done, which runs smoothly, I'm given an appointment that coincides with the arrival of my new high-tech leg. This leaves me with a spring in my step as I say my goodbyes and leave.

Since the Bombings I've become more aware of my surroundings and people around me. Because I was brought up in Brixton I've had to be observant, but I'm even more vigilant now. As I'm driving through Brixton I clock a car behind and get a sense it's tailing me; it continues to follow me all the way past Crystal Palace Football ground. Feeling a little edgy about being followed I take the next right to see what happens, they also turn and are still behind me. Okay, so what if I take another right and pull over. The car drives past and I think there are four plain clothes Police Officers inside, looking my car up and down as they pass. I do a quick U-turn and go back the way I came to see what happens next.

Before long I can hear sirens coming my way, so I continue quickly onto the main road, where I feel safer, pull over and get out of my X3 taking the keys out of the ignition. I sit on a wall waiting with my arms folded. After a couple of minutes sure enough they pull in behind my car.

"Good evening Officers, so why are you following me?"

"We noticed you driving erratically." I frown shaking my head.

"No I wasn't but if I was, shouldn't you have pulled me over ages ago? You've followed me all the way from Brixton."

"No, we only noticed you at Crystal Palace Football ground."

"Yeah really, anyway how can I be of assistance Officers?"

"Is this your vehicle?"

"Yes it is." One of the officers looks around my car.

"Okay then you can go now." They get back into their car and drive away.

"Hmm." Strange they didn't even ask me for my name. I suppose they did a CRB check from my registration. Still, I can't help but wonder how many times Police pull over young black men for suspicion of driving a nice car … 'erratically' *KMT!*

14th March 2006
Home Croydon

Just spoke to Carlton; one of the major tabloids is looking for me to do an interview. They have to be joking right?! There is no other news so they want me fi turn news. Me nar talk to no press, painful lessons learned!

20th March 2006
In My Car

I'm driving to work feeling apprehensive about my meeting with HR. Thinking it over, after taking into account what I've gathered from previous discussions, I don't think it looks good. My conduct has been called in to question as well as the revelations in the Media about my past. The question is will the company keep me on in spite of the bad press. I don't know what something that happened twenty odd years ago has got to do with my work now and I really don't want to be going through all that again at this stage in my life. I've been working for them for four years and have been regarded as an asset to the company, but now this is all on the line.

They liked me so much that when I was made redundant by the Finance Department, other members of staff and even customers pleaded with HR to find me another job. So the Head of HR told me to hold tight, give him a few weeks and he would find something for me, he was as good as his word too, I started working for them again in a different department within a couple of months. This made me feel like part of the family, I got a permanent contract and really felt valued, until now. It's interesting how the four months after the Bombings they were singing my praises, telling everybody and anybody they knew me. Then as soon as the Press mob turn against me, so it seems did they. Well, let's see what happens when the dust settles, maybe I'll find some true diamonds amongst all the fake stuff that glitters. Hopefully!

20th March 2006
Central London

Walking through work for the first time since the revelation feels uncomfortable. There are a few guys sitting having breakfast in the Canteen area; one guy I used to sit with sometimes in the mornings is at our regular table with his mate. He looks up and glares at me, so I walk over to him.

"What's up?"

"What you done was bang out of order!" I think for a second, do I really need to explain myself to him for something that happened when I was seventeen. This individual in front of me was not even born then.

"I suggest you don't believe everything you read in the papers mate, and you should know better coming from Liverpool, remember Hillsborough?" Turning my back on him I just walk away, I don't need this today.

After the meeting I'm feeling deflated, wondering why I have to go through more of this investigation scenario. Robby says he should have the results by the middle of next week. All in all, it wasn't too painful, but yet another fence for me to jump over. As I walk back through the building though, I'm reminded that not all is doom and gloom, in amongst the stress Pippa, as always, puts a smile on my face, telling me I need a bra? WTF! Perhaps I'm getting 'moobs' or lets just hope its muscle! Either way she pencils me into her diary on the 5th May for a lunch date. She's lovely! It's funny how giving little compliments to women makes me so popular at work, for me it's all about stimulation of the mind and it makes the day go along pleasantly; compliments lift the spirits and don't cost anything. Why wouldn't you?

20th March 2006
In My Car

I'm gonna focus on the positive, I'm glad to be alive and the way I managed to walked around the company was great; I can move along quite smoothly now, so let me focus on that. Maybe someone who didn't know me wouldn't even realise I'd lost a foot, that's a good feeling to hold on to. Maybe because I've got so much going on in my mind, instead of trying to walk, I'm just walking! Anyway it makes me feel more confident.

On the way back home, passing through Brixton I bump into a few of da Man dem, all I can sense from them is much needed love and a lot of respect! "It's a shame the way it ended Sugar, but you looking good, your Mum would be proud."

Mentioning my Mum being Proud puts a big smile on my face! "Thank you Bruv."

"No need to thank me, you're my real life inspiration, trus' me, not a lot of da Man dem could of gone through what you gone through big man, *you* pick me up." He nods sincerely.

"Stop dem talk man," I reply embarrassed and laughing.

"Real talk Sugar and look at you, looking 'ealthy, toned and radiant, ah man wouldn't believe say yu go truu dem ting de, da Fardah ah guide and protect you." It's heart-warming.

Those same touching words seem to echo everywhere I go. I feel the Brixton vibes and it's like after the knee-jerk reaction from the public, the dust is beginning to settle. Can they once again remember me as the person they saw straight after the London Bombings and the positive effect that

I inspired for the four months that followed? Maybe things are beginning to turn around again, who knows? I can but pray and wait for the time to share my truth, without being exploited.

21st March 2006
Outside Home Croydon

As I leave my house to go to the shops, I notice a huge white guy staring right at me from across the street, he must be at least six foot six, strong build and severe grade one haircut; this guy looks very menacing. But you know what, I can't let him intimidate me, I'm one of God's soldiers, I've died and come back to life, its gonna take more than him to scare me now.

"You are Garri Holness?" he raises his voice and makes the question sound more like a statement.

"Yeah my name's Garri Holness" I approach him switching on a bit of attitude, cos as Mum used to say *'duppy know who to frighten'*. His face cracks into a smile and his eyes soften. "You've been a real inspiration to me man!" I'm taken aback, as I was preparing to defend! I'm like, "Really?"

We have a pleasant and somewhat deep conversation and somehow I seem to find a few comforting words for him, to help him continue on his journey through life. I carry on my journey to the shop, taking on the lesson that you can't always judge a book by its cover.

March 2006
Home Croydon

It's about time to call my Family Liaison Officers Cagney and Lacey at Scotland Yard. Those aren't their real names but as I'm sworn to secrecy, that's as much as I dare say! Giving Cagney an update on my progress she tells me that a few of her colleagues have been asking after me. It's really a nice surprise considering the onslaught of the Press. I've a great rapport with them both; they show such compassion and a joke is never far away.

Whilst on the phone I can hear that the Postman is at the door. Picking up my post I notice a very official envelope. 'Who dis?' It's an invitation to Highgrove from the Prince of Wales and the Duchess of Cornwall they request the company of 7/7 Survivors. Wow, they didn't leave me out, credit to them and friendlier than the letter I was expecting!

23rd March 2006
Home Croydon

The post arrives bringing the dreaded letter from work, as I open it I'm getting a funny feeling in my belly, but no matter what, I know I've got to roll with the punches. A deep sigh escapes as I begin to read it.

Long story short, they say there is a fundamental breakdown in the trust necessary for the employment relationship to continue. Due to the seriousness of the allegations in the press and the potential implications of this situation on their business, they have come to the conclusion that they will dismiss me on the grounds of Gross Misconduct. I'm sacked because they read in the Newspapers I was arrested for a burglary in 2004. Shocked, confused and very upset, I think back to 2004 …

Winter 2004
Outside Knollys Road Nursing Home

After signing out of Mum's Nursing Home, I'm on my way to Carlton's house to create some music. Only a few hundred yards down the road I notice a black guy and what looks like his son have been stopped by two Police Officers. As I try to walk around them a young Police Officer stands in my way.

"Excuse me, a burglary has just taken place and we have reason to believe you may be involved."

"Not possible Officer, I just left my Mums Nursing Home, I have witnesses there and I had to sign in and out, so there's a record of how long I was there, I'll show you if you like, come and see, it's just there." I point to the building.

"No sorry, we're not going down there."

"Okay I'll be on my way then." As I walk away the young Police Officer pushes me.

"What you doing? Don't push me, I've done nothing."

"Just stay there, we need to talk to you, as you fit the description that came in over the radio, tall black man wearing blue jeans." I'm in disbelief. "Are you joking, listen man you just need go to the Nursing Home, where I've been all morning until now. Like I said before I don't know anything about a burglary, I've been with my Mum just there, you can see the Home from here." I point again to the building down Knollys Road. I try again to walk away as I don't feel there's anything more to be said, I'm obviously innocent, but he pushes me again. I feel myself starting to get annoyed this time.
I decide it's best to walk into someone's garden and close the gate, making

the gate a barrier between him and me, in an effort to stop his pushing and diffuse the situation.

We continue our debate whilst I'm behind the gate but he get's more and more heated. It seems he's just not interested in what I'm telling him and I feel very aggrieved. I decide to leave anyway, knowing I'm completely innocent and that I have cooperated for long enough with this nonsense, but as I try to open the gate, the young Officer pushes me for the third time. This time I fall over backwards, not realising how close the steps are behind me. As I get back to my feet I check to make sure I didn't lose my keys or damage my phone as I fell.

"Take your hands out your pockets," he shouts, then the whole thing escalates and before I know it, there are thirty Police Offices on site. At least twelve of them surround me. I tell them again that I've not done anything, and that I just left my Mum in the Nursing Home literally two minutes before I was stopped. The next thing I know they all rush me, and try to put me on the floor; there's a big scuffle as I try to defend myself. It results in four Officers sitting on top of me, while the young one pulls my arms back to handcuff me. Blood is pouring from my mouth and nose as I'm taken to the waiting Police van.

The black guy and his son are also arrested, but we were never charged for the actual burglary they supposedly stopped us for. We are charged with threatening words and behaviour as well as assaulting a Police Officer, because we stood our ground and protested our innocence of the burglary. The verdict in Court, not guilty for assaulting a Police officer but guilty of threatening words and behaviour, a complete fit up!

We didn't even fit the description that came over the radio, other than being Black men, so I decide to appeal and counter sue for assault as they roughed me up without just cause. After winning my appeal, I was acquitted on all charges, so I dropped my counter charge of assault and wrongful arrest.

23rd March 2006
Home Croydon

It's hard to believe that an inaccurate Newspapers story is the cause for me losing my job, it seems very unfair, but there it is, the power of the Press.

Being stopped by police isn't unusual for black men in London, I really had no idea this incident would cause such a problem. Particularly when I knew I had a cast iron alibi and the Agency had supplied me with a character reference during the trial. Part of me wanted to believe they would find a way to keep me on, despite the bad press, but I guess that's just the side of me that wants to believe the best in people.

Even though I had already sensed my job was history, I can't help but feel the pain as I read it in black and white. It feels like I've lost my livelihood, my sanctuary, and my last strand of hope for a normal life. What's gonna happen to me now, left out in the wilderness? Didn't I pay my dues in accordance with the Justice System, when I was a teenager? Why am I being punished again?

Anyway I can't afford to dwell on this negativity, I have to stay focussed, it's time to sit and do my affirmations; it helps.

After clearing my head I realise I have to calm down; I can't let the Press beat me, any more than I let the Terrorists beat me! Like I said I have to roll with the punches otherwise I'm gonna break; and that's not gonna happen! I have come to believe some of the Press are just as misguided as the bombers; they are supposed to be educated people who know what they are doing, and are meant to report the truth, not cherry pick to make a profitable headline at the expense of others. There's no excuse for what they've done and even their own peers say the main culprits have been very unfair. I believe in Divine Justice and I'm pretty sure they will attract exactly what they deserve sooner or later. No good can come of such behaviour!

In contrast I can understand where my work place is coming from, they have to protect their company. The Media is very powerful and their dubious headlines could affect the company's reputation, even if they aren't true. They've already said my work record is very good and that I get on well with all the other staff, so obviously it's not personal. I realise they have to look at it from a business point of view, and so do I, that's life.

27th March 2006
Home Croydon

I escape my gloom for the excitement of getting my new high tech leg this morning. I'm good to go in my blue and white tracksuit, as it makes for easy access to my stump, much easier than struggling with jeans.

27th March 2006
Queen Mary Roehampton Waiting Room

As I sit here pondering how my life has changed and the challenges I now face, my level brain kicks in. Jumping, can I still jump? Will it be the same? How will it feel? Can I run? I must be able to run, I'm gonna try anyway. The Gym? Football man, I wonder if I can still play Football after all I'm a baller; you can't lose that ability. Lost in my own world, which seems normal these days, I catch myself smiling just as Dr Lawrence walks in with my new leg. I'm so excited, like a kid on his birthday.

"Well Garri, here it is, are you ready to have a go?" He seems pleased for me as well.

"More than ready Sir." I can't get the leg on quick enough, as he's explaining about the shock absorbers. A spring like device in the foot as well as an air ball in the calf area that can be filled with air and adjusted, he then gives me a pump for self maintenance. What? I can pump it up myself, now that's cool; it really appeals to me!

I get up feeling very confident after all the practice I've had on the basic leg. I walk around the fitting room for quite a while, another epic moment. Lawrence stops me from time to time to adjust various parts of the new leg and I quickly become more accustomed to it. After he finishes tightening it I walk out into the corridor feeling the desperate need to run, so I do, from one end to the other with a big smile on my face! Oh wow, I did it, I ran up and down the corridor and I'm feeling great, no discomfort at all. This leg really cushions my stump perfectly. Lawrence makes one more adjustment before he takes it back to check everything's ok.

I'm already planning to test jump off a couple of small walls to feel the impact and start re-thinking what's possible. I feel like I've been upgraded and as well as that, I've also been given a waterproof leg, which although is basic, means I can have a shower standing up! "Lawrence thank you very much mate, it's been a pleasure as usual" I can't wait to get out of here and try them out.

"Okay Garri, do you have enough socks and nylon covers?"

"No, I don't think so."

"Good thing I got these for you then" he pulls out a stash, looking pleased.

"Thank you very much Sir." I'm elated and so grateful to him.

"Any problem Garri, give me a call but you should be okay with both prosthetics."

"Once again, thank you and have a great day"

"You too Garri, take care."

All this excitement builds up energy in my legs; I'm good to go!

As I leave with my stash of goodies all I can think about is running. I sit in my car and reflect a while on how fast I used to run.

April 1984
Stockwell Park Estate Brixton
On Barrett House Near Skate Park

Out walking with my German Shepherd General, we bump into my mate Didly on his own, in the street rapping quietly, trying to compose. "Didly you can't chat no lyrics man." I tease him.

"Of course I can Sugar, hear dis one, who control Brixton Wackod and the Raiders"

"Shut up you joker, ah l'il Andy lyrics dat." We start laughing, we're always joking around, but two Police Officers coming along the road shout over to Didly. "Excuse me, stop right there, we have reason to believe you were just involved in a street robbery." They start questioning Didly using the stop and search Sus Law as they approach us. Didly is having none of it answering in a flippant manner and backing away, which doesn't go down well with the Officers so they move towards him. My dog General barks, so the Officer's step back alarmed. Didly sees an opportunity to get away, and legs it to the end of the square, jumps on the wall, then leaps across onto a garden wall, and over another wall, running as fast as he can. The Police chase him, but lose their bottle at the high wall, knowing if they put one foot wrong it's a long drop onto concrete; Didly disappears.

Having lost their prime suspect, they come for me. "It's your fault he got away!" They are furious and red-faced.

"What you talking about?" I'm surprised.

"Because of your dog he got away, so were going have to arrest you for obstruction."

"You're having a laugh Officer!" They move towards me, General growls, so they back off again. Then one of the officers gets on his radio talking about a dangerous dog and needing reinforcements, exaggerating the whole event. That's my cue to do a runner as well. General knows his way home, so I let him off his lead. "General go home," he doesn't need telling twice; he takes off with me close behind. I'm running flat out as fast as I can down Barrett House balcony with the Police in hot pursuit. We cross over the bridge leading to Burrow House balcony; it's a straight run. There's a group of boys in front of us and as I get closer I see my big brother Hector; our eyes meet. He calls out,

"General, General!" General pauses for a second and looks at my brother as I run past, but quickly decides it's safer to run after me; it's like he knows we're in danger. We reach the end of the balcony, run down the stairs and come out through the garages. We stay there for a few seconds checking the road both ways, no sign of the Police. They must have stopped or we must have outrun them, no time to analyse, we quickly sprint over into Crowhurst garages oposite. Next up the stairs, onto the balcony, a quick left and a quick right, ducking down behind the balcony walls leading to my house, so I can't be seen from the other side. I manage to crawl along past six doors, to get home; it's like mission impossible. Keeping low I reach up to put my key in the lock and just manage to open the front door. General pushes in first, we're safe. He rushes through into the kitchen and as I follow him he pushes his head up under the curtains and peeps out of the kitchen window; this dog is something else. General move man, raaaahtid the Estate is crawling with Police searching for us!

27th March 2006
Driving Through Brixton

As I pull up outside Zak's Tyre shop, the Man dem are outside playing football. Trying to score goals between two cones on the forecourt, but they keep missing.

"Yo give me ah kick der." I'm keen to try out my new leg.

"No sugar, allow it." TZ answers, he's concerned about my leg.

"Kool noh man, kick the ball, gimme." TZ chips the ball over to me, without letting the ball bounce I half volley it in between the makeshift goal with my right leg, standing steady on my new leg. The Man dem hails out my name Sugar, Sugar!! Pure noise! The looks I'm getting from everyone, I see the surprise and amazement in their faces, and I feel great; but hey once a baller always a baller, you get me? Alfie comes running out of the office.

"Sugar man I was watching you on the CCTV. For real you got to take part in the Paralympics, you've still got it. That goal was messy!"

On a high today it's funny how small things I took for granted can brighten my day and inspire me, kicking a football and running!

31st March 2006
Home Croydon

It just dawns on me that it's my last official day employed, and I feel a sense of sadness that my twenty-year-old conviction continues to haunt me. It's hard to believe the savagery of the Media cost me so much, yet I must remember to be thankful I still have my life. And very importantly, I've had a spiritual wake up call, inspiring me to see life from a new perspective.

Scandal in Press – £loss of reputation, *respect and opportunities*
2004 Police incident, although fully acquitted – *£loss of a great career, trust and financial security*
Compensation for 7/7 – *£reduced due to sensationalised headlines about past conviction*
Spiritual Wake Up Call – *£priceless!*

4th April 2006
Home Croydon

Listening to some music samples, which help to keep me positive. I've not written a new song for ages, but a hook is playing around in my head and it's deep; it's taken twenty minutes to get it together. First time in a long time I'm showing raw emotion. Wow man I am choking up, feeling very tearful let me take a break. *Note to self; must face my demons to be fully cleansed.*

A letter from my Housing Officer arrives. She's arranged a viewing of a three-bedroom house on 27th April. Fingers crossed please, please, please this could be just what I need, a completely fresh start.

5th April 2006
Home Croydon

It's funny what I used to take for granted; standing up having a shower with my waterproof leg on is bliss, a great way to start the day. As I gather my thoughts, I decide to get my paperwork in order, filing and shredding well overdue!

15th April 2006
Brixton

Miss Campbell, a family friend of my Mother walks past me in the street. "I'm glad everything is out in the open Garri, there's nothing to hide anymore, you should feel free, a weight has been lifted off your shoulders."

I'm taken aback by her straight forwardness. Bless her, sometimes the truth hurts but hearing it from her, someone who knows me from childhood, I know she only has my best interest at heart.

16th April 2006
Home Croydon

My crazy side is out, I've got a little soft foam football in my front room doing 'kick ups', just done six in a row. "Braps!!"

25th April 2006 11:11pm
Home Croydon

About to go to sleep when I manage to knock the tip of my stump with my heel. Argh, Chaa man! Hot and cold sweats overwhelm me as I breathe in and out fast trying to manage the pain. Bwoy it's painful. It takes a while to ease off but I trust it will sort itself out by the morning because I've got a busy day.

26th April 2006
Royal Free Hospital

The Plastic Team who did my skin grafts assess my progress. I'm in and out pretty quickly though as Dr Floyd says my graft is healing very well and that I'm making great progress. I'm relieved and happy at his assessment, despite the slight pain in my stump from last night's incident; I just have to solider on.

While I'm here I go up to the eighth floor onto the 'George and Mary ward' to say hello to the lovely nurses that looked after me. I step out of the lift and open the double doors leading onto the ward that was my home for just over two months after the Bombings. Some nurses manage to recognise me straight away, and are very glad to see me. The others are just looking at me confused; it's as if they can place my face but can't remember how they know me. One nurse in particular is really puzzled and she should know me well as she used to bathe me! When she finally realises who I am she lets out a scream! I can't stop laughing. They all agree I'm taller than they remember and I look younger. Come to think of it, some of them only ever saw me lying in my bed, so no wonder they think I'm taller!

26th April 2006
Driving

Through Hampstead, Camden, Euston to Russell Square where I make a stop to pick up some Silica. I take it to repair my nails and hair. I park outside my old office, but I'm short of cash so I pop into the Post Office to use their cash machine. As I leave the Post Office I inevitably bump into a few work colleagues who are very pleased to see me. I don't know if drinks have got anything to do with it, as they are outside the Pub on the corner. I'm joking!! We exchange niceties on my way to the health food shop.

When I get there the woman who I remember from before the bombing is serving, and she gives me a gorgeous smile. "Can I get a large Silica please?" I'm determined to regrow my fingernails.

"Ahhh come here!" I wonder what's going to happen next. My heart starts thumping in my chest and I freeze. The woman comes out from behind the counter, hugs me and then kisses me on the cheek whispering in my ear,

"You're looking really good, it's so nice to see you again." My knees turn to jelly and butterflies flutter in my stomach like a kid, and me a big man!

"Thank You" is all I can manage to say as I pay for the Silica and walk quickly out of the shop with a big grin on my face. Wow what a lovely woman, I needed that hug. I felt deep warmth and compassion from her; it was a tender moment.

26th April 2006
Brixton

Back on the Endz; I pull up outside the Church on Brixton Road feeling like I have to give thanks. Bwoy, I was christened in this Church, but can't even remember the last time I walked through these doors. It's empty inside so I walk to the front and take a seat. Knowing I'm here but through the grace of God I thank the higher powers for my life and this second chance to shine a spark of his light. He gives me strength so I wanna pay it forward. I meditate and before I know it half an hour has passed.

I feel inspired to get up and light two candles, so I find some change in my pocket and put into the candle box. I light one for my Mother, my rock, may she Rest In Peace, but wait, no that ain't right; Mummy won't just rest peacefully wherever she is, she's going to grow and evolve, so I say from the heart Evolve In Love Mummy! The other candle is for me from me, a signal that I take back my power and re-emerge like a rite of passage from darkness into light. I'm drawn to a statue of Jesus on the cross. I know now how it feels to be persecuted, I overstand; I feel close to him. I am in the 'State of Jesus' I feel like I've been crucified by the powerful Media, but can I rise again?

26th April 2006
Home Croydon

Everywhere I drive I keep seeing adverts for a big dance coming up at Brixton Recreation Centre in two days time, General Trees and U Roy among others. I'd love to go and it tempts me, but because of my leg it's very unwise right now. Chaaaaaa!!! Although I really wanted to go, maybe it's a sign to sit my backside down and stop fasting up the place. About I want to go an' dance, I need to meditate!

27th April 2006
Norwood Junction In Traffic

It's just past two o'clock and I've finished viewing a beautiful house in South Norwood. It could be perfect for me, it's got a lovely big garden, spacious rooms and is in a fantastic location with it's own drive. Let's see what happens, but I think it could be out of my price bracket. Dream on!

28th April 2006 2:45pm
Home Croydon

After a lot of running around, it's time to take off my leg and relax, as my stump hurts. In a way I'm glad I hit it, as it's made me realise how vulnerable it is when I'm unaware, I've got to learn to be more careful. Time to bathe and comfort it with a hot flannel, like Mummy would've done. I'll use the flannel that belonged to Gran, how old must that heirloom be? Mummy was born in the 1920's. Wow, my ancestors knew what to do!

Just as I'm thinking of family, Tony calls. "Sugar you know I keep thinking about Mummy." He sounds sad.

"Funny that, Tony I've just this minute been thinking about Mummy as well." Then he cracks and begins to get emotional, even big tough men can connect deep with their Mother it's natural. Tony was very close to Mum; she helped him in so many ways. I try to offer soothing words, but I know he's really missing her; I can feel it in his vibes. "Tony it's good to cry Bruv, let it out, it shows you care. And when you're done, remember that Mummy's in a better place now, right? She ain't got to suffer no more man." I give him the time so he can let go cos I can feel it too.

3rd May 2006
Local Newsagents

My mobile rings. "Hello."

"Hello, this is BBC London can I speak to Garri Holness please?"

"Hmmm, speaking" I feel nervous.

"We've just read an article about you and wonder if you'd like to do a live interview with us." I can't believe it, so unexpected.

"Mmmm I see, well thanks, but no thanks."

"Can I ask why Garri?"

"I'm just not ready, I've been through a lot as you may know."

"Okay then, take my number if you change your mind."

"Fair enough, thanks again."

Ten minutes later a text comes in from the BBC, giving me their number and saying when I'm ready, they will be waiting. I think it will take me a long time to be 'ready'!

5th May 2006
Russell Square London

Driving to my old workplace I get a text from Pippa about our lunch date, she's so sorry but something urgent came up at the last minute and can't make it today, but we will reschedule soon and kisses. Although disappointed I continue anyway as I need a quick word with HR. Once inside, at least I'm getting a friendlier greeting now the knee-jerk reaction is over, several people are notably offish but I'm learning that people are all different and the one's that are genuine show themselves head and shoulders above the rest.

As I leave I pop over to the Pub, as I know the Dispatch Crew will be there 'my people dem' amongst others from work. I find Rusty sitting at a table outside so join him, then I feel hands on my shoulders from behind me. It's Sue* the big boss's PA what a warm greeting and quite unexpected! A kind touch can make such an amazing difference to me at the moment.

After a few minutes, I need to visit the Gents, which is inside the Pub. On my way in, I notice a couple of men in suits looking at me, and I remember them from a fun snowball fight we had one winter. They obviously recognise me too; as they come over they shake my hand and have some very kind words to say. It seems as though more people I speak to recently, say they're also relieved that the negative Media Circus is over and done with, and I have to agree!

10th May 2006
London

I'm attending a meeting with representatives of C.I.C.A again, Tessa Jowell MP, the Met Police and other survivors of 7/7. After the question and answer section has finished, I mingle for a while with the other survivors and their compassion for my situation is simply breath taking. It's strange how some of the people I thought were my friends, were taken in by the Media and stood back, and those I hardly know have surprise me with their kind words and positive gestures. Life, one big road with a lot of signs!

16th May 2006
Mini Market Croydon

I've been on a creative vibe for a little while now, doodling at night to help me sleep and I've designed a massive tattoo to go on my back. I've finally decided to have it done, so I make an appointment at the tattoo parlour for 1st June. As I walk past the football souvenir shop, the woman inside calls to me. "Why you limping?" I stop in my tracks, pause, smile at her and walk away, but then I stop again feeling compelled to go into her shop to tell her my story. She listens silently, eyes filling up as I speak. There's another customer in the shop as well, who comes over also listening in quietly. After the tale is told, she asks the other customer to take a photo of her and I together.

"You know you are an inspiration, whenever I'm feeling sorry for myself, I'm gonna look at this photo to help me remember to stay positive like you."

"Thank you, that's nice." I feel uplifted and grateful myself now; like the storm has passed and as if God has put these people in front of me, to restore my faith. Almost as if he is showing me the way forward is to tell my story.

1st June 2006
Tattoo Parlour Croydon

Stripped off to the waist the Tattooist starts work on my back. "Don't move!" He sounds firm.

"Yeah okay." He seems a nice enough guy. He continues for around an hour and a half, chit chatting away and I don't move an inch as instructed.

"It'll be done in five minutes, you okay?"

"Yeah, okay but how much longer?" For the next hour he keeps saying the same thing; five more minutes, just five more minutes. He's a real joker. Two-and-a-half hours in, he finally stops.

"Finished!" I have to admit it's bloody uncomfortable, so I'm glad it's over but I knew it would hurt a bit! Still soldier it through, been through worse!

"You know you gotta come back as we still got some shading to do." He looks hopeful.

"Really?" I'm unconvinced.

"Yeah mate it will look awesome." Still hopeful.

"Hmmm." I dwell on it as he shows me my tattoo in the mirror, before he puts a cling film wrap around me to protect it.

"Mate, don't think I'll be back for the shading, I've had enough!"

"Okay, your call, remember to look after it though."

"Yeah, yeah I will, great tattoo, thanks very much." I pay the cashier and leave, rather sore but with a blinding tattooed on my back that I designed myself, result!'

1st June 2006
Clapham Common

As I walk through the Common enjoying a very pleasant day, looking for friends I've arranged to meet, the cling film wrapping that's protecting my tattoo is making me double hot, as a complete stranger stops me. "You're such an inspiration man, keep it up and keep going."

"Thank you." I say surprised and he smiles as he walks on. Straight after another guy standing in a group approaches and introduces himself, "Bradley." He holds out his hand in a gesture to shake mine. "It's a pleasure to meet you Garri."

"Thanks Bruv."

"Me and me mates over there, are from North London, we've been watching what's been happening in the news and just can't understand why the Media turned on you. Trust me there's a lotta people out there backing you. You're one of us mate, from the street, a real solider."

"Humbled by your words my brother." We embrace then part, fist to fist.

I catch sight of my friends under a tree and head over. Really pleased everyone I meet today has only good words for me. Clapham Common is really the place to be right now, as I catch a vibe under this tree in good company and in the shade!

3rd June 2006
Home Croydon

While sorting out some papers I come across the Royal Invitation. It's an interesting gesture for the Prince of Wales and the Duchess of Cornwall to invite me to High Grove for a memorial with the rest of the 7/7 Survivors. But I'm anxious even just looking at the invitation, which gives me doubts about going at all. I think I'll follow my intuition and stay out of the limelight at this time. Maybe it's better for me to take a short break away somewhere out of sight. Actually I'm in desperate need to get away from the Media Circus, and I have been invited to go to Spain.

13th June 2006
Queen Mary Hospital Roehampton

It's a regular check up day and it gives me the time and inspiration to think about the future of Prosthetics. I end up wondering, hoping, and dreaming in fact that I can one day get such an amazing prosthetic leg that is even better than my original leg… Perhaps one with a tracking device, a voice activated Sat-Nav that can take me home on cruise control if I get tipsy! Whichever one they invent going forward will surely get better and better. I'm up for whatever challenge lays in the future, I am willing to test drive anything, and I'm even willing to fly!

I'm prone to daydreaming these days. Some friends' say I'm going through a cleansing period, others say you cannot buy this experience. I reflect, and on the whole I think I'm okay, but I'm just drifting along without much solid direction. After July I'd like to take a year out away from everyone, find some peace of mind. Rediscover who I am, and understand my calling, my path, my new journey in life. I'm just feeling this constant vibe, I'm drawn to my spirituality; the am that I am. The Student is ready, Teacher please show yourself!

16th June 2006
Gatwick Airport

Heading through departures with Halle, as we approach the metal detector, I figure the machines will go crazy as soon as my leg goes through, so I knock on my leg and put it through first in front of me to show them it's prosthetic. Sure enough it beeps loudly. I must look like a cause for concern, a big black guy setting off the security machines. Everyone looks, wondering what's going on. The Security Guard approaches me. I get in first and state the problem. "Alright mate, prosthetic leg."

"Could you step over here for a second please Sir." Fortunately he's polite and calm. He pats me down and uses a hand scanner to scan my legs. The left leg understandably goes off the scale, but to my surprise the right leg also sounds off. "Hmmm, that's funny, I must still have shrapnel in that leg I didn't know. It's from the London Bombings Mate."

"Oh! All right, sorry to hear that Sir, please go through you have a pleasant flight."

All clear and we're off to Spain to stay near Marbella. It's the first time I've ever been on a plane and I am getting very excited, now that I've passed through security. Boarding the plane, I try to position myself into my allocated aisle seat, just as a Flight Attendant walks past me. "Excuse me." I smile at her.

"Yes sir." She stops and gives me her attention.

"Would it be possible to change seats, I need a bit more space" I tap the hard plastic part of my leg making a noise so she can hear that it's a prosthetic.

"Oh ok, let me see what I can do once we have all passengers on board. I'll see if there are any spare seats with more leg room Sir."

"Thank you very much."

When all passengers are on board, my wish is granted, and I'm escorted towards the front of the plane where seats 11a, 11b and 11c are empty. We are given the whole row to ourselves.

"Thank you, that's very helpful." I'm well pleased and give her a big grin.

"My pleasure." She smiles back and continues walking towards the front.

Sitting here is much more comfortable, as I can rest my leg to the left side. After a few minutes the Cabin-Crew start whispering, and looking over, until one of the Stewardesses approaches discretely. "Excuse me sir, are you the guy, who was involved in the London Bombings?"

"Yes, shh don't tell anyone!" She laughs and nods back at the others watching, from then on no limits on special service! The crew is so very nice to me and we are treated like VIP's. A few magazines, a newspaper, several free drinks and a quick nap in-between, it's fasten your seat belt time again as we begin to descend.

It's late afternoon as we arrive at Malaga airport and when the doors of the airplane finally open a wall of heat hits me, it feels good and I've got almost a week to lap it up. Once we clear Customs, I'm eager to explore Spain.

Halle's brother picks us up and takes us to his place. I take in the beauty of the colours around me so bright and full of life and the sunshine feels amazing. We decide we'll need food so stop off at a few shops on the way. The fresh fruits and vegetables in Spain appeal to me, it all looks delicious. By the time we arrive at Aromie's apartment I'm more than impressed with what I've seen so far. His home is beautiful and a good size too. The view from the windows is stunning, it's so high up I can see for miles and straight away get a sense of peace. Although it's not green like England, the variety of trees and brightly coloured flowers is awesome. Halle unloads the shopping before we hit the road again with Aromie. We're going to his bar Terra Blues, so he can open up and meet up with the others. He is also the founder of Lick FM, a radio station in Marbella that he runs with a group of like-minded guys and girls; the Lick FM Crew.

I'm loving the laid back chilled vibe of Terra Blues as I sit here in the bar, taking in the vibes, drinking a juice and generally chillin'. I can't keep still for long though I'm excited to discover more! Come let me take a one walk, to the Square across the way to check out the clothing and jewellery stalls. Mmm. Spanish style ah gwaan. The men's jewellery store is offering some fantastic one off 'tings!

Looking up into the blue skies, I realise it truly is a Godsend that I'm out here at this time. I needed to connect with nature, sea, sand, sun and the amazing plants and trees. Some of the blossoms look as if they aren't real; so brightly coloured, it doesn't seem possible.

17th June 2006
Marbella Spain

Aromie knows of a good restaurant he suggests we try, so we head off to 'Rays Caribbean Restaurant'. The food is lush; the vibes and environment are on point. They're playing some old skool studio one, Dennis Brown and Freddy McGregor; I drift off in heaven.

Next stop Sonora Beach to catch up with the rest of The Lick FM Crew. As we eat, talk, drink, laugh and smoke, it's as if all the stresses and strains are miles away and they are my extended 'family'! I begin to enjoy my life again. I take Halle by the hand and stroll down the long sandy beach, which to me is amazing. I've not seen anything like this before, so take in every inch of the scenery as we slowly walk along going nowhere in particular.

18th-20th June 2006
Marbella Spain

A fantastic time with fantastic people, weather, shopping, beach party and Halle's Birthday! We've had a truly amazing time, on so many levels.

21st June 2006
Marbella Spain

Time to leave, it's been fantastic to get away and as we get into the cab I look back with fond memories of Marbella. The Spanish cabbie is in his sixties and he's playing some wicked R&B. At the same time he's trying out his English chat up lines on Halle. He's got some front, yet I can't help but laugh! We reach the airport in plenty of time and as the cabbie takes out our luggage, he points at something behind me. I turn around to have a look, but there's nothing there, as I turn back I catch him giving Halle a quick kiss on the cheek. Feisty! Laughing I shake his hand and wish him well. I should've given him 'two kick' you see, I smile to myself.

21st June 2006
Malaga Spain Airport Departures

Walking through duty-free I notice a cowboy hat in one of the accessory shops; gotta buy it! Cowboy hat, now on head, Halle is giving me some strange looks. I'm immune!

Security is laid back, no problems letting me through. As we're about to board the plane to London Gatwick there's a little boy behind us giving his Mum the run around. "Ocean, Ocean, come here."

"Excuse me, did you just call your son Ocean." I can't believe what I think I've heard.

"Yeah." She replies very matter of fact.

"Fantastic name!" I smile.

"Thanks, and her name's River" the young mother holds a baby girl in her arms looking like proud mother's do!

"Wow, how fantastic!" I love it when people move outside the norm it's inspiring!

We are directed to our allocated seats by the Cabin Crew; time to relax and reflect, I so needed this holiday, I feel like my battery has been recharged as I kick back to enjoy the flight home. As we fly over London I notice everything is dull and grey, in comparison. I must admit to feeling down; the sunshine in

Marbella was uplifting for sure. Getting off the Plane and clearing customs my mood stays grey, I guess this is what they call the holiday blues!

June 2006
Home Croydon

During the next few days, I get back into the London vibe slowly. It's okay really and the sun is shining here too as the temperatures rise. Also I have memories of Marbella to reflect on and the sense that life can go on.

2nd July 2006
Royal Free Hospital Hampstead

I'm a bit apprehensive even though one of the top Surgeons will be performing my ear operation, but ever since I've known it was possible, I've been looking forward to this day. After settling down in the ward I notice a few familiar nurses floating around. We have lovely conversations and again I can't thank them enough for the help and support they gave me straight after the Bombings. At exactly one-thirty I'm taken down to the Operating Theatre, given an injection and told to count sheep. Sheep this time!

"One sheep, two lambs!" I laugh, "three sheep… four, five, six…."

I'm already on the ward when I open my eyes again, its five o'clock. "Garri you okay?" The Doctor is standing over me.

"Errrr… yeah okay, I think." I'm still trying to focus and not fully awake yet.

"The operation was successful Garri." Now I hear him.

"Fantastic!" I think there is a slight improvement already.

"Let's put this pack into your ear, it will help protect it. And we're going to keep you in overnight as a precaution; can someone be here to pick you up in the morning?"

"Yeah, I'm sure someone can and thank you so much." It's exciting to think I can regain some of my hearing.

"My pleasure Garri, you'll need to come back for a check up, so I'm going to book you an appointment, which you can collect in the morning before you go, okay?"

"Oh okay, thanks again and have a great evening." There's nothing to do now but relax and catch up on some much-needed Mediation.

3rd July 2006
Royal Free Hospital

Sitting in the waiting area near the canteen, I see Halle arriving to pick me up. As she approaches the entrance I'm already up and walking towards her, I greet her with a hug.

"You alright Babe, how'd it go?"

"Well, the Surgeon said it was successful, just waiting for it to settle down." As we go towards Halle's car, I notice a lorry driving towards us at speed, so I move Halle to the inside of the pavement and stand between her and the lorry. 'Swoooosh' I *hear* the lorry pass my left side.

"Ih-eeah! I heard that, I heard that in my left ear!" Smiling from ear to ear with excitement I turn to Halle, and kiss her!

7th July 2006
Central London

Here I am one year after the bombing driving to Russell Square. I've been feeling mixed emotions on and off for the past few months; aloof, anxious, cautious, persecuted and now the Anniversary is here. I park up and walk to Russell Square Tube Station. En route I bump into a woman from my old workplace, we chat for a while; it gets emotional. The kindness she shows and her feelings towards me are heartfelt. It reminds me of something I read once that touched me, I can't remember where. *'Real tears don't fall from your eyes and cover the face they fall from your heart and cover your soul.' - anon* my eyes well up … 'Whoa! Man up!' Control yourself; the inner voice rescues me just in time.

My work colleague continues into the supermarket and I resume my journey to the Tube. I know this day is going to be very emotional, the first Anniversary of 7/7 and I try my best to be centred. As I reach the meeting place at Russell Square Station, people have already started gathering. As I approach, two men smile and welcome me. "Garri isn't it?"

"Yeah." Looking carefully I don't recognise either of them.

"Jason from Islington Fire Service and this is David, the manager at Russell Square Tube station. We were part of the team that came down to help get you guys out."

"REALLY!" I'm so pleased to meet them and I shake both their hands appreciatively.

"Yeah Garri, I'll always remember you! When we first saw you, you were so cool and calm, we thought you were okay, so we just walked past." They laugh, but at the same time I feel their respect.

"Ah yes, I remember that." I also remember thinking why the hell didn't I tell them I wasn't okay. My inner voice was screaming get me out, while my 'Man dem Ego' was saying I'm okay. Lesson learnt, always ask for what you need!

Jason and David continue to explain what happened underground and David has since received an MBE. Sounds like he deserved it. It's so great talking to these guys and seeing real people, who were just voices underground in the darkness and confusion of the aftermath. Finally around twenty people arrive at Russell Square and we all set off together for Hyde Park for the unveiling of the new Memorial.

7th July 2006
Hyde Park

In the park Tessa Jowell, the MP assigned to deal with the 7/7 Survivors, calls out to me and waves. "Garri, Garri!"

"Oh hello Tessa." We meet and she kisses me on both cheeks, such a pleasant woman. "Are you okay?"

"Yes I'm okay thanks, all the better for seeing you though." She smiles as we walk towards the monument and seating areas. I take a seat and then the Ceremony begins with the Choir singing; I drift off.

As I think back over the months building up to July itself, I realise my frequency was erratic and I sought refuge deeper within. Almost as soon as 2006 started I'd already begun to get agitated about the Anniversary. Now I'm in July feeling extremely fragile. Thankfully the little break in June to sunny Spain charged me up in preparation for July, which is a double whammy month for me after the bombing on the 7th and Mummy dying on the 21st. And as if it wasn't enough to deal with, by November the Tabloids were dragging up my past without compassion for my loss or mourning.

Nobody in this world is perfect or we wouldn't be here, we learn from our mistakes and everyone's path is different. I remember being in Streatham Police station in 1985, accused of the sexual assault the press are so keen to sensationalise. I told the officers involved over and over again I didn't do anything. They got so angry because I wouldn't admit to assaulting the girls they threatened to take me up stairs where no one could hear how they would deal with me. They said there would be no tapes to record anything that happens. I remember being absolutely terrified I was just seventeen, still a kid. Then they did force me up some dark back stairs and into a small room that was dimly lit. I could feel my heart pounding in my chest wondering what was going to happen. Tears well up inside me as I remember such intense memories. My eyes were opened to Police brutality.

January 1985
Streatham Police Station Upstairs Dimly Lit Room

During repetitive questioning about the assault, I repeat over and over to the two detectives questioning me that I was not involved. One of the detective's stands over me and the other is writing notes. I ask for my Mum or a Solicitor, but I'm denied. The detective standing is unsympathetic and shows anger, which quickly builds into aggression. He grabs me by the hair and violently jerks my head down towards the floor. As I go down I see a boot coming towards me, so I curl up into a ball and cover my head with my hands. A barrage of kicks punches and racist swearing rains down on me, I hear the dull thuds, but I'm numb, in shock and disbelief that Police can do this. It continues on and on relentlessly for what seems like a very long time until I'm dragged up from the floor, shaken and very distraught. They continue questioning me again over and over for another twenty minutes, but I still refuse to give them the answers they want. The Policeman that roughed me up pokes his finger hard into my chest with every word he shouts. "If-that-was-my-Daughter-you-wouldn't-fucking-be-alive!" He throws me back onto the seat and a pen is slammed on the table in front of me. The other Policeman offers me a way out. "You better sign this statement, if you want this to stop." He puts the statement he was writing on the table in front of me, so I start reading it. "I didn't say that." I protest, but then he becomes menacing as well. "I didn't say you should read it, I said *sign* it here, here, here and here!" Slamming his finger down on the statement at the places he wants me to sign.

"But I didn't say that." I insist, reluctant to sign the fabricated statement.

"You better fucking sign the statement now, unless you want more of what you just had?" The first Police officer unnerves me by growling through clenched teeth as his face turns red and contorts in rage. I sense he's ready to explode so I sign the false statement in fear of my life!

7th July 2006
Hyde Park

Loud applause suddenly brings me out of my thoughts and back to the surface. The Choir members smile to acknowledge the applause; the ceremony ends. I find a quiet spot to pay my own personal tribute to the victims but I'm not hanging around. The Press being here makes me uneasy.

8th July 2006
Home Croydon

This time last year I was having blood transfusions in a coma and on life support, fighting for my life. A few people thought I wouldn't make it, but here I am, God is great!

9th July 2006
Home Croydon

The Press onslaught starts up again straight after the anniversary just because some of the Politicians shook my hand. The mainstream News Papers start the headline and a Local Paper runs with it, like a dog with a bone. One local Reporter seems to be a particularly vindictive individual, who doesn't know when to draw the line; I may have to get my Solicitor onto him… Meanwhile I stay in.

14th July 2006
Home Croydon

Crash! My car alarm rings out! I rush to the window to see some boy racer has crashed into my X3, my heart drops and I go outside to check out the damage.

"Bruv you alright?" I remain calm, but firm.

"Yeah, yeah, yeah." He seems okay, but angry with himself, he obviously took the corner so fast he was out of control.

"You insured?" I frown.

"Yeah." He rubs his face and looks genuinely sorry.

"Okay then just give me your details and let the insurance sort it out, lucky no one got hurt."

"Yeah man, no problem." As he walks towards his car I walk around my car to inspect the damaged, oh well, good thing I am fully comprehensive and I wasn't in the car at the time. The young guy gives me his insurance details as well as his address and mobile number, everything seems in order, but I need to say something to make him stop and think.

"Hey yute man, you fi tek time drive."

"I'm sorry man." He looks sorry too.

"It's ah'right man juss kool." No point getting angry, no one got hurt, but there's something about July!

17th July 2006
Home Croydon

I'm constantly thinking of Mum today; it's a strange feeling with all that's been going on. I feel I haven't had the time and headspace to mourn her properly due to being upset over the Tabloids. They continue to repeat the same negative story about me all over again and no authorities are out there helping me. I feel persecuted and disconnected with this world right now. There's a major dip in my vibe again; everything is unfamiliar.

21st July 2006
Home Croydon

The pain of losing you Mum is deep I so miss you. I really miss you and 'those talks' we used to have. But you're in a better place now, where there's no suffering, so it would be selfish to want you back. It's been a year since you've been gone, all week I've been feeling your vibes, July is a very deep month for me and I just need a sign Mum. Please give me a sign, what shall I do? All writing stops as I reflect … it's depressing.

Over two months pass as I try to keep my head above water. It's not easy!

3rd October 2006
Home Croydon

It's my birthday and once again I'm reminded that I might not have even been here. I receive a hand full of birthday cards in the post; one of them is particularly intriguing and makes me giggle; some women! Not in the mood to celebrate outwardly though, simply to give thanks internally for my life.

4th October 2006
Home Croydon

Back from Roehampton with my latest prosthetic, I'm so grateful they keep me moving forwards. Now I'm the proud owner of a blade running leg, which will enable me to run and do other more active sports. Maybe even run in the London Marathon if I can get my mojo back. I'll have to go and test-drive it when I'm more together. It'll be interesting to see what I'm capable of with this power tool!

It's all about rising to the challenge and I feel that I need a positive new vibe in my flat, I think I'll use my stored up anger to motivate me now, rather than allow it to make me depressed.

26th October 2006
Shopping Centre Croydon

The idea of decorating my flat is on my mind, I'm out and about looking for inspiration, perhaps some art for my walls, but the next thing I know I trip down five or six marble steps going into a Department Store. I fall heavily! "Shit!" I sit up on the stairs, trying to regain my composure, but I've twisted my right ankle and my left knee badly, and the intensity of the pain almost immediately causes hot and cold sweats. With perspiration already dripping down my face, I feel embarrassed and disappointed with myself, how could I fall? It seems the shoe on my prosthetic leg got caught up in the covering they put on the steps to make them non-slip.

Several of the shop assistants kindly rush over to help me, asking if I'm okay. A teenage girl that watched me fall laughs her head off and seems to be delighting in my accident. I focus on her with a disapproving look, eye to eye, as I deliberately roll up my trousers and removed my artificial leg, still looking at her. As expected the shock factor totally disarms her. The look on her face is priceless, as if she wanted the ground to swallow her up. I smile as she receives a valuable lesson. Some young people!

My stump feels hot and looks swollen already, I need to let it breathe for a while allowing cool air on it. After fifteen minutes or so, I try to continued my shopping, still feeling the painful effects of the fall but soldiering on. Fortunately I find everything I need quickly and manage to carry my heavy bags back to my car. After loading up the shopping I drive home via the Chemist to stock up on pain relief. It's a good thing I drove into the Town Centre today, my disabled drivers badge comes in handy for moments just like this.

27th October 2006
Home Croydon

My stump is twice the size and too painful to walk on today. I can't even fit it into my prosthetic, so I have to use my crutches and stay home to recover. Bloody non-slip stairs!

11th December 2006
Home Croydon

I've been housebound for six weeks, boy it's been painful on many levels but like they say, everything happens for a reason, and I think the reason for this must be to teach me to slow down, be more alert and more careful, that's the last time I'm gonna fall over! I will pay more attention to everything I do from now on. On the upside, during this time I've managed to meditate and nurture myself back to health and also find time to decide how I want to decorate my flat. Although I feel I'm getting fitter now, I do need to find a gym and do some workouts on my legs to strengthen the ligaments and muscles. Maybe if my muscles were stronger I wouldn't have fallen over.

25th December 2006
Fulham

Although I'm at Halle's Mum's house for Christmas, I'm not really present. I feel sad inside, it's the second Christmas without Mum and I feel lonely and family-less. My support structure has fallen away bit by bit; the good I was appreciated for has been quickly forgotten. Although Halle and her family make me feel very welcome, and are warm towards me, I'm introduced to them only as a friend and I realise something is missing inside. Self-doubt creeps in through the back door and the realisation hits home that this is not *my* family. I feel a need to belong, someone to love me unconditionally, so I don't need to worry what they really think of me. I wonder what the future holds, if I'll ever be regarded by anyone as boyfriend material, rather than 'just a friend'. My mind is on overdrive and I just want to withdraw and get home into my own space so I can relax my guard.

31st December 2006
Home Croydon

New Year's Eve alone with my Mum's ashes, talking to her about my rollercoaster ride since her passing, I'm feeling more spiritually in tune though and my mediation is becoming easier and more powerful.

New Year January 2007
Home Croydon

First week of the year, I find myself trying to relax, the meditation helps, but I also need to get into a regular exercise routine. I know I must stay focused on my health, but I just can't motivate myself. I get a sinking sense of depression just around the corner and I can't seem to shake it. Here I am with a nice car and a bit of money in the bank so I can go shopping if I need something, but retail therapy doesn't work for more than five minutes. Money is no compensation for losing my leg. Yes, it makes it easier to buy food to eat, to drive somewhere I need to go and park close, but then what about if I don't feel like eating, or even going out at all, what then?

As I look back, my thoughts dwell on all those people that boarded the Garri Holness bandwagon straight after the bombing in 2005. So many Birthday cards in 2005 and yet only five Xmas cards now. Truthfully though, I'm glad I can see more clearly. At least I know these five people are genuine, that's precious. I've learned so much this year and I'm grateful for that. It's been like a rite of passage, or a spiritual awakening, glimpses of the Bigger Picture.

7th January 2007
Home Croydon

Music is my positivity in adversity, so it's handy that I can put some beats together and write a few lyrics. I'm grateful to have developed this know-how, but wonder if I still have the passion for it inside, or perhaps it's been crushed? It could go either way, but I am aware it's my choice, and I absolutely know music feeds my positivity. I just have to take it one day at a time, small steps and choosing Love not Fear. I'm reminded of an old Native Cherokee Indian Story, 'The Two Wolves'. They say a Cherokee Elder was teaching his grandchildren about life. He told them there are two wolves inside of us all. One is the Wolf of Love, the other is the Wolf of Fear and they constantly fight. One of the Grandchildren interrupts asking him 'Grandfather, which one will win?' He replies, 'the one that we feed'.

11th January 2007
Home Croydon

I'm feeling so down again it's getting beyond a joke. I'm desperate for something to lift me up, even just a little bit. What can I do to feed the Love and defeat the Fear? Shall I try sleeping it off, or is that giving up? I decide exercise will help and I've just the thing lurking somewhere! Where's that running blade? It's a new challenge that just might inspire me. I fit the leg and stand up putting my weight slowly onto it. Whoa, it certainly gives me a bounce in my step, but I don't feel very secure. Running on the spot for a while seems to be okay, but the stability and balance is so very different. Guess I will get used to it if I keep practising. Let me try a 'ting, go for a little test jog around the block.

It's all about getting the balance right, and it's easier if the ground is even so I run on the side of the road. After a while I'm surprised how light and comfortable it is. I begin to pick up pace. Bwoy! I reckon I could run fast using this leg, so I sprint along the road for a short stretch and it feels amazing. Just then a tram comes along behind me, 'let me see if I can get to my gate before the tram passes me!' I start running and it inches up on me gradually. People wave from the train smiling, and then someone calls out from across the road encouraging me as I run alongside the tram. "G'wan my son!" I'm causing a bit of a stir with this new leg and I manage to get to my gate only split seconds after the tram. Wow, pretty good going for a first attempt!

Well, that worked and I feel much better emotionally and physically now. This is the first time I've actually been able to run fast in a very long time, what a great feeling. I'm proud of myself. It's interesting how running lifted my vibe back up. We have the technology, Garri Holness the Bionic Man!' I feed Love not Fear, and I have a laugh.

15th January 2007
Brixton Zak Tyres

After the uplifting success with my running leg, I'm in the mood to take on more challenges. TZ's mountain bike is lying outside on his forecourt unattended; so I pick it up. I just feel the need to test myself. T just finishes dealing with a customer and walks out as I'm getting onto his bike. I shout over to him. "TZ, soon come."

"Sugar, what y'doing man?" He watches me wobble a bit on the bike and looks worried, so I smile and wave taking one hand off the bars. "Kool noh' man, me ah try a ting."

"Mind you kno', Sugar." I ride off on his bike getting the hang of it as I go along. My balance is really good since learning to walk again so I'm quietly confident. My own leg pushing the pedal on the ball of the foot, while the high tech leg sits central on the pedal. I decide to ride into Stockwell Park Estate to see if I can see my brother Tony. I would love to show him I can ride, but unfortunately he's not about, so I just ride around for a while and then back to TZ's half hour later. By the time I get back he's waiting impatiently and looks anxious."Where d' you go man?" He asks shaking his head.

"Check me brother innit."

"You went that far?" Still shaking his head he laughs.

"How you mean?" I act as if it's nothing.

"You're a gangster Bruv! Yo Jay you know Sugar just rode my bike?" TZ's brothers face lights up in surprise.

"Sugar man ain't nothing holding you back!"

It's such an exhilarating feeling to ride the bike through the streets and the sense of being able to do something normal gives me a buzz.

18th January 2007
Croydon Town Centre

Walking down the escalator in a department store I notice a very smart woman with her young daughter looking over at me smiling, so I smile back and continue about my business. As I look back towards them, they're still looking at me, so I quickly look away. I'm self-conscious about the way I walk and presume people will notice; some do even mention it. After a little shopping I bump into them again. This time, the woman has something to say, but I'm ready for it. "Hello, you're a lovely young man, *tut*, if only I was younger." I didn't expect that though! She leaves me with a broad smile on my face. She doesn't even ask me why I'm limping! Its moments like this that help to bring back a little self-esteem and hope after everything I've been through. Thank you!

22nd January 2007
Clapham

Having lunch with my great friend Dom. Over lunch it's time for a good old chat, this guy is one friend I know I'll have forever. They say true friends are like the roots of a tree no matter what the weather they will always be there for you, deep rooted. A fair weather friend is like a leaf on a tree, depending on the season, will depend on whether or not they are there for you, they go with the wind you can't depend on them!

22nd January 2007
Home Croydon

KMT Traffic Warden man, you know me by now, how can you give me a ticket outside my own house? Chaa! Sometimes I forget that I have to show my Blue Disabled Badge on the dashboard. But they know my car, bloody job's worth! I scribble a short note on the Penalty Charge Notice, as I want to send it off straight away, hoping the situation can be sorted out without me having to pay a fine. On my way to the post box I bump into my friend and her son. "Alright Portia?" She smiles and so does her son.

"Yes Garri I am, and how are you?"

"Bloody parking tickets!" I rage playfully about the ticket and her son laughs.

"Only you Garri" she laughs too.

"Do you want to race up to the post box?" Her son sets off running and I can't ignore the challenge.

"Yes I do!" I catch up and race him to the postbox just holding back a little to let him win, mind you he's only five! Never mind I can still outrun a five-year-old! Whoop! Whoop!

24th January 2007
Croydon Home

Cleaning my car is still challenging but it's good for me to keep active and get outside in the fresh air, so I reckon it's a good idea to try and clean it every week. It's like a workout and while I'm at it, I've also decided I'm gonna wash an elderly couple's car today. They nearly always park behind me, and sometimes we have a little chat while I'm busy cleaning. They joked last time that I should clean theirs too. They are so very friendly and I'm feeling well today, so it'd be a great surprise for them when they get back from their shopping trip in town to see their car nice and clean.

Looking out from my window later, I notice the couple get off the tram and head for their car. The look of surprise on their faces warms my heart! I'm smiling from the inside out, so delighted to make someone's day!

25th January 2007
Croydon Home

There is a firm *rat-tat-tat* on the inner door to my flat; it must be one of my neighbours, because no one else can get in from the main door. As I open it, to my surprise it's the elderly couple whose car I cleaned yesterday. "Hello." The lady says quietly and with a shy smile.

"Oh, hello, what you doing here?" I'm happy but surprised to see them.

"Thank you so much for cleaning our car dear, we brought you a packet of teacakes to go with your afternoon tea."

I smile in appreciation. "You didn't have to do that, I said I'd clean your car one day. I'm glad I could do it really, shows I'm getting better."

She looks across at her husband who is smiling too. "You did miss a bit though!" He jests, we all laugh together.

"Thank you, I'll enjoy these later. Have a good day."

"And you too dear."

Nice people!

26th January 2007
Croydon Home

Mobile ringing and showing an anonymous number on caller ID, but curiosity tells me to answer it anyway, even though I don't usually. "Hello?" There's a pause before it connects.

"Hello Garri, it's the Weekly Post* we just wanted a catch up to see if you're okay." I'm so shocked I can hardly say anything, "Yes thanks, I'm okay, bye." and I only just manage to keep a civil tongue! I hang up straight away struggling to stay levelheaded.

Unfortunately my mood dips, just like that! Perhaps I should have given them a piece of my mind. I feel the Tabloids have been exploiting me unashamedly and they even have the cheek to phone and ask if I'm okay; what are they thinking? The main culprits have been repeating the same old story over and over again about my past conviction! *'KMT'!"*

Let me not allow this to undermine me or bring me down. People have told me that my interviews helped calm the Nation by being a voice of reason in times of anarchy, they said it rippled around the world. I have to hold on to that. I received messages from all over the world saying my message was a shining light in the darkness and fear, that my positive energy renewed their faith. It really hurt when they knocked me, but this experience is making me stronger, wiser and more determined.

13th February 2007
Croydon Home

Flight booked to Jamaica in March to fulfil Mummy's last wishes, she always told me she wanted to go back Home and this feels like the right time to take her. Oh yes! One-stop Jamaica very soon! Ms Holness it's your time, I'm keeping my promise to take you home soon and I'm feeling happy to be alive again. Jamaica, Jamaica!

16th February 2007
Home Croydon

On the phone with TZ, discussing our trip to Jamaica!

"Yes my brother, weh yu ah sey"

"Yes Sugar I'm good to go you know, I need this holiday me bredrin."

"Kool noh TZ." I'm so happy he's coming with me.

"Sugar I got a link as soon as we get there, truss me." He seems excited.

"I'm on a one move still, my Mums ashes, got to drop them off at my Sisters."

"Big-man when you're doing your t'ings I'll be on da beach getting some rays; it's all good."

"One stop 'Yard' T. Ya done kno' Rudebwoy."

"Ya done kno' Sugar." We both start laughing; I'm determined to create better times!

5th March 2007
Home Croydon

It's the big day, my long awaited trip to the land of my ancestors! One-stop Jamaica and so excited I've done three separate checklists to make sure I've got everything. Good to go as the cabbie rings the buzzer right on time and I feel butterflies in my belly. I am going to visit my parent's island that I've heard so much about for so many years!

It seems fitting the cabbie is a Muslim guy, and he's very interesting. We talk life and politics and he opens my eyes to a few things. He moves on to the 7/7 Bombers, he despises them and goes on to explain about real Muslims, not extremists. He offers a completely different perspective on the Muslim community.

Anyway before I know it, we're at TZ's yard.

"TZ wha'ah gwaan, everything criss?" He comes out with his luggage.

"Everything criss my Lard." The cabbie gets out and opens up the car boot.

"Rudebwoy this cabbie's deep, truss me."

"What's he going on with?"

"Political affairs, seen!"

"Sugar, you're a joker man." My conversation with the cabbie continues all the way to Gatwick, while T just chills in the back probably daydreaming about chillin' on the beach.

After checking in we head for Security, before I get there I roll up my trouser leg so they can see my prosthetic leg and I glide straight through without any questions. As my hand luggage goes through X-ray, it crosses my mind they will spot the most precious cargo of all, the ashes. I can't put them in the cargo hold, it wouldn't feel right, so I just pray they get through. After collecting them on the other side we make our way past Duty Free, then TZ stops to buy some food. I'm excited, this is my first trip to the land of my ancestors, Jamaica here I come!

"Can passengers for Thomson Airways flight to Montego Bay Jamaica please go to departure gate 23, where your aircraft is ready for boarding."

"Okay T ah fi we time."

"Yeah man." We head for the gate like a couple of kids on an adventure!

On board the plane I manage to find a gap for my bag and calmly take my seat, I've flown before so I know what to expect this time. TZ is across the isle from me, we have space. As we take off, I settle in for the long haul, thinking of everything I've gone through and the important mission I'm on, taking my Mum back to Jamaica to be amongst her own. TZ must sense something, as he keeps looking over, concerned, eventually he leans over and asks, "Sugar, you alright?"

"Yeah, yeah." I answer quickly, no need for a fuss.

Four hours into the flight it hits me, I feel tearful about this mission, the loss of Mum and also my foot. The idea of taking my Mum's ashes to Jamaica with part of my own leg, to the land were she was born, in a place where she went to school and grew up, seems beyond belief. It's going to be hard to leave her there, but I must fulfil her wishes; at least there's a strange sense of comfort knowing part of me will always remain with her. Wow! I said that? It really is the end of an Era and I feel emotional, still I gotta stay focused on the task ahead. Closing my eyes I hear a little voice inside telling me to stay level by imagining the task ahead is already completed and it feels good.

When I open my eyes again there's a fantastic view to behold, my first sight of the beautiful island of Jamaica, surrounded by the Caribbean Sea with so many shades of turquoise blue, just as Mummy had described it. My roots are here in this truly awesome place! I can't wait to get off this plane and stand on my family's soil.

5th March 2007 Early Evening
Jamaica, Montego Bay Airport

We land safely, and I give thanks for that. "TZ we reach Jamaica safe and sound." I'm wearing the broadest smile.

"You done know Sugar… but are you alright?" He cocks his head to one side as if listening intently.

"Honestly bruv it's kinda dawned on me what I'm about to do, and I had a moment back there, but I'm okay now thanks."

"Sugar I've got respect for you man. Trust me your Mum would be proud of you." As the door opens the heat and humidity hits us full on, it's incredible. But wait!! I'm sweating already.

"Ih-eeah!"

Going through Arrivals is hectic, so crowded, and the Staff are so serious, which doesn't help the flow; a smile wouldn't go amiss. *KMT*, anyway my inner voice steps in.

'Relax Sugar you're here on a higher mission'. It keeps me in check. Finally we reach Passport Control and I show the young guy on duty my passport. "Hello sah, see my passport yah?" I smile, trying to be friendly, but he remains straight faced.

"Weh yu 'ave inna yu hand luggage?" He points at my bag.

"Just some documents an' my Mother's ashes." I smile again.

"Your Mother ashes, yu 'ave papers fi it?" He frowns.

"Weh yu sey, if me wha', 'ave papers? Papers fi da ashes?" I frown too.

"Yes sir, yu need official papers from your Government fi dat."

"Wat! I never know dat?" I'm astonished.

"Sorry sir, but yu kyaan pass through wid dat."

Now I have to do something, I'm not going to be stopped at the final hurdle. Rolling out my best Jamaican I try to reason with him. "Weh yu ah talk 'bout, ah me Mudda you kno', she born inna dis country and here wha' noh, me 'ave dem yah papers." Reaching into the side pouch of my holdall I pull out the front page of the South London Press covering my story at Mums' funeral, and her Death Certificate. I hand them to him,

"See wha' me go through inna my life, me kyaan leave me Mudda 'ere, me come from far, all me wan fi do is bury me Mudda inna her home town." He looks at the paper and looks at me again. "Bwoy, me feel yu pain, here what 'appen, me no see nuttin'." He pretends to look the other way with his arms folded. I have to smile Caribbean folks can be so endearing! "Well ah'right den, kool noh man, reespek!" I walk through quickly before he changes his mind.

"Yes big man do yu ting; 'member me noh see nuttin'." He shakes his head and cracks half a smile, still looking in the opposite direction, pretending not to see me. It's hilarious!

Smiling I wonder how I just got away with that! TZ's waiting a little way ahead of me in Arrivals, but looking back anxiously.

"Sugar what was that all about?"

"Mums ashes, my brother, he said I need proper official papers from the government to bring them through."

"What?" He looks shocked.

"Yes Rudebwoy." I calmly nod.

"So how you pass through then?"

"Come on T, you done kno' I got papers innit," I hold up the South London Press Cover. TZ roars with laughter.

"Sugar man, only you could get away wid dat, your Mum's watching over you, you know that?"

We reach baggage reclaim, and our luggage doesn't take long to come through. Then out to the arrivals hall where TZ's link Richie, is supposed to be meeting us. As we walk through we both look out for Richie, even though we don't know what he looks like. My eyes suddenly fall on a sign! *'Tony and Sugar England',* it's a handwritten note on a piece of A4 printer paper that Richie proudly holds on his chest, how funny!

"Yo Richie?"

"Yeah man!" Richie escorts us to his car, and chats to TZ all the way, while I'm quietly looking around taking it all in.

"Yo Tony weh you sey yu want?" Richie asks.

"Money exchange, phone sim, payphone card, the *Blessed.* You can do that for me Richie?"

"Yeah man simple t'ings dat." He nods and smiles.

Standing by the car outside the airport building, we look over to see the other passengers that came in on our flight, getting into the hotel minibus. It's a great sense of belonging to be here without feeling like a Tourist, I've come back to my roots and we are going to take the scenic route with one of the locals. That's how we do; we are ghetto yute's out to explore.

The strong Jamaican accents feel welcoming, bringing familiarity and a sense of warmth. Memories of Mum, Dad and my childhood flood in. We haven't even left the Airport yet and it's like a heavy weight has already been lifted off my shoulders. TZ jumps in the front seat next to Richie and I'm glad to chill in the back. The colourful shrubbery and tropical trees form dark silhouettes against the warm orange and yellow hues of the sunset, which lights up spectacular views of the mountains off into the distance.

Richie starts up the engine and he's off, like a Formula One Rally Driver, I hold on to steady myself, and sit back securely in the seat. He's really vocal as well as impatient, but he's confident and seems capable, lets hope! As we approach the hillsides around Montego Bay, I come to understand these roads aren't easy to drive on, especially at dusk. I catch a glimpse of the edge of the road and I'm shocked to see a sheer drop only a matter of inches from the wheels of our car. My stomach turns over; a mixture of excitement and sheer terror! But hey, I'm in the land of my ancestors so it's all good!

We pass through Trelawney, I always heard that name as a youth in Brixton, I imagined it to be just like Brixton, but I can't tell now cos even with the streetlights on it's suddenly very dark. We bypass Falmouth and join the Motorway. I'm surprised to find even the main roads are totally dark! So they have Motorways with no streetlights, really? All I see is cat's eyes in the centre of the road; so, this is Jamaica, very interesting. I'm like a sponge taking it all in. This country is deep man, the rawness, the natural beauty; I'm catching ah vibe.

Our driver Richie seems like he's just having a laugh, he hasn't taken his hand off the horn since we started and he's constantly cussing people. '*Beep, beep, beep,* move over!' That's all he's doing, he's cracking us up, then without warning he suddenly slams on the breaks! We've stopped outside a money exchange; I take a stroll, while they go inside. I can't help but notice the wonderful colours of the buildings and a few shops. The heat is pleasant causing a beautiful warm undercurrent, which is relaxing, even though the sun is down.

Currency exchanged, we leave for the Phone Shop, as a Jamaican phone sim is badly needed. Mobile shop found and we are hopeful they'll have a suitable sim. I go in with them this time; the temperature is still smouldering! Wow Jamaica, I'm filled with curiosity about the shops here, they look so colourful. As TZ gets his phone sorted I browse, this Mobile Shop is all right, it's got all the latest top of the range phones and music equipment, probably from the US. As I overhear TZ's conversation with the shop assistant I feel we're in the right place, she's very knowledgeable and helpful.

Hungriness starts biting my belly-bottom I need some food real soon!

"TZ, Richie unno ready fi move me hungry you see?"

Happy with his purchase TZ is ready to head back to Richie's car and his madness. *Beep beep beep!*

"Move noh' man!"

5th March 2007
Sunset Rio Grande Holiday Resort Jamaica

Two hours after landing in Jamaica we arrive safely at the Hotel and I am thankful. The other Passengers who were on our flight have now changed into lighter clothing and look more relaxed. They watch in surprise as we come strolling in so late, I smile at them and head straight for Reception.

"Good evening Sir may I help you?"

"Good evening," I hand him my documents, while he's checking our documents, I have a quick look around; it's a nice hotel.

"And what room will I be in?"

"Room number 716 on the seventh floor sir."

"What, 716 on the 7th Floor?" I can't believe it!

"Is that okay sir?"

"Yeah, yeah that's great thanks." My mind goes into overtime now with the number thing, I'm thinking sevens! 716 on 7th floor, first 7 then 1+6 = 7, then 7th floor 7/7/7! The London bombing 7/7/2005 2+5 is 7 7/7/7! That's freaky! Anyway we go up to the seventh floor, but we only have one room, I'm sure there's got to be a mix up, T and I sharing a room, no man! Even though the room is big though twin double beds with balcony, neither of us are comfortable sharing, that can't happen.

"T, I'm going downstairs to try a ting, must can get another room, soon come."

"Yeah man chat some lyrics Sugar. Do your ting Meng."

"Ok Antonio" we joke out the Scar face movie and laugh.

Without much effort at all another room is secured. I'm grateful for the Receptionist's help and I go back to tell T the good news.

"Oops there it is! TZ you have room 719 on the seventh floor. Twin double just around the corner."

"Seeeeen! You done kno' Sugar." He takes his stuff out of my room, and down the corridor to his room, privacy at last. I feel more relaxed and walk out onto the balcony to take in the view. I can see the swimming pool lit up below, and beyond that the flat calm sea meeting the star laden sky on the distant horizon. I hear Bob Marley, Buffalo soldier floating in on the wind from somewhere out of sight; I am at peace.

"I'm here, I'm in Jamaica Mum, yu hear me?" I look up at the stars.

Ah'right I had my moment, so now I go looking for TZ to explore, find food and unwind for the evening.

"TZ weh yu de?" We start at one end of the resort taking in the array of colourful shops, jazzy bars, fast food grills, posh dining rooms, relaxed games area, and swimming pools, then end up wandering off onto the white sandy beach for a leisurely smoke. If only I could bottle this moment, my first night in Jamaica. Taking in the view, where the sea meets the sky over the blue yonder!

6th March 2007
Sunset Rio Grande Holiday Resort Jamaica

I can't believe this breakfast selection it's fit for a King! 'I & I' is all-inclusive, oh yes! All the food looks more than delicious.

"T, I'm 'olding a porridge rude-bwoy, line the stomach."

He looks around at the feast for a moment, "Tru dat."

"Then we can hold a proper food."

"Come on Sugar man, I know how dis thing go, me ah tell you bout dem ting yah."

"You joker you don't know about dem food 'ere."

The oats porridge goes down a treat. TZ just laughs, as I leave him to go back again in search of some fruit. After filling my belly I return to my bedroom, pockets filled with fruit; I unload the cargo and grab a book to read by the pool. TZ takes in some sun on a lounger close by, and the day passes at a leisurely pace Caribbean style, as we relax and get in tune with the time line.

7th March 2007
Sunset Rio Grande Holiday Resort Jamaica

After breakfast TZ goes out sunbathing again, but I'm off to check out the gym. It's a small gym and basic, but it's got what I need. I take another look around to familiarise myself with the resort, until I pretty much know where everything is. I find a secluded little spot to sit under an old coconut tree on the beach and meditate; I'm feeling so much better.

8th March 2007
Sunset Rio Grande Holiday Resort Jamaica

After breakfast, I hit the gym and try to encourage TZ; he's having none of it. The gym although basic, is helping me keep me in shape. It's not what you've got, but how you use it. After the workout I eat some fruit and rest for a while before taking a shower and making my way to the beach to find TZ.

Wearing my shorts for the first time, as I stroll down to the beach, I can see people staring at my leg but I don't mind, I would look at me too. It's actually quite amusing, as the younger kids look baffled but I just smile and carry on. I find TZ and we chill out on the beach for a while, there's always something to eat, at any time and the drinks flow constantly day and night, but the punches are lethal man, they creep up on you unexpectedly; time for a nap under the sunshade.

After my nap, I go for a walk along the beach and it's wonderful to see the various stones, shells and pebbles in the water and on the sand; I pick a few up, taking in their smooth textures, the shapes, colours and sizes, then throw them into the sea. It's a great feeling to be walking, and especially walking along this beach, occasionally running away from the waves coming in so as not to get my trainers wet. Sensing someone looking at me, I turn to see TZ trying to get my attention, he's about to go on a jet ski. I make my way over to him and he hands me his phone and cash. I sit watching his antics when a tall man approaches smiling. "Jet skis me friend?" He smiles and shows me a leaflet.

"No thanks." I smile and look back at TZ.

"So why yu no waan spend money, yu must 'ave money man."

"Why do you say that?"

"Well look noh, yu lose yu foot, yu must get nuff money fi dat." He irritates me, so I get a little firmer putting my London accent aside. I've found it's quicker to communicate with the locals in Jamaican. "Yo sah, me noh waan go pon no jet ski." I step into my power, being assertive yet cool and calm.

"But, da Government must gi yu nuff money?" He still won't give up hassling me. Time to get heavy with this guy, who does he thinks he's talking to? "Yo! Mek me tell yu sum'ting." As I raise my voice, his friend who's standing close by pays attention as well. "First ting, no amount of money will gimme back me leg, second ting, di greatest gift in our existence is life, an' t'ankfully me 'ave dat. God give me a second chance. Thirdly, no amount of money can buy happiness; happiness is a state of mind! Yu hear weh me ah sey?" His friend looks with eyes wide open, and digs the first guy in the ribs with his elbow. "Come, dis man di pon ah higher level, yu can't talk to dem man yah."

I'm feeling satisfied, as the two of them walked off deep in discussion.

9th March 2007
Sunset Rio Grande Holiday Resort Jamaica

Usual routine, off to the gym, I'm gonna try skipping with a rope for the first time since I lost my foot. I start slowly, but then manage to get a rhythm going. As my confidence grows I make a plan to try a little run on the beach later in the week. Life is a challenge, but can also be seen as an adventure and I'm more than willing to participate. I feel I'm doing okay; my mojo is returning.

I really enjoy going for a walk late in the evening to look at the stars, smell the sea and think about life. Walking down the seafront I'm once again drawn to my spot under the old coconut tree to commune with the 'erb. 'Blazing the grade neatly' I feel at one with the Universe. After an hour or so I make my way back towards the hotel for late night snack.

In the queue for food, a middle-aged couple in front take an interest in me. I'm still in my own sacred space until the woman speaks and pulls me back into focus. "Excuse me, if you don't mind me asking, what happened to your leg?" Feeling relaxed I'm happy to share my story. She hangs on my every word and looks amazed, and when I finish he joins in too. "I've been watching you, and I'm really impressed by the way you walk and carry yourself, I'm Bob by the way and this is Irene." He smiles and his wife smiles too.

"Nice to meet you, I'm Garri."

"Yes Garri very nice to meet you also, you're an old head on young shoulders, I didn't even notice your leg at first, it was your smile I noticed as we walked past you. I said what a lovely looking young man, which made Bob turn to look at you. It was only then that we notice your leg. I told him we must stop you for a chat next time we see you. Anyway I agree with my husband you do walk really well, you're such an inspiration."

"Thank you! Thanks so much for your kindness."

"No, no thank you, it's been a pleasure talking to you."

"Enjoy the rest of your evening."

I head back to my room feeling light and remarkably content.

10th March 2007
Sunset Rio Grande Holiday Resort Jamaica

The Entertainments Team are rehearsing and putting the last touches together for the show later on. After watching for a while I'm tempted up on the Stage and grab the mic. I sing a duet with one of the Staff, having a laugh and enjoying the experience with no pressure. Afterwards it becomes apparent that some people must have heard us, as they stop me on the way past. "Hey Garri, are you gonna take part in the show tonight?"

"No, no mate, I was just having a laugh."

"Oh come on, that sounded good man." I back away quietly, knowing I'm not ready to sing in public yet.

Later in the evening the Events Coordinator approaches me smiling all over her face. "Hello sir, will you be singing with us tonight?"

"No thanks." I shake my head.

"I hear you can sing?" She says smiling and touching my arm.

"Yeah, yeah, but I'm not ready to take part."

Now pouting, she seems a little disappointed. "Ah, okay Sir what a shame, but I understand." She walks away, looking back every so often and smiling. I need to make a swift exit so go for a walk along the beach to meditate, but suddenly I feel like running, so I find an area of firm sand and start jogging, slowly at first and then it seems quite easy; I can do it! Oh yes I can! It's been a good confidence-building day today and I fall asleep feeling good.

11th March 2007
Sunset Rio Grande Holiday Resort Jamaica

My sister Toria arrives from Spanish Town to check me. We have some business to sort out and I've bought Mums ashes down from my room. There's an open plan seating area near the front desk with seats and tables, so we find a free table and get comfortable. "Sit down Sis, relax, weh drink you want? Any drink!"

"Yu can get me a soft drink?"

"Yu sure yu no want somet'ing lickle stronger."

Smiling, she shakes her head. "No man me ah'right, just get di soft drink fi me."

Leaving Mum's ashes with Toria, I go to order our drinks at the bar. Sipping several drinks slowly, we stay at the Hotel for a while having a chat, and my sister gives me a bag of fruit she brought from her garden. We decide to go for a walk outside the complex and into Ocho Town, before we leave, I take my bag of fruit up to my room.

I know the area already; it's like home from home! After walking for a while Toria says she's feeling hungry so we stop off for lunch together.

After ordering the food we sit at a table outside watching the world go by, 'Caribbean style'. I love the vibes here, proper feeling it, real life. I'm taking it all in, soaking up the essence of the environment. After we eat, I walk my sister to the bus station, which isn't too far; it's time for her to take Mum's ashes back home. "See you soon Sis phone me when you get there."

"Ah'right me lickle bredder, good to see yu, we will talk soon."

"Take care Sis and look after Mummy."

"Noh worry man, noh worry she de wid me." She nods and waves me to go, "G'wan." I smile and stroll slowly back towards the Hotel.

I feel so at ease, comfortable, at home, lost in my own world that I forget about my leg for a moment. However wearing shorts with my bionic leg in full view, brings on inevitable attention. Two women walk passed talking about me. "Him walk good eehh?" Her friend nods and they both smile looking back.

Next a guy walking towards me from the opposite direction catches my eye, raises his hand as he shouts, "Gwaan my yute!" He gives me a grin and we high five as we pass each other continuing to walk, without even looking back. I'm conscious other people are looking now.

Then two small boys, no more than seven or eight, pop up from nowhere, and in thick Jamaican accents, start questioning me.

"Wa'ppun to yu foot?" They frown looking worried.

"I lost it." I'm flippant.

"Nar man, yu kyaan lose yu foot." They pull faces at me as if I'm stupid and the smaller one cocks his head to one side in disbelief putting his hands on his hips, he's hilarious.

"I did yu kno'." I hold in my laughter, wondering what they'll do next.

"Da whole of da foot?" The taller one responds and bends down curiously to have a closer look at my leg.

"Yeah man da whole ah da foot."

"Tu'Rhaatid!" The smallest one exclaims, shaking his head and the other scratches his head pausing to think before he continues the inquisition. "How yu manage fi walk den?"

"Bionic foot my yute." I reply but they look totally unconvinced and actually reach down to touch my foot.

"But yu still 'ave yu foot?" They point at my shoe with broad smiles and make a face as if they've caught me out. I keep a straight face but I'm really dying to laugh.

"No man it gaan, it get blow off." They still seem unconvinced egging each other on even more.

"How yu mean yu get blow off sah?" The taller one looks at me intently raising his eyebrows, as the other continues to inspect up and down my leg.

"A bomb blow it off pon di train my yute." I raise my eyebrows and they gasp in horror. They look at each other then back at me in shock with wide eyes. The taller one shouts, "Bomb? Bumbaclot!" He puts his hand over his mouth.

"Ih-Eeah!" The little one joins in, and then they both stand perfectly quiet, hands over their mouths. The taller one quietly whispers, extending his words. "An yu still livin?"

"Yeah man, I'm still here!" No longer able to hold it in, I walk away chuckling so hard my cheeks hurt. What funny little kids.

Okay, so it's about time to relax in the sun, but as I approach the Hotel a black woman who was on our flight, gives me an obvious double take and stops. "Hello my name is Sue."

"Hi Sue, I'm Garri."

"Sorry to stop you Garri, but when I first saw you I thought you were just 'bopping along' I didn't realise you'd lost your foot."

I don't know what to say, so I just smile as usual, realising that for the first couple of days I wore long trousers, not wanting to draw attention to my leg.

Anyway as we talk she realises who I am, and already knows the whole story from the newspapers. "Garri keep your head up, you've been a true inspiration to millions don't you forget that. The bloody newspapers thrive off fear mongering, you was just too positive for them. Why did they turn against you? Maybe because you're black they conveniently forgot you're a victim of a terrorist bombing. I believe you still have the Lord's work to do on this Earth, and with that lovely smile you have, well, just keep smiling."

"Aw thanks Sue."

We reach Reception together and some Staff members start joking around with me. I've noticed they are so much warmer since I've been rolling out my Jamaican Patios. Pure jokes! Even Sue laughs at what goes on.

Using my London accent again, my conversation with Sue continues into the lift until she reaches the fourth floor, where she gets out. "Thank you so much for a great conversation Sue, enjoy the rest of your day!"

"I will, and *you* Garri take care," she hugs me.

I dwell a while on what Sue said and try to imagine what I could have achieved if the Press hadn't sabotaged me in such an ugly way. Still, everything happens for a reason and like Sue said, maybe God has a bigger plan for me. In a strange yet wonderful way I'm thankful about what happened, it's allowed me to discover who my true friend are. Those who could see beyond the headlines, those who know me!

Back in my room I delve into the bag of fruit my sister gave me earlier, I find three lovely ripe mangos and a huge coconut that whets my appetite. I've got to go down to the kitchen now to chop off it's head…

"Yo de big man! Chop dis fi me noh'." As I hand over the coconut to one of the Chefs in the kitchen, he pulls a curious face. "Ah weh you get dis?"
"Just kool noh man, me need a straw an spoon toh."
"Okay, right over da so." He points me to the spoons but frowns. "Yu' know dis coconut not s'pose to be in 'ere?"
"Kool noh sah, yu nuh see nuttin'." The Chef shakes his head smiling at my idea.

As I go in search of TZ drinking the delicious water from the coconut Toria brought me, I'm pretty sure I'll find him along the beach sunbathing. 'Dat bredda ah go black fi ah Greek yu see.' As I continue to walk along still wearing shorts, my bionic leg is still getting a lot of attention. An attractive woman catches my eye, I'm pretty sure she's Latino and a hot Latino at that! "Ello, 'ello, you're lookin' mighty fine, indeed!" I raise my eyebrows and smile at her.
"Aww thanks." She smiles back.
"You're welcome." As she walks off I can't help watching and thinking, Ih-eeahhhh dat woman look nice yu see. I'm getting braver!

I find TZ exactly where I thought he'd be, on the beach lying in the sun, so I take the seat next to him. "TZ what's good? Yu ah take in some rays?"
He opens one eye and looks up at me, "Yeah man, but wait Sugar, where you get the coconut?"
"Just kool man… I just see a hottie fink she's Latino."
"Wha' J-lo sister?" He wears a huge grin.
"Did you see her?"

He nods enthusiastically, "Yeah I saw her, did you get her digits though?" He sits up on his lounger.

"I wish!"my smile widens as I remember her, "So fine!"

"Easy Sugar."

I finish the coconut and decide to go for a walk, "T you're browned off already! Come we take a walk outside, check out the market."

"Tru dat," he gets up "Come we go Sugar, I need some high grade."

"Kool noh me bredrin, tek time."

We go off the complex and towards the market. The backdrop here is unbelievable, good thing I've got my camera with me. It looks like an oil painting; I have to stop to take pictures, the colours around me are so bright and vibrant. I stand on a bridge leading to the market capturing the beauty of the surrounding area, the clear blue skies above, the luscious greenery, the mountains in the distance, the partially dried out lake in front and the sun glistening on the remaining water; heaven!

As we carry on walking a guy approaches TZ pestering for money. I sense he's making TZ feel uncomfortable, so I get involved. "Yoh! Ah my bredrin dis, kool noh!" he pays me no mind so I step in between him and TZ and screw up my face at him, "Yoh big man back off noh!" The brother backs off straight away thankfully, but we've not even reached the market yet and the hassle has already started! As we walk through the market it's a full on frenzy as everybody attempts to sell us their stuff first. "Come 'ere, come 'ere man, come. 'Ow much money yu'wan spend?"

"Nothing thanks, me just ah look."

"Wha' typa ting yu ah look fah? Who ya'ah buy it fah?"

"Me ah browse fi see weh yu 'ave, maybe sum'ting will catch my eye, an' me ah come back t'morrow, seen?"

Jamaicans are interesting people, their intonation and the way they speak may sound loud and appear aggressive if you don't know them, but they aren't like that at heart. Really they are kind and helpful, when you understand how they express themselves. Even a joke can sound aggressive to the uninitiated!

After walking through the market, we head downtown looking for the Blessed. We see a likely source in the distance, five or six guys on a corner drinking, smoking and playing dominoes! As we approach, they all stop and look up suspiciously.

I whisper discreetly to one. "Yo we ah look for di blessed yu 'ave 'im?" he smiles, relaxes and nods.

"Yeah man we 'ave him, weh yu ah look fah?" TZ takes over the conversation with him and finally they shake on a deal.

"Mek me just finish off da hand, dun off dem bwoy yah."

We stand watching for a while. They are totally animated, slamming the dominoes on the table, cussing loudly at each other and sometimes they slam them down so hard the dominos fly up and fall on the floor! Then they lean down to pick them up and quickly slam them back down on the table, to the onlooker it looks like full-on battle!

Suddenly the Top Shotta takes a deep breath and leans back in his chair full of confidence. He pauses for affect looking around the table at his rivals and smiles at us, his audience. "Ah me ah di King yu kno'," he says tapping his chest, "Me run dis, watch how me lock down dis game yah!" He leans forward again fully animated and slams his last four dominoes down, sliding them into position in quick succession without bothering to look up. "See it yah, Key Domino mi friend, who unno ah try test, *KMT*."

One of the others answers, "Wah! Ah so you ah gwaan Bredrin!"

There's a lot of muttering, dissecting of the game, cussing and slamming of palms on the table, but he wins fair and square!

Business quickly concluded we head back to the Hotel. On the way back we bump into the same guy who was pestering TZ on the way out, this time I just have to look at him and he moves away fast. As we pass by a derelict shop, a bag of rubbish in the doorway moves. As I look closer it look's like a man, no, two people! Tu Rhaatid! I thought I was seeing duppy. This must be the Jamaican homeless, it didn't occur to me; I had no idea!

Almost back at the Hotel I remember I meant to pick up a Tenor Saw CD in the market, I must find Tenor Saw.

"Yo TZ I forgot the music hut in the market, got to check it out, yu ah come?"

"Bwoy I'm going back to put down this ting."

"Ah'right, me soon come."

I go back to the music hut and find an Elder Man chilling outside with his head down, his face completely hidden beneath a mass of long dark locks as he subtly and rhythmically moves his slim body to the beat of the music streaming out from his stall. As I approach he looks up and grins, parting his lips to show flashes of gold in his teeth, his face wise and weathered with a few silver roots escaping from the locks at his temples.

"Yes Fardah how it ah go, yu 'ave any Tenor Saw?"

His eyes light up at my question, his voice gravely as he speaks in a gruff Jamaican accent. "If me have Tenor Saw? Yes my yute, see it yah! T'ree dollar. What else yu want, me 'ave him."

"Dennis Brown, Al Campbell?" I ask.

He acknowledges nodding confidently. "Yeah man me 'ave dem man de yes. Listen, 'ere weh me ah go do fa yu. Wan ol' skool compilation, seen? Me ah fling in some Freddie McGregor, Sugar Minnott, Beres Hammond, Yamma Bola, Jnr Reid an' some more." He smiles seeming pleased with his plan and it sounds perfect to me; I can't wait!

"Yeah man, me can come fa dat t'morrow?"

"Yeah man." Still nodding in agreement.

"Reespek Fardah, any time?"

"Yeah man yu criss, any time after ten."

"Ah'right lickle more Don."

I'm well pleased with my Tenor Saw CD and the many more unexpected tracks to follow tomorrow.

On the way back from the market, I clock a hairdresser opposite the hotel and it reminds me I really need to re-twist my hair, so in I go. A pretty mixed race woman, perhaps Caribbean and Chinese is standing near the till in a red flowery dress with a full skirt. Her natural hair pulled tightly back in a high ponytail.

"Excuse me, would you be able to re-twist my hair?" I ask, bending forward to show her my head.

"Come lickle closer, mek me see yu 'air." She runs her fingers through my hair to check it and smiles. "Yeah man, me kan do it."

"How long will it take and how much?"

"Bout hour n half, me 'ave fi wash an' blow dry it. An' because yu cute, just gimme fifteen Jamaica Dolla."

I smile back and pop in a Jamaican phrase. "So weh yu ah sey, ten o'clock tomorrow?"

She cocks her head to one side and looks at me grinning as she takes it in. "Yeah man dat al'right." Giggling, she watches me intently as I leave the shop. I look back and smile again; she's still watching curiously.

12th March 2007
Sunset Rio Grande Holiday Resort Jamaica

Oats porridge, scrambled eggs with two slices of toast, various fruits and a cup of hot water, great way to start the day. Then I take a slow walk down the beach, to gather my thoughts before hitting the gym.

12th March 2007 10:00am
Hairdresser's

Pure jokes, they chat so fast I can't catch all of it, but picking up body language and facial expression I can understand a lot of what's being said. There's an older man with a bundle of DVD's sitting on a chair near the door, and he's watching 'Shottas' on his portable player. I yell out to him from the hairdresser's chair. "Yo sah! Me ah look fi ah copy of 'Shottas' yu 'ave 'im?"

"How yu mean big man, see it yah. Fresh, wid new soundtrack." He waves the bundle of DVD's at me smiling.

"Reespek Fardah. How much fi it?"

"Just gimme ah change man."

"Well alright!"

When my hair is fixed up, I'm good to go. "Thank you!" I pay the hairdresser and the DVD man, then taking my new DVD I move on to the market to get my music.

Finding the Music Man sitting outside near his stall. "Yes I... yu 'ave him?" I'm starting to feel like a local here.

"Yes my yute, see it yah another Tenor Saw an' two bad boy compilation wid Bob Marley, Peter Tosh, Freddie McGregor, Al Campbell, Dennis Brown, Sugar Minott an' nuff more; ah you dis." He hands me the package.

"How much fi dat?'

"Call it twelve Jamaican Dollar."

"Reespek Farda." I give him fifteen. He checks it and puts it in his pocket with a half grin on his face. "Yeah man, any time yu inna di area, come link me. Guidance."

Just as I step out of the market, TZ strolls up.

"TZ come we go little further into the ghetto. We noh de pon no tourist t'ing."

"True dat Sugar, come we go." I lead him beyond the market and we find top grade 'erb, and a bar to have a drink. Jamaica nice!

13th March 2007
Walking Ocho Rios Jamaica

Out and about again, I catch the eye of a light skinned middle-aged man sitting on his veranda, looking directly at me. I smile, but he looks serious. He stands up and holla's over at me, his voice strong and clear, and a little abrupt. "Yo man, come yah." "How yu mean, come yah? Ah me yu ah talk to?" I say light-heartedly, wondering what he wants. He seems harmless enough, medium height with short dark curly hair, his belly slightly overhanging the waistband of his shorts. He stares at me curiously. "Yeah man, come yah, you know sey da whole of us ah watch yu? Watch how yu ah walk up and down like its nu'ting, yu ah move good big man. If yu 'ave on long trouser, yu not even kno' sey yu lose yu foot! 'Ow yu manage fi lose yu foot?" I thought it was about my leg and I'm prepared. I decide to tell my story.

An audience of about fifteen to twenty people gather around listening in. I feel like the village storyteller. Their energy rises and falls and some express their emotions. "Ih- Eeah!" They hang on my every word fully focussed. Listening intently, no one interrupts, until occasionally there's an outburst of surprise such as "Oh Jesus!" or "Lawd 'ave mercy," and "Backside!" It makes me chuckle. "De greatest gift in life, is life itself and me have dat. I'm here tru' di grace of God. So me kno' me de yah fi a reason." When I finish, there's a short silent pause until several men start reasoning about what I've been through. One guy touches my shoulder as he speaks."It wasn't yer time." Another agrees, "Yu 'ere weh me ah tell yu, it wasn't yer time Jah kno'."

"Yeah man, how yu mean, yu de yah fi ah reason, yes?"

"My Don! You know sey, ah some big blessing you get, Jah know!"

Then the first man who called me over speaks again. "Twenty-six people dead 'round you bumbaclot! And yu still de yah, yu 'ave ah higher purpose! Truss me pon dat." He looks reflective.

Then a younger guy adds, "Yoh Sah! Yu sey anytime, you de ah Jamaica. Anytime, any place, any where and yu want anything, see my cell number yah, call me an' me will give yu ah link, cos yu blessed big man, yu see me ah sey?" He hands me his number and I put it in my pocket smiling, "Hey listen noh', me 'ave fi mek ah move, lickle more."

"Yes Don man, do yu ting, guidance and protection, Jah Rastafari!" I walk away looking back at the small gathering waving me a fond farewell.

I feel honoured about the assembly as I head back to the Hotel, but before I get very far it suddenly gets darker and darker as the clouds gather. 'Rain ah come!' Within seconds the downpour of warm straight-down rain baptises me. Walking in the rain never felt so good! I feel reborn and blissfully purified. Yes true healing for me both mentally and physically and this warm liquid sunshine tops it off. I'm in a very good place.

13th March 2007
Sunset Rio Grande Holiday Resort Jamaica

As I step out of the lift on the seventh floor a strong smell of high-grade from across the way hits me 'TZ is in da house.' I laugh to myself. After a rest I head out to the beach for my late evening walk, through the foyer and bar area, and passed a few members of staff, who start bantering with me as usual.

"You smell sweet eehh, what type ah cologne yu 'ave on?" She leans in to have a sniff.

"Unforgettable! P. Diddy" I chuckle kinda knowing what's coming next.

"Lef' it fi me noh?" She smiles.

"It's man's aftershave." I try to put her off.

"Me kno' business."

"Ok when I'm leaving I'll give you what's left in the bottle."

"Mek sure yu kno." I'm still chuckling.

I kick back on the beach under the coconut tree at my spot overlooking the sea. This is my quiet little spot on the beach away from everyone. My place to commune with the sand, the sea and the stars above, time to reconnect; time to mediate. I feel free, like more weight has been lifted off me today, and it feels good. There's a sense of belonging and peace within. You know when you have found peace within; it doesn't seem to matter what time it is.

On the way back to my room I notice there's still a lot going on, entertainment, singers, dancers and comedians. There are also nightclubs in the complex and because it's spring break, it's packed with Americans from high school having fun. Anyway it's time for bed, the end of a very good day and I'm so looking forward to going to St. Mary tomorrow in search of my roots. My Mum was born in St. Mary and I'm pretty sure I'll find relatives still living there. I must remember to book a cab before I go up.

14th March 2007
Sunset Rio Grande, Ocho Rios Jamaica Holiday Resort

It's a lovely morning so I get into my shorts and out for my first ever

Above
Mum and I at a family event, 1996

Right
Toria, my sister in the Eighties

Left
Mum's funeral, August 2005

Above - Brother Tony proudly leads funeral procession, August 2005
Below - Releasing doves with my brothers at the funeral

Above - After burying Mum's ashes with the ashes of my leg, Jamaica 2007
Below - Training with the Paralympic Squad for 2012 Games, 2011

Left - King's Cross Station - a minute silence, 2005

Right - Shaking hands with Kenneth Olisa the first black Lord Lieutenant of Greater London, 2015

Below - Meeting Prince William at the 10 Year Memorial, 2015

swim in the Caribbean Sea. Mummy always told me its healthy bathing in seawater, especially in Jamaica, I'm psyched up and ready to go for it. The sun and sea will definitely help my skin heal from the wounds the bombing has left on me.

I look for somewhere not too far from the sea to sit down and take off my leg. I find a perfect spot where I can get in easily, but far enough away so my leg won't get wet when the waves come in. People watch me shuffling along the sand on my bum, using my arms to drag myself towards the sea. I guess it's an unusual sight, so I can't blame them for staring. Moving closer and closer to the water, I turn to face the sea putting my legs in front. The waves push against me as I edge in deeper and I do my best to stand up using the buoyancy of the deeper water to support me. Finally I just let go and swim out, splashing and feeling free, it's truly amazing, although it doesn't taste very nice! Looking back at my bionic leg laying on the sand, I remember the little jog along the beach I did on Saturday night and the memory of it uplifts me. I spend some time just floating on my back, looking up at the bright blue sky and enjoying my first ever experience of being in the sea. After a while I swim towards the shore as far as I can into the shallows until I ground my body on the sand, then I start sliding along the beach towards my prosthetic leg. I reach out to grab my towel…

7th July 2005
London Kings Cross Underground

Suddenly it's dark and I'm sliding through dismembered dead bodies as I haul myself along with wet sticky hands. The deathly silence is overpowering and my stomach churns, there's a nauseating taste in my mouth and I freeze.

14th March 2007
Sunset Rio Grande Holiday Resort Jamaica

I close my eyes and shake my head, somehow trying to reboot my brain. A sudden rush and it's daylight again, but I'm trembling as I recall this nightmare scene. I manage to snap back and reach for my towel to dry my hands. I don't know if dragging myself along triggered this experience, or because my hands are wet, but it caught me totally off guard and I don't like the feeling of being out of control. The mind is a funny thing and I have to acknowledge that although I feel good being here, I'm still deep in healing and these *flashbacks* are part of the process. At least I managed to bring myself out of it quickly this time; perhaps I have gained a little control.

Strolling down the beach to meditate most nights with 'a little strapped one' may be teaching me to deal with the dark corridors of my mind? Anyway, thoughts of the cabbie due to collect me soon brings me quickly back to centre, as I rush to get ready for the exciting day ahead.

14th March 2007
In The Taxi

We drive to Richmond and pass through Highgate, then through a few more Districts while I take in the scenery. Stalls along the roadside, sell everything from woodcarvings to Bob Marley t-shirts; from breadfruit to oranges and mangoes, it's a sight to behold. We pass by Port Antonio Prison, into Louisburg along Kendal Road, which is lined with mango and coconut trees as far as the eye can see! It's like a dream seeing places I heard about when I was a kid, and now being able to put colour and scenery into the stories is awesome! Suddenly the cabbie shouts out of his window to a man on a hill beside the road. "Bigga!"

The man looks round, "Yoh me boss!"

"Wha' ah gwaan?"

"Me just de yah." He stops the car and I get out of the cab to have word with this local guy, as we chat I suddenly realise that he is 'The Bigga' Mummy talked about, which means we're related. I'm putting faces to names as Mummy's stories come to life in a lovely way.

We continue driving some 200 yards further, when a man with weathered skin and white hair comes into view holding a massive machete! I would be shocked if this was London, but I know they use these in Jamaica, for chopping sugar cane etc. The cabbie shouts at him too. "Yu know any ah di 'Olness family?"

"Yeah man, me ah 'Olness yu kno'." He's nodding.

"Wha'?" I get out of the cab again, he's a Holness too, amazing!

"Me busy right now, but 'ere weh yu do, turn da car round an' folla di road straight, nuh tek left, nuh tek right, go straight into Louisburg, yu will see wan Clinic. Miss 'Olness runs da Clinic, she must kan 'elp yu." He points in the direction we must go.

"Thank you Sah." I shake his hand and get back in the cab.

"'Member straight, nuh come off di road." He points again and we drive off in that direction.

When we arrive there's a woman sitting outside the clinic, and I figure this must be her, so I get out to ask. I explain who I am and she tells me she's Maureen Holness, one of my first cousins, we are overjoyed to meet, she remembers Mummy so well her Father was my Mum's brother. Now I really feel at home! As we talk we share a weird coincidence; she has also had her left leg amputated, but hers taken above the knee. Wow! What are the chances? I can't believe it!

We sit together for a while discussing life and our history. This is definitely, one of the special days in Jamaica, seeing so many family members I've heard about but never met before. It's magical to be walking along the same roads that Mummy did, it's like going back through time; truly a blessing that brings me a much better understanding of the way Mum was bought up in this environment; and I've found my roots!

After freshening up I'm ready to go back to the Hotel, so we say goodbye and the cabby starts the engine. "Okay my Don, one stop Ocho." The cabbie smiles and pulls away, as he looks in the rear view mirror at me quizzically.

"Yu ah'right son?"

"Yeah man, me ah'right."

"Me ah put on some music fi yu?" He plays Beres Hammond.

"Tank yu sah." I sit back and chill singing along♪ *"Who sey dat big man don't cry…"* as we start on the long drive back to Ocho. By the time we finally reach the Hotel, I've already replayed my mini adventure several times in my head. I pay the cabbie and thank him dearly for his hospitality, so he hands me his business card; I'll certainly book him again. What a day!

14th March 2007
Sunset Rio Grande Holiday Resort Jamaica

I need to savour my day, so go straight up to my room to be alone. When the lift door opens on the 7th floor the pungent smell of Sensemilla hits me, TZ's such a joker, he's at it again! I go straight to my room as I just need to sit down and think through the day, starting with this morning's first ever swim in the sea, to seeing part's of my family I've only heard of and the uncanny coincidence of my cousin's leg. Today was deep man, what a day, what an extraordinary day!

Quickly out of my clothes I run a bath while sorting out what I'm gonna wear for dinner. '*Knock, knock, knock*' but wait, who's that knocking down my door?

"Hello, hello! Hotel Security, hello Security here, open up please!" I wonder what they want. "Yeah, hold on a minute man, I'm not dressed." I pull on some shorts and open the door. A couple of big guys face me and TZ is behind them with a sorrowful look on his face. "Do you know dis man?" He points at TZ frowning.

I lift my head in acknowledgment. "Yeah, he's my bredrin."

"Where yu documentation dem?" The overpowering smell of Sensimilla sets off alarm bells in my head as it dawns on me, they must have raided TZ for the weed. "Here you go." I hand them my Passport and holiday documents. By now they're in my room giving it the once over, nothing found. So they start on TZ again.

"Yu kyaan smoke no weed in 'ere, it illegal." They don't look happy.

"No! It's legal here innit?" TZ protests his innocence.

"No man it illegal! And anyway how comes ah small man like yu ah smoke so much weed?" TZ grimaces as they give him a written warning to sign; he signs the papers and they leave taking his weed with them.

"Sugar man they took all me weed y'know, I'm pissed man."

"Big man go on better than that, you're too hot."

"But Sugar the weed sweet me, you see." He smiles, trying to win me over.

"About the weed sweet you, *KMT!*"

"Kool noh, we de ah yard, me bredda, me 'ave fi sample the proper tings, seen?" Laughing.

"What did you tell them anyway?"

"I thought it was legal blud." He raises his eyebrows trying to play the fool.

"You're a joker you know. Only you!"

"So, how was your day Shuggs?"

"Yeah man all good, but me and you will chat a likkle more, I need a bath now and it's ready and waiting."

"Seeen!" He leaves for his own room and looks back, but I have to say something more to him, "Don't mek dem catch yu again." He gives me the thumbs up.

I close the door shaking my head in disbelief on my way to the bathroom. Easing myself into the bath slowly after propping my leg up against the wall, I relax back to soak and it feels good. As I look down, I'm faced with the blank space where my leg used to be. I ponder on it for a while, I don't usually as there's no point to feel sorry for myself. I just have to stay positive and be practical, so I get on and wash my leg sock as I do every time I have a bath, leaving it to dry for the next day. If I don't rotate the socks they smell and I hate that smell. I start to wonder why I hate it. It's a strong word hate, why hate it? Since the Bombing, I've become very sensitive to smells, especially of sweat on rubber or plastic, it takes me back underground and is a constant reminder of the 7/7 nightmare. After bathing I dry off and hop to my bed so I can cream my body. Twin double beds make life easy as I can spread out my clothes on one and relax on the other.

Once dressed it's time to find TZ to go for dinner and a walk down to the beach. We chat about my day and he's pleased for me.

15th March 2007
Sunset Rio Grande Holiday Resort Jamaica

I've booked the same cabbie again today to visit my sister in Spanish Town and right on cue the phone rings." Yeah,'ello."

"Mawning Mr Holness yu cab is 'ere."

"Tank yu fi dat, me soon come."

I arrive downstairs pretty sharpish not wanting to keep him waiting. We greet each other and it's good to know he's someone who seems to enjoy helping me reconnect with my roots.

As he drives, I take in the scenery. I can't get over the beauty of this country as we drive from district to district. When it's time to stop off for a drink, I get out to stretch my legs and take plenty of photos, taking in the realness of Jamaica. It's still some distance to my sisters but the sun is revitalizing. I can just imagine what it would be like living here. Before long we're back in the car and the journey continues, it's taken longer than it should have, because we've taken a few wrong turns, but I don't mind it's part of the adventure and he's a nice guy.

15th March 2007
Spanish Town Jamaica

I see my sister Toria outside in front of the house using a stick to pick mangoes from a massive mango tree; we pull up along side. "Yo big sis, yu kno' weh you ah do." I call from the car window taunting her.

"Ah who dat ah ask, if me kno' weh me ah do." She yells back laughing.

"Den ah kno' your lickle bredda."

"Ah my tree and me kno' weh me ah do, you kno see me 'ave me stick, mind me noh lick you wid it." We laugh together as we all enter the house; the cabbie asks to use the toilet before he leaves.

It's so great to see my sister again and especially at her yard in Jamaica, she gives me the Grand Tour. My niece and her daughter are inside so we sit chatting for a while until my nephew Steve walks in. "Yes Uncle Garri, wha'ah gwaan?" he shakes my hand.

"Den me noh de yah ah gwaan."

"What ah weh yu sound like ah Jamaican." He's surprised.

"Den kool nuh man, Jamaica inna me Blood."

"So weh yu wan fi do Uncle, come we go ah di Mall in ah Kingston?"

"Yeah man, how you mean."

Steve and I drive a few miles to Kingston in his car and it's good to visit places with family, and not as a Tourist. "Yeah man yu car drive nice, ah so yu ah move, Stevie Wonder."

"Well me ah try ah 'ting Uncle, come we go inna di shop dem." We browse around a few clothing shops, nothing really takes my fancy, so we do a bit of food shopping before heading back to my sisters for dinner.

Toria serves up salt fish, run down, renta yam, green banana and roast breadfruit, washed down with yard style lemonade, ah so we grow! Wow! Imagine this I'm at my sister's yard in Jamaica eating dinner. I'm actually sitting with my sister at the same table in Jamaica; Mummy would be so happy. I look over and see Toria crack a smile with a far off look in her eye."Wha' ya' ah 'tink 'bout?"

"If Mum could see us now, Ih-eeah!"

"I know Sis, I was thinking di exact same ting." We both smile.

"Her first born and her lickle washbelly together after so long."

After dinner we browse through some old photos and reminisce. It's great to see the family and how some things have changed and some have stayed exactly the same. "Mek me go an pick a coconut noh." I love fresh coconut water.

"Den gwaan noh." My sister leads me to the back of the house, where there's a small goat munching on the grass and several chickens running around. It's such a surreal moment in time as I look around for the coconut tree in her garden. I can't quite reach the coconuts, but I manage to clamber on top of an old crate so I can reach up easily to get one down, and I'm very pleased with myself.

We talk a lot more before it's time to leave and before I go my sister hands me a bag of goodies to take with me. We say our goodbyes and I take in the vibe, there's a connection, a sense of family and love. The ashes are here now and I get a sense of security. Part of me just doesn't want to leave this place, and it won't, my ashes are staying. As I look around the neighbourhood, I notice the other houses along the dirt road and a huge unfinished property opposite.

When it's time to go, Steve and his Wife drive me back down to my hotel, we have to go through Fern Gully and across Flat Bridge on the way. This bridge is infamous and not only is it flat, as the name suggests, but it's apparently haunted. My nephew explains that when it rains the road is closed as the river runs right over the top of it and quite a few people have been killed there. Some of these Caribbean roads are not easy and there are various myths about the bridge being haunted and cursed, even one about a Mermaid who lives under the bridge and grabs people as they cross at night-time. Some of the locals dread to cross it once it's dark and won't even attempt it without praying first.

Anyway, it's been a brilliant day today connecting with my family, and my history makes perfect sense to me now. We don't find the Mermaid at Flat Bridge, and arrive at the hotel safe and sound.

15th March 2007
Sunset Rio Grande Holiday Resort Jamaica

After we say our goodbyes, I head straight out to my coconut tree on the beach and lie down underneath, it's peaceful and quiet here. Looking up at the leaves with their wondrous array of colours and shapes I feel free and at peace with the Universe. Time to meditate, I light up and drift off!

May 2005
Dulwich Care Centre Nursing Home London

I catch my first glimpse of Toria, my sister, sitting with her back to me on Mum's bed in the nursing home as I walk in. I watch her for a second or two taking in that she's my sister, before I sit opposite without saying a word. I can't help staring as she interacts with our Mum, I'm so glad she's here. The resemblance is uncanny, just like a younger version of Mum. Bloody hell, my sister in front of me now for the very first time! I catch her gaze as she moves off Mum's bed and sits back on a chair facing me.

"Al'right sis?" I smile.

"Garri weh yu ah look pon me so fa?" I'm taken aback.

"What weh you sey?"

"Yu 'ear me."

"Hey Mummy, Mummy, she trying to rough me up." I'm directing the fun at Mum, who is looking so peaceful propped up on pillows in her bed, and then a little wry smile appears on her face.

"Yu stay deh." Toria retorts.

"You know what, I'm thinking how much you and Mum look alike." I just have to say it.

"Den ah noh me Mudda." She cracks a half smile.

"Mummy she bright, eehh." In the midst of our laughter and teasing Hector walks in closely followed by Tony. This is a first, all of us together in one place! "Mummy Holness you never thought you'd see this day innit?"

"Leave 'er be an' mek her rest." Toria interjects.

"Kool noh big sister."

Even though Mum can't really talk, I want her to be involved with us all. She's not seen my sister for some twenty odd years, which is a long, long time. I feel it's good for her if I joke around, to overcome any awkwardness there might be. I so want my sister to feel welcome. Looking at her is like looking at Mum as a younger woman, it's amazing!

15th March 2007

Sunset Rio Grande Holiday Resort On The Beach

I become aware something hot drifting across my face, I wipe it off and open my eyes to check where its coming from. "Rhaatid, ah di ashes from da 'erb', time to hold some zed's Rudebwoy!" I make my way to bed, the end of an awesome day!

18th March 2007

Sunset Rio Grande Ocho Rios Jamaica Holiday Resort

I decide to spend the last few days of my holiday doing some of the tourist things in the hotel complex. After watching the Arsenal v Everton game on Sky, I'll take in some of the in-house entertainment. They're teaching the holidaymakers how to dance the 'butterfly' and 'dutty wine' and inevitably they try to involve me, but I'm still not having any of it. I go in search of TZ to catch some sun on the beach.

19th March 2007
Sunset Rio Grande Ocho Rios Jamaica Holiday Resort

Up early to have a relaxed breakfast, before we travel home today. Strap a little one and link TZ; he's already got a fat one strapped from his reload. I can't believe it; he's really taking liberties, even after he's been warned about it, he's going all out on the last day! We go for a pleasant walk on the beach to finish up, Jamaica, peace out until next time! We order a cab, one stop Sangster Airport Montego Bay.

On the way to the Airport the cabbie plays some wicked tunes.

"Dat CD yah ah play wicked, mek me buy it off yu noh."

"It ah di only one me 'ave wid dem tune yah."

"Okay no problem." I smile, even though I'm disappointed, I'll always remember this journey the vibes are nice and the CD would have been the icing on the cake, but never mind. As we reach the Airport, the cabbie helps with our suitcases, I pay him and leave a nice tip and he looks pleased, "Yo! Big man 'old dis." The cabbie hands over his precious CD.

"Weh yu ah sey?" I can't believe it.

"Gwaan with dis man."

I take the CD smiling. "Reespek Fardah, reespek in every aspect." He breaks a smile too, showing broad white teeth with a gap at the front. "Likkle more."

Montego Bay check-in is such a commotion! TZ gets through okay, but the 'eagle-eye' ground staff lady starts on me as soon as she sees my leg.

"Tek off yu foot." She points at me.

"Excuse me you want me to take off my prosthetic leg so you can search it?" I'm shocked.

"Yes! 'cos yu could ah carry anyt'ing inna it."

"*KMT!*" My mouth falls open and I'm speechless. I'm not even gonna try to answer this woman. I look round for someone else to reason with. An older woman in a uniform sitting down about fifty yards away catches my eye. As I look at her she beckons me over. "Come 'ere."

"Hello Miss."

"Noh mind her yu 'er, wha' ah happen to yu foot?"

We have quite a long conversation; I briefly mention my mother, and all that happened to me. I can see she's deeply moved.

"De next time yu come ah Jamaica, mek sure yu come see me first. Yu 'ear? Me ah boss fi dem."

"Oh yeah definitely. Thanks." I'm relieved and reboot my smile.

"An 'ave a good trip yu 'ear son."

"Yes I will, and tank yu Mummy."

I catch up with TZ at Departures and feel the need to rant.

"T, some woman wanna give me trouble, bout I must take off my foot, *KMT*! She's lucky I never cuss a bad word." I'm still a little irritated.

"Kool Sugar man, don't mek the woman upset your holiday"

"Ah true dat, Rudebwoy." I see sense, he's right.

"At dat me ah sey Sugar."

"Come we ah go."

While waiting, we notice a group of Monarch Air Staff looking over at us. Then our flight is announced.

"Monarch Airlines Flight to London Gatwick is ready for boarding." We get on board and settle down.

"Hello Sir, my colleagues and I were just discussing whether we knew you, as your face is very familiar. Are you Garri from the London Bombings?"

"Hmm I saw you lot staring at me before and wondered what was going on." I frown playfully shaking my head.

"Well, are you Garri?"

"Yes it's me." I smile, "but shh!"

They are so kind with their words and compassion towards me and we get lots of freebies for the journey. I feel like a bit of a celebrity and TZ also gets a 'bring in'.

After a while I become the focus of a playful stare from a woman across the aisle from me. It's one of the woman who wanted me to sing on stage in the hotel, she keeps teasing me. It's fun and passes some time. Actually it turns out that quite a few people on the flight out to Jamaica knew about my story, but I didn't realise it until I spoke to them at the hotel; now we're all going back together, like one big happy extended family. Nice little vibe on this plane.

It's a bit of a downer arriving back into England on a cloudy grey day. Everything out of the window seems grey, the vehicles, trees, landscape, the roads, what a stark contrast to Jamaica. All the colours are washed out.

"Fasten your seatbelts we are now approaching London Gatwick." Finally! I can't wait stretch my legs.

20th March 2007 7:00am
London Gatwick England

"TZ wake up my yute." I prod his shoulder lightly to wake him.

"Wha' ah gwaan?" He opens one eye.

"We reach, fix up yourself!"

"Seeeen!"

Passport and documents at the ready, we pass through Arrivals, one stop baggage reclaim. As we walk and talk I feel reborn, spiritually, my soul and my aura feel different. I feel energised, despite the grey day in London. After a short wait for our luggage to come around the conveyor belt we sail through Customs. On the way out to the passenger pick up point I catch sight of the cabin crew. TZ and I thank them for their hospitality and kindness. Still engrossed in conversation, I hear TZ shouting from outside. "SUGAR!" He must have gone out and already found his mate who is giving us a ride home.

"Kool noh man, me ah come man, me ah come." I say my goodbyes to the cabin crew, and then make my way to find TZ.

TZ is already in his mates Range Rover and he left the back open ready for me to put my suitcase in before we roll out. The Range Rover drives beautifully, and it feels good to be back in good 'ole Blighty. Next stop home and TZ asks for the CD I got from the cabbie in Jamaica. He says he wants to make a copy, so I pass it over to him. Before I know it we are pulling up outside my house in Croydon. I take my suitcase and as they pull away I shout after them. "Hey my Bredrin! 'member you have my CD."

"Yeah Sugar! I gonna copy it and give it back to you! Don't worry." But, I've a feeling I'll never see it again!

"Alright say nuttin'! Me 'n you will talk lickle more. Seen!"

20th March 2007
Home Croydon

As I walk up my garden path checking out my overgrown garden, it feels very satisfying to have completed my Mission; I took Mummy home along with my foot to keep her company. As I put down my suitcase at the front door, I feel content and at peace for the first time in a long time. "Yeah man, one foot in yard and one foot here, I suppose that's how it's meant to be. A foot in two different worlds on so many levels."

As I unlock the doors to my flat, it's still only half past eight, so time to relax for a while. I sit on the sofa with a cup of tea, scanning the flat thinking again about the improvements I want to make going forwards. I'm getting really excited about creating a new vibe in my place. I drift off with thoughts of a new sofa on my mind.

20th January 2000
Mum's Home Stockwell Park Estate

"Wha' kinda official letter dat yu get Garri?" Mum looks over my shoulder.

"It's mortgage papers Mum."

"So everyt'ing ah go tru den?"

"Well it looks so." I ponder over the papers.

"Look pon me lickle Garri go buy house, well yu worked hard fi it, but ah shudda two bedroom, cah me wan move in too."

"Mummy you mek me laugh yu know."

"You t'ink ah joke, me need ah change too, yu kyaan tek me with yu?" I sense loneliness in her voice and look up at her.

"You can come and stay with me anytime you want Mum, my house is your house, and I know you'll like the garden as well."

"But Croydon too far Garri." She frowns.

"It ain't that far Mum."

"Who me goin' talk to when yu gaan?"

"You can phone me Mum, Tony's only across the road and Hector ain't too far either."

"Den yu kyaan stay 'ere wid me?"

"I would of loved to stay Mum, but I've just bought a place, so I have to move in and be independent as you taught me."

"Me ah go miss yu, yu kno' Garri."

"I'm gonna miss you too Mum, but I'm always gonna pass by here from work and on the weekends."

"Anyway 'ere weh me ah go do, me ah go buy you wan settee." She smiles.

"Mum I don't want you to buy me a settee, you always taught me to be independent, don't depend on no one, you said." She loses the smile.

"Garri! Yu shut up yu mout', me ah go buy yu wan settee." She screws up her nose.

"I don't want it Mum, I must learn to do everything myself."

"But me ah give yu ah start."

"You help me with the deposit, that's a good start, and anyway you're getting that back, it's just a loan."

"Why yu noh wan tek nutting from nobody?" She glares intensely looking deep in my eyes.

"It's the way you grow me Mum." I smile cocking my head.

"Anyway me ah buy di settee gi' yu, so no boda ears hard, cos yu ah femmi pickney an' me must help yu."

"Alright Mum." I give in.

"Yu stubborn yu seh Garri, yu noh want noh help from noh body."

"You taught me how to be independent, cook, clean, wash and iron from I'm lickle bit."

"But yu must kan tek lickle help sometimes."

"You done it though Mum, no one helped you, you done it yourself, and I'm just following your lead."

"Well me kyaan sey nuttin' 'bout dat." She sighs a deep sigh.

"Arrrh so me win yu de soh." I jump up laughing in celebration of my victory.

"Well yu 'ave a good point but listen noh, when yu ah go outta road, yu tek out di dustbin."

"Yeah, yeah."

"How yu mean yeah, yeah, mind me noh lick yu wid di frying pan." She takes a playful swipe and I duck.

20th March 2007
Home Croydon

Waking up on the sofa Mummy bought me an hour later, with a cold cup of tea, bloody hell I fell asleep! Although I'm tired the idea of improving the flat is still on my mind. As I wander through I decide how I want to sort out the front room, the hall, and the bathroom; I'd also like a new kitchen. My bedroom just needs a lick of paint; in fact the whole place needs a lick of paint. I'm getting excited thinking about the makeover, it will change the vibes completely. With that in mind I begin to unpack my suitcase and sort out what needs to be washed and what can be packed away. Let me check my post and get settled.

21st March 2007
Home Croydon

I'm uploading my pictures from Jamaica, but while I'm online I might as well research the equipment I need for my flat and maybe order a new kitchen. Yeah I'm gonna do it! I've got my washing on and I'm gonna cook something at the same time. Talk about multitasking!

2nd April 2007
Brixton

Life moves along fairly balanced, even the Doctors routine health check is good. The zone outs are reducing and I'm generally keeping on top of things, as long as I don't get too stressed out.

9th April 2007
Home Croydon

My casting agency, who I've been working with since 2000, call and I'm pleased they've decided to put me forward for a feature extra in a popular soda advert. I take this as a sign that my life is coming back on track. Whether I get it or not doesn't really matter, just to be asked is a good sign!

12th April 2007
Roehampton Walking School

Looks like I'll be back here a few more times this month as they assess my walking on the new leg and socket. It's going to be an active month, fitting everything in amongst my home improvement plans and a few lunch dates, as well as the Hospital, but it's good for me to keep busy and keep my mind occupied while I'm still healing.

8th May 2007
Battersea Wine Bar

Lunch date with an old work colleague Chelsea we go way back, in fact she was the one who helped me get my first job after finishing my AAT qualification in Accounts. It's so great to see her and catch up. We chat non-stop and then she looks deep into my eyes, "D'you know Garri that haunting distant look you had in your eyes the last time I saw you, has been replaced with your old sparkle. It's good to see you looking so much better."

"Thank you very much, I must admit I feel better. I can understand what you say about that distant look in my eyes, no surprise really after everything that I've been through."

"Yes Garri, when I first saw you a few months back, you could actually see in your eyes that you had been through something really horrific."

Again it dawns on me what I have been through; the eyes don't lie. The conversation flows until Chelsea has to get back to work. We say our goodbyes.

Now to find my car keys, as I head back for the car patting my pockets as I go, can't seem to find my car keys. Spontaneously I burst into song.

♪ "*Zim zimmer who's got the keys to my bimmer!* See it yah, I found them, as if by magic." I turn the corner. "Now where did I park? No, it's not even this road!" As I get to next road my car's still not visible, so I lift the key fob up high in the air, point it down the road and press the unlock button to see if my car will holla back. *Bleep bleep*, "Yes!" The indicators flash and the clunk of the doors unlocking sounds up ahead, thank God for electronic alarms. I jump in, start him up, and one stop Endz.

15th May 2007
Queen Mary's Hospital Roehampton

I love driving myself here, the scenery is so beautiful and it's very uplifting, it feels like a life-time away from the days when I had to rely on the minibus to bring me. It's certainly been an interesting journey learning to walk again. From my first glimpse of the lovely lady walking on her two prosthetic legs in hospital, to the day I almost kept up with the tram on my running blade in Croydon!

Anyway back to today. They're gonna update my fittings, I suppose this is going to be a part of my life forever now, but at least it's a pleasant place to come and the people are lovely too. I love being independent again and I find it strange how Mum's sayings keep popping into my head every so often. The way she was and what she said makes more sense now though, much more than it did at the times when she said it. Obviously it went in, she set the seed and now I reap the benefit. I am an independent man! I reflect on the day and I'm happy as I fall exhausted into bed; sleep comes easily.

4th June 2007
Home Croydon

My nephew Steve arrives from Jamaica to stay with me for a week, it's wonderful to see him in London, after our meeting in Jamaica a few months ago. After a couple of hours to settle in I take him to my local pub 'The Cricketers', it's only a minute walk away from home. I introduce him to the bar staff and landlord as I order two pints of Guinness. It's a lovely day the sun is shining with a nice warm breeze so we go back outside and sit down at a garden table. It's his first experience of an English pub, and it looks like he's impressed. The locals certainly like him and enjoy his Jamaican accent, as he tells his stories.

"Who you here with?" one of the locals asks.

"Me Uncle Garri!" They all know me.

"Yu want another pint Uncle?" It's funny to hear him calling me Uncle when I'm younger than him.

"No thank you Sir, I got a few things in my house I have to do."

"Me kan stay yahso Uncle Garri."

"How you mean, of course you can stay, you know how to get back to my yard innit?"

"Yeah man, straight walk." He looks happy.

"Alright me see you lickle more, and look after him lads." The locals laugh.

"He's a big lad, he can look after himself."

Steve doesn't get back till late, it must be after closing time, obviously he had a good time and a few beers. Anyway he gets back as I'm finishing up my chores, so we sit chatting stories about Jamaica, his past and the family. We're going deep and I love every minute of it, the family history is being fitted together like a jigsaw puzzle, piece by piece.

5th June 2007
Home Croydon

I take Steve to see my brother Tony and no surprise, he's outside cleaning his car. As I pull up he looks up to see who's in the car with me. Steve jumps out. "Uncle Tony, wha'ah gwaan?"

"Rhaatid, weh yu ah sey Steve ah when yu come yah?"

"Yesterday, but me ah stay wid Uncle Garri."

"Stop the Uncle t'ing, just call me Garri."

"Ah'right kool noh."

Tony finishes cleaning his car as we chat, and then we all go up into his flat. He's got a little mini sound system all set up with a mic in his front room As Steve and I walk in I just know it's going to be pure jokes! Steve's a music man, Tony's a music man and I'm a music man too. I head straight for the mic, done kno, I have to bless the place. After Tony sorts us all out with drinks, I take a sip of rum, Blunt ah burn! There's a beautiful atmosphere; lyrics are flowing. Oh yes, the Caribbean vibe's come to London!

A few hours later the three of us take a walk into Brixton, giving Steve the Grand Tour of the Endz. We show him Stockwell Park Estate, Crowhurst House, where we used to live, straight up Aytoun road, past the skate park. The Academy, TZ's tyre shop, Brixton Market where my Mum used to shop and the two riots hot spots in the 1980's. We end up outside a newsagent on Coldharbour Lane and catch sight of Hector coming along.

"Yo! Stevie wonder, yu wanta juice?" I'm thirsty.

"Me all right you know."

"Me kno ask if you all right, me ask if you wanta juice?"

"Ah'right uncle Garri, me ah tek a juice."

"Tony, what you saying?"

"Bwoy I'm going back home you know, to finish off some things."

"Ah'right me Bredda, gwaan easy."

"Lickle more Uncle Tony."

Tony goes home and I leave Steve to chat with Hector while I get the drinks, and it suits me fine as things are not so good between Hector and I at the moment. When I come out of the shop Hector's already gone so I hand Steve his drink and we head back to the car. I'm going home, but Steve's going to the pub; he's got a fascination with the tall blonde barmaid!

10th June 2007
Home Croydon

Steve's leaving today, his dad's cousin is coming from New Cross to pick him up this morning; it's been a blessing having him here and I have really enjoyed our week together. I'm sorry to see him go.

12th June 2007
Brixton

At the GP for my regular check-up and I get a new prescription for my psoriasis; I'm glad to have something new to try for it, as every little helps and it's quite upsetting when it gets bad. I've also been without fingernails for a very long time now and have recently become a little more self-conscious about how my hands look. Fingernails are much more important than I thought, we need them to scratch, squeeze a pimple, pick up things from the floor, ring pulls on tins and so on! 'You never miss the water till the well runs dry!' as Mum used to say.

16th June 2007
Local Shops Croydon

It's a hot summer day. I'm just chilling as I walk down the road catching some rays alongside a parade of shops, when a woman in the florists shop catches my eye. She's sitting making a floral wreath but as I look at her feet, which is my habit since the Bombings, I see she's wearing some really funky shoes. Now she has my full attention and I stand watching for a while. I take a look around the shop through the window, and notice an Aloe Vera plant. I've always wanted one of those so I consider going in to buy it. After a little while the woman looks up and sees me, she beckons me in. Standing near the counter I admire her work, there's a nice vibe!

"You know what, watching you close up, gives me an idea."

"What idea, what do you mean?" She looks alarmed.

"Sorry how rude of me, my name's Garri by the way." I smile.

"Ah, my name is Tanya." She speaks with a charming Eastern European accent, then smiles and holds her chin as she looks at me quizzically.

"Yeah what you're doing creating that wreath inspires me, I'd love to have a go, I think I could do it." She looks surprised.

"Really? Okay, we'll give it a try, you can be my assistant!"

As we chat I help her choose different flowers to arrange in the wreath, and it inspires me more. Pretty soon I get the hang of how she does it, and have a go myself; I can actually do this. A good hour passes with me in my creative flow, how unexpectedly rewarding! I feel good again and before I leave I end up purchasing the Aloe Vera plant. What a lovely way to start a friendship, and I love her funky shoes!

1st July 2007
Home Croydon

I decide not to buy flowers for the Anniversary this year. I'm gonna make something myself. Inspired by my new Florist friend Tanya, I feel like embracing my creative side. So, sketch pad and colours in hand, I start doodling and carry on with different ideas over the next couple of days. It's a pleasant distraction from the foreboding tension that has surfaced before at this time of year.

3rd July 2007
Home Croydon

The wreath design is complete and I decide to fill it with green moss and then assorted flowers. It's in the shape of a heart and I think it will look really different and personal to the situation, that's good.

July 4th 2007
Tannell Florist

I go back to see Tanya and ask for her advice on my project taking the sketch with me. Tanya is very supportive and also offers to give me a hand to start it off, if I come back tomorrow. Brilliant!

5th July 2007
Tannell Florist

I hurry to see Tanya and I'm feeling good about my project. Checking she has everything in stock Tanya helps me to start the wreath. After putting the base together for me, she lets me take a handful of different flowers as well, so I can continue working on it when I get home. I'm inspired and totally focussed; it feels great!

5th July 2007
Home Croydon

Embracing all the creativity I can muster, I set to work on my tribute for Saturday. I've taken a few photos along the way and looking back at the progress makes me feel even more determined and honoured to be able to design and put together something with so much feeling, meaning, love and attention. It really is a pleasure. Proper job satisfaction!

6th July 2007 3:30am
Home

I can't believe the time; it flies by when I'm focused on something creative. Anyway, I must tidy up, as I need some sleep. I'll do the last little bits in the morning; it's been intense but also the perfect distraction from the stress!

7th July 2007
Home Croydon

Waking up I feel good about what I've been doing over the last few days and rush into the lounge to take another look at the wreath. It's given me a focus away from the negative aspects of the day ahead and has left me with a real sense of achievement. It's time to sort myself out now, a long day ahead. The 7th of the 7th 2007!

7th July 2007
Hyde Park, London

As I arrive, I'm ushered towards a tent with a group of the other survivors and the bereaved. The Steward tells us that we will be driven across the grass to the Memorial by buggy before the Ceremony starts. Wreath in hand, I take a seat feeling very awkward and anxious until a woman from the group kindly approaches me. "That's beautiful Garri, I really like it, my name is Joan by the way, nice to meet you." She smiles warmly.

"Hello Joan, that's a nice thing to say, I actually made it myself."

"Really, wow it's very beautiful, well done."

"Thank you, it took me a couple of days and an early morning to finish it."

"Worth it in the end though." She takes it all in.

"It certainly was." The transport arrives and we make our way to the Memorial site together. As we move along in the buggy my tribute is the centre of more positive comments along the way, I'm proud.

Putting the wreath down next to the communal headstone, I get a sense of strength and achievement. Even more lovely comments come my way and I acknowledge them, but I'm lost in the moment.

Remembering what the victims went through and wondering what their last thoughts could have been before they died, a cold shiver runs up my spine. I find a seat and sit down. As the Ceremony begins I drift off deep in thought; I can't understand why lives are deliberately sacrificed in the name of wars. War spreads fear like a highly contagious disease, so why do we have war? What is its purpose? Is it really about Homeland Security or is it more about Money!?

The sound of applause jolts me back to reality, and I too applaud for the Choir who have just finished their last song. It's time now for the Press and the Public to get closer to the Memorial site. As the barriers are lifted, people descend; it's certainly time for me to leave. By now I know exactly how it works, sadly I regard the Press as birds-of-prey in search of a meal, and I don't want to be cornered so I duck out towards my X3, which I parked near the Dorchester Hotel. I jump in and drive away quickly without a plan.

Ending up at my work place, habit I guess; I park up to reflect again. Seems fitting to come here, as in 2005 I wasn't able to finish that fated journey to work, but I'm here now, and need to stay in the now. I take a walk around the area, to fulfil my need for familiarity. I smile and say hello to a few people, pop into a few shops that I used to frequent at lunchtimes, and return back to my X3 parked outside the office. I sit in the drivers seat contemplating a life I feel lucky to have. I must remember 52 people were killed and I'm still here; it's my duty to make the most of each day God sends me. I'm gonna go on holiday, yep that's what I'm gonna do!

19th-24th July 2007
Spain Puerto Banus

The Spanish sun feels hot and inviting, I so need this break to get away from the papers and headlines again at this time of year. It's great meeting new people, making new friends. I'm growing more confident; my mojo seems to be returning. This is a beautiful experience in Spain.

19th August 2007
Home Croydon

My holiday flew past as good times tend to do and before I know it, it's a distant memory. Now its time to focus and get my home in order; let me organise the things I need for the makeover.

21st August 2007
Home Croydon

My latest toy arrives, Paint Runner, a spray paint gun and I'm very keen to get started! I know it'll be a challenge, but even so I'm planning to do all this decorating by myself, I don't want any help, as I want to sit back later and say I've done that myself. What an accomplishment it will be!

Wearing my goggles, paper boiler suit, decorating gloves and old trainers so I don't get messy, I put the Music on and get started. Bedroom first, I'm a bit wary to begin with but eager to unleash the paint gun onto the ceiling. Braps! The ceiling looks good in no time; so let me extend down the walls, no joins visible, what a machine! No drips, runs or spills. Result! The only thing slowing me down is when I get hot and sweaty in the boiler suit, my leg gets wet and starts slipping and squelching around in the socket so I have to keep stopping to dry off so I don't fall. It's annoying but also a good excuse to stop for a cuppa and a bit of a rest.

24th August 2007
Home Croydon

It's taken four days, well into the early hours of the morning to finish the ceiling and all the walls, I'm very happy with the results. It's a release for my creative energy and I must say it looks better than I'd thought. It's really brightened everything up. Bit tricky around the windows, but I managed in the end. It's all about the careful application; after all it's my home! The sense of achievement is enormous and very satisfying.

17th September 2007
Croydon Home

Next stop kitchen shopping, heading for my local retail park at Purley Way, Croydon. After a bit of research and negotiation, I order a Kitchen due for delivery at the end of October. Job done, just like that!

Back home to start on painting the woodwork, this is gonna take time.

30th September 2007
Home Croydon

Painting the doors, taking care to ensure there are no drips. Finally the last door gets it, as I daydream about how my kitchen's gonna look.

The buzzer rings and I find the lovely Halle standing at my door with a big smile on her face. "Hello busy man, how's it going?"

"I'm okay Babe, I'm nearly done." I feel weary now I've stopped.

"Show me then, give me a tour." She looks pleased, which lifts my energy.

"Careful Babe, a couple of doors still have wet paint." Halle looks around admiring my work and I feel proud of myself.

"Wow you've done well, really well!" That lifts me more.

"Thanks Babe, I'm knackered though, need some sleep. I've been on a mission, staying up till the early hours to get it done."

"I can tell, you've got bags under your eyes." She laughs.

"Bags darlin', I've got suitcases! But it was worth it. Does it feel different to you?"

"Yeah, it definitely feels different, in fact the flat looks much bigger." She's excited!

"Yeah I thought that. All that's left to do is the kitchen and bathroom and it'll be like a new flat, I really need this change."

"Yeah I understand a new start. Well done Babe, I'm proud of you!" Halle hugs me and I try not to get paint on her.

"Guess what?" She looks at me with a sparkle in her eye.

"What?"

"No, you've gotta guess." She smiles a lovely smile, but I'm way too tired to play. "Babe, I can't be guessing now my heads hurting me, what is it?"

"I've got you a birthday treat."

"That's sounds good, tell me more."

"We're gonna spend your birthday in Spain." She smiles and I'm smiling too, now she looks even more excited.

"Spain for my birthday? Wow! That's great Babe, fantastic news, and thank you so much! Come, give me some sugar." I get a kiss and another big smile.

2nd October 2007
Puerto Banus Spain

We're in Spain, staying at a great Hotel. The vibes are relaxing and it's fantastic to be back here in time for my birthday. Halle and I both know the blue sky and sunshine makes such a difference to my well-being, even though it's not as warm as it was in June, I'm so happy to be here.

Halle sets out the plan. "Terra Blues opens later tonight, so my brother's coming round to take us for a meal first, after that we can go for a walk and check out the shops."

"Sounds great, I want to check out the Port too."

We have a lovely evening but I'm ready for an early night, I'm so exhausted from all the decorating.

3rd October 2007
Puerto Banus Spain

Happy birthday indeed, it's a relaxing day in the sun and I have an afternoon nap, still catching up from all the hard work I put in decorating my flat. After a lovely meal we end up in Terra Blues again. They sing Happy Birthday to me and Halle produces a cake with far too many candles on it!

It's a beautiful warm night as we come out of Terra Blues and head for the Hotel. We take a different route for a change and I have to carefully navigate down some very steep steps. I'm slightly merry and in a light playful conversation with Halle. Almost at the last step my left leg gives way and I slip but manage to recover without falling.

"Be careful." Halle looks concerned but I feel merry and in a really funny mood. "My left leg's drunk babe."

"What did you say?" She comes in close to listen again.

"I said, my left legs going one way and my right leg's going the other way, I'm pretty sure my left leg's drunk!" Halle can't stop laughing and tears start rolling down her cheeks. She starts me off too, so we laugh and joke all the way across the Square and to the Hotel. Fun times, although I'm so glad I didn't fall!

4th-5th October 2007
Puerto Banus Spain

We spend time relaxing on beach, which is walking distance from the Hotel. Time out to take in some rays and chillax, it's a great place to meditate. We also get together with a few friends and form a convoy going to a Caribbean Bar-B-Que at Senora beach. A bit of a distance away but worth doing as I like to visit new places; life is to be enjoyed, especially when you've nearly lost it!

6th October 2007
Puerto Banus Spain

Our last night in Spain at Terra Blues Bar, I feel like stretching my legs after a while, so I take myself off for a walk down the strip. There are a variety of buildings with fast food outlets, bars, clubs and nightlife along the strip and narrow pathways leading off to small shops or back to the dock which houses many beautiful yachts. Walking along further I find myself in an area with loads of skimpily clad girls and guys in vests flexing their muscles at passers by. They give out flyers that offer free admission to a club and a free drink. A couple of the guys try to encourage a hen party of around seven girls into their club and I watch their performance, I like to people-watch. They try everything to get the girls involved, but they ain't having none of it! What a shame. "Nice try lads!" I laugh and they shrug their shoulders defeated as the girls walk away. Next thing I know I'm suddenly getting the attention of several girls offering a very different type of service. Time to leave I believe, swift exit back to Terra Blues!

7th October 2007
Homeward Bound

After a three-hour flight, we arrive back at Gatwick, and once again everything seems grey and washed out, why is it always a grey day, when I return from the sun?

19th October 2007
Home Croydon

Once over the holiday blues, it's good to get on with life in my freshly decorated flat. As I go into the kitchen to make a cuppa, I look around trying to imagine how my new kitchen will look. It won't be long now till it arrives. I'm interrupted from my musings, *ting ting* as a text arrives from my casting agency, saying they have put me forward for an advert again. That puts a smile on my face, fingers crossed!

22nd October 2007
Home Croydon

In the middle of the day I receive another text from my casting agency, put forward again for another advert and as a feature extra this time. Now my fingers and toes are crossed!

24th October 2007
Home Croydon

Unfortunately I'm not picked for either of the adverts, but at least my face is getting out there now in association with something positive. I'm getting fed up of seeing my name on the Internet search engines associated with negativity, it can be soul destroying if I let it get to me. I have to pull myself up when I notice the dip. Not so easy to do sometimes though.

30th October 2007
Home Croydon

My kitchen arrives at last, flat packed so the deliverymen leave it in the communal hallway. I've not made arrangements to have anyone fitted yet, so it will have to stay there for now, but hopefully not for long. I don't want to cause any problem for my neighbours, but as its not obstructing anything, I'm sure it'll be okay for a little while. I've hadn't even thought about when I will get it fitted. I just know it will be done.

1st November 2007
Norwood High Street

Walking along, I bump into an old friend, I knew Corey back in the day. I'm very happy to see him and he looks well, "Yo, what you saying man?"

"Raaah Sugar what you saying?"

"It's been a long time Mate."

Corey and I used to play football together; I haven't seen him for years. He's a brilliant footballer as I remember and we had some great matches, but that was a two-footed Garri, I don't know how I'd play now, another challenge to come perhaps?

After a brief catch up, it turns out he is a builder and the ideal person to find me someone to fit my kitchen. The Universe conspires to help me! We exchange business card and arrange to meet Tuesday for a consultation so his guys can start work fitting my kitchen. An unexpected result!

6th November 2007
Home Croydon

Corey's workmen arrive and I'm feeling amazed at how it all worked out so easily. I stand watching them for a while as they dismantle the old kitchen cupboards. I get a feel for them and their energy is good. They are very focused on their work and I'm comfortable with them, so I leave them to it and head to Croydon to do my errands. When I get back, the kitchen is almost gutted and it looks like a bombsite!

8th November 2007
London

Having lunch with an ex-boss. It's great catching up with such a refined gentleman, I always feel warmth and a fatherly energy when he's around. I mention my new kitchen and that I'm hoping it will be completed soon. I can't wait to start cooking again, although so far it's only been a couple of days of take away foods or eating out.

9th November 2007
Home Croydon

They are a few small problems fitting the kitchen, so it's going to take a little longer than I thought.

14th November 2007
Home Croydon

The word on the street is that burglaries are on the increase on my corner, so I've decided to have a security gate fitted to my front door and I know exactly who to call to find out where to get one. I ring TZ and he answers straight away. "Yo!"

"Yo T, d'you know where I can get a security gate for my yard?"

"Easy Sugar, what d'you want a gate for?"

"Kool noh mi Breddrin."

"The geezer that fitted mine is good, I could give 'im a one ding fi yu?"

"Yeah do dat man."

"Just let me finish with the car I'm working on and I'll call you back in fifteen."

"Ah'right mate, no problem."

15th November 2007
Home Croydon

Phone rings "Who dis?"

"T man, wha'ah gwaan?"

"T your backside, what happen to fifteen?"

"Big man, it's fifteenth today innit?" He laughs.

"About it's fifteenth today!" I laugh too and it's okay, I know he works hard!

"I had so many cars to sort out and I totally forgot Bruv, it's only when I was leaving my yard this morning locking my gate, I thought raaaah, Sugar! Anyway my Bruva take down his details, I have arranged for the guy to link you if that's alright?"

"Yeah man, it's all good Bruv."

Writing down his details I realise the man lives close to me. "Thanks for that T, have a good day mate."

"Pass up if you got time."

"Yeah man." I call the guy and he arranges to come over tomorrow to measure up. Things are moving swiftly.

16th November 2007
Home Croydon

The security gate guy arrives and gets on with measuring up, while I make a cuppa. Once this gate is on, there is no way anyone will be able to come through my front door uninvited.

"Ah'right mate, you got all you need?"

"Yeah, now I've taken the measurements, I can figure out the size and cost, hold on." He scribbles down his figures and passes me the paper, "I could have it fitted Monday, if it's all okay for you?"

"Brilliant mate, morning or afternoon?"

"What do you prefer?"

"Morning please and I'll have the money ready for you."

"Okay mate, nice, have a great weekend, see you Monday."

"You too have a great weekend and thank you for your time."

19th November 2007
Home Croydon

I'm relieved the security gate is being fitted to my door. It's better to be safe than sorry. Plus if I decide to travel again, I need peace of mind while I'm away.

21st November 2007
Queen Mary's Hospital Roehampton

Having a check up and we discover my stump has changed shape slightly, but they suggested it might, so I'm not concerned. I felt it rubbing recently and that happens when the socket is too big. They can re-do the casting for a new socket to coincide with the most recent hi-tech prosthetic leg coming in. It has extra built in shock absorbers, which sounds fantastic. It should be ready for December, and it's an exciting prospect. Something to look forward to.

21st November 2007
Home Croydon

Early afternoon, I've got my drive and creative energy flowing again at last, and I'm working on two music tracks at the same time. Figuring out the lyrics on one, the other I'm creating the beat. They sound quite good, but everything takes time. Feels good to break away for a while and do something I've got a passion for.

23rd November 2007
Home Croydon

After a few minor hiccups the fitted kitchen it's complete. Looking around it was worth all the discomfort and take away food. Bwoy it looks great; light wood cupboard doors and contrasting dark countertops. Its taken time but the workmen did well and now my flat has got a completely different feel. That's a good job, money well invested. It's so light, clean and more spacious now that it's finished what a contrast. I'll be cooking this weekend!

26th November 2007
Croydon Natasha's Office

I'm doing some part-time bookkeeping for my friend Tash. We get on very well, she's such a lovely woman and clever too a winning combination. Tall with long dark hair, sparkly eyes and always has a lovely smile for me. It's so great to put my accounting experience to work again; use it or lose it they say.

2nd December 2007
Croydon Natasha's Office

Working for Tash is very good for me; it keeps me busy, and my brain ticking over. Today she introduces me to one of her girlfriends Angel, who I instantly click with. It's a pleasure to spend time with a new circle of friends.

Anyway I've got letters to write and accounts to do so I leave them to get on with it.

11th December 2007
Queen Mary's Hospital Roehampton

Reading the football page of a tabloid whilc I wait for Lawrence in one of the small consulting rooms, it's the only part of the papers I bother to read any more. As Lawrence arrives I stand up to greet him, we shake hands and exchange pleasantries. He's already brought the leg with him and hands it to me straight away. "Well here you go Garri try it on, tell me how it feels." Carefully slipping my stump into the new leg, I get up and walk around for a while, up and down the corridor, noticing the reduced impact on my stump as I stand on it. I can hardly feel any pressure at all, which makes it very comfortable. The extra shock absorbers offer a cushioned landing or a spring in my step depending on how you look at it. One small thing that bothers me though, is that I used to be pigeon toed and this leg is not! I wonder… "Lawrence, this may sound funny, but can you adjust the leg so the foot turns in slightly, that's the way my foot was before?"

"Yeah, I don't see why not," he does a simple adjustment, "How far in shall we turn it Garri, about that?"

"No man that's much too much! Stop playing games with me man." It feels really weird, so he adjusts it again laughing. "How about now?"

"Yeah man, that's exactly right, it actually feels really familiar now. Thank you so much Lawrence" He smiles and shrugs his shoulders. "No problem, we aim to please."

I'm good to go, that simple little thing makes such a huge difference.

13th December 2007
Home Croydon

Once home I jump backwards off my small garden wall getting use to the landing and feeling of my new leg. I drop to the floor to practice falling over; anything can happen at any time, preparation Rudebwoy that's the key!

17th December 2007
Home Croydon

Laying on my bed just analysing myself, reflecting on my life. Fate is a funny thing, this time of year I would have been socialising and Christmas partying, but now I just feel alienated, disconnected from the world. I wonder if better times will return, I wonder what the future holds.

18th December 2007
Home Croydon

Still feeling disconnected from mainstream society and the working environment, the interface of connection that evades me. I reflect on the spirit of Christmas past, present and future and get a sense of longing to be part of something, but not really sure what I want to be part of anymore. I know I've had a lucky escape from a life of pretence. I would really enjoy a genuine connection, with genuine people again, who enjoy me for who I am, not for the Media attention that surrounded me. It's truly a gift in itself having that level of awareness.

24th December 2007
Fulham London

Lunch with Halle at her Mum's house is always pleasant. Miss Lilly* makes me laugh; she's such a cheerful and caring woman, with a funny sense of humour. I'm greeted with a big smile and "Merry Christmas!" She hugs me and I smile responding to the hug."Merry Christmas Miss Lilly."

"Merry Christmas Daughter." She approaches Halle with a hug and kiss.

"Merry Christmas Mum."

Halle leads me through to the dining room. Even though there is so much food on the table, my eyes stop at the Christmas Crackers and I remember the last time I pulled a cracker was at a work party. I can't seem to shake off the memories of work and the anxiety I feel about losing my job and the sense of security and belonging.

Distracted by flashing miniature Christmas trees at each table setting, I feel a smile coming on, I certainly haven't seen that before, bless Miss Lilly.

"What you smiling at?"

"The lickle trees dem Babe." We both chuckle as Miss Lilly brings in some hot plates, telling us to help ourselves. The food is lush!

"You're going to love the desert Babe." Halle whispers.

"Why what is it?"

"Mum will bring it in soon."

Sure enough in walks Miss Lilly. "Garri would you like some desert, Halle tells me you like apple crumble."

"Oh, yes please." I beam a smile from ear to ear.

"I've also got mango crumble, I made it myself."

"What mango crumble as well? Okay I'll have some of each please." It gets better and better.

"Ice cream or custard?"

"Thank you!" She smiles, I laugh!

25th December 2007
Home Croydon

It's a quiet start to the day, and I'm still full from yesterdays feast. I've got some old skool classic house music on low as background music as I call Halle to see what time she's coming over. We plan to spend some time together before we fly out to Spain again on Thursday to celebrate the New Year there.

27th December 2007
London Gatwick

It feels different leaving the country at this time of year; I've never spent the New Year in another country before.

27th December 2007
Spain Marbella

It's quite a bit cooler, but the sky is still blue with odd clouds scattered about. The atmosphere is different though, it's strange to see all the Christmas decorations adorning the shops instead of flip-flops and sunhats. It gives the place a different feel. The people are awesome as usual and there's an extra sense of cheerfulness in the air. When I'm here I enjoy being part of an extended family and it's just what I need right now. I have nothing but love for these people.

31st December 2007
Spain Marbella

Celebrating New Years Eve in Spain is a new experience; the place comes alive with even more merriment than usual. We are given twelve grapes to eat at midnight, a tradition said to bring good luck, as fireworks light up the skyline and the dazzling and colourful effect is doubled as the sea mirrors the sky. It's a fantastic way to spend New Year and as I eat my twelve grapes on the beach, one at a time at exactly midnight. I pray that 2008 is a better year, a new life filled with awareness and empowerment!

1st January 2008
Spain Marbella

Ano Nuevois! Happy New Year! For the first time in my life, I spend New Year's Day walking along the beach and it feels great but really different. It's a good day to reflect and make intentions for the year that lies ahead. It suddenly occurs to me that Mum wanted her ashes buried in Jamaica with her Parents. Although I've done the first stage and taken her ashes to Jamaica I need to fulfil the last part of her wishes somehow. Therefore my New Year's Resolution is to go to Jamaica and spread her ashes over my grandparent's graves in St. Mary if at all possible. The property now belongs to a family, who can apparently be very troublesome, which means I'll have to arrange for Steve to go with me on that mission. That's gonna be my plan for this year. My New Years resolution is set!

13th January 2008
Home Croydon

I find the law of attraction becoming more and more interesting as I see how things unfold in my life. I'm reading a book called The Secret, but I've not done any reading for ages; the last book I read was The Celestine Prophecy I'm sure it was my friend Kirsty that introduced that book to me, I wonder how she is. Anyway I'm not sure about this book, nice cover, great marketing, I've heard so much hype about it and I'm curious what it has to offer, but reading through it just doesn't grab me.

25th January 2008
Home Croydon

I'm reading and watching videos on YouTube; researching spirituality. Connecting the dots and becoming aware is high on my agenda these days. Of course if we are really all one, as some Wisdom Schools would have us believe, any increased awareness is self-awareness! I have been through so much weirdness; I need to find answers. I am being spiritually guided now and it feels good.

27th January 2008
Home Croydon

It's funny when you research one thing and then you're drawn into a different direction. I'm reading a story about French Freemasons and the Statute of Liberty. Talking about chains, I read that the Unicorn is representative of all that is good and pure within humanity. Is it then a significant thing that on the front of the British passport is a Unicorn in Chains? Not to mention the Unicorn tapestries displayed in a famous Museum. I have to get off this Internet man before I get too deep!

3rd February 2008
Home Croydon

I can't get away from the computer but they say knowledge is power so I want to gain my share. Ancient Kemet is now known as Egypt and on my bucket list. I also want to learn more about the Nubians in Africa. I should have learnt some of this stuff at school, I wonder why I didn't, God knows Mum forced me to go every day! I have to wonder if I wasted my time, what did I actually learn?

Okay maybe a waste of time is a bit harsh, I learned to read and write, and I'm pretty good with numbers and that is a blessing, but I also learned how to follow the rules mindlessly, understand the History lessons ('his'story, who is 'he' anyway?), and geography. Hmmm, I just discovered even the map of the world is probably distorted.

Science, well that's a whole new ball game since Quantum Physics came into view. We may have to rethink everything we think we know! I also learned how to pass exams, again without thinking, just repeating like a sheep and being compliant. Mis-Education is not helpful, especially when it doesn't even cover the basics of cooking, washing, cleaning, making a fire, survival skills, creativity or running a business and keeping your accounts! How are we meant to get on in the real world? *KMT!*

11th February 2008
Croydon Riches Sounds

Just got myself 'Cubase' music software, and I can't wait to get it home to see if I can improve the two music tracks I've been working on. My creativity is flowing again, which is a good thing.

11th February 2008
Home Croydon

I'm amazed at the sounds that are in this package. Hours pass unnoticed when I'm being creative, until my belly grumbles and I need a food break; I eat quickly and get back into it as soon as I can as music feeds my soul!

18th February 2008
Croydon Natasha's Office

Back into my accountant's brain today, reconciling rental accounts and putting the landlord letters together with a statement to be sent out. As the last one is completed, I get a great sense of job satisfaction; it's good to have variety in my work it keeps me level. I couldn't work full time doing the same thing everyday because I still zone out sometimes, but the part time stimulation, seems to work well by giving me some wiggle room. If there are some days when I can't cope, I can always make it up on another day. I start to wonder how long the 'zone out' attacks will continue; will I always be like this?

23rd February 2008
Home Croydon

Outside in the fresh air today, giving the X3 a good wash, as I pass through the garden I notice signs of life appearing. My poppies have already got green shoots showing through and on the Marley tree small green buds flourish at the ends of the branches. Some green tips are breaking through the soil as the bulbs start to sprout into life. Making my way back and forth to the car with the clean water for rinsing, I keep stopping to take in the amazing energy in my garden; I love it.

25th February 2008
Norwood Travel Agent London

Searching for flights to Jamaica, but every time a good deal comes up on the system, it quickly vanishes. But I'm not giving up! 'Me nar let yu down Mummy Holness.' After great length, and some frustration we grab a cheap flight to Jamaica on 11th March. Part 2 of my mission is now underway.

"Thanks for your time and your assistance Lee."

"No problem Garri you have a wonderful trip, I'm so glad we finally managed to grab that flight."

"Yeah, me too thanks, this is a very important trip!"

As I go out onto Norwood High Road, a car showroom on the right side distracts me. Of course before I know what's happened I'm inside browsing around; my attention is taken by a hot looking BMW, but then I realise it's got a manual gearbox and I lose interest. No good for me, I can only drive automatics now. The little things we take for granted! Anyway I've got my brochure and documents from the Travel Agent, I want to get home and focus on my trip. I'm putting my savings to good use; life is for living.

3rd March 2008
Home Croydon

Tidying up the front garden and doing some weeding, gardens need constant attention. With my hands in the earth I feel at one with the Universe, so I really don't mind. Even watching the ants as they form a line and move things along that seem far too big for them to carry, is really quite inspiring. The hive mentality takes working together in cooperation to a whole new level of understanding; Ants know what time it is!

5th March 2008
Croydon Garden Centre

Buying some flowers for my garden, the perennial type, I've got to get the right colours to fit in. It's very therapeutic walking amongst the plants and garden accessories. I notice a large spider sitting on its web that's glistening in the light. Just as I get close enough to have a good look, a bright green grasshopper jumps straight into the web. There's a struggle as Grasshopper tries to break free and Spider dashes in closer trying to tie him up in a parcel of webbing. I watch in awe as the little green guy battles tenaciously to get away, while Spider seems eager for a meal. Desperate to survive Grasshopper leaves a leg behind on the web and leaps away! Wow it makes me shudder; he lost a leg, just like me! But for him, he has five more to jump on and the Spider gets a tasty snack, the Natural Order!

5th March 2008
Home In The Garden

I manage to plant all the flowers in one day, even though it wasn't easy; my lower back is suffering though. Hot bath in sea salt needed, and then I may research what message Grasshopper may have brought me today, perhaps it was a sign? I've learnt the Animal Kingdom can bring messages for us, when they show up and get our attention. The Native Americans, call them Totem Animals, they regard animals as teachers.

After my bath and contemplations about the enormity of going to Jamaica alone to bury my Mum, I look online to find out about my encounter with Grasshopper. I find quite a few similar messages that offer this - *If Grasshopper has jumped in front of you, it's a good omen, you are being shown there's a bigger picture and it's a good idea to take a leap of faith. Go for your goals without worrying about the outcome. Even if it's something that you have been avoiding, which may be linked to large-scale changes in your life path. It can mean good changes in relationships, career or a change in how you are being in the world. Know that you have all you need to jump over any obstacles and it will so often lead to a positive outcome.*

Fascinating, I can't quite believe it, yet on a deep level it resonates with me. Even the act of this particular Grasshopper, sacrificing his leg to save his life rings true for me. I'm deeply moved and need to digest this magical message. Some times fact is stranger than fiction; you just couldn't make this shit up!

6th March 2008
Home Croydon

I'm staring through the window admiring the work I did in my garden yesterday; the plants that I bought look great. Now the garden is more evenly balanced. There's a sense of stability when I create pleasant things around me. I will take on the message from yesterday, go for my goals and I am certain I will find a way to bury Mummy on the land she once owned.

9th March 2008
Home Croydon

More computer research; this time I find the Dogon tribe of Africa; the Sirius mystery, which leads me to the Mayan civilization. These people are deep and this research is a good education for me. It's a whole new aspect missed out during school history lessons. I'm in the mood for learning and feel it's important to get at the truth, rather than rely on spoon-fed bullshit.

10th March 2008
Home Croydon

Let me check my checklist for Jamaica one more time before I go to bed. Passport, money and documents are in my bag. Suitcase locked. Good to go; now time to sleep. This journey truly feels like a huge mission, Mummy Holness it's your time, seen!

11th March 2008
London Gatwick

As I board the plane I look around at the other passengers jammed into economy and try to make myself as comfortable as possible for the long haul to Jamaica. I have an aisle seat so I should be okay. But after a while we experience turbulence, the Pilot informs us of a delay as we have to take a slightly different route. Eleven hours in, I start pacing up and down the gangway; I'm going stir crazy up here!

It's another hour or so before we finally come in to land. What a flight, twelve hours, Imagine that! And I did it all by myself, thank you Lord for my safe arrival! As the doors open and the heat hits me, I feel at home and my spirits lift. Out into the warm breeze and so pleased to be here again in the land of my Ancestors.

After collecting my luggage, I'm ushered to a mini bus; it's part of the all-inclusive deal I booked this time. Within fifteen minutes we arrive at The Rosehall Iberstar Hotel, it's impressive; I did well thanks to my travel agent Lee. The young Jamaican guy on reception greets me. "Hello Sah documents please."

"Here you are Sir!"

"I'm so sorry, because of the late arrival you've missed dinner, but, there are a few snack bars near the beach."

"Couldn't be helped, turbulence, anyway snack bars are good I'll check them out thanks."

"Your Room is 1112 and here's your key. Take that lift over there to the 5th Floor. Enjoy your stay sir."

"Thank you very much and you have a pleasant evening." The repeating numbers of my room get me again 111! And 1+1+1+2=5 and on the 5th floor, what's going on?

Taking my luggage towards the lifts, I see a few people drinking in the bar, looks like it's still open so I locate my room quickly. Leaving my suitcase and hand luggage inside I hurry back to the lobby, bwoy I need to get a juice and some food. Strolling through the lobby, I can smell food! I follow my nose to a snack bar outside the main building. Great place to grab a quick little snack and a fruit punch to keep me going.

Back to my room to check it out properly and unpack. There are two double beds to choose from and plenty of space with all the mod cons. Let me just fix up the iPod, plug in the speaker, and oh yes, Gospel house music, proper! The view from the window is impressive even though it's dark, the spotlights highlight exotic plants and meandering water. It's all about chillin' tonight!

12th March 2008 Early Morning
Montego Bay Jamaica

I'm awake far too early, but checking the view as I sit up makes me smile,

I see the swimming pools that sit between the Palm Tree lined gardens that house brightly coloured exotic flowers. Beyond that the Turquoise hues of the Caribbean Sea glisten in the morning sun. Perfect! I reach down the side of the bed for my leg, slip it on, and head for the bathroom.

After a little pampering, I dress and head out in search of breakfast. The dining area is a fairly a long walk, over several paths and open areas so I work up even more of an appetite than I already had. As I open the door, a mountain of Pineapples greet me and there are a variety of other fruits laid out on the main tables. Further into the dining room I see the open buffet, which looks delicious. Scanning the various trolleys with their array of food, fruit and cakes, I decide to settle for my usual porridge oats to line my stomach to start me off. I find an empty table, sit down and eat my porridge, which is followed by a mint tea, couple of pastries and a fruit salad. Satisfying and delicious! Breakfast, oh breakfast, so needed after yesterday's long flight. The rest of the day I take time to explore the resort, chill out and get in line with the time zone.

13th March 2008
Montego Bay, Jamaica

Seems everyone's smiling at me; either I have a friendly face, or I must be smiling all the time as well. It's quite different from the London vibe, which can be quite insular. It doesn't take long before banter starts up with the Staff working at the Hotel and I enjoy it, pure jokes. The Man dem here support Manchester United, but me, I'm a Gooner for life! They start calling me Arsenal and instantly there it is, 'friendly' rivalry between us, which we all enjoy. The 'women-dem' love the smell of my aftershave, they keep asking me to leave my cologne for them. It happened last time, so I know they're serious! I decide I will leave it for them when I go home, it's gonna cost me a new bottle every time I come at this rate! A cute little girl around five or six looks at me innocently with big brown eyes asking "Wha' happen to yu foot? Dat not 'ur foot."

"Den who foot is it?" I answer with a smile. She giggles and tries to grab my foot so I pull it away laughing, and move quickly away from her heading to the beach. It's good to be here and relax for a while before I organise my mission.

14th March 2008
Montego Bay, Jamaica

I bump into a group of five Canadian women, and everywhere I go they seem to be there. Although a friendly, and fun loving bunch, they can surely drink and get very friendly really quick. They invite me to get involved with their drinking game. Me? I don't drink much so it ain't gonna happen, I prefer just enjoying their company from a distance, it's too funny what's coming out of their mouths while under the influence! Time to go for a walk along the beach and find me a nice spot. "See you later girls, don't overdo it." I wink as I make my escape.

"Where are you going?"

"For a little walk, you just stay there and enjoy yourselves."

"Okay Garri, see you later."

16th March 2008
Montego Bay Jamaica

Back from the gym, I throw my towel on the bed and head for the bath. While I'm in the bath it suddenly dawns on me, the lovely woman working out next to me in the gym was flirting with me. As I think about the things she said it's pretty clear looking back, but why didn't I see it in time to banter with her, too focussed on my workout perhaps? Still it's a nice confidence to boost!

17th March 2008
Montego Bay Jamaica

Walking through the foyer there's a group of people standing together; the Assistant Manager, the little girl who tried to grab my foot, and a few others. I wonder if the child is his daughter. As I approach she comes after my foot again, obviously fascinated, but she just won't stop this time and it gets awkward.

"Stop it, hey pickni leave me alone noh."

"It not yours," she's insistent.

"Then who it belongs to?"

"It not yours!" Standing on the other side of her is an Empress, the beautiful mother I suspect. "Leave di man alone, yu noh' kno him, me sey fi leave di man alone." She turns to me, "I'm so sorry Sir." She smiles and I'm captivated.

"It's alright, don't worry, she's funny." Wow! It is the Mum and she is beautiful, the baby's father is lucky! I walk to the beach with a little strapped one.

18th-20th March 2008
Montego Bay Jamaica

The next three days fly past as I continue my holiday routine; breakfast, gym, snacking, relaxing, sun bathing, showering, and meditating. Getting into the general holiday spirit, watching some of the in-house activity as well as reading a book from time to time. I'm keeping myself calm and relaxed as I mentally prepare for part two of my mission.

21st March 2008
Montego Bay, Jamaica

Leaving the gym I literally bump into an English woman. "Oops, sorry."

"Waay heey no need to be sorry Hunni!" She exclaims.

"You're funny!"

"And you're well fit, aren't you?" I think she's talking about my physique.

"Excuse me?"

"We should meet up again in the morning and work out together." She winks and walks into the gym without looking back. Women can be so forward sometimes I can't believe it. My heart's thumping in my chest, this one's so obvious it's impossible not to notice! Is someone up there trying to help me? Yeah man! My confidence builds, but not quite enough to go back and continue the conversation. The damn confidence issue is at an all time low since the bombing and the on going Media onslaught, but anyway it's a nice way to start the day!

22nd March 2008
Montego Bay, Jamaica

Settled in nicely and everywhere I go it's fun and jokes with the Staff, but I've got to focus on the second part of my mission, Mummy Holness. I ask one of the Hotel workers to line me up with a good cabbie to take me to my Sister's house.

Turns out the cabbie is a very tall man, around six foot, four inches at least, it's not often I have to look up at someone. We have a good in depth talk, as we drive to my Sister's place in Spanish town. Some of the things he says will resonate with me for the rest of my life. He thinks way outside the box, he's a deep thinker and I'm soaking it up! Like I said before, I'm ready, Teacher where are you? By the time we reach Spanish Town and stop outside my sister's place, I feel like I've had a whistle stop education. I pay him and he hands me a business card with his contact details. Richie Rich,

Mr Kool N Kalm.

"Yoh sah, everyt'ing ah'right?"

"Yeah man everyt'ing criss."

I ring the bell on the gate and my niece Ava pops her head around the front door, recognising me she comes out to open the gate. "Hi Uncle,

"Hi Ava, how you doing?"

"Yeah I'm okay, Mum did say that you might be coming, how you keeping?"

"I'm good y'know."

"Mum's still at work."

"Yeah, she did tell me she wouldn't be here, but I just need to collect my Mums ashes."

"Oh okay, she said something about Steve picking you up and I spoke to him earlier, he'll be here soon."

"Yeah that's right, we're on a mission."

"Ah'right as long as unno know weh unno ah do." She shrugs smiling.

"You don't mind if I wait just out here do you?"

"No, no you should be ah'right nobody nar trouble yu."

"Wah yu mean I should be ah'right! Member yu know, duppy know who fi frighten!" Ava laughs and goes back into the house.

While I'm waiting I notice the building works at a house opposite, it's slowly coming along since my last visit. What type of house would I build if that was mine? I start imagining how it would be and I get lost in thought until Steve appears pulling me back from my dream world. "Yes, Uncle Garri."

"Wha' ah gwaan sah, you ready for dat mission ya?"

"How you mean Uncle? What ah weh you ah talk Jamaican hard eeeh?"

"Kool noh Stevie Wonder."

"Ah'right Uncle, me ah go pick up me bredrin Shakespeare and JR just in case anyting ah gwaan."

"Den kool nuh man, den me noh kno' sey ah yu ah run t'ings."

We set off to St. Mary picking up the Man dem on the way, first Shakespeare, a tall light skin guy, and a serious bredda, then JR, another big man. We stop off outside his house but JR invites us in. He is cooking fish on a barbeque up on the roof and it smells delicious, so we're happy to join him. There is a lot of banter going on between the three of them, its fun to watch and then JR offers me a piece of fish. "Reespek big man," and a big man he is too, quite stocky as well as fairly tall. "Yo big man da fish yah taste nice yu see." It's delicious and I feel happy to be here.

"Kool noh man."

After eating, we all jump in JR's SUV. The Man dem are giving me pure jokes, what comfortable and beautiful surroundings I find myself in, on such a daunting day. We drive from parish to parish Bog Walk, Linstead, Troja and Highgate getting ever closer to our destination. All I can do is take in the beautiful scenery and the sweet mellow vibes of Jamaica. As we approach a service station JR pulls over; he needs to pump up his tyres. Great opportunity to stretch my legs so I jump out and decide to have some fun with these guys. Stretching out my legs, like we do when we are gonna play football, I look around the forecourt and off into the surrounding neighbourhood. It's quite a rural town, the garage sits amongst trees, shrubs, and there are a few eateries as well as single and two storey houses close by with small porches and shutters on the windows.

After I take a quick little jog across the forecourt, I start my fun.

"My leg feels flat I need some air in it!" They look at each other puzzled as I expected, then look back at me.

"Stop yu stupid-ness, weh yu ah gwaan wid?" Steve replies.

"Me foot need some air Rudebwoy!" I say seriously.

"Yu ah joker yu nah." Shakespeare creases up laughing and it's infectious, the others join in, but I keep a straight face and continue with my performance, walking slowly and methodically over to the air pump. I stand waiting my turn and when JR finishes, I can feel them all watching to see what I'm gonna do next. I act it out, rolling up my left trouser leg I reach down and undo the air cap on my artificial leg, I put the nozzle of the air pump towards it and top it up to the right pressure, occasionally taking a sneaky peek up at the others watching me. The garage is at a standstill by now with all eyes on me. I have quite an audience and it's hilarious, I'm chuckling inside. "Okay that should be enough, now to test it just to be sure." I announce, jumping up and down on the spot, kicking my legs out to each side, and finally do a quick sprint from one side of the forecourt to the other as fast as I can.

One of the Man dem pipes up "Bumbaclot, 'im nuh easy!"

When I do look up properly at my audience, I can see the puzzled looks on people's faces and I can't help laughing. Shakespeare finally comes over with a big smile on his face. "Bwoy me nuh waan lose me foot yu kno', but if me 'ave fi lose it, me waan one like Dat!" I laugh harder!

One of the local Elder Men watching shakes his head, as he approaches me. "But see yah." Holding out his hand to shake mine he continues. "You is a God bless yute, yu fi kno' dis, you mek my day, what did happen to yu?"

I give him a condensed version of my story, knowing that we're pushed for time.

"God 'ave yu 'ere for a reason, yu work nuh done yet. Yu go ah Church?" He looks into my eyes.

"No Sah, but me ah spiritual yute, me kno God ah walk wid me and me Mudda too."

"Okay, but yu 'fi go ah Church!" I see kindness in his eyes.

"Yeah, yeah but the Temple of God is within."

"Still, you fi go ah Church." He won't be deterred so I Shake his hand and wish him well before we hit the road again!

22nd March 2008
St.Mary's Jamaica

As we reach our destination Steve and I leave the others in the SUV and approach the house hoping to get permission to see my families graves. An older women opens the door, so I explain who I am, and as if offering some kind of proof, I turn to show her the back of my Arsenal Top 'HOLNESS 7', then go on to explain my mission. She is very caring and compassionate, allowing us the time to do what we came here to do; there is no trouble in this house!

We venture into the forest, Steve leading, as he thinks he knows vaguely where his Great Grandparents are buried. As we climb a steep hill we move deeper into the forest and a feeling of excitement overrides my anxiety. I watch every step taking care and holding on to branches whenever I can; there is no pathway to walk on and it's pretty rough under foot. It's turning into a rare adventure searching for my Grandparents graves out here in the middle of nowhere!

After twenty minutes or so we find the graves covered with plants and leaves, and the first thing I do is take a few photos. It's like Raiders of the Lost Ark and it's a very good thing Steve bought a machete. After five minutes or so of intensive machete work, with sweat pouring from us both, we manage to clear away the foliage. In the clearing, Steve begins to dig a hole; I take more photos as we take it in turns to dig until the job is done. I open the Urn containing Mum's ashes and those from my leg and scatter some over our ancestor's graves reciting Psalm 23 'The Lord is my Shepherd I shall not want.' Laying Mum at peace is a very overwhelming task, I feel emotionally shattered as I place what's left of the combined ashes into the hole we dug in the ground. "I love you Mum, may you Evolve in Love." I grab a handful of earth and place it carefully on top of the ashes. Steve steps forward to say his goodbyes too, adding more earth and I take a couple more photos. We stand silently for a moment and finally fill in the hole.

I take a quick look at the photographs to make sure they have captured the situation and we're done. To say I feel drained would be an understatement, but I know that this is the most challenging thing I've done in my life so far. I've managed to carry out my Mother's last wishes, against all the odds and in spite of all the drama.

As the sun goes down, we know it will get dark quickly and we don't have a torch. We can't afford to be stranded out here so quickly make our way back towards the road, navigating through the thick hillside jungle. It's not easy but I'm walking confidently leading with my 'bionic' left leg. I manage better than expected and some how it feels like I haven't lost my leg at all in this moment. Surprisingly Steve is the one that falls over, not once but twice! I feel at one with this land now, the ashes of my leg scattered amongst the earth. It feels strangely satisfying!

As we reach the road and civilisation, the Man dem are having a smoke. They look relieved to see us, as I guess it took longer than we expected. Before leaving I call Tony and Steve calls Hector to keep them in the loop.

In no rush to leave, we stay for a while at the side of the road drinking, smoking and reasoning. I'm still trying to get my thoughts together and the others offer up words of wisdom. After half an hour or so, we decide to head back to JR's house to pick up Steve's car and go home, yeah, now it really does feel like *home*!

Not even five minutes into the journey, I feel a presence, a vibe close to me. I'm pretty sure it's Mum come to tell me something.

'Me glad yu bring me home Garri, t'ank yu!' Goosebumps and a shiver runs up my spine and around my neck towards my ears. I shudder but feel proud and honoured I was able to do this, thank you God!

22nd March 2008
Kingston, Jamaica

Pulling up outside JR's house, Shakespeare, Steve and I say our goodbyes to JR and leave him as we all jump in Steve's car. On the drive back to Steve's house I'm actually starting to feel relieved. The more we drive, the more the underlying pressure that the mission had on me is lifting, I've actually completed it, after everything I've been through, give thanks and praise! I reflect on this sacred mission to Jamaica, to reconnect my Mother with the land of her birth and to know that from now on part of me will always be with her. Now that's deep! I smile from the inside out and in this moment I understand, that Mummy is only ever a smile away!

22nd March 2008
Steve's House

Looking out of the window, I notice how quickly it's become dark, we left the hillside just at the right time and now I have another pressing mission!

"Steve, where is the bathroom?"

"Dung de so pon de lef'." As I freshen up in the bathroom, I take a long look at myself in the mirror, noticing my eyes, I'm not really present in my body right now, but I must keep it together, it'll be okay.

Steve's voice jars me back to reality. "Uncle Garri, yu ah'right?"

"Yeah man me kool, me ah come."

"Ooh, me just ah check pon yu."

"Yu nar fi check pon me, me ah'right."

"Ah'right, yu waan ah drink, cos me feel it, so yu must feel it too." He hands me a beer with his eyes full, as I take a seat.

"Yoh Steve, yu kno' sey ah wan big ting we do de soh, end of an Era!"

"Yeah man, me kno' yu feel it, me ah put on some Studio One music fuh yu." Slim Smith singing Turning Point comes on. Sitting here contemplating in my own little zone, the sweet smell of cooking tickles my nose, where's it coming from, wha' ah gwaan? Taking a walk around the side of the house I see Steve's got a barbeque going with some jerk chicken. He's created a nice little ambience with Studio One playing in the background, so I join him. Shakespeare's killing us with jokes and roughing up the frogs. Time passes easily on this warm night as I gradually return from that distant place within me to join the others here in Jamaica.

Shakespeare's son arrives; he just flew in from Miami. During the discussions it comes out that he's a good singer, this of course sets off some old Jamaican rivalry!

"Weh yu sey, wan fi wan yute?" I challenge him to a singing dual, he accepts. The rules are loose, but basically we have to take it in turns to outdo each other, singing the best songs we know, to find out who's the better entertainer. "Yeah man me ready." He accepts with a wide self-confident grin, but I'm confident too.

"Uncle, mek sure yu deal wid de bwoy yu kno'." Steve urges me; the family honour at stake.

"Hey son, no mek dis man come from foreign, pon fi we corner, an' ah talk wicked, member ah Miami yu fly in from, kill 'im wid lyrics!" Shakespeare boastfully incites his son.

The sing off begins at once as I take the lead, it goes on for quite some time; lyrics I'd forgotten come back to mind as well as some current favourites. Even people from neighbouring houses start clapping and cheering us on, as our songs float out into the neighbourhood, while Steve does his thing with the barbeque. It's turning out to be an unexpected and powerful night. Fathead would be proud that I used one of his lyrics in the sing off!

♪*'Makeup cake up overnight'* everyone's laughing. Then I add some of my old lyrics, along side the Johnny Dollar song, everyone joins in; there's new depth to my connection with Jamaica and I like it.

After a while it seems everybody within earshot is singing, there's quite an array of voices sounding out through the community from near and far, and it's making me feel like I belong, my soul feels at home. Where do I come from? Where do I live? It's so surreal being here. The vibes sweet me and as for the jerk chicken, it tastes fantastic! "Yes nephew, yu kno' weh yu ah do." I enjoy the tasty food Steve has cooked.

"Kool noh Uncle." He looks well pleased.

"Yeah man, you have use." I tease him, he raises his eyebrows and grins.

I may be a little lean and tired but it's to be expected. Sweet Jamaica. I decide to stay overnight with Steve, living proper, like one of the Man dem, we won't chance going over Flat Bridge tonight! Steve's wife kindly makes up a bed for me and exhausted I leave them all to it.

23rd March 2008
Kingston, Jamaica

Sunday morning breakfast Yard Style fit for a king. Stomach lined and feeling good I'm ready for the road, Steve's going to take me to the Hotel via my Sister's house.

After greeting Toria, sharing our adventure yesterday, and showing her the photos, she seems happy with the mission. She asks if I want to pick fruits from her garden to take back to the Hotel. A couple of coconuts and several mangoes later I've a bag full hand picked straight from the source. Loading up my goody bag in Steve's car, I hug my niece and sister saying goodbye till next time, I know I'll be back.

En route Steve decides to take a detour, to introduce me to more family members. I recall names that Mum often mentioned; once again it's so precious to put faces to the names she deposited in my memory banks! I'm getting a little family history lesson as we approach the area where Mum was born and find the house she first grew up in. Small chickens, baby goats, and various other livestock walk freely around the property. I just have to pause for a while and take it all in; this is where my mother grew up. The longer I stand here, the more and more family members pop up, very unexpected! My cousins Blossom and Precious are last in line to meet me and I explain the family connection. As soon as Blossom realises who I am, she grabs my hand and won't let go. I can feel the love and respect they must have had for my Mum, which they now extend to me. It's so great my Mum kept in touch over the years writing letters to her family in Ewarton. The family is huge; I've already met seven cousins in such a short space of time. It's been really great to catch up with these long lost cousins. I can really feel Mummy's essence while connecting with my family.

23rd March 2008
Hotel Montego Bay, Jamaica

I get out of the car in the car park, "Steve t'ank yu so much fi ah come pon dah mission wid me. Yu kno' di great Vera Holness ah look down pon we, God bless yu."

He gets out to hug me. "Kool noh Uncle Garri, yu kno' how di plan set; simple t'ings."

"Tek time drive, big up di Man dem fi me, lickle more."

"Yes Uncle Garri, easy yu self, man."

As Steve drives away from the hotel a feeling of sadness creeps in; we had such a good time together, I got to know him well and we shared a very precious moment. Anyway, let me carry on with the rest of my holiday and not get too sentimental.

The same group of Canadian women catch sight of me as I walk through the lobby and try pulling me into their drinking game again, the smallest of the bunch of women is dancing and trying to gyrate against me; she's way too drunk to dance. As I step back another of the group starts being a little too touchy feely as well. I guess they're all tipsy and mean no harm, but I'm not in the mood for inebriated women right now, so I make my escape upstairs for a while to relax, have a wash, then I'll come back down for my walk along the beach to my spot under the tree.

Waiting for the lift to come my phone rings "Who dis?"

"Sweetness weh yu ah gwaan wid?" I don't recognise the voice. "Ah who dat?"

"Noh Gary G man."

"Bucker! Weh yu ah sey, yu de ah yard ?" Gary G aka Bucker is an old and genuine friend from Stockwell Park Estate, the Endz in London. I told him I'd be here before I left.

"Yes mi Bredda an me ah come link yu tomorrow when me 'ave time."

"Yes, yes me friend, yu kno' weh me de?"

"Me kno' Jamaica, Sugar how yu mean."

"Kool Noh." I look forward to linking up tomorrow.

24th March 2008
Montego Bay Jamaica

Bucker shows up early morning. I've known this man from my youth in London and here we are linking up in Jamaica! It's a blessing seeing him, but he's wearing a Liverpool shirt, I suppose someone has to! We spend a good time reasoning over a juice, in the sun at the front of the hotel, but Bucker has a busy day, so we say our goodbyes and he leaves.

The sun's blazing and I'm so bloody hot, the sweat is running down me, so I head down to the beach for a swim. Once in the water I feel good, I've never been in the sea before I came to Jamaica, but I will always swim when I'm here from now on. Thinking about getting out makes me uneasy, I'm aware of the flashback I had last time. Thankfully I'm distracted by one of the lifeguards who named me Arsenal.

"Yo Arsenal, Chelsea ah win 4-3!" I'm surprised, so I shout back. "Wha!" Tottenham were winning 3-1 earlier, what a come back!

As I get out of the water all is well, so I head back up the beach. The Entertainment Team try to get me involved with their activities again, but I decline, letting them know I prefer just to watch. One or two of the girls are nice so I'm tempted, but I just sit tight and watch until they finish their dance routine.

The little girl who tried to grab my foot is with her Dad, the manager of this hotel. I wonder if she's going to give me trouble again. I don't mind though, it's worth it if the Empress isn't too far behind; and here she is! Her husband walks off and she is left with the child, who makes a bee-line for me. "Lef di man foot alone, noh pickney." I smile and try to catch her eye; this woman is simply gorgeous.

"It's alright, I know she means no harm, but yu kan come play wid me foot any time." I'm shocked at what just came out of my own mouth, so I laugh to make light of it. She smiles back, and walks off with the child, only looking back once still smiling.

As I approach my little secluded corner on the beach, I realise it could not be more perfect. Behind me they are building an extension to the hotel, so no one is allowed through; Security has it blocked off. Because my spot is just past the security point, it takes some sweet-talking to get through, but I manage. It's so calm here in my little mediation spot, just sand, sea, sky, my tree and God. I sit peacefully facing the sea, me ah do my 'tings in peace. This vibe I'm feeling right here, right now, is the healing of my soul and the memory of it will live forever within me. Wow there goes a shooting star, it must be a sign!

25th March 2008
Montego Bay, Jamaica

Chaa! I don't want to leave, but everything is running smooth. Suitcase packed, breakfast is yummy as usual, I really am gonna miss my breakfast!

In reception waiting for the minibus to arrive, one of the staff reminds me to leave my cologne for her. I tell her I've put it away in my suitcase, but that seems to upset her, and I remember I said I would leave it, so I dig it out and give her the half full bottle. She looks amazed, and hugs me with a big smile on her face. Bless.

The tour guide arrives ready for us to board the mini bus. One stop Montego Bay Airport and it's only a fifteen-minute drive. Never mind, something tells me this isn't my last visit to the land of my heritage.

All airport checks done and my luggage on its way through, just waiting to board the plane back to Blighty, back to reality! I know what I have just done in the past few days will stay with me for the rest of my life, I'm so proud that I've managed to carry out my Mum's last wish. 'Thank you Mummy Holness for your guidance and protection!'

Bing bong "All Passengers for London Gatwick please go to Gate Seven." Before long I'm on the plane relaxing in my seat, I pull my jacket over my head to catch some sleep. It's another long haul back to London.

March 26th 2008
London Gatwick

As I look out of the window over London it's a stark contrast to the sun-kissed land of Jamaica, yet it's familiar, this land my Mother chose to spend her last days. This is my home, where I was born and brought up, and where I choose to live my life too.

After landing I take a train from Gatwick to East Croydon, I reach home safe and sound, pick up my post, unpack my suitcase, put my washing in before calling my brother Tony to let him know I'm back. Build a lickle ting and relax; sleep comes easy.

27th March 2008
Home Croydon

I check my diary to get up to date with my schedule, I have a Hospital appointment on Monday, a meeting on Wednesday and on Thursday I'm seeing my friend Jo in Hampstead for lunch. I try to keep busy, it's not good being unemployed, it's bloody hard trying to find work, especially when your name is all over the Internet associated with bad press. Although search engines, are not my ally, I'm not going to allow them to dictate my life.

31st March 2008
Royal Free Hospital Hampstead

After the specialist, Doctor Quiney, examines my ears he looks thoughtful and pauses for a second. "Garri the first op gave you an improvement in your hearing, but it seems there's been a slight movement which has adversely affected it."

"Ah, I thought something wasn't right."

"So, with your permission I'd like to operate again. What I'll be doing this time, is putting three prosthetic bones together to create a tunnel, then insert it into your ear with keyhole surgery."

"That sounds interesting, I knew my hearing wasn't as good as it was when you first operated." I feel uplifted, after all I've been through, another keyhole surgery seems like a walk in the park.

"Okay Garri, see our receptionist before you leave for your appointment so we can get it done."

"Okay that's great thank you," I'm so looking forward to being able to hear in my left ear again.

"See you soon Garri." Doctor Quiney leaves me uplifted.

"Yeah, see you soon Doc." On the way out I get the booking confirmed for 21st April and I'm feeling more than hopeful.

2nd April 2008
Holborn London

I spend the day discussing compensation with Solicitor. Too long!

3rd April 2008 13:00
Hampstead London

I enjoy a light lunch with my lovely friend Jo; it's great to socialise with an intelligent person. I consider myself lucky to have friends on so many different levels. After lunch and a nice chat she has to head back to work,

"Take care hunni and have a great afternoon." I smile as we hug, she's warm and caring.

"Thanks Garri I'll do my best and thanks for lunch, it was great catching up with you again." I watch her walk back towards work. Who would of thought I'd have a friend who is a Human Rights Solicitor? Maybe I'm a product of my environment, but I can surely mix with a wide range of people.

Anyway, let me focus on driving home. Seat belt, start my X3, but before I pull away, which house CD shall I put in? Ah yes I found just the one. Cruising back home to the sounds of 'Kphil House Party Lick FM', it's good to be alive as I drive through Camden, Euston, Russell Square, Bloomsbury, Holborn, The Strand, Westminster, Lambeth Bridge, Kennington and Brixton. It may not be colourful like Jamaica, but I do like London.

3rd April 2008 15:00
Brixton London

I can't drive passed TZ'z without stopping. Brixton has special memories and will always remind me of Mum. I walk into the reception area and find Tony just finishing off with a customer. I catch his eye and wait until the customer leaves.

"T, wha' ah gwaan?"

"How are you Shuggs?" He looks pleased to see me.

"Very well my Brother, but I'm still hungry I need proper food, I'm going outta road do you want anything?"

"You paying?" He laughs raising his eyebrows mischievously.

"Just kool man, what d'you want?" I lift my chin as I grin back

"Just get me a beef pattie in a coco bread."

"What yu kno' 'bout dem food dey?" I'm surprised he asks for Caribbean food, but then he's been in Brixton all his life, something had to rub off.

"*KMT!* Sugar man, hold me a Guinness punch as well, any size will do."

"You really think your still in Jamaica innit, anyway me soon come." I hurry away to pick up the food.

Back from Brixton Market, we sit together talking and sharing the food until it's time to leave him to his work. The customers are waiting."TZ, me gone ah me yard Rudebwoy."

"Thanks for this Shuggs."

"Easy my Brother."

"It was bloody needed, so busy today man, I'll call you later."

"Alright mate." Jumping back in my X3 I head home feeling satisfied with a full stomach.

21st April 2008
Royal Free Hospital Hampstead

I arrive early, my belly's rumbling as I couldn't have breakfast but it's worth it, if I get my hearing back. The procedure goes ahead smoothly and it's completed soon enough. I feel good, but they tell me I must rest here 'til late evening when the anaesthetic has worn off. It's a good opportunity for reading and meditating. The more time I spend meditating the better I feel. We have a choice; think about that which feeds our creative imagination or else allow fear to castrate it. We choose. And as castration is out of the question, I have to feed my creative imagination; if I can imagine it I can do it. My mind goes back to my high jump record and I can't help but smile,

I really did imagine myself going over that high jump and I did it!

It's late evening and time to go home. Still feeling a little dizzy as I get into the car, but pretty much back to normal. Even though my ear is covered in a cotton wool dressing to protect it, I can definitely hear sounds as vehicles pass my left side, very much louder than I did before the operation. It feels like it did after the first op, but this time I hope it's gonna last. Let's see what happens, I'll have to wait two weeks before they can remove the dressing, until then fingers crossed.

I'm very careful over the next couple of weeks monitoring my healing by singing and listening to music, in between exercise and meditation. The meditation keeps me centred and it's useful for visualising my ear healed and my hearing better.

7th May 2008
Royal Free Hospital Hampstead

The ear specialist is happy with my results and the level of hearing he's reclaimed for me is remarkable. It will take time to fully heal but the operation is a complete success. I'll need to use a hearing aid, but that's okay, I can hear a wide range of sounds even without it and that's the main thing. It makes such a difference.

June 2008
London

During the next few weeks my hearing slowly but steadily improves. As the warmer weather arrives I spend time out having lunch with a few friends. It's good to get out of the house and I especially enjoy meeting up with my fantastic Solicitor Caroline and her friend Karen; it's always very interesting and informative to spend time with them. I'm also delighted to get the all clear to fly again, so I book a holiday to Spain next month and can't wait to catch up with the Lick FM Crew and drink two drinks at Terra Blues bar.

July 2008
London Gatwick Airport

Time for a short break we board the plane for Spain and I relax back in my seat. My hearing is already around 30% better and I'm excited to think it's gonna last, and possibly improve more. An hour into the flight my ear pops and my full hearing returns instantly. It's quite amazing to be able to hear the sound of a sweet wrapper being crumpled two seats away! I haven't been able to hear this well since before the bombing. I figure it has something to do with the air pressure.

July 2008
Marbella Spain

As usual Spain is beautiful, the Sun is beating hard and there's a warm breeze. I'm chilling out on the beach with a few friends joking and laughing. The enhanced hearing I experienced on the flight only lasted for a few hours after landing. Still, it's much better than it was before the op and I'm loving that I can hear music, coming from somewhere up the beach.

I'm excited to be invited to The Sisu Hotel, apparently this is a place where celebrities come to party. Lick FM are hosting Kphil, a celebrity DJ from the US, and he's busting up the place with big tunes! As I glance around I see various young TV actors and a few footballers posing as they floss with their big bottles of champagne in the middle of the afternoon; it feel like an interesting life-style as I sit looking in from the outside.

As I mingle, I enjoy people watching, several people including a few of the more famous acknowledge me as I walk past their little groups. I guess I might look as if I fit in with my one away mesh top on, but it's clear to me now that this life-style is not for me and I'm glad I'm not part of it.

We leave soon, as we have lots on the agenda with food shopping to get done, and I want to pass by the port shops to take in the sale, on the way back to the hotel in time to fix up, shower and put on some fresh clothes ready for this evening. I love Spain so vibrant and carefree.

My time in Spain is a great boost to my healing as always and puts me in a better space to go home and get on with re-building my life. I don't know how I would manage without these short trips to the sunshine.

20th August 2008
Croydon Home

I get a call from my casting agency to do an advert in Chiswick on 22nd August; it's going to be a long day but it's work and I agree to do it. I will face it with positivity and an early night under my belt. I look forward to meeting new people, which is an added bonus.

22nd August 2008
Croydon Home

After a good breakfast I'm well prepared for my long day. Now it's time to sort out my Sat Nav. Also in case of wardrobe malfunction, I'll need clothes to change into. Finally on my way, first the petrol station, tank up then off I go to Chiswick. But before I set off let me find my Jazzy Soulful House CD. Music is such a beautiful thing.

I have to take the motorway, even though I don't like driving on motorways, and the M25 is a huge motorway that circles around the outside of Greater London. It's actually one of the busiest in the UK. Still, I do know it's good to get out of my comfort zone and confront my fears, every now and then. It's the only way I'm gonna rebuild my confidence and my life!

22nd August 2008
Chiswick

It's a good day filming and socialising, I always enjoy being on set. I have a little chat with one of the main actors Normski, from back in the day, which is apparently unusual as there tends to be an us and them divide. I try to be just the same with everyone I meet regardless of who they are. It helps me regain my confidence and shows me I get back what I put out. Most of the other extras complain they are ignored, and I'm glad that doesn't often happen to me.

It's been a long, full on day and I'm cold and knackered, so get ready to drive home. I can't wait to get home after filming outside all day with only film set food from the caravans on site. I need some warmth and proper food inside me. Although it's summer there are no guarantees of summer weather in England. As I pack up my car my phone rings. "Who dis?" The line crackles.

"Yo what you saying Sugar, its Platts."

"What's good bruv?"

"I've got a G4 Mac I'm letting go of, are you interested?"

"Link me tomorrow an' we chat, I'm driving an yu know what di Bwoydem's like."

"Ah'right Sugar, tomorrow den."

23rd August 2008
Croydon Home

I call Sanj aka Platts to discuss the G4 he's selling.

"Yes my Brother I'm interested, I do need to upgrade so I can start recording some proper tunes, but I need some help y'know. I've never used a Mac, I'm a windows man."

"Sugar that's standard man, I can help."

"That's great thanks! I've been writing some songs but I want to start again, be a blank canvas and write from the new space I'm in, but I need some guidance Bruv."

"Sugar, I can write, produce, build beats and mix the tracks, didn't you know?"

"What?" I'm surprised to hear how much he can help me.

"Yeah man."

"So what you saying Sanj, we're good to go?"

"Yep."

"We can arrange something where we link twice a week, so we can start to get something going, if that fits in with your schedule?"

"Yeah that's kool, I could start in September but we have to work something out payment wise."

"Yeah man no problem, so what you saying Monday, Tuesday, say twelve till six in the evening?" I'm excited to get a different level of creativity again; it's been a while.

"Yeah, good for me." What a blessing, getting an upgrade on my Studio and assistance as well. Now I can get back into singing and writing much more seriously.

Over breakfast I zone out thinking about song writing as the Sun shines in through my window.

11th June 1984
Home Stockwell Park Estate

The Sun's shining in my room and it's warm, such a beautiful day. I hear the ice-cream van's tinny jingle in the distance. I open the window and let in some air. It's all about the music today, where's my version tape? After rummaging around I find it, and turn on the amp, echo chamber, equalizer, tape deck, and the mixer. "Mic check one. Mic check one," my voice echoes.

Music sounds out, Little John, instrumental 'In the Ghetto'♪ *"I was born and raised in the ghetto."* I am disturbed by loud banging on the door and Mum shouting, "Garri! Ah 'ow yu 'ave on di music so loud, yu ah keep dance? Ah me ah pay di light bill! Ah outta road me ah 'ear yu ah sing." She looks vexed.

"Sorry Mum, I'll turn it down."

"Ah better yu go fine' work 'bout you in yah ah sing, yu kan sing?" She says flippantly.

"Den me noh sound good Mummy?" I'm fishing for a compliment, tongue in cheek.

"All me ah sey, when yu done weh yu ah do, me left di money yahso, buy four bottle of milk fi me outta Sidney Road."

"But Mummy, you can't tell me ah sound good?" Still fishing.

"Yu sound ah'right but is betta yu go find work, it pay better an' member fi go buy di milk." She brings me back to Earth with a bang, crushing my dream!

23rd August 2008
Croydon Home

Sanj drops in to deliver the G4 and after he leaves I just stare at it! This one hard drive, screen and keyboard can replace all those old machines I used to have. My technology upgrade is fantastic! I clean it up and find the perfect spot for it in my bedroom; look what I'll be singing and recording on now. I'm so happy!

Once it's ready, it's time to unwind. What shall I watch this evening? A documentary I think, 'The Anunaki'.

26th August 2008
London Pimlico

I have lunch with my friend Annabel today. I met Annabel a few years ago at a BBC event with Carlton. We just clicked and stayed friends ever since. She's from a completely different background to me and they say opposites attract, I can but hope; she's beautiful and also physically fit, I feel fortunate to have her as a friend. Annabel arrives punctually on her bike. We have a funny kinda trade off; I'm making her more streetwise, she is making me more articulate and professional. She keeps reminding me I've got to teach her to dance as well. It's lovely catching up with Annabel, a breath of fresh air; she brings out another side of me. They say it's all about the company you keep! Swim with sharks, you become a shark!

29th August 2008
Home Croydon

Friday already, this week's gone fast. Getting ready for Brick Lane and The Magic House Experience tonight, Tasha invited me along and I'm looking forward to it.

29th August 2008
East London

We arrive in a convoy of cars, all dressed up as we do. Once inside I feel the vibrant energy and beautiful vibe of the more mature crowd. "What you drinking Tash?"

"I'll have a glass of red wine please Garri."

Walking over to the bar a few familiar faces stand out. As I wait for the drinks I notice Tash engrossed in conversation with a woman. As I return with the drinks, she introduces me to Rose Windross, the lead singer of the Magic House Experience, who used to sing with Soul2Soul back in the day.

Rose leaves us to go on stage and sing with the live band. Song after song she nails it, she's a great performer and is really getting my creative juices flowing; what an experience, she's right where I want to be, singing live. It's the perfect time to have upgraded my own mini studio. Now I feel inspired to actually get on with my music and work towards performing as well.

I'm having such a laugh with this group of people; they are so much fun and it's good to see several old skool faces. Norris 'DaBoss' Rose's brother, Creed and Spoony. I used to see these guys regularly at 'Twice as Nice' in the Colosseum at Vauxhall, when it first started. The crowd there were lovely too, the same type of people as here, it's real. Big up the Magic House Experience, Brick Lane; you got it going on!

31st August 2008
Home Croydon

I've washed the car, tidied up the garden and now it's time to chill and get engrossed in pre-season football. Not much is gonna get in the way of this today.

1st September 2008
Home Croydon

Sorting out my paperwork and bringing my diary up to date, gives me the sense of getting my life together; more Doctor's appointments this coming week. At least I've got this paper work done and out of the way so I can make time for my music.

8th September 2008
Queen Mary's Hospital Roehampton

During my check-up with Dr Soori, I mention the slight discomfort caused by the blister on my stump. He tells me not to worry, as the skin will harden in time. However as a precautionary measure, they decide to slightly adjust the inner plastic of the socket. They call it a 'blow out', which involves remoulding the shape of the plastic fitting that sits next to my stump, so it's not as tight. The prosthetic guys get it sorted out while I wait, which saves me another journey. After they've made the adjustment it feels so much more comfortable, but the only way I'll know for sure is when I've walked on it for a few days.

15th September 2008
Home Croydon

In between working with Sanj on my music, I've been sending out my CV to test the water, trying to get back into work, but so far it hasn't been fruitful. I guess when any prospective employer searches me on the Internet, it pulls up pages and pages of the same old headlines. It's a real disadvantage and I really could do with some help, so I decide to email Tessa Jowell. As she is assigned as a point of contact for the Government to assist the 7/7 survivors, I figure I should ask her for help. I write expressing my disappointment about my unfruitful attempts at finding a job and my desire to get back into the work force; I feel I've so much to give. Lets see what happens now.

16th September 2008
Home Croydon

The adjustment to my leg has made a big difference; it's definitely more comfortable than it was before. The way I walk is getting better and better and relatively pain free. The day also gets better and better as I open an email from Tessa Jowell, she has responded to my email already and her assistant has sent me details of a youth project that may offer me some voluntary work, as a way to get back into the business world. I'm so pleased; at least I'll be putting my experience to good use. I call them straight away and speak with the main guy; he says he loves what I have to offer in terms of my experience and would like to see me on Wednesday. Result!

17th September 2008
Lollard Street Kennington

I arrive for my appointment early and think how funny life is; here I am back at my old secondary school. Taking in the old building from the parking area provokes memories that flood back in. 'Penny up the wall', 'Run outs' football round the back on the green and sneaking out at break time to go to the sweet shops on Lambeth Walk. I chuckle to myself, as everything looks so incredibly small, I feel like a bloody giant! As I walk into the assembly hall, which from memory was huge and quite daunting, probably because it leads to the Head-Masters office, it seems different now, very different. As I sign in, I'm directed to the main office to meet the boss.

He's a nice guy and we have a brief chat about the job before he introduces me to other members of staff. I'm asked if I would like to stay the whole day, to see how things work. Willingly I accept, as I'm keen to make a start, what a place to be though Beaufoy Secondary School, how ironic. I'm back where it all started, but this time, maybe I can help guide the youth of today stay away from trouble. That would be worthwhile indeed.

I'm given a form to fill in for a CRB check, they say it could take eight weeks, but the boss assures me that it is still possible to work three days a week until the CRB has been done. I feel so good to be given the chance to get back to work.

22nd September 2008
Lollard Street Kennington

My first full day officially going out to work since the Bombings feels so great. After a busy morning I'm in the kitchen making a hot drink, when I hear a commotion coming from the corridor.

Opening the door I see two teenage boys scuffling and a female member of staff looking on helplessly. She obviously can't separate the boys and looks like she has no intention to even try.

Quickly sizing up the situation, and mindful of the CRB not yet in place, I move in and stand in between the two boys raising my voice. "You lot calm down."

"What, wha'?" They look surprised.

"Just calm down." I'm firm and alert, watching both boys.

The taller boy whinges at me, "He's taking liberty's, doh."

"Allow it man." I remain firm, looking straight into his eyes.

"Nar blud." He looks back at the other boy.

"Rise above it Rudebwoy." I insist, but they try to move around me, to start fighting again. I react quickly lifting him up and putting him down in the corner. "Stay there!" I shout, he seems shocked and stays put, so I turn my attention the other boy.

"And you, don't bother with it." Looking him in the eye and using a tone they both understand, he listens. Realising he is dealing with an Elder from his own culture, he knows he isn't going to get away with it, the squabble is over and they move on.

"Oh gosh! Well done Garri! Thank you! I didn't know what to do."

"Its okay, don't worry about it." I feel empowered, as if I'm in the right place at the right time. But at the same time, I'm concerned to think that a woman is put into a risky situation like this; I suddenly realise why they want someone like me here!

24th September 2008
Lollard Street Kennington

I have another great day at work assisting other members of staff; I'm starting to get the hang of things. I like being useful, a new sense of purpose.

26th September 2008
Lollard Street Kennington

It's training day for some members of staff, but because I'm still waiting for my CRB check to go through, they've left me in the office to file and answer the phones. Guess I'm in for a busy one then!

29th September 2008
Lollard Street Kennington

Out with the kids to an Art Gallery; brilliant day, I love art. This new sense of purpose inspires me and I enjoy the day very much, I'm so grateful to Tessa.

1st October 2008
Lollard Street Kennington

I find myself deep in conversation with a boy who has a personal problem hopefully my advice will help resolve it. These kids are starting to open up to me, I'm so grateful for that. I can understand them; after all I was one of them. I get where they're coming from and I recognise their uncertainty, so maybe I can make a difference. To plant one seed of positivity, that grows flourishes and blossoms, will be a joy to watch. If only someone had been there to guide me through the pitfalls I faced, it could have been life changing. All these kids need to know is how the system works and given a little guidance around the pitfalls so they can stand a chance of creating a successful and worthwhile life. We are part of the human race; and it is a race, so the point is to win! Who said a black man can't win a race? Look at Usain Bolt. Yes we can!

3rd October 2008
Lollard Street Kennington

It's my birthday and I'm at work. But at least I have a purpose. When I get home a little low-key celebration and then it's all about my music.

6th October 2008
Lollard Street Kennington

I feel very disappointed to learn I can't continue working at the school today. It's a huge blow as I was settling in so well. The boss tells me he has overlooked a company policy that states you cannot even be on the premises without a CRB in place. This means I wouldn't be able to come in again for another six weeks or more until the CRB comes through and they need someone straight away. We agree I should look for something else, rather than wait around doing nothing; it's very disappointing.

It takes me a few days to reboot; but when I do, I realise that this is another blessing in disguise, as it will give me more time for my music, which is improving week on week! Positivity in adversity, its always there if you look hard enough.

13th October 2008
Queen Mary's Hospital Roehampton

"Okay Garri, Dr Soori would like to see you now."

"Thank you," I make my way down a small corridor to his office and I'm greeted with a smile. "Hello Garri, how you keeping?"

"Well thanks, as well as can be expected Doc."

"Good good, today I have a colleague here with me. Let me introduce you to Dr Jones; he's a Prosthetics Sports Specialist. I wonder do you mind if he sits in with us?"

"Yeah, yeah that's okay; sounds interesting, I love sport."

After the consultation, we decide I need to be more active and I should join a local Gym. I've got to strengthen my core as well as my legs and arms. It's time to really come out of my comfort zone by joining a regular gym. It's time to put my focus back on me again; it's got to be about my well being and improving my health.

20th October 2008
Local Gym

Turning my car into the car park, I find a disabled bay right outside the entrance, how lucky is that! As I go in through the glass doors reception is light and airy with very high ceilings. It's got a nice vibe. I just know people are going to look at me, especially in my shorts, but I don't care, I've come to work out just like everybody else. I offer the receptionist the pass I downloaded from the Internet. She's cute and smiles at me warmly before calling for one of the Trainers to come and give me my orientation. We exchange pleasantries while I wait.

The trainer arrives looking lean and fit, he shakes my hand and smiles.
"Follow me then Garri, let me show you around."
"Okay man, lead the way." He leads me up three flights of stairs to the first floor, passing a wall of windows to the right side that offer a view of the swimming pool and spa area. Looks like there are three Jacuzzi's, steam room and a sauna as well. The whole swimming area has a feeling of spaciousness as the ceiling goes right up to the roof. It's impressive, no chance of feeling claustrophobic in here. At the top of the stairs he continues around the mezzanine floor into the gym area. I scan the machines as he shows me around, and my eyes rest on a bike in the front of the main Gym. I feel the need to stretch my legs as I've got loads of energy to release. Once he finishes showing me around the three Gyms, I get on the bike and put my towel over the handle bar so that I don't see the screen time. I'm going to test myself to see how long I can cycle without stopping.

Pretty soon sweat drips down my face and body but it feels so good. I really need to let go, as I haven't done that for ages. The things we take for granted are sometimes such a joy when we lose them then regain them. A guy approaches and stands behind me, "You really gave that some welly Mate."
"You what?" I look up, unsure of what he means.

"The bike, you really gave it some welly."

"Oh yeah, yeah the bike, I haven't used my legs like that in a very long time!"

"Did you realise you were pedalling so hard the bike was lifting off the floor?"

"What, really? I didn't feel it, I must have been miles away." I smile at the young man as he walks off, but he's brought to my attention that I have an audience; the pressure is on.

Phew, I don't even feel my legs right now, I must be on a high; maybe I'll feel it tomorrow. I look around trying to decide what I can and can't do before I set up a program in my mind to follow. I have to be careful not to hurt myself, but at the same time I want to show that I am more than capable; time to be focused and zone in.

27th October 2008
Home Croydon

My brother Tony's number comes up on my phone, but there's a pause when I answer. "What's going on bruv?"

"Bwoy Garri I've got some bad news y'know." He's solemn.

"What's that?"

"Dad's in King's College Hospital man."

"What?" My vibe dips.

"Yeah I just found out." He sounds upset.

"Ok bruv I'm going to call and see what's going on, do you know what ward he's in?"

"Yeah…" He gives me the details and I call Dad's wife straight away. She tells me that the Doctors told her he only has a short time left with us, so Tony and I have to go and see our Dad as soon as possible.

28th October 2008
Kings College Hospital London

Looking at Dad in the Hospital bed is not a pretty sight, as I remember the handsome, charming, fun loving, strong man he once was reduced to an insecure, frail man with only a dim sparkle left in his eyes. He eyelids flutter as I draw close, then as he catches sight of me, a faint smile appears, its heart warming.

"You all right Dad?" he shakes his head slowly. I get up close so I can whisper in his ear, "Dad always remember you're a great Father. Even though there were ups and down, I'm proud to say you're my Dad and…" I go on.

I have much to say to him before he goes, along with a message to give Mummy when he catches up with her. I wonder how that must sound, but anyway it feels right to me.

We leave the hospital in a very sombre mood, as I reflect on the deep and meaningful things I said to Dad. It feels like closure, and I am grateful to have had the chance to say goodbye to him. That's something I didn't have with Mum. There's a strained silence in the car as we drive back to Tony's flat and I park up next to his car on the Estate. "You alright Tony?" I put my hand on his shoulder.

"Yeah man, I'm alright." He turns to look at me with sadness, yet strength in his eyes.

"You sure?"

"Yeah, yeah." He taps my hand to acknowledge he's okay.

"Ah'right, lickle more."

"Drive safe Bruv."

2nd November 2008
Home Croydon

Late afternoon my Dad's wife calls, to tell me he's passed away. Even though we were expecting it, there's a sudden dip in my frequency as it dawns on me I'm now an orphan!

November passes quickly, finding me deep in contemplation. I reflect on my past, my life now and how my future may unfold. I decide to bury myself in my music, meditation and the Gym to try and uplift my spirit.

1st December 2008
Home Croydon

Today is all about perfecting the song Sanj and I have been working on since September. Studio turned on, mic position sorted, it's all about singing the 'guide vocals', I've gotta get the opening right. After a few vocal warm up exercises with the beat playing in the background, it's time to go in. Yes I'm going in remembering to pronounce my words clearly and with character like Sanj has suggested. Using the skeleton melody we have already put down, its time to play around with the vocals, let's see how this goes…

"♪*From the Day*… nah! *From the day*… hmmm… *From the day our love was borrrrn*. Mmm nearly there… *From the Day our lovvve was Borrrn*, yep that's it.

My intercom buzzes and stops my flow.

"Hello"

"Ello der, is Sugar der pleeze?" I don't recognise the strange accent. "Who dat?"

"We got ah meeting twelve huh'clock, to do di muzic ting."

"Sanj! Stop with di stupidness and come in." Sanj walks in laughing.

"Easy Sugar, how are you Bruv?"

"I'm good mate, I was just practicing the beginning of the song."

"Good, when you get dat, the res' will follow, truss' me."

"Funny you should say that, I was thinking the same thing earlier, d'you wanna drink?"

"I wouldn't say no mate, got any coffee?"

"Yeah I have, two sugars, milky?"

"Sugar, how d'you know dat?"

"I don't know mate it just come to me…soon come!"

Sanj sips on his coffee while he listens to the track.

"Sugar, your vocals, yeah man you're gettin' there, I'm starting to feel it more now, but tighten up the beginning."

"I know man, it's hard work though."

"I know Sugar that's why I'm pushing you man; you've got a great tone to your voice but you need to express it more. It's gotta grab them from the first word. Like dis. ♪*Frrum the Dhey, our lovve was Bournnnn…* you get me?"

"Alwight mate, I get it!" He makes it sound so easy!

2nd December 2008
Home Croydon

Sanj is working on our track in detail today, changing the sounds of instruments putting some on mute and adding others; it's interesting to watch him at work.

"Sugar, how does that sound?" He plays the beginning.

"Sounds alright."

"I don't want alright Bruv, I want to know how it sounds."

"Play it again." I listen more intently this time.

"You preferred the other one though innit?"

"Yep." I have to be honest.

"Ok let me try sumtin', what about dis Sugar?"

He plays a different version. "That sounds messi!"

"Okay, bear with me while I make a few minor adjustments"

"Yeah man do your t'ing, I'll sit back and observe; I need to know how to operate the system as well." I watch as he goes into detail with the Logic software, which was already on the G4, he engineers the tracks with various effects. It's fascinating to me and I am eager to learn.

8th December 2008
Home Croydon

The music Sanj and I put together is playing in the background. We still ain't got a name for it, but I'm sure it will come to us.

"Sugar try this… ♪*Even though we just got started; don'no if the end is cloSsse.'* remember to pronounce the ends."

"I've got dis Sanj."

"That's the confidence I wanna hear."

"♪Even though we just got Started; don'no know if the end is cloSsse."

"Messi, gwaan Sugar, alright you're ready to lay down some guide vocals."

"Oh yes!" It turns into a long day, but we manage to put down a rough version that I can use as a guide.

It's not till we listen back to the track that I understand why he asked me to redo certain parts and how to emphasise certain words; to push the dynamics in my voice, It's to give the song a certain feel, this is a learning curve and I'm lovin' it. As we listen to it over and over the title drops in unexpectedly 'Live 4 Now' of course. Good advice too!

9th December 2008
Home Croydon

In the garden checking out my plants, I can hear my song floating out through the window. It's turned up loud on a loop, so I can hear it from out here. It helps me to understand it so I can learn how to sing it better. Sanj shows up right on time for todays session, but we stay outside for a while taking in the sounds. Suddenly Sanj frowns, straightens up, and becomes more alert. "You alright bruv?"

"Yeah yeah, I just heard something I didn't like."

"Where?"

"In the beat, very faint, let me go and check."

Back in the studio Sanj discovers the problem. "Sugar, look you see that." He shows me the problem.

"Oh yeah."

"Overlapping! That's the noise I heard." He deletes it and plays the music again; he doesn't miss a thing. We continue to write the rest of 'Live 4 Now'.

15th December 2008
Home Croydon

My mobile rings out, the introduction of Starvue, Body Fusion so I start moving to the rare groove classic and nearly forget it's the ringtone so I should answer it, before it goes to answer-phone. "Hello."

"Yeah Shugg, it's me man, I'm running late, turn on the system till I come."

"Yeah mate no problem, where you at?"

"The trains are running late again innit."

"Alright mate I'll see you soon."

"Easy."

Okay that gives me more time to work on holding those long notes. '♪*So we gotta live for naaaawwwh, so we gotta live for the moment…*'

Warmed up nicely and feeling confident as Sanj arrives.

"You good bruv?"

"Yeah man the bloody trains, sorry Sugar mate let me just deal with this." He takes off his jacket and hat then adjusts his scarf, before sliding out of his trainers.

"Here you go mate" I hand him a cup of coffee and bowl of biscuits. "Cheers mate." He smiles!

"No problem, you need to relax first. After your coffee can I redo the middle eight?"

"Redo the middle eight Sugar?"

"Yeah man, I know I can do it better, smoother, now that I know what I'm suppose to be singing."

"Alright let me finish this and I'll get the track ready."

16th December 2008
Home Croydon

As we come out of the kitchen clutching cups of lemon and honey, the middle eight I did yesterday is playing; it sounds so much better. "Sanj what do you think Bruv?"

"Sugar I must admit you've improved a lot, what I like about you is that you listen, you're willing to learn *And* you practice."

"Thanks for that Bruv."

"Yes, you're right it sounds much better."

We continue to work on the track until six o'clock, the honey and lemon really soothes my throat and makes the transitions smoother.

"Hey Sugar, I won't be around over the Christmas period and New Years.

I gotta few jobs to finish off, but while I'm doing that I'll try to book you into a recording studio in the New Year, so in the mean time, practice hard on your vocals so that you're ready and good to go, you get me?"

"Yeah man." It sounds exciting and I feel motivated.

"Your hard work's paying off, trust me music's not easy."

"I know man, I know."

"Ok then Bruv have a good Christmas, keep up the hard work and I'll see you in the New Year."

"Yeah Bruv, thanks for all your guidance and the work you've put in, have a great Christmas, you know I'll be practicing and I'll see you in the New Year."

We fist pound, in a gesture of friendship and mutual respect.

17th December 2008
Croydon Home

All I can hear in my head is the lyrics to 'Live 4 Now' repeating over and over; time to practice but first I've got to warm up my vocals. Mouth exercises, breathing exercises, vocal exercises for around ten minutes before I'm good to go.

I start singing and recording. Four hours later, I wonder where the time has gone. I need to eat, turn off the set and relax for a while. For the next couple of weeks this is to be part of my routine, so I'll be ready for the studio.

The last part of the year ends as a blur and the days roll into each other, from music to the Gym in amongst the inevitable build up to Christmas and New Year running on in the background.

5th January 2009
Home Croydon

Mobile rings, I still love my ringtone and can't help but dance as it rings.

"Sugar mate I haven't forgotten ya." Sanj sounds tired.

"Sanj! I kno' you haven't forgotten me mate, wha' ah gwaan?"

"How you been Sugar? Did you have a good Christmas and how was the New Year?"

"Yeah my Christmas was alright, I watch the 4400 series, interesting!"

"What did you watch that on?"

"Hard drive Mate. Then New Year, what did I do? Apart from singing and going to the Gym a few times, I just chilled man and watched a couple movies what about you?"

"Same ole, same ole Shuggs, Family ting you know how it goes. Anyway, I'm waiting for my Bredrin Mike to get back to me about availability at his Studio in Thornton Heath, don't worry mate he's a good friend and we'll get a good price."

"Ok my brother, I'll leave that with you, but let me know asap, so I can fit it into my diary."

"No problem mate, easy."

"Kool noh'."

11th January 2009
Home Croydon

It's Monday morning, back from the Gym and greeted with a note pinned on my inner door. I open it to find that the Metropolitan Police need to see me urgently. I'm confused and curious so I make my way over there, still in my gym gear. On arrival they call me to an interview room, and then caution me! WTF, I'm baffled. Then the plain-clothes officer from S.O.C.A says he would like to talk to me about class A drugs.

"What you talking about man, class A drugs, are you serious?" It's like a nightmare and I can't help but think it's a distasteful joke. He starts showing me some photographs of POI's. (People of interest) "Do you know any of these men?" I don't know most of them, but some I do. They tell me that unbeknown to me, I've been under Police surveillance for the past eighteen months! I'm shocked and speechless. My mind races over what I've been doing over the past eighteen months that involved any of these men; I can't think of anything. Finally it dawns on me, I was on my way to hospital passing through Brixton and I got a puncture; I went to a friends garage to get it sorted, where some of these guys sometimes hang out. I left my car there to sort out the wheel and borrowed a car. I continued my journey to the hospital in the borrowed car apparently with the Police tailing it. So it seems I inadvertently was dragged into the umbrella of their investigation for eighteen months!

Anyway the Police leave me locked up in a cell, while they go to check out my house for drugs paraphernalia. I spend a while exercising trying to keep warm as I didn't shower after my trip to the gym earlier, and the exercise keeps my spirits up.

After a couple hours they return and take me back in the interview room. The only evidence they find is a bank statement, showing a transaction that links me to one of the POI's.

"Further to what you've told us, I am now charging you with money laundering Mr Holness."

"Money laundering, are you kidding me!? Where do you see evidence of money laundering in my account? There aren't any credits at all, only a debit because I made an investment in this guys fashion business. The stock I bought is still in my flat."

"Hmmm. "They aren't happy, so bang me up in the cell again and leave to check my flat a second time. This time I'm getting pissed off.

The first time I took my mind of it with exercise, but now I'm feeling tired, stressed and uncomfortable. Before I know it I find myself rocking back and forth on the bench and knocking my head against the wall; it seems comforting somehow. They're taking liberties, look how long they're gone. I need to get outta here; I need to get out now! I put my finger on the buzzer needing to get attention before I have an episode of zoning out. The Duty Officer comes to the hatch. "What's up?"

"I want out please, I'm feeling claustrophobic."

"What?"

"I need to get out of this cell now, do you know I have stress relayed problems caused by the bombing? Can you please get me one of your bosses, they've got to let me out?" The flap shuts promptly and I hear him hurry away. Within five minutes one of the top boys comes down, and opens the cell door. "You alright Garri?"

"No I'm not!"

"Okay then come and sit in the waiting area."

"That's better, thanks Officer, I'm not in a good place right now."

It's some time before the officers return from my house, once again with nothing, except a flippant comment about liking my DVD collection! Bloody cheek! This time they let me go home, telling me to return to the Police Station on the 9th March to find out if they are going to charge me with supplying class A drugs and money laundering. Really? I'm actually feeling proper angry with this now.

"So, if I'm found guilty, what am I looking at?" I want to know the worst that can happen.

"Maybe ten to twelve years."

"Ten to twelve years! But wait, you know I'm really not involved in this don't you?"

"We'll see."

Very shocked indeed at the thought of Prison, but as a feeling of dread starts rising one of the Officers pulls me to one side quietly and tries to comfort me.

"Garri we know you've got some very powerful friends; you know we've been following you, up in Hampstead, Holborn, Victoria etc." He winks.

"Raaah! All those lunch dates I had?" He nods, I smile.

"We're just dotting the 'i's and crossing the 't's, you should be okay Garri, don't worry." Again I see the more compassionate side of Policemen.

"Ahhh! Okay, thank you, I appreciate that." I'm a bit relieved, but that's not the point, I don't need this unnecessary stress. Stress causes us to make chemicals that aren't good for our health at all, and I'm not going to be able to relax until March, when all this is sorted out. *KMT* Chaa man!

19th January 2009
Home Croydon

My mobile rings, "Who goes?"

"Sugar, I just spoke to Mike, you free next Monday?" It's Sanj.

"What dates that?"

"Err."

I look in my diary,"26th, yeah man that's good for me."

"So I can tell Mike to book us in for this Monday, yeah?"

"Yeah mate Monday 26th no problem."

"I'll try to arrange more dates with him when I see him later."

"Okay so we are good to go."

"You ready Sugar?"

"Yeah man."

"You were practicing?"

"Of course man."

"You sure?"

"Come off my phone Sanj!" Laughter, then the line goes dead. Hopefully this will help take my mind off the pending Police investigation.

25th January 2009
Home Croydon

Got to make sure I get a good night's sleep tonight bwoy, tomorrow is a big day, me ah cut me first tune! I take a sip of honey and lemon and sit back to listen to the guide for 'Live 4 Now' paying very close attention to the change of melody and the dynamic one last time before we record. I'm totally focused on this now.

26th January 2009
Home Croydon

Eating oats for breakfast to line the stomach, as is my habit, it's going to be a long day so I must prepare myself. I check my stuff; lyrics, pen, water, phone, wallet and a broad smile on my face, I've got butterflies, I'm going to the Studio. As I take out a Live4Now CD that I've just burned on my G4 Mac my mobile rings. Withheld number, I don't answer those calls. CD in hand I head for the X3.

Getting excited as I drive to the studio listening to myself singing through the sound system. "♪ *From the day our love was born, I never had to look back, you always made me know that, this is forever...*"

26th January 2009
Mike's Studio Thornton Heath

Sanj and Mike are outside smoking as I arrive.

"Yo what's up, I ain't late am I?"

"Naa Sugar man you're safe, we're early!"

"Ah!" I'm relieved.

"So what you saying, what's good, you ready?"

"Yeah man, I've been looking forward to this."

"That's what I want to hear, Sugar dis is my bredrin Mike. Mike, Sugar."

"Nice to me you Sugar."

"Good to meet you Mike, respect for letting us use the Studio."

"No man, that's no problem, Sanj is one of my long-time friends, anything I can do to help this man it's done."

"Easy Sugar man, come we go, lets get this cracking."

The studio has a nice vibe inside with cream walls, a black mixing desk with silver trim and silver spotlights. It's simple but has all we need and I clock a small statue of the Buddha sitting beside the Mac on the mixing desk, smiling with approval. Sanj sits on one of the large sofa's and Mike leads me through into the sound booth, with it's textured walls. I take a seat and get comfortable, watching them through the glass.

Eight hours later...

Talk about grueling, no time to think about anything else I'm exhausted but for a first session, it was good, although Intense! Heading for home with food on my mind. 'Live 4 Now' is still playing on the car sound system and the reality of cutting my first song hits home and gives me goosebumps!

26th January 2009
Home Croydon

Just starting to unwind after having a bath and eating. I continue to practice parts of the song for a while before dropping off to sleep.

27th January 2009
Recording Booth Mike's Studio Thornton Heath

Sanj beckons me through the glass, so I take off the headphones and go through to see him. "Sugar man, just relax."

"I'm trying Bruv but it's hot in there." I sit on one of the large sofas, thankful for a break.

"I know its hot in there Sugar and there's a difference in your tone, take a break and listen to what we did yesterday." I take a sip of water and lean back for a while to listen.

"Ok Sanj I hear the difference."

"Alright! What you saying, you good to go?"

"Let's do this." The booth is bloody hot, must be the lighting in such a small space so I undo my shirt.

"Turn the mic up a little, I can't hear myself."

"That okay?"

"Little more, yeah, yeah that's right." I give it all I've got.

I'm struggling, the next few days feels like I'm just drifting along, I can't seem to anchor in or concentrate for long, I'm constantly distracted. I'm still mourning my Dad and I'm still numb. Somehow I manage to stay outwardly cheerful as if I don't have a choice, but even the music feels flat.

30th January 2009
Home Croydon

It's bitterly cold and I feel it deep in my bones, especially my knees, I guess this is how it's gonna be from now on. There was so much damage to my body it's likely I'll feel the cold more than I did before. The Weatherman says snow will fall, but how many times have they said that, and got it wrong? So let me get something to eat and turn on the heating, I have to look after myself as best as I can. Good day to stay in practicing my vocals and watching a few old films on DVD.

31st January 2009
Home Croydon

Damn last night was cold! I believe the weather forecast may be right after all. I'd better get to the shops and stock up on food today, I won't want to go out in the snow. I put an extra sock on my right foot, tracksuit bottoms, padded trousers, vest, t-shirt, two big jumpers, hat, scarf, and gloves. I ain't taking any chances of catching a cold.

What a mission, I'm so glad to be home; I got sweaty in my warm clothes and now my stump feels sore and wet in my prosthetic leg, it kept slipping, but I had to soldier on. At least I got my supplies in. I can't even function properly in the kitchen I'm actually shivering, bwoy it's cold but a hot drink, and a bath will warm me up.

By late evening, I'm looking out of my bedroom window and the weather forecaster was right, light snow is already falling; it's beautiful to watch from here, with the heating turned up and nice and warm inside.

1st February 2009
Home Croydon

As I get out of bed and pull the curtains the brightness hits me. Everywhere I look is white and I mean everywhere! Snow completely covers the cars, trees, gardens, roads; it must be at least six to eight inches deep. I make my way into the front room on my crutches excited to look out; this is unusual for London. As I open the front room curtains, damn it's just white everywhere! I am so glad I went shopping yesterday, cos I sure ain't going out today, I'd most probably fall over! But what a beautiful picture, yeah I should take some pictures! I get snappy through the window.

After breakfast, I decide to put on several warm layers of clothes and take the camera outside, in the name of art. Although my stump is still sore I'll take it slowly and carefully, after all it's one of the challenges in life I have to deal with, luckily not very often.

As I open the front door the world seems unexpectedly quiet. The snow dampens sound and of course there's little to no traffic going past except for the odd four-track, driving along slowly. The people who have ventured out are smiling and seem excited; snowballs fly through the air. The grass hill opposite is transformed into a snowy ski slope as kids with snowboards have fun trying their best not to fall over on the way down.

I grab a couple of handfuls of salt from the plastic bin by the front door and throw them along where the garden path should be, slightly flattening the snow down. I grab a few more handfuls and carefully make my way along the path towards the gate, scattering the salt as I go. I get some great photos from the gate, but I won't venture any further. Man it's cold, time to go back inside for a cup of hot chocolate, perfect weather for it!

I call Sanj "Hey man, what's good Bruv?"

"Sugar man! I'm snowed in, I can't get out my house."

"So no studio work then, Mate?"

"You got that right Bruv," He sounds irritated, "so what you sayin'?"

"Let's see what the end of the week brings."

"What you sayin' Thursday?"

"Yeah, lets play it by ear?"

"Easy."

By late evening I hear the frantic wheel spin of a car from the back of my flat. It continues for a while and in the end I peep out of my bedroom window to see what's going on. A Mercedes is trapped in snow at the top of my road. I watch for a while as the driver keeps trying to maneuver out of the ice and snow. At one point he gets out and tries to move snow from around his wheels with his bare hands then has another go at driving out, but still no luck. I feel sorry for him and decide help, so I dress up in my warm clothes and venture out. I grab my shovel and a bag of salt then walk towards him. "You okay Sir?"

"No, not really, I can't move my car, it keeps slipping backwards."

"Okay let me try something, wait a minute." I start shoveling some of the snow away from the wheels and put salt down in its place clearing a small space in front of his car. "That's better, try it now."

"Okay, thank you." He starts up the engine and the car moves forward, freed from the snow trap. Both the driver and the female passenger beam broad smiles at me through the windscreen. The driver's window opens and he pops his head out. "Thank you so much, may Allah bless you!"

"It's no problem, I'm glad to be of service." I smile back.

"You live there?" he points to my house.

"Yeah, why?"

"I've got to give you something, to pay you back for your kindness."

"No man, we are all one, God's children and I'd like to think I'm here to help, so that's enough." The man gets out of his car and gives me a warm hug, then, before I know what's happening kisses me on each cheek. I figure it must be a cultural thing. "Thank you so much, my wife will be delighted now!"

"Enjoy the rest of your evening." I wave as I head back for home smiling about my good deed for the day.

2nd February 2009
Home Croydon

The snow's been falling constantly throughout the night again. Damn! You can't even see the tramlines anymore. Everything has a fresh new layer completely white and at least ten to twelve inches of snow lies on the ground. No form of transport can get through by the looks of it, and it's still snowing; no car, no bus, no tram, hold on a minute. What the hell is that? I see something rush past my window; I dash to the window and catch a glimpse of the back of a woman disappearing on her skis! Really skiing? Well at least she's getting through!

Okay, I'm ready for some breakfast, so I wash, put on some clothes, eat and then try to find out what's really happening out there. As I look out, I decide to see if I can make it to the shop, the skiing woman inspired me. What a great test for my stump and me. There's always a first time for everything, can I walk in the snow? Let me try!

A few extra layers of clothes and green wellington boots later, I'm good to go. The dull ache in my stump slows me down though. In fact it probably doubles the time I take to make it to the shop but I am determined. On top of the discomfort I have to keep stopping to adjust the sleeve at the top of my leg, it's so frustrating. Every time I exert myself I sweat, then my leg gets so wet it slips out of the socket! Still, on the bright side I manage to get there!

I've passed so many snowmen and also snow-women on the way that I feel inspired to take photos of them on the way back. It's a good thing I brought my phone.

The mood is lighter on the way back, everyone is talking to each other; it's a friendly vibe, such a difference in people. Somehow the snow brings people together, how great! As I absorb the stillness in the air, my friend Lorna comes to mind. She's a local lady in her eighties, who I befriended after seeing her with a black eye. She apparently fell, so since then I've told her to let me know if she ever needs help. I wonder how she is coping with the snow, think I should call in to see.

Lorna's Care Assistant answers the door. "Hello, can I help?"

"Hello, I'm Garri, a friend of Lorna's and I've just stopped by to check if she's okay." And as soon as she hears my voice Lorna comes straight to the door smiling. "You okay Lorna?"

"Oh yes Garri thank you and how are you with this cold weather?"

"I'm coping, I just thought I'd check in on you to make sure you're all right."

"Oh you're such a lovely young man. Yes I'm all right thank you, I have help." She smiles at the lady who opened the door.

"Well that's good, take care now and remember you got my number if there's any problem, you look after yourself."

"Okay Garri will do, you take care out there." She peers out into the cold pulling an 'I'm glad I'm not out there' face. I smile at both of them before I leave, "Nice to meet you Garri, it's kind of you to drop by, take care."

"Nice to meet you too, bye for now."

As I tackle the short distance home, it feels odd without any cars, buses, or trams around. The white blanket softens everything. In fact I can't even see the pavements or anything else for that matter. I don't even recognise the place!

As I approach my house a group of boys are having a snowball fight; they throw snowballs at anyone who walks past. I can see they're starting to annoy people so when I get to my house I call them over and encourage them to help me build a snowman beside my garden. They happily get involved and as we create our snowman I chat to them about life. Some of my neighbours, I've never even spoken to before, stop and talk to us and several people take photo's as we work on the snowman. The atmosphere is surreal in a time where technology has all but taken over, it's enjoyable actually talking with people you don't know in person. I feel a sense of community spirit that's long been missing; it's a beautiful thing.

A guy I do know, who lives at the end of my road is walking past with his girlfriend, and they stop to take a photo of us. "Garri, I'll drop the photo off to you later."

"Thank you very much, Sir."

His pretty Asian girlfriend is getting lots of attention from the young guys. I'm not at all surprised, she has a cool way of dressing and a very lovely smile. She smiles in my direction and the young boys clock it. As they walk away, the youngsters start on me, "Is you dat bruv."

"You're in there. You see di way she look at you man?"

"Stop dem talk." I close them down shaking my head; they're far too hyped!

3rd February 2009
Home Croydon

As I look out of my front room window this morning I notice the snow is melting, then I spot a giant snowball about five-feet high. The kids must have had fun making that last night, but it's turning slushy as it melts. Our snowman is melting too, he looks like he's lost weight, poor guy! Then I notice a middle-aged man walking up my garden path, wrapped up warm and smartly dressed, he's possibly Middle Eastern. I listen as he pushes on a few buzzers before he gets to mine. I answer, "Hello."

"Hello, are you the guy that helped me the other day get my car our of the snow?"

"Oh yeah man, it's me." I didn't recognise him, I go out to the front door to greet him, and he shakes my hand warmly. "You saved my life, how can I repay you?"

"Don't worry 'bout it man, it's all good. Do you live locally?"

"Yes, just at the corner."

"The corner? So is Sam your son?"

"Yes, you know my son?"

"Yeah man, me and Sam get on great."

"Oh, that's very good, you and my son are friends I didn't realise. Anyway I'm not going to keep you out here in the cold I was just on my way to the shops and wanted to thank you once again. May Allah continue to bless you."

"Thank you Sir, and you have a good day."

4th February 2009
Home Croydon

As I look out this morning, I see the ground peeping through again, it looks like the worst is over and the roads are clearing. The phone rings somewhere in the flat and I have to hunt for it.

"Sugar, you good?" It's Sanj.

"Yes Bruv I'm good, glad the snow's clearing. What you saying?"

"I'm good Shuggs, ready to get back into studio mode?"

"Most definitely my brother, most definitely!"

"Tomorrow and Friday good for you?"

"Yeah man, lets do it."

"I'll phone Mike to confirm, easy."

"Tomorrow Bruv!" I hang up feeling a flutter of excitement about the music again.

5th February 2009
Mike Studio Thornton Heath

Today we record the lead vocals; another 8-hour day!

In the evening at home I continue to practice the second verse, I've got to nail it by tomorrow. This is very intense.

6th February 2009
Mike Studio Thornton Heath

I'm singing my heart out and give it all I've got.

"Woyyyyyy! Gwaan Sugar!"

"Yeah Sugar that sounds good." Mike agrees and I'm pleased to hear their approval at last!

"That's a good take Sugar, I wish all the takes were like that."

"Easy bruv, I've got to make you work innit?" We all laugh; I'm feeling better and more confident. I smashed it!

"Okay mate enough of that, it wasn't a break, get back in, same vibe Sugar." The whip cracks!

7th-8th February 2009
Croydon

Over the weekend I'm in and out of the Gym, still not happy with my routine, but I'm not going to give up!

9th-10th February 2009
Mike Studio Thornton Heath

Working on the last bits of the lead vocal before we move on to the harmonies, another long day in the Studio, but the sense of achievement is mounting.

"Sanj play me the tune so I can record it on my phone."

"Alright Bruv, but Sugar don't let no one hear the tune yet, remember it's not finished."

"Yeah, yeah."

Mike has to pick up his daughter so we finish early.

"Next Monday come at twelve, we haven't got much left to do."

"Okay Mr. Engineer." I head home hungry and tired, but again with a sense of satisfaction, we are well on the way.

16th February 2009
Queen Mary's Hospital Roehampton

Today I'm getting another new leg and I'm as excited as ever. Each time, it just gets better and better! This new high tech sports leg has proper put a spring into my step. It doesn't have the pump like the old one as it's a closed system but it's meant to be even more comfortable and easier to run with. I can't wait to go for a run in the Gym this afternoon. On the way to the car park, I notice a poster announcing trials for the Paralympics. It makes me think!

16th February 2009
Gym Croydon

Being at the Gym helps me get my mind into focus and away from the outcome of the Police accusations I still face. I'm pretty sure I'll be okay, but you never know what can happen these days, my own history is a testament to that!

Anyway, I've finally sorted a workout routine that I like and I had a really good work out on my upper body last time. Today I'm doing legs, so it's good timing that I've got this new leg to test drive. I enjoy my workout, I always feel better after exercise. It's a good contrast to sitting in the studio all day and I'm so grateful I can still take part. The Paralympics comes to mind again… Hmmm.

17th February 2009
Mike's Studio Thornton Heath

Sanj is working on the track editing and mixing. I'm just sitting back now and taking in the whole experience. My work is done and overall it's been a joy to be involved, even though I was frustrated with myself and had to dig deep at times, I did it. As I listen to the track, I feel it's been worthwhile even though it still isn't quite finish.

18th February 2009
Home Croydon

My leg muscles hurt this morning. Maybe I pushed myself too much on Monday; yes I've over done it. There's also a dull ache in my stump and the blister looks angry. I take a hot sea-salt bath which is a great way to soothe my body and unwind, closest thing I've got to the Caribbean sea in London!

Feeling better and chilling in the front room with my leg off, I get the sense my stump needs a breather. Time to relax with some DVD's.

22nd February 2009
Gym Croydon

On the rowing machine, I find myself looking out into the car park and the field beyond deep in thought. I hope this bloody stupid Police case gets sorted out; it's stressful. I must remember though, I'm lucky, lucky to be here, lucky to be alive. That's one thought that will always make me smile. When I finish rowing the sweat is pouring off me, and my whole body aches, but it's a nice ache, Gym pain is good pain, it means my muscles are working. As I make my way over to the water fountain, there's a sudden sharp pain in my stump, it stops me dead in my tracks for a second, this seems like more than the usual discomfort, but it goes off again quickly, so I decide to ignore it and continue to do some floor work. It's all about the core today.

23rd February 2009
Mike's Studio Thornton Heath

Sanj is adding the backing vocals; this is the final part to be added. The song sounds wicked and our voices really compliment each other. The excitement builds!

24th February 2009
Mike's Studio Thornton Heath

All that's left to do is make the master mix before we leave. Our song is almost complete and I feel fantastic; can't wait to get home and listen to the completed track on my sound system and share it with my friends! Talking of friends I discover that my old school friend Tippa has a studio in the same block. Tippa is a talented veteran Reggae Artist who was a DJ with Saxon Sound System in the late eighties and nineties and still DJ's worldwide to this day. A true legend in the game so I figure I'd like to get his opinion on our track. Sanj and I take a walk to his unit around the corner to ask if he has time to have a listen. I pop my head in and Tippa is there. "Wha' ah gwaan?"

"What you saying G, what you doing 'ere?"

"Just passing through man, doing some work."

Sanj jumps in, "Yeah Tippa, I've got something here, I'd like you to listen to. You 'ave time?"

"Yeah man, did you work on the track?"

"Yeah."

"Ah'right, let me hear dis." He smiles. The track plays and he listens intently, moving to the beat.

"Well to tell you the truth, it sound good, you kno', see me ah tap me foot and ah shake me head, I don't often do that straight away and me hear a nuff music; yeah man it sound good."

"Thanks for that Tip"

"Ah you dat?" He asks me,

"Yeah man me ah try ah t'ing."

"Your not trying, yu ah gwaan!" Tippa inspires me and we all laugh; I'm on a high!

25th February 2009
Home Croydon

It's not been easy to cope with all the stress of the past few years, so I tell myself it's better to live in the moment, not to dwell on the past or drift too far worrying about the future. I'm still suffering and sometimes zone out when things get stressful. I really need to live in the now!

My workouts at the Gym are going very well and my body is definitely getting stronger, when I feel fitter my mind is clearer. I'm getting to know a nice bunch of people at the Gym and I fit in without any awkwardness, in fact I'm making some new friends there and that's always good. I even bump in to some of the Man dem from back in the day who seem pleased to see me; we often work out together. So the message is, live for now, live for the moment!

I feel my song coming on. 'Live 4 Now' is pumping out of my sound system on the way home. I'm on a high singing along to my first recording. I've actually done it! What a great feeling. I'm in a good place; I know the music helps to reduce my stress.

Once home it's food time! 'Yeah! Mek me go fry two dumpling fi go with the fried sprats, me hungry ya'see!' In the kitchen I add water to self-raising flour to make the dough before adding a few secret ingredients. Mum's dutch pot is on the fire with oil in it, and I'm good to go. Got a plate full of fried sprats to deal with, one of my favourites, Mum would always cook them for me, and she showed me how to do it too, bless her!

2nd March 2009
Home Croydon

Sanj arrives grinning from ear to ear.

"What's going on?" I feel Sanj's excitement.

"Easy Sugar."

"Weh yah ah kin teeth fer, wot, sweet you?" I'm curious.

"Sugar, don't make your head get big but everyone I've play the song to loves it, the lyrics, your tone everything!"

"Really, that's nice to know." I get a sense of achievement.

"Sugar they're even singing along with the chorus. ♪ *'So we got to live for nowwwwwwww, so we got to live for the moment,'* messi!"

"So what's the plan Sanj?"

"Bruv you been cooking fish in here?" he sniffs the air.

"That was yesterday's food Bruv, your nose too good you see."

"I can just smell it."

"What you hungry?"

"I'm hungry now."

"How you mean you're hungry let's talk business, man!"

"Ok put the kettle on Mate."

"About put on kettle. *KMT!* D'you want piece of bun as well?"

"Yes please." He smiles and rubs his hands together, "Right Sugar, I want to do an album with you based on your experiences and your view on the world since the Bombings." He seems keen to continue our partnership.

"What? Sounds interesting but what made you think of that?"

"I think people want to hear your story."

"Hmm, I started writing a book before, but when the shit hit the fan I figured that was the end of it, people wouldn't want to read anything that happened to me after what the Press did."

"Yeah I see that, but I don't agree Sugar, I think you need to tell your truth so why not tell it in song, I mean Bob and Peter done it, why not you?"

"True dat!" chuckling from my belly, as he refers to Marley and Tosh like they're his best mates. "Yeah man lets do dis!"

"Okay, I've got a few things in mind, bear with me while I get a new project up." Without another word Sanj opens a new project in Logic and starts work. I sit and watch him in awe as he starts making a few tracks. He's building the beats I want to hear and the lyrics I wanna sing, I'm loving it.

He creates a new beat based on an old nineties song *'Headline News'* he keeps asking me to sing some of the lyrics he puts down to try them out, then we change a few until we agree on what's being said; to top it all the sax it's awesome!

3rd March 2009
Home Croydon

Sanj is still working on the beat to the second track as I begin to write down my thoughts, which we'll add to the lyrics as we go on, we found a good way to co-write.

9th March 2009
Croydon Police Station

I report to the desk sergeant as arranged, but he tells me to come back in ten minutes. *KMT*. As if I hadn't waited long enough for this nonsense to be sorted. A small crowd have gathered outside, and I wonder what's going on. As I walk past I recognise a few News Reporters in the crowd.

"Garri what you doing here?"

"I'm local innit, why what's going on?"

"We're waiting on a News Conference about a murder suspect."

"Oh, I see."

"How are you though Garri?"

"Yeah, I'm really well thanks."

"It's a shame what happened to you."

"Yeah I know, and it saddens me to think it was probably all for the sake of money, or maybe it's because I'm black; check it who really benefited?"

"Don't worry Garri you still have a lot of admirers out there."

"Hmmm." I fake a smile and walk back into the station.

As I approach the desk, the Sergeant tells me the CPS has withdrawn all charges. Thank God! I can stop worrying and get on with my life. What a ridiculous waste of time and energy, I have to wonder why I attracted that. Seems I must be more careful who I borrow a car from, you never can tell!

My next mission is to get past this lynch mob without being seen again, or else I'll be back on the front-page tomorrow! '*Garri Holness Zaps Paparazzi With High Tech Running Leg In A Clash Outside Croydon Police Station!*' Yeah that might sell a paper or two!

11th March 2009
Local Computer Superstore

Looks like I need to upgrade my G4; it's running far too slow with all the music that's stored on it now. I've had this plan in mind for quite a while and it's time to make it happen! I buy the latest machine with a big memory! New Mac in da house!

Next, I'm off to Croydon to get a new interface for my studio. I know exactly what I want so it's quickly acquired. Upgrading my home studio is now accomplished; I'm good to go on a more professional level.

11th March 2009
Home Croydon

Sorting out the new studio, out with the old and in with the new. Check everything is in working order first then transfer all music files ready for tomorrows session with Sanj, I'm feeling excited to test it out. I try to figure out how to make the best use of the available space. Although the system looks great in my room, I start wondering if there's enough space for us both to sit comfortably where I've placed it.

Halle comes over in the evening and she raises a serious subject in a very caring way. She thinks I should go to see my GP about the stress of the recent events including the recent passing of my Father. I wonder if she's right, I know I can't see myself from the outside as others see me and it's hard for me to know how I'm really coping. What I do know is I've been deliberately keeping busy so that I don't have time to sit and think. Halle also says I should socialise with more people, I spend too much time indoors and she notices the sparkle has gone from my eyes. I guess I needed this pep talk, I do know it's in my best interest.

We spend the rest of the evening watching a movie before she makes her way home. She got through to me and I decide to make an appointment to see my Doctor as soon as possible. I figure it can't hurt going for a chat.

12th March 2009
Home Croydon

Sanj just called but he's feeling ill, so I'll take the time to practice and get used to my new system.

16th March 2009
Brixton Doctors

The GP believes that I have Post-Traumatic Stress Disorder, and he wants to refer me to Maudsley Hospital. Although it shocks me at first, I wonder if in fact they could help me. I'm aware that I can't see the changes that Halle can obviously see in me, and I'm grateful to her for caring enough to raise the subject. It probably wasn't an easy thing for her to do.

23rd March 2009
Home Croydon

Sanj arrives at the usual time "Sugar what you smiling at?"

"Just kool man go turn on the system." I'm eager to show Sanj the new equipment and see his reaction.

"Raaaaaah! Is that how you're going on Sugar. Messi! Now we can do some proper work Bruv."

"Yeah, I knew the old system would slow us down Mate."

"The old one couldn't handle it all Sugar, but where is it?"

"Behind you, why you wan' it? You can take it if you like."

"What!?" He looks very pleased.

"Yeah man, take it, yes."

"Huh! It's a good thing I drove here today, help me get it into my car mate." We get the old G4 out and into his car leaving more space for us to work on the new machine. It doesn't take Sanj long to become familiar with the new Mac and interface.

24th March 2009
Home Croydon

My buzzer rings, it's Sanj he's early.

"Sanj what you doing here so early Bruv?"

"Shuggs, I've got work to do and your new system gonna make it easy." He sounds excited.

"You just want to test out the new system innit?" I understand his desire to play with the new toy!

"Sugar I've been thinking about your system all night."

"You're nuts Bruv, but I must admit, me too!" We both laugh.

"You good though Mate?"

"Yeah man, I'm good wha' ah gwaan?"

"I've got a CD I want you to listen to," Sanj slides it into the side of the Mac.

"Ohhh, that's were the CD's go now!" I can't believe how technology is advancing so fast. His track sounds out and I listen carefully. "Yeah, wicked!"

"Thanks mate, I'm still working on them but one of them gave me a spin off idea we can use." Sanj opens up another new project on Logic and begins to add instruments before sorting out a beat. It would appear he has bits of lyrics already in his head as he writes them on the note pad.

"You're on one today, do yu'want a drink, are you hungry?"

"It's not me, it's the new Mac, and yes thanks to everything else."

"You joker!"

He starts singing bits of our third song. *"♪Cos forever I've been holding out for you to say the word..."*

I love it, and it sounds much easier to sing than the second one. Looks like we'll be having another long and creative day in the studio, only stopping to eat!

25th March 2009
Home Croydon

I pick up my post and there's a letter from the Maudsley Hospital, I've got an appointment on 31st March at 11.00am. I feel anxious and slightly reluctant, what if they tell me I've got physiological problems? I suppose its better to find out than not to know. What I already know is I've been through a lot of shit; and sometimes it shows. The second post brings me a book, 'The Monk Who Sold His Ferrari'. I open the pages, look through and start to read. Although I'm reading, I can't concentrate and I'm not taking it in; time to meditate.

30th March 2009
Home Croydon

I've decided to move my studio equipment out of my bedroom and into the front room today. I only put it in my bedroom so I could work on it without having to put my leg on, but I don't want to work where I sleep any more. It has a disturbing effect on my energy at night and thinking ahead, I get the sense that we will be working a lot more together, so I need to have a different sleeping and work space.

It doesn't take long and I notice a huge difference once it's moved; there's so much more space in my bedroom, and it's much easier to move around. Also looking into the front room with the studio equipment now on top of the table near the window seems like a perfect fit, with a lot more space for both the mic and the chair to maneuver.

As night falls I feel much better, everything is more comfortable to work with as I do my practice, and the icing on the cake is that I can leave it to go off to bed whenever I'm ready.

31st March 2009
The Maudsley Hospital

In a deep discussion with the Doctor I start opening up about my fears, feelings and thoughts, it's intense! His prognosis is severe Post-Traumatic Stress Disorder (PTSD) as well as depression and a mild case of epilepsy. He wants to put me on a program using Cognitive Behavioural Therapy (CBT). It's based on the idea that certain patterns of thinking can trigger or fuel certain mental health problems such as PTSD. The Therapist can help me to understand my current thought patterns and in particular to identify any harmful, unhelpful and false ideas or thoughts I've taken on. The aim is to change my ways of thinking in order to avoid these false ideas, while helping more realistic and helpful thought patterns to immerge. It can apparently help to counter recurring distressing thoughts and any unhelpful avoidance behaviour.

The therapy will start on Thursday 9th April in weekly sessions, of about 45 minutes each, for several weeks. I'll be taking an active part and the session will be recorded for me so at any point if I feel lonely or stressed at home I can listen to them again. I'll be assessed after three months to check the developments.

Wow, it takes a while to sink in. There was me thinking I'm doing okay but apparently the tests tell a different story. Although it's not easy to accept, I suppose it's only to be expected in the circumstances. Getting bombed and losing Mum was bad enough, but what followed was unnecessary and unbelievable and I wouldn't wish it on my worst enemy!

6th April 2009
Home Croydon

I'm in the garden weeding, when along comes Sanj nice and early again.

"Sugar, what's good?"

"Go in the front room and find out." I follow behind him.

"Yes Sugar, that's so much better." He's smiling.

"Easy."

"Yeah now we have space to work." We high five triumphantly!

"Shuggs' you should of done this long time."
"Just kool man, anyway what you drinking?"
"I need some Rizla Rudeboy!"
"In the tin, there." I point him towards the coffee table.
"A soft drink would be nice too Shuggs."
"You want me to drink it for you too Bruv?"
"Nah, I'll manage."

We start work and I manage to put down a small part of the guide vocals for the second song; it's not easy though. We call it *'Don't take it to heart'*.

7th April 2009
Home Croydon

I finish laying the guide vocal with Sanj for *'Don't take it to heart'*

"I can see you're having difficulty with this song Mate, break it down and learn it bit by bit."

"Tricky song Sanj."

"I wrote it with you in mind, only you can sing that song Sugar."

"Thanks bruv, no pressure then."

"I know you can do it." He seems confident.

We work for a while until, *Beep beep* sounds from the road out front, Sanj's cousin has come to pick him up. Saved by the beep!

"Alright Sanj see you later Mate, thanks very much, lickle more."

"Easy."

8th April 2009
Croydon Town Centre

My lovely Russian friend Tanya calls to ask a favour; she needs me to look after her flower shop while she's out at a meeting. I've agreed; this should be fun, I jump in the X3 and drive directly to her shop.

She's waiting anxiously and meets me at the door with a quick hug. "Thank you so much for coming over, how are you Bambino?" But before I can answer she goes on. "Good yah, I've already prepared a few bouquets so you don't run out, okay? All the plants got prices on them so you know. You know where the toilet and kitchen is? And the till, she's very simple to work, here, let me show you." She leans over the till, presses a few buttons and smiles looking at me.

"Calm down Tanya one thing at a time please."

"No no no, I'm running late, were you watching me?" She hands me a set of keys. "Err yes, why you giving me the keys?"

"In case I don't come back in time, you can lock up please?"

"Tanya!"

"Bambino!" Tanya hugs me again without another word and quickly runs out of the shop!

I find myself alone in her shop, with only half an idea how everything works, but then I'm sure it's not Rocket Science. I've always wanted to have my own shop, I would sell men's fashion jewellery, I know flowers ain't quite jewellery but it'll be good practice interacting with people and that's what I need at the moment, just like Halle said. I make a cuppa and position myself at the counter, the day passes quickly, I really enjoy it and all goes well. Tanya is back before I have to lock up and I must say I'm relieved about that!

9th April 2009
Maudsley Hospital

First day of my program and I'm filling in the forms, but the questions are deep. After much deliberation, I hand the form to the receptionist and sit down to wait. After a few minutes a young man approaches. "Garri Holness."

"Yeah that's me." I stand up.

"Hello Garri, I'm Dr Blue*, please come this way."

"Okay, Doc." He leads me up some stairs and into his office, where a woman is already seated. She smiles and gets up as we enter. "Garri this my assistant Doctor Jones, if you don't mind she'll be sitting in with us."

"I don't mind." I smile back at her then take a seat.

"How've you been since you were last here?"

"At the moment things are okay, the Media onslaught has eased off, so that's a big relief."

"Well that's good, Garri I'm going to put the tape recorder on now okay?" We talk and talk; it's good to talk.

14th April 2009
Home Croydon

The third song is coming along nicely; I so love the vibe. "♪*This is the time, for us to evolve.*" Big tune and I like to practice before Sanj gets here; it's always good to see improvements.

Sanj arrives later than usual this morning, as the trains are running late again. As he walks in I sense a change in his vibe, a frustration, but I ask no questions. I figure he's just frustrated with the trains.

Although we have a very productive session, I still sense something's not right with him. Maybe he's having an off day, we all have them.

16th April 2009
Maudsley Hospital *Treatment*

They ask me to relax, close my eyes and imagine being on the Underground travelling to work. Then, with my eyes still closed the Doctor moves in quietly and taps me lightly on my shoulder. My reaction is unexpected and I quickly realise all is not well!

20th April 2009
Home Croydon

As I arrive back from pruning a neighbours garden Sanj is already waiting outside my front door.

"Yes my top producer." He looks pleased to see me.

"What's good Sugar?"

"You're here innit, everything's good, let me go have a quick wash, just go through man and do your ting." After fifteen minutes I'm back, clean, fresh and ready to go.

"Oi Sugar did I leave my lighter here?"

"Don't try that one Bruv, you know how many of my lighters you teif." I raise my eyebrows and look at him accusingly, with a half grin.

"Funny you should say that you know, just the other day I was in my house and I used a strange lighter that lit up with all different colours."

"Yep, that's my lighter you crook." Still sensing uneasiness in his vibe I leave Sanj engrossed in the beat as I head out in my car to do some shopping.

Once back, I unload the shopping and empty the dustbin outside. Sanj has opened the front room window slightly and the tune sounds *bad* from out here. I stand listening for a few minutes, before heading back inside.

"Sanj that sounds wicked from outside."

"Yeah, I'm gonna leave it on a loop, while I have a break outside." Sanj starts to walk out picking up my lighter.

"Alright, Bruv where you going wiv me lighter?"

He stops, "I need a light innit."

"Mek sure you come give me back me lighter."

"Easy." He's flippant.

"About easy, I want it back!" I laugh, seriously!

He leaves me in the front room listening to the loop, and I'm thinking that bass line sounds even better inside. Damn! What has he done? It's awesome!

On the way in, he makes a point of handing me my lighter. "Here you go Mate." I take it, throw it in the air, and catch it, before putting it back on the coffee table. "Thanks Bruv."

"Cup of tea?" he asks hopefully.

"You know where the kitchen is Mate help yourself."

"Don't be like that Sugar."

"Don't be like that Sugar? But you know where the kitchen is." He goes to make tea and brings one back for me too.

"Shuggs I should finish this off by tomorrow."

"That's good. What did you do with the bass?" He smiles proudly. "Easy my Brother."

21st April 2009
Home Croydon

Sanj arrives and I still sense something's troubling him, so it's time to have a heart to heart. We strap one and talk as we smoke. Eventually he opens up to me, it's a personal problem. I try to advise him as much as I can, and tell him I'm here if he needs to talk again. I knew something was troubling him. I picked up on his energy. I'm starting to sense people's energy more and more. Bwoy! We all got our problems.

Back into the music groove, it helps.

23rd April 2009
Maudsley Hospital *Treatment*

I start to learn the triggers that set off my anxiety attacks. At night I often spend 30 minutes to an hour trying to sleep through my body and legs shaking uncontrollably. The Doctors tell me this is on the spectrum of an epileptic fit, but can be dealt with through the training they are giving me. I feel reassured, and more self-aware.

28th April 2009
Home Croydon

Sanj is away working on other projects, which gives me time to practice. Practice makes perfect, innit?

30th April 2009
Maudsley Hospital *Treatment*

I'm learning my mind creates my reality! It's all about choices and it sits well with what I know about the law of attraction. Paralympics could be part of my reality, let me try a t'ing.

4th May 2009
Home Croydon

We are recording take after take of the third song. Sanj will pick out the best to edit later. The song is proving difficult for me to sing. I can't get my head around it, the dynamic and interchanging melodies is a real test of my ability and patience. I'm truly outta my comfort zone, and feel pressured, as Sanj wants to record at the Recording Studio soon. I know I can do it better than this, if I take my time. I don't want to waste money on studio time going over the same things again and again.

"When you're ready Sugar let me know."

"Will do, this one is not easy though Bruv, I'll need more time to prepare."

"I know Mate but you can do it, break it down, learn it bit by bit, like I said."

"I'm doing that like you said before, but when we record its wrong. "
I can't help but sigh as the frustration builds.

"Take it easy don't beat yourself up Mate, it will come." He pats me on the back encouragingly.

Sanj seems in a better mood today as I watch him run down the road to catch his train. I practice for another couple of hours before I eat, then try to relax watching a documentary on the black Pharaohs of Kemet Africa, in Sudan. It's certainly a great distraction from the frustration, very interesting!

5th May 2009
Home Croydon

The sun is shining in through the window and naturally I'm practicing, *Don't Take It To Heart.* It's got a real tricky beginning, so I go over and over and over it. Eat then go over it again and again. It's all about getting it right! It's stressful but that's what happens when you strive to do your best.

7th May 2009
Maudsley Hospital *Treatment*

I'm still struggling to apply the techniques to my daily life, the doctors remind me to listen to my tapes at home; sometimes I just get frustrated!

11th May 2009
Home Croydon

It's a difficult afternoon, Sanj and I are still going over and over the same song, I thought I was a perfectionist, but Sanj takes it to another level! When I think I've got a verse right, he points out a problem with the phasing of a word; one word you know, chaa! I'm thinking he can just drop it in, but he's not having any of it and I'm getting more and more frustrated.

"Sugar I think you should take a break now."

"I need it Bruv, this is a big tune."

"I know it's a big tune Sugar that is why we've got to get it right."

"It's taking longer than expected innit?"

"You can only do it when you're ready."

"So what are you saying Mate?"

"You need to practice it more, we can't record yet."

"The tune's bloody hard you know."

"I know but here's what, I don't want to waste your money or your time going to a recording studio if you're not ready."

"I hear you, but I've also got personal stuff going on at the moment, it's not easy for me to focus."

"I've only got your best interest at heart."

"Yeah okay, here's what, to take the pressure off me until I'm ready, what if you bring some of your other artists here; hire my studio to them?"

"That's messi if you're sure Sugar? I could make this like a little base for me."

"Yeah brother, no problem let's work something out."

"But Sugar that doesn't mean you can stop practicing you know." He smirks.

"I know Bruv, but I'll be able to enjoy it again, when there's less pressure."

"The music business isn't easy, you gotta focus 100% on what you're doing."

"To tell you the truth I can't be 100% focused right now; I've still got a few things going on with my health."

"I knew something was up, yeah I see, we need to keep the pressure off you. It'll work well then if next week I bring one of my other artists here and give you a break."

"Yeah man, I can learn too."

"Easy."

14th/21st/28th May 2009
Maudsley Hospital *Treatment*

Making progress.

4th /11th /18th June 2009
Maudsley Hospital *Treatment*

They help me to become even more aware of my reactions and the patterns that trigger them. It's not easy, but I can see it's possible to apply this awareness to help myself. I feel calmer now I'm aware that the zone-outs are helping me digest what happened.

25th June 2009
Maudsley Hospital *Treatment*

Today is a big step in my treatment they decide to take me back on the Tube! Although I've already been for a trip by myself, this time they will monitor my behavioural pattern and use it towards my final assessment.

2nd July 2009
Maudsley Hospital *Final Assessment*

I'm signed off from the treatment plan, unless I feel the need to come back at a later stage. It feels good to be signed off in time for the Memorial, but I also know I'm still not 100% and wonder if I'll ever be back to my old self. I feel like different, yet in some ways dare I say it, better than I was before the Bombings, a change of perception maybe. I've come to realise looking for comfort in material things doesn't work; happiness is an inside job!

5th July 2009
Tannell Flowers Croydon

Tanya is making a bouquet for a customer so I wait outside. After the customer leaves, she catches sight of me and shouts,

"Bambino, come!"

"Tanya, what are you saying, you good?"

"Yes I'm very well, very busy though."

"Yeah I can see that, anyway I've got a present for you." As I hand her a bar of chocolate, she squeals. Women and chocolate!

"But I need a favour, the 7/7 anniversary is in a couple of days, I need to take a wreath, do you have any suggestions?"

"Hmm, what size, big, small, medium, do you have a design in mind, price?"

"I've got an idea, the number 52 made from twigs or stems standing in the center of a bed of flowers with 52 small white doves sitting on the numbers."

"Oh okay, let me see if there is anything here we can use to start you off. But first please do me a favour and drop this bouquet around the corner?"

"Tanya man!"

"Bambino!"

6th July 2009
Home Croydon

Under Tanya's instruction I'm putting together the last bits of the wreath. I'm using old poppy stems and ivy as well as a few more flowers from my garden to construct the numbers. The small white doves look great sitting on the framework, which forms the numbers five and two. As I think of 52, I suddenly realise 5+2=7 and the number seven is very significant. Not least because there are seven days in a week and it took seven days to create the Earth according to the Bible. 52 people died on the day 7/7/2005 2+0+0+5=7 again! Perhaps there are more things that happen in life than we are aware of? Seems there are patterns everywhere if you have the eyes to see them! Anyway Tanya and I make a great team; I use my phone to take photos that I email to her and she offers advice along the way until finally its complete, it's a job well done!

7th July 2009
Home Croydon

Wreath safely in my car as I set off to Hyde Park. I'm a bit numb as I drive unsure of what's to come. The idea of seeing the Press still ties my stomach up in knots, making me feel a potential threat at every turn.

7th July 2009
Hyde Park, London

As I pass through security, I look for a space to park. Wreath in hand I head to the Memorial site quietly acknowledging those I know around me as I go. I put the wreath down next to the plaque, the significance of the 52 white doves playing through my mind. The inevitable *click, click, click*, as the photographers sound off from a little grass mound close by. Still apprehensive about being around the Media, I quickly walk away.

As I find a seat in the designated survivors area, I feel a strain in my right knee, it often happens when I walk too quickly on grass. Sitting quietly with my eyes closed I try to unwind, until someone sits next to me. "Hello

Mister." I open my eyes to see Alison smiling. "Hello my little Angel." I'm so pleased to see her. "Oh Garri!" She laughs every time I call her my Angel.

"How are you Alison?"

"I'm very well Garri, how are you?"

"I'm good Alison, it's just the bloody Press that get me down."

"Garri don't let them worry you, whatever they write will be chip paper the following morning, you know that right?"

"Yeah I know, but it don't just affect me, it affects my family and friends as well, not to mention the general public."

"Garri don't ever forget your positive contribution to 7/7, you're an inspiration." I slowly take in what she says.

"Thank you Alison." She smiles and looks over to the VIP seating area. The sight of the Dignitaries arriving distracts us. Prince Charles and Camilla Parker Bowles arrive together, then Gordon Brown, David Cameron, Nick Clegg and several others. The ceremony and unveiling begins immediately. Songs from the Rock Choir sound out in between speeches from three of the survivors; finally the names of the deceased are read out solemnly.

I glance over to the seating area where the bereaved families are seated, and focus on the two large elegant vases, that sit regally each side of the red carpet that leads all the way up to the 52 steel memorial columns. One vase filled with red roses the other with white. After a moments silence the first bereft family member moves forward, picks up a red rose and carries it towards to the steel columns, closely followed by the others, who choose either a red or a white rose to take with them. The columns are grouped in four clusters to reflect the separate locations of the Bombings at Tavistock Square, Edgware Road, King's Cross/Russell Sq. and Aldgate; each family member places a rose beside their loved one's name and walk slowly back along the red carpet to their seat.

The Frenchman, who lost his son, catches my eye and nods his head at me, so I respond respectfully. I might well have been the last living person his son had contact with before he was killed. As he walks down the red carpet towards the memorial he takes a red and white rose with him. I guess sometimes it's not easy to choose, he lays down the red rose next to his son's name and lingers for a while before turning to walk back down the red carpet still holding the white rose. Before returning to his seat he step off the red carpet looking in my direction; everyone watches him, wondering what he's going to do next. I feel a little awkward when I realise he's approaching me.

I remain seated as he stands in front of me not wanting to tower over him; he bites his lip as if biting back his emotions and looks into my eyes handing me the white rose. I accept it willingly, and he leans over to kiss my brow before hugging me in towards to him. I lift off my seat slightly as he pulls me in, and I can see over his shoulder to the VIP area opposite. I find myself eye to eye with Prince Charles for a second; all eyes are on us. I lower my eyes downward, unsure of what to do next; it's a powerful moment. I feel he has publically acknowledged, without restraint, his support for me, and all the distress I've been put through, not just the Bombing itself, but everything that happened afterwards as well. I feel extremely emotional, and can't stop a tear running down my cheek. From his perspective I guess I must be a kind of connection to his son, that must create a special bond.

Once all the victims' families have laid roses, they signal for the survivors to come over. We file along one at a time to do our part, as I struggle to stay in control of my emotions.

With the ceremony completed it's time to mingle in the marque, which offers refreshments and a change of energy. Trevor McDonald comes over for a quick chat and I take a photo with him, such a nice man, why can't they all be like him. Next Gordon Brown offers a few encouraging words and advice and I'm truly surprised. Then I see Ken Livingston, but he walks past awkwardly, he seems somewhat distant and disconnected from what's going on; Alison notices and comments on it too. As I turn back towards Alison I see David Cameron standing behind her, so I move forward to greet him.

"Hello Mr. Cameron." I reach out to shake his hand.

"Hello, what's your name?"

"My name's Garri Holness."

"Hello Garri, nice to meet you, is there something you'd like to talk to me about?"

"Hmmm."

"You can talk to me about anything Garri." I think for a second and decide to go for it, well he did ask.

"Sure okay, how about Institutional Racism?"

"Err?" His face drops from a smile to a look of concern.

"Don't worry, I'm not talking about the Police racism, that's another story."

"Okay, so what are you talking about?"

"Society!" I pause for emphasis.

"Society?" He repeats, looking more confused.

"Yes! For example look at that bus passing, see the advert on the side. Can you see what's missing?"

"No Garri?" He frowns.

"When you drive home after this, have a look at the billboards around you, ask yourself where are all the ethnic people? When you go clothes shopping, do you ever see an ethnic mannequin? Even the makeup and hair adverts on TV are all geared towards non-ethnic consumers."

"Hmmm, interesting." His face reddens slightly but he keeps eye contact and I can see he's still listening.

"The problem is that what I'm pointing out to you is an invisible advantage to those people who benefit from it, many of them don't even see it as racism even though it's in plain view. As a politician, it can't be helpful to ignore this part of society can it? Meanwhile I'm sure you want the ethnic vote, right?

"Well, yes of course, but really-" I don't want to be fobbed off so I continue. "So you see black youth need successful role models to have a visual impact that shows them they too can enjoy the privileges of being valuable members of society. You must know everyone needs to feel valued and part of society. The Inner City youth only join gangs so they can belong to something, and this has been going on for decades."

"I see your point Garri, so what do you propose we do about it?"
He listens with interest.

"Okay, I'm glad you asked, I suggest a program which includes ex-offenders who have managed to turn their lives around, are trained to help and mentor the youth before they choose gangs and crime over study and a career; we have to change that mind-set. We have to show them they have a chance of success, despite their background."

"Have you been inside Garri?"

"Good question, yes I have, and I know the changes we want to see start within our community, but if we don't voice them to people like you, nothing will be done, so excuse my rant, but as you see I'm passionate about this." He offers a look of acknowledgement and I hope I've given him food for thought. Alison steps forward perhaps she senses he's had enough for one day. "Garri smile, let me take a few photos of you two together."

Such a sweet girl, she's been close by me all morning, making sure I'm okay. She snaps away taking several pictures of David Cameron and I, before he makes his escape. She then gets the attention of Gordon Brown and asks me to take a photo of her with the Prime Minister; I oblige.

8th July 2009
Home Croydon

On my way to the shops I pass a few familiar faces. A guy shouts from across the road. "Oi mate, you're on the front page of the Star!" My heart sinks.

"What?!"

"Yeah Mate." I hurry to the newsagents to see for myself. The owner knows me well so she lets me look through all the papers. I feel totally deflated; will they ever stop? The major Tabloids and the local rag condemn David Cameron for shaking my hand and talking to me. Headlines state, *'Rapist who lost leg in 7/7 blast meets Cameron as guest of honour at memorial service'* and *'Should Garri Holness have met David Cameron?'* Thankfully the front-page story in 'The Star' is actually focused on the Memorial, but it's the only one. Unbelievable! It's seems that every year after the anniversary these hateful reporters have a dig at me; like I haven't been through enough already, they want to pour on even more hate! I'm really pissed off!

Walking back home feeling crushed, the landlady of my local pub is sitting outside having a cigarette and smiles when she sees me. "You alright Garri?"

"Yeah, I'm alright Linda."

"You don't look it, what's up?"

"The papers are at it again." I put my head down and sigh.

"Yeah I heard, but don't worry, if anyone asks me about you, I always put them right, it's horrible what they're doing to you; you're a hero really."

"Much appreciated Linda and thank you."

"Well it's true." I kiss her on the cheek and try to produce a smile; it's good to have some support at this time. "Bye for now."

"Bye Garri, keep your chin up, you're a good man." I walk the short distance home still feeling utterly deflated.

July - September 2009

I keep my head down, feeling the need to let the drama blow over yet again. I also meet a spiritual teacher, at the Gym of all places, who is also an author and we make an agreement to write my book together, I feel inspired. They say when the student is ready, the teacher shows up!

Meanwhile the uplifting music goes on in my home studio as Sanj introduces me to various up and coming artists he brings in to record. It's interesting to watch Sanj giving them direction on voice projection whether it's singing or rapping. He's hard on them sometimes, I think he's too hard, but hearing their recordings, I appreciate the results of giving them that push. Even they are amazed by how they sound. I can see why he's good at his job and how he gets the best out of his artists.

I stay in the background, making mental notes and it's great having music to uplift me, when life throws its curve balls. I'm like a sponge taking it all in, and learn so much by just watching. I find it fascinating when Sanj asks an artist to remember a life experiences as they sing to get more emotion into their voice. I can definitely hear the difference, and it inspires me as I certainly can do that after all that's happened!

My practice starts after six when the studio closes, and they all go home. The system cools while I have dinner. Then I do my thing, using whatever I've learnt that day. It's good to have this time to focus and escape from it all.

Thoughts of the Paralympics inspire me to go to the gym as I've decided to take part in the trials. I focus on my exercises, keeping my conversations to a minimum and my exercise to the max. I'm determined to concentrate on what I can do to make life better.

29th September 2009
Brunel University Uxbridge

After a long drive I arrive at the Paralympic Potential Day. It's a great day to test myself and I'm well excited. After I change and enter the main arena, I see the iconic Olympic Games flags and posters everywhere. The hall is huge and divided into sections hosting different disciplines and as I look around I see many potential Paralympians with a variety of disabilities taking part in numerous trials. I'm amazed!

The excitement in the air is electric as I give the assistant my details and she gives me a number 137. I scan the arena to find a seat and put my bag down. Space found, time to start warming up. I see so many extraordinary people, their dedication and how they overcome their disability to excel in their chosen field of expertise really impresses me.

After a quick warm up I decide to compete in my first event, the Sitting Volleyball. Even though I've played volleyball in the past, it's a whole different ball game sitting on the floor, ouch!

Next I try my hand at weight lifting, and because I've already been lifting weights in the gym since the Bombings, I'm more confident with this event.

By the time I approach the running track I'm warmed up and raring to go for the 60-metre sprint. One of the woman watching beckons me over just before I start and curiosity pushes me to see what she wants. "My friend and I have been watching you. We think you'll be good at the sprint, in fact I think you'll have the fastest time." I smile shaking my head, "No pressure then?" Now I feel self-conscious but try again to focus on the trial.

I've got three attempts to get my fastest time down. I'm nervous, imagine competing in the Paralympic Games as a Sprinter, wow! The starter pistol goes off and I run as fast as I can, my left leg stays firm and it goes well, 5.15sec. But they say my time could have been faster if I'd continued to sprint past the finish line instead of slowing down towards the end. He says it's a mistake most people make the first time, so I'm not deterred.

Second sprint I really go for it, but I'm going so fast on my bouncy running blade, that my right leg can't keep up and I pull a hamstring. As I fall to the floor in agony, I'm so disappointed. Suddenly three women surround me, all trying to massage my leg at the same time, and they keep asking me where it hurts. One runs off to get ice, and brings it back quickly placing it on my hamstring. She's wearing an England tracksuit and it turns out she's one of the coaches. Playful remarks fly at me as they all have a laugh at my expense, but at least I can join in and laugh at myself too.

3rd October 2009
Home Croydon

The studio work with Sanj slows down as the projects are completed one by one. This gives me the chance to get back to my own thing now the unnecessary pressure is off. Although my hamstring is still sore, I manage to put the system on and practice until early evening. Then I have a rush to get ready as Halle is taking me out to the Blue Elephant, in Fulham Broadway for a bite to eat as a birthday treat, I hope I can walk okay, we'll just have to take it slow.

30th October 2009
Home Croydon

With my hamstring now healed, I spent most of the day at the new

Westfield Shopping Centre in White City, it's like a massive maze of retailers. It's spacious, clean and smacks of luxury, offering many of the big name brands in stand alone stores. The variety of restaurants is also impressive. I must admit I was tempted into buying two wan away jumpers to add to my collection as well. Definitely worth the trip! Anyway let me put away my clothes and go back into music mode.

1st November 2009
Home Croydon

Most mornings I wake up between five and half past, it's my time to meditate and contemplate; amazing insights flood in, and I even reflect on some relevant quotes that I've seen recently on Facebook. Just this week both my mates Kevin and Troy, who are very active on Facebook, posted several things that inspired me. I think I'll start putting some of my insights on my Facebook status updates when I can remember them.

3rd November 2009
University of Roehampton

The guys keep asking me to attend a Sitting Volleyball training session. I was a runner, footballer and high jumper, but as I can't really do any of that now, I've finally come to watch them. After a while, I realise that the circuit training will be very good for my core so I decide to join in. During the last half-hour they ask me to play in a friendly game; man are they competitive! It's bloody tough but really enjoyable. Glad I came!

5th November 2009
Home Croydon

Sanj is engrossed in a track editing and mixing, while I'm in the kitchen, preparing jerk chicken, sweet potato chips, and a salad.

Although I ache from head to foot from Volleyball, while I'm cooking I make the mad decision I'm gonna play with the team regularly to see how it goes. The training is on Monday's so I have to switch music days.

"Oi Sugar, that smells nice."

"Just do your ting man, and by the way any chance we can change days to Thursday or Friday instead of Monday?"

"If you feed me!"

"If I feed you? *KMT*!"

6th November 2009
Home Croydon

Sanj is mastering a track and is fully focused in the studio.

"Gonna clean my car, soon come."

"Yeah alright." I make my way outside and play my music as I begin cleaning just as a friend pulls up alongside.

"Hey Garri, you fancy doing my car while you're at it, I'll pay you." She smiles, how can I resist! I end up cleaning her car as well my own and make sure both cars sparkle.

10th November 2009
Home Croydon

Today I decide to start sharing some of my insights on Facebook *Assumption...you should never assume what others are thinking. Just as others cannot assume what you are thinking.* I get several likes straight away; it's addictive!

Facebook status 8.30am *"Don't dwell on the past, look forward, and focus."* More likes come my way; it makes me smile.

Facebook status 8.45am *"Whatever you're doing come from a place of Love. World Peace!"* I'm enjoying sharing my thoughts on Facebook, but I don't want to get too addicted!

13th November 2009
Home Croydon

My buzzer goes. "Who is it?"

"Shuggs is me Mate." I buzz Sanj in.

"What you saying?"

"I'm good you know." He's carrying a carrier bag.

"What's that?"

"Pack lunch Rudebwoy, I have to bring my own, cos I told my Mum you ain't feeding me." He laughs "Try this my Mum cooked it." He hands me a little pattie and I take a bite.

"This taste messi Sanj. I'm glad I didn't feed you, your Mum can keep making your lunch and we can share it! " He grins.

"Yep we can 'av a cup of tea and eat a few of them later on."

"Wiv a cup of rosy eh?" We laugh together as I appreciate the delicious home cooked Pattie.

Sanj turns the system on to continue where we left off yesterday. "Sugar you know it's a blessing being here, it's so convenient, I do my best work here because I'm free to do what I need to do I have no restriction, I'm in control."

"I think you should start looking at working on your own music Bruv."

"I enjoy helping other people though."

"I hear you, but you've got to do you some time, surely?"

"I know and I've got nuff tracks, let me just finish off these works first because it's bringing in the money then I'll start my thing, but I need a studio."

"Bruv you can use this don't be stupid, we can work something out."

"Respect for that." Back in he goes, more editing and mixing before tea and patties.

16th November 2009
University of Roehampton

Volleyball training and I really go for it, but I'm gonna need a hot bath with sea-salt later. I can feel my muscles ceasing up already!

20th November 2009
Home Croydon

Facebook status "*Be Positive in your mind, body and soul, try not to let unknown forces take control. Have a great weekend folks!!!!*" This time I get comments as well, people wish me a good weekend too. I find the smiley icon, and I'm not afraid to use it! Later I watch the movie 2012, great movie. Wicked effects!

21st November 2009
Home Croydon

No sign of Sanj this morning, so I give him a call, but no answer. I'll call again later, but for now let me try singing the other song *'This is the time'*. The beat is wicked; love this tune, headphones on, time to go in. Three hours later, doesn't time fly when you're in the zone! I call Sanj again, still no reply and I'm a bit worried so I leave a message to call me back. Wish I had my dog General here at times like this …

20th November 1983
Stockwell Park Estate Brixton

Our dog Rolex has been missing for nearly an hour and it's unlike him to run off. I start thinking something must have happened as I help Mum prepare Sunday Dinner. I know he knows it's Sunday and he ain't missing his Chicken dinner for nothing. I go out onto the balcony again to call and whistle for him, but it feels like my efforts are in vain. Where the hell is he?

"Garri, Garri!" Mum calls me back in, "wha' ah gwann?"

"I'm worried about Rolex Mum, he's been out a long time."

"General!" Mum calls and General comes running into the kitchen straight away. He looks at Mum with adoration, thinking he's getting a treat. "General, yu fi gwaan fin' Rolex before Dinna, gwaan noh, go find Rolex!" She opens the door and he rushes out. Within half-an hour General brings Rolex back in time for dinner. This dog is something else!

22nd November 2009
Home Croydon

Mobile rings, but don't recognise the number. "Hello"

"Ello der" It's Sanj, and it's a crisp clear landline so he's obviously not on the mobile as usual.

"Sanj, where you been?"

"I lost my phone and wallet innit."

"Arrh!"

"But my bredrin just called me and said he found it in his car, so I'm going to link him. Plus I've got some work to finish at his place as well."

"As long as you're alright Bruv."

"I'll pass you later, if I can get there."

"It's ok Bruv, it's all good, we'll chat soon."

"Easy."

24th November 2009
Novello Theatre, London

Halle and I are watching *'Cat On A Hot Tin Roof'* featuring some of my favourite actors James Earl Jones, Adrian Lester, Phylicia Rashad and Sanaa Lathan. What a great, great, play, we both thoroughly enjoy it. It's nice to get out and about, making the most of living only a short distance away from central London. It's good to take in the London vibe.

1st December 2009
Home Croydon

Focus back on the music, Sanj is in da house again, it's truly a blessing being around him. I look at music now in a completely different way.

"Sugar you got any Rizla Mate?"

"You're supposed to come with Rizla Rudebwoy."

"Don't go on like that Mate."

"Alright see it yah." I give in.

"Thank you very much."

"Don't take the piss!"

We laugh, but as I reflect on Sanj I can't believe he hasn't had a break yet. Sometimes it's not easy to understand why people without talent seem to do better than those that have.

4th December 2009
Home Croydon

Outside doing a bit of gardening, I love feeling close to nature. Everyone I greet on my corner this morning is full of smiles. The build up to Xmas is in the air, but it's not the usual stressed vibe this year, there's a community spirit. Once my garden is tidy I'm back to writing and researching. I'm getting my autobiography together. I've been writing a diary since the Bombings; it's a big job though piecing it all together.

This evening I'm going up to central London again with Halle to the Theatre to see a hip-hop play; quite excited! She's doing her best to get me out and about and I'm grateful.

4th December 2009
Central London

"The play is wicked, yeah man!! I am proper captivated, I'm sure I could do couple of dem moves."

"Behave yourself Garri." Halle smiles.

"Dem man move skilful, so glad we came." It feels like life is getting back on an even keel.

5th December 2009
Home Croydon.

The post arrives bringing a letter from Volleyball England. They invite me to train with the Paralympic Sitting Volleyball squad preparing for the 2012 Olympic games. Wow, I have to sit down! Imagine that, what great news; I obviously did better in the trials than I thought. Things are looking up after all the crap I've been through. I have been given a chance to represent England in the Paralympics! Very nice way to start the weekend!

15th December 2009
Home Croydon

It's bloody cold this morning and I'm sure it's gonna snow. I can feel stiffness and pain in my joints, and I've learnt by now that's a sign, so I make a decision to have a lie in and an easy day. I'm grateful British Gas serviced my boiler a few weeks ago; at least I know the heating is okay. It's so cold I need a hug, Halle! Where are you?

21st December 2009
Home Croydon

Taking time to write and organise my thoughts. I understand I am the creator of my life and it's time to focus on thriving now, not just surviving!

24th December 2009
Home Croydon

Facebook status, *A time for Caring, Sharing and getting involved in the Festive Spirit but spare a thought for those that are less fortunate and those that are not with us. Please note the Love that you're feeling at this moment amongst your love ones, shouldn't stop there, Spread Your wings as far as the eye can see and touch as many hearts you can, elevate, inspire. Remember we are vessels of God. So we can create a better future. Have a very Merry Xmas.* Many lovely replies and messages are posted during the day.

25th December 2009
Home Croydon

Home alone on Christmas Day but that's the way I want it to be, in my own space. Mum and Dad drift into mind, I really miss them. Another Christmas without them, but I suppose when it's your time it's your time. Time? I begin to contemplate time...

How long is our human shell built for? What is our purpose here on earth? Maybe it's to find the path of true enlightenment, and be at one with body, mind and soul. It feels like I'm going through the process of reprogramming my mind; no brain washing or spoon-fed information allowed. The alternative books and documentaries I've been studying have really opened my mind, along with the CBT treatment at Maudsley and my increased spiritual awareness. It's like I'm slowly lifting the veil from my eyes. I continue to analyse my life, my family and the change in my perception. I'm hopeful.

27th December 2009
Home Croydon

Facebook Status, *Watching the Arsenal on sky. Yes we are winning. Can I get ah Wooooh Hoooh from all of my Gunners!*

I get a lot of comments and not all of them favourable!

9th-10th January 2010
Bath England

I'm training with the Paralympics sitting Volleyball Squad this weekend. There's a great feeling of comradely amongst the boys. Bath is a wonderful place but I'm not here to see the sights, I'm here to work. The training is hard, very hard; this is a whole new level of fitness! Muscles hurt that I never knew I had, so much pain! Sitting Volleyball is really not easy, especially on my poor butt. My triceps, shoulders and abs are agony, oh man! And that's before we even play a single match. If this doesn't get me back into shape, nothing will!

On my journey home I reflect on a great weekend. I've trained hard and played some good Volleyball, but I've got to practice. Some of the lads, who are much more experienced, gave me advice and encouraged me, they made me feel like part of the team, which is nice, but I have to practice the spike. Spiking is when you slam the ball hard down towards the opponent's court in order to score, I must master that before I can be good enough to feel like I'm really part of the team. The next training session on Monday 18th is back in Roehampton, glad it's a little closer to home.

Life goes on at an interesting pace in-between Volleyball, the Gym and my Music, as well as getting my Autobiography together; it's keeping me more than occupied!

18th January 2010
University of Roehampton

The team fitness instructor is a very regimental woman; she even walks like a solider, and it seems she's taking liberties with me, although she does it with a smile on her face. Everyone else is asked to do sets of 10 to 12, but she's pushing me to do 12-15, maybe she's trying to test me, or something. Anyway I won't surrender, but I'm surprised how much fitness training is involved. 70% of Volleyball training is fitness work, mostly on the core, 20% playing volleyball, and finally 10% talking tactics and cooling down. In time I'll get the hang of it, as painful as it feels at the moment, but I've already got a reward, my England Olympic kit to be proud of!

20th January 2010
Home Croydon

I'm in agony and feeling weak, I've overspent my energy and my muscles feel like they've totally ceased up, I can't even get out of bed this morning my back is giving me grief! "Arghhh!"

The Trainer pushed me way too much, and I must be crazy to do what she asks! She's got me aching all over, I don't think there is any part of my body that doesn't hurt. Everytime I try to get up, I fall back down again in agony. I have to run a hot bath with sea salt, and then somehow find food; I'm so hungry! Maybe I'll get back into bed after that and sleep the pain off!

"What I am doing man, beating up my body? All those guys so much younger than me, yet she's trying to keep me on par with them. Chaa!" But I smile proudly.

22nd January 2010
Home Croydon

I figure the hot bath yesterday saved my life, I can actually move around a little bit today! Gotta do some food shopping though, and I badly need a wrist support, as well as a pair of padded shorts my bum hurts too much when I'm sliding around on the floor for such a long time, it needs protection!

23rd-24th January 2010
Kettering Northamptonshire

Training over the weekend with the Sitting Volleyball squad again, God help me!

25th January 2010
University of Roehampton

Training yet again, I'm a sucker for punishment yes, but at least I'm getting fit in the process. I catch a glimpse of a familiar face at the other side of the hall and it makes me smile. It's Martine Wright in her England kit too. I wave and shout over, "Hi Martine, fancy seeing you here!" She looks round and smiles as she sees me. "Garri, what are you doing here?"

"Playing Volleyball," I laugh, "and you?"

"Same!" We laugh and chat for a minute before she heads back to join up with the women's Paralympic team, what a coincidence, it seems we have several parallels.

I find a space at the edge of the hall next to a heap of the guys clothes and prosthetics, drop my tracksuit bottoms and step out leaving my leg standing up in them, ready to step back into later. It's much quicker to get in and out this way; the other guys do the same. Shuffling along the floor to join the guys in the middle of the hall already warming up, I hear a loud clatter behind me. When I look back, my leg has fallen over and knocked several other legs over in a domino affect. There's now a scrum of undone clothing and limbs sticking out in all directions that looks like escapees from a yoga class, I laugh out loud!

Five minutes or so later the Fitness Coach arrives and puts us all into pairs to start Training. Here we go again… no laughing matter now!

26th January 2010
Home Croydon

Aching all over my body again, it's intense but this time I know the routine. Hot bath, eat something and relax for a couple days to let my body recover.

28th January 2010
Brixton, London

I'm feeling physically better today, and as I walk along Brixton High Street I see an old friend coming towards me. "You alright Babe?"

She stops to chat. "Yeah, I'm alright; look at you though, you look so well, healthy and proper fit, haven't seen you for ages."

"Thank you very much Hunni." I smile. "I'm doing okay."

"Sugar you look good man, well done!"

"I'm training hard and it's helping."

"For real, I'm going to tell my sister I saw you."

"You tell her I said hello and take care."

"I will." It feels good to be acknowledged. Today is another confidence building day.

30th January 2010
Kensington London

I'm in the Iconic Royal Albert Hall with Halle as part of a packed audience watching the Cirque Du Soleil. The building is magnificent, and it's the perfect venue for this kind of show because it's round. The acrobatics are absolutely fantastic, breath taking in fact. I like the comical parts too, what a great event to attend. I'm so grateful to be here in London having fun and living life.

March 2010
Home Croydon

It would have been Mummy's birthday on the 28th and Dads on the 30th, it's not an easy month emotionally, but at least I can express myself with music; it's the perfect release.

20th April 2010
Home Croydon

Just given my car a good wash and wax, sparkling! It brings a smile to my face. There's a magical feeling about the motorcar industry and I can't put my finger on it, but I think it's the closest thing many of us men get to emotion. Apart from football of course!

22nd April 2010
University of Roehampton

After telling the Volleyball Manager everything about my youth conviction, I'm filling in a CRB application form so I can play without restrictions. I need to be two steps ahead of the Tabloids, so they don't spoil this opportunity for me as well. I don't want any more headlines, and especially not stating I shouldn't be allowed to represent England because of my conviction. Anyway, time for the gruelling training to continue!

24th April 2010
Holborn Hogan Lovell's Solicitors

I've been blessed with some great and influential people in my life and my solicitor Caroline is definitely one of them; she is a real diamond. She's put together a Team in case of further Tabloid intrusion, which includes a Human Rights Barrister, who doesn't take prisoners, she tells me straight and doesn't pull any punches, with me or anyone else. I admire her for that. Karen too, is another diamond team member in the Press department, and I can't forget Paul their boss. I think of them as my new extended family, if things go wrong they'll be there to pick me up, dust me off and put me on the road again.

"Garri we're here for you, any problems you have, at any time of day, call us." It's such a comfort knowing I've got heavy weight people like that in my corner. This is not a service I'm paying for either; it's about love, compassion, justice and the kindness of hearts, it's truly a blessing I'm grateful for.

27th April 2010
Home Croydon

I ask the Press Office at Roehampton to liaise with Hogan Lovell's my Solicitor. I've learned it's no good ignoring what might happen, I need to be prepared and I have a feeling the Press may have something unconstructive to say about my inclusion in the Paralympic Squad. A letter will be drafted in advance so that we are ready for any negativity that may come my way. It's a great sense of empowerment like a Boxer, who has trained and is prepared for the fight this time!

"Yes, me ready fi unno rass!" It feels good!

6th May 2010
University of Roehampton

Volleyball training again tonight, although it murders me I'm up for it. It's a challenge and I know it's very good for my core strength, I can feel the difference in my body and arms already. I have to say it's hard work though trying to keep up with Justin & Charlie. These guys have lost both legs, which make them lighter than me, but there is no denying they are both exceptionally fit. The bleep test, which assesses our stamina, is the ultimate, and they are my inspiration, the benchmark if you will, where I'm heading as far as my fitness is concerned. I'm relatively fit already, but this is a whole new level of fitness; it's all about stamina and staying power!

I arrive home just after eleven, absolutely whacked and clutching my jerk chicken take-away. I could hardly get out of my car and walk into the take-away shop tonight but I need to eat, and then have a hot bath so I can rest.

7th May 2010
Home Croydon

It always takes me two or sometimes three days to recover after Volleyball Training, but this morning I've got a severe pain in my back that won't shift and I can hardly move. In fact I can't even get out of bed, but at least I don't have to force it as I've got an easy weekend to look forward to. It feels like the old pain I had in the Hospital when I was first injured and I start to worry if I'm overdoing it.

June-July 2010
Home Croydon

The Volleyball Team are away in the US without me as I'm still waiting for my CRB to come through, but I have to admit, it's a welcome break from the pain and punishment, although tinged with a sense of missing out; I would have liked to go as well.

5th July 2010
Home Croydon

It's that time of year again, but rather than flowers, this year I've framed a poem as my tribute to the 52 Beautiful Souls who lost their lives 7/7/2005....' *I wish Heaven had a phone so I could hear your voice again. I thought of you today but that's nothing new. I thought about you yesterday and days before that too. I think of you in silence, I often speak your name. All I have are memories and a picture in a frame.*

Your memory is a keepsake from which I'll never part. God has you in His arms... I have you in my heart! ~Unknown. It strikes a chord with me over losing my Mum and I hope it will comfort others who have lost loved ones too.

7th July 2010
Hyde Park, London

I will not allow the Press to stop me from paying my respects. I make my way to the Plaque and lay my framed poem down next to it. There are a few women standing close by and they look over. "Hello, are you Garri Holness." I detect an American accent.

"Yes I am." I answer cautiously, unsure of what's coming next.

"Me and all my friends in the States were wondering why the English Press turned on you. It seems to us you are at a total different place in your life than you were as a seventeen-year-old teenager." She looks into my eyes sadly.

"Yeah your right."

She goes on, "You're a man now and a victim of the biggest terrorist attack to hit London since the War. Why would they bring up your past of twenty years ago like that?"

I shrug my shoulders but find nothing to say.

"We all think it's because you're black, but listen you've got a lot of support across the pond, Stateside. You are a true inspiration!" Her face lights up with a smile and sincerity.

"Wow! Thank you very much for your kind words, that's nice to hear, you've really lifted my spirits today." I return the smile.

"My pleasure Garri and remember to keep the faith." I acknowledge at least not everyone has been turned against me. I find a seat as the Ceremony begins.

8th July 2010
Local Newsagent Croydon

I scan through all the papers with a sense of relief, it's the first year they haven't written anything condemning about me, it feels like a victory!

July 21, 2010
Home Croydon

Facebook Status, *My Mums Prayer, A little bit of faith, kept me from my fear, when I think of you Ma, down my cheek runs a tear, my love my dear will always increase, as your spirit lives within me, may your soul evolve in peace. Bless you Mum.* Lovely replies abound, especially from my community and those who knew Mummy.

20th August 2010
Regents Park London

The Volleyball Team invite me to join them for an exhibition match in a central London park; it's all about getting members of the public involved. It's a fantastic day and feels so great to be here as part of the Great Britain Team, having photos taken and signing shirts. Even though I'm not officially one of the senior team players yet, a lovely black girl specifically asks me to sign her shirt, so of course I feel obliged!

11th/12th September 2010
Kettering England

I'm involved in my first 'friendly' tournament; we're up against Military Teams in the North East of England. The first match will be at noon, the second at two o'clock and the final one at four o'clock. This repeats over two days and it's my first full-on experience of competing, so an ideal opportunity to see where I fit into the Team.

It's tough and very competitive, yet a chance to compete again, which is exhilarating. Although my Team only win a few of our games, winning isn't the priority for our manager Matt. He's observing our fitness and skill levels, as well as ironing out any tactical problems. I do okay for a first timer, but I know I could do so much better going forward. Watching Ben, Charlie, Rob, Justin and Jabba perform is inspiring, and clearly shows me I've got plenty of room for improvement.

I'm absolutely shattered after another full on weekend. A hot bath with the essential sea salt to ease my muscles followed by a good night sleep sounds like music to my ears.

13th September 2010
Home Croydon 03.33am

I wake up needing to go to the toilet and open my eyes to see my clock illuminating the time in the darkness. It's far too early to get up but I need to go. I can hardly move at all after the Volleyball weekend, so I get up carefully as the back pain rips into me. I slowly make my way to the bathroom on crutches, not at all balanced and still half asleep. I'm so disengaged I almost fall, and on top of that, there is a strong sense I'm being watched.

I have a cursory glance around the flat on my way back to bed, just to make sure, but it's all clear. Back in bed, but unable to sleep I reach over for my drawing pad and start doodling, nothing in particular, just drawing to help me relax, as I often do. Before I know it, there's a familiar face looking back at me from the page, it takes a moment to realise who it is. Wow! It's Mum, how the hell did I do that? As I look into her eyes I hear her memorable voice loud and strong in my head.

'Garri yu need fi stand inna yu power, yu roots dem strong, yu ancestors dem, de behind yu ah support yu. Know who yu are and pick sense from nonsense, know dat yu are love an dat love kept yu here fi a reason. Learn fi use yu intuition, fi be a Free Man, an' stand inna yu Sovereignty!

Whoa! Where on Earth did that come from, Goosebumps rush up and down my arms then all over my body, what a message! I speak out loud an acknowledgement of this powerful message, "I love you Mum, and me ah listen!"

20th September 2010
Home Croydon

After breakfast my CRB arrives in the post, its very good news! It says I have no restrictions, which means I'm free to play Volleyball with the GB team anywhere in the World! I'm keen to call Matt and tell him that it's finally come through.

I grin from ear to ear as he confirms I will indeed be travelling the World with the Team wherever they go. It feels like the shackles have been taken off. I have the opportunity to be part of the Olympic Games and I would not have thought that possible after all that's happened. I feel free!

Looking back at the moment I first heard the Olympic Games were coming to London in 2005, when I was busy at work entering data onto SAP. I remember wishing I could have taken part in the Games. Okay it's not track and field, which was my dream, but it's so exciting that I have the opportunity to take part as a Paralympian.

As I reflect back on my life I can still hear the voice of one of the Man dem ringing in my ear. *'That's it your life is fucked up now, and you can't do nothing!'* He will never know how much his words both challenged and inspired me; it was a prediction that I had to prove wrong!

EPILOGUE - JULY 2015

Against all the odds, I've made it through to 2015 with my mind still in tact and a positive mental attitude! Co-writing this book has been such an interesting journey, I didn't expect that telling my story and writing about it, could have such a healing affect.

I'm also excited to have launched my career as a Motivational Coach sharing 'The Art of Positive Thinking Despite Adversity'. Using my testimony of life, I try to help and motivate others who are in a dark place or going through a traumatic experience, to overcome the challenges and fears they face. I talk to people who are in rehabilitation for addictions, others with regard to grief and mourning the loss of loved ones. I've even been back to Roehampton Walking School helping recent amputees to embrace their way forward. I aim to continue spreading positive thinking for as long as I am invited to do so, and wherever that takes me; it's more than a job it's a calling from within. If you'd like to invite me to talk at your venue or function, please do contact me through my website.

When I was twenty-three, you might say I followed a calling then too, when a few friends from my regular Sunday League Football and I started winning trophies and medals, which gave me a sense of accomplishment and team pride. Also several of the team had turned their lives around, finding good jobs and working hard; some even started their own businesses, which inspired me. I needed to share this positive energy of group achievement with my local community, so I got together with a few friends from Stockwell Park Estate and opened the unused Community Centre as a meeting place for local youths. Back in those days I didn't need a CRB check, just the will to make a difference in the lives of the next generation, and I had more than my fair share of that. After all I had experienced a challenging start in my life; it was hard to swallow, and it was an important lesson I felt the need to share so that other youths didn't suffer the same fate as me.

The richness I felt during my time spent building up the Youth & Community Centre in Brixton was huge! I ended up liaising with local Government to receive grants used to buy recreational items such as pool tables and gym equipment. We also arranged various trips for under privileged kids that they would never normally afford. I clearly remember the day we went to Alton Towers, when the kids persuaded me onto one of the biggest rollercoaster rides of my life and frightened the shit outta me! And I don't mind admitting that now! We showed them glimpses of how a better life could look, without criminality at the center. Giving them reason to say no to gangs and yes to learning and earning their living using their talents and abilities.

During those years, I became Vice Chairman of the organisation and got involved liaising with Brixton Police who became inspired by what we had managed to achieve. A far cry from the police brutality I had experienced as a youth. The value of those years spent helping kids continues to bring rewards even today, when the youth of yesteryear still stop me in the street to thank me for the inspiration and knowledge that helped them to get out of the Endz and move on with a more fulfilling and successful life. I'm pleased to say The Youth & Community Centre is still alive and kicking today!

Knowledge may be power, but understanding how to apply that power to life is priceless. It's enlightenment I seek now; this is the richness I value most. A very different perspective than the one I had before 2005.

After careful consideration, meditation, and being honest with myself, I made the very important decision that playing Sitting Volleyball in the Paralympics was not my calling. The stress on my already damaged body was taking its toll. My back was constantly hurting, and it was proving more and more difficult to recover after each training session. So I listened to my intuition and allowed it to lead the way. Back pain can be a sign of lack of support in life, the spine being the supporting structure in the body. So perhaps in this case it was telling me I was over extending myself, not supporting, loving or caring for myself, while I was chasing after the need for approval that could result from being a Paralympian, and especially a medal winner.

Since giving up the grueling training, and the need for recognition, I've gone from strength to strength, so I know I've made the right decision. Of course it's disappointing not to have competed as a Paralympian, but over the recent years I've managed to listen to my inner voice, guiding me forwards through life. Helping me explore in more detail the strange and wonderful experiences that have come my way, and continue to come my way. This is exciting indeed!

After everything that the Tabloids did to discredit me year on year, I would never have believed I could meet and have a chat with Prince William at the recent ten-year Memorial. The thoughtfulness he showed was surprising, and the empathy I felt from him over the loss of my Mother was touching. We even managed to have a laugh as we posed for the photograph I've included. I also met the first black Lord Lieutenant of Greater London, Keneth Olisa, who both inspired me and offered to help. It was a great leap forward since the conversation I had with David Cameron back in 2006.

I still look at the picture I drew of my Mum in 2010 and it continues to bring forward inspiration and guidance whenever I meditate with it. I still don't understand how I was able to draw it, but it's one of those extraordinary experiences that came my way, which I can't explain, yet I value immensely.

I no longer chase material wealth, but neither do I turn my back on prosperity. I like to be comfortable, yet I live by the 'Moral Compass' that people mean more than profit or status; knowing that keeps me right on track. I have come to believe we are spirit living inside a human body, yet in a world of high-tech computers and virtual reality, our communications can be sadly without spiritual essence or soul. I believe we need to check the ways we communicate and whenever possible make more of an effort to get together and talk to each other or occasionally write letters rather than emails. It's my opinion our handwriting, sketches and doodles, which we seldom get to share these days, contain the essence of who we are; that spiritual aspect we all share. It's such a shame we don't reach out to communicate more through the written word. I have therefore found a way to offer you my closing thoughts for this book in my own handwriting.

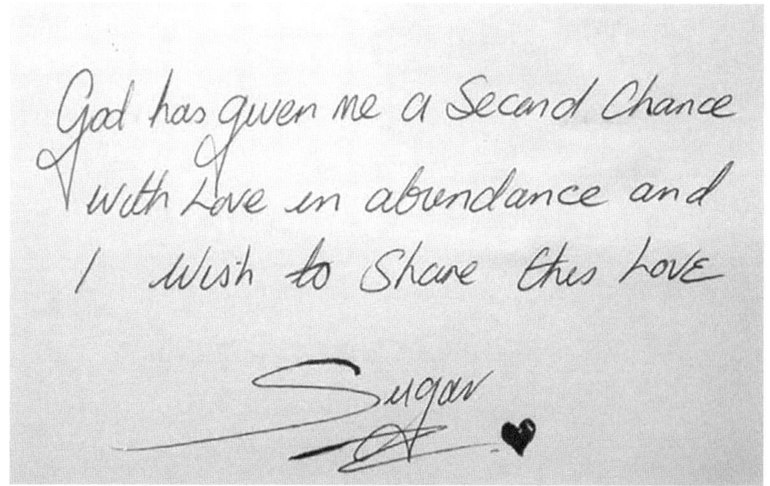
God has given me a Second Chance
with Love in abundance and
I Wish to Share this Love

Sugar

Please use the glossary at the back only for guidance, remembering that Jamaican Patois or Creole is primarily a spoken language. It is not easily written and we have tried here to explain the words used in this book based on the sounds or phonics. Also you will find 'Lomaican' words, a mixture of Patois and London Cockney, born from an assimilation of the many Caribbean heritage folk who have been raised in London.

Remember there are few, if any consistent rules, as there are in English, and therefore words can change pronunciation and spelling depending on the context yet still mean a similar thing. For those readers who already use the language, please have fun with our attempts at writing what you already speak so well, hopefully you'll recognise most of it! For those readers who have little or no idea, please enjoy learning more, if you wish, about the culture and language of the remarkable little island in the heart of the Caribbean called Jamaica. This language is often at the root of much of our urban slang. For such a tiny island, it has had such a huge impact on the world

GLOSSARY

Ah	It's, to, is
Ah fi we time	*It's our time*
Ah yu dis	*It's yours this,* this is for you
Arr	*Or else* A threat
A wan wash	*One wash* a quick wash, to freshen up
Bad	*Great, complimentary*
Banging Tune	Proclamation of a great record
Batty	Bottom
Beg yu	Ask you to do something with humility
Bless'ed	An endearing term for exceptional or sacred thing
Big man	Adult, not related to size but concerned with status, bravado, age and experience
Bopping	Walking with a bounce
Bredda	Brother
Bring in	Get involved, include
Brixton Bop	Injuries that cause a limp sometimes faked to appear more 'gangster' or tough
Bumbaclot	*Bottom cloth* used as exclamation, expletive or insult, King of curse words
Bwoydem	*Boy them* Police, derogatory term that diminishes Police authority
Crisp/Criss	Context dependent, anything from okay to beautiful, cool or in style
Crookified	Become a smart crook, trickster
Dat	That
Dem	Them
Den	Then
Den gwaan nuh	*Then go on now*, carry on your way
Depan	On, on top of, upon
Desoh	There so
Deh	They or There
De'ah	I am here
Di	The
Dis	This
Don	Important man earned status, well respected
Dun off	*Done off,* to finish, over with
No badda ears 'ard	*No bother ears hard,* don't be stubborn

Dung	Down
Duppy/Doppy	Ghost
Eediot	Idiot
Easy	Take it easy
Endz	Your area, hometown, sometimes Ghetto
'Erb	Weed, Cannabis, Marijuana, Sensemilla
Fa/Fah	For
Fardah	Father
Fi	*To,* This is the main Jamaican Preposition. Mi naa waan fi do it. (I don't want to do it) fi mi, fi she, fi yu, mines, hers, yours shows possession.
Firing	Fantastic
Flex	Context dependent to make move, plan an activity or flirt by showing off (muscle flexing)
Folla	Follow
Frowsy	Unpleasant dirty smelly condition
Fa	For
Gaan	Gone
Gi	Give
Giya	Give you
Gwaan	Context dependent, go on, going on
How ya mean	*How do you mean*, how can you ask that, it's obvious!
I & I	Me myself and I The 'I am' God within, Creator, Sovereign
'im	Him
Ital	Natural vital food, no artificial additive, pure unprocessed, no chemical salt, etc
Inna	*Inner,* into, used as being into other peoples business
Ih-eeah!	An exclamation to emphasise something
Jah	God, The Creator, Deity
Kyaan	Can't
KMT	*Kiss My Teeth* suction sound on teeth as exclamation of disapproval!
Kool	Cool
Lef	Leave, left, passed

Link	A connection, getting or meeting together. Mi link yu up layta (I'll meet you later)
Lickle	*Little* , small or young
Lickle bit	*Little bit,* as in a small or young child
Lickle more	*Little more (time),* later, saying goodbye
Man dem	*Man them,* an associated group of friends
Made up	Delighted
Me / Mi	*Me or mi,* me and I can be interchangeable
Me sey	I say
Me 'ave fi gwaan a way	*I have to go on that way*, I have to behave like that
Me fi turn news	I make the news
Me noh di ya ah gwaan	*me here what's going on*, I'm here what's happening
Me naa talk	I won't talk
Messi	Great, real, good
Mudda	Mother
Mussi	Must be
Naa	A variation of the word no
Nar	Not
Nuh	Now no and know
Nuff	Enough, plenty, too much, a lot
Nuttin'	Nothing
Overstand	To have an overview, knowledge
'Ow	How
PPAM Aid	Pneumatic Post-Amputation Mobility Aid
Phat	Full round and appealing, can refer to the bottom
Pickney	Young child
Pon	On
Pure Joke	Lots of fun, having a laugh
Rhaatid	Mild expletive, exclamation of surprise
Rass	Meaning your arse
Reespek	Respect
Rudebwoy	*Rude boy* – Pal or Mate, a term of endearment also a term of respect given to address bad boy or 'gangster' status
Sah	Sir

Seh	Say
She de wid me	She's here with me
Soh	It is so
S'pose	Suppose
Sum'ting	Something
Sum'tings yu nu fi talk	Some things you shouldn't say
Sum 'tings yu talk	Some things you should say
Strapped one	Spliff of high-grade weed
Tek Time	*Take time,* take your time, slow down
T'ing	Thing
Tru dat	*True That,* that's true, agreed
Typa	*Type of,* category
The Bless'ed	Sensemilla
Tu Raahtid!	An exclamation used in place of Wow, Damn, Gosh or Heck when you are surprised or when you get an understanding like an Ah ha moment.
Top Shotta	Alpha male
Tree	The number 3
Truu	Through, true, truth, threw
Two box	Two slaps or hits in quick succession
Unno	You all, you lot
Wan	One
Waan	Want
Wan a way	One off, unique
Wa'ppun	What happened
Wah	What
Washbelly	Youngest child
Weh	Context dependent where or what
Wha' ah gwaan	What's going on, how are you
Wid	With
Whata weh yu tief	You're such a clever thief
Weh yu ah kin teeth?	Why are you laughing?
Yah	Here
Ya'ahh	You are
Yard Food	Traditional Jamaican food, home cooked food such as rice and peas, fried snapper, plantain, breadfruit etc.

Yard	Home, where you live, but often referring to Jamaica
Yahso	Here so over here, right here
Yer	Your
Yo/ Yoh	Hey, greeting
Yu	You
Yu 'ave 'im	Have you got it
Yute	Youth
Yu'waan	You want

GARRI HOLNESS

Garri Holness was an Accounts Executive in London for over 20 years. He had a near-death experience in the 7/7 London Bombings in 2005. After a leg amputation and re-learning to walk he was inspired to change his life and become a Motivational Speaker and Author. He knows how it feels to be at rock bottom and having picked himself up, placed his focus firmly on positive energy, he has moved towards his external and internal healing at full throttle. He offers compassion along with the practices he used to overcome the nightmare he lived through. He now inspires professional business people with positivity, as well as mentoring underprivileged youth and those with addictions. He hopes to be seen as relatable, thus inspiring to those people living in the inner cities. He considers good exercise and diet as an essential part of his teachings and lifestyle, using them to engage and drive others forwards. His aim is to draw out a person's potential, guide them through their personal transition to fulfil that potential and coaches them to maintain it. He offers talks and workshops on how to stay positive despite adversity, along with help and advice on how to overcome all types of trauma in particular for those who have lost limbs.

You can connect with him on Facebook, Twitter, LinkedIn and via his website www.garriholness.com